W9-BMJ-170

Baptists in North America

Religious Life in America

Published

The Black Church in America: An African American Spirituality
by Michael Battle

Baptists in North America: An Historical Perspective
by William H. Brackney

Forthcoming
Methodism in America
by Douglas Strong

BX
6235
.B629
2006

Baptists in North America

An Historical Perspective

William H. Brackney

Blackwell
Publishing

AUG 2 0 2007

© 2006 by William H. Brackney

BLACKWELL PUBLISHING
350 Main Street, Malden, MA 02148-5020, USA
9600 Garsington Road, Oxford OX4 2DQ, UK
550 Swanston Street, Carlton, Victoria 3053, Australia

The right of William H. Brackney to be identified as the Author of this Work has
been asserted in accordance with the UK Copyright, Designs, and Patents Act 1988.

All rights reserved. No part of this publication may be reproduced, stored in a
retrieval system, or transmitted, in any form or by any means, electronic, mechanical,
photocopying, recording or otherwise, except as permitted by the UK Copyright,
Designs, and Patents Act 1988, without the prior permission of the publisher.

First published 2006 by Blackwell Publishing Ltd

1 2006

Library of Congress Cataloging-in-Publication Data

Brackney, William H.
    Baptists in North America : an historical perspective / William H.
Brackney.
        p. cm.—(Religious life in America)
    Includes bibliographical references and index.
    ISBN-13: 978-1-4051-1865-1 (hardcover : alk. paper)
    ISBN-10: 1-4051-1865-2 (hardcover : alk. paper)
    ISBN-13: 978-1-4051-1864-4 (pbk. : alk. paper)
    ISBN-10: 1-4051-1864-4 (pbk. : alk. paper)
        1. Baptists—United States—History. 2. Baptists—Canada—History.
I. Title. II. Series.

    BX6235.B629 2006
    286′.0973—dc22
                                                        2005024134

A catalogue record for this title is available from the British Library.

Set in 10.5/12.5pt Sabon
by Graphicraft Limited, Hong Kong
Printed and bound in Singapore
by Fabulous Printers Pte Ltd.

The publisher's policy is to use permanent paper from mills that operate a sustainable
forestry policy, and which has been manufactured from pulp processed using acid-free
and elementary chlorine-free practices. Furthermore, the publisher ensures that the
text paper and cover board used have met acceptable environmental accreditation
standards.

For further information on
Blackwell Publishing, visit our website:
www.blackwellpublishing.com

Dedicated to the members and friends of Blue Ridge Baptist Church in Falls County, Texas whom I served as minister in 2004–06

Contents

Foreword

Cecil Northcott, a British scholar, opined that an important source of our heritage of religious liberty "lies in the witness of the Baptist churches whose devotion to this idea, through years of persecution in Protestant Europe, makes their place a foremost one in the history of liberty" (Northcott 1949: 48). The conspicuous role of Baptists in the cause of religious liberty was deemed by Sanford H. Cobb to be the greatest contribution of Baptists to Protestantism (Cobb 1920: 64ff.). Writing more than a century ago, the distinguished historian, George Bancroft, wrote that "the paths of Baptists were the paths of freedom" (Bancroft 1902, 1: 608). Writing in the mid-twentieth century, Leo Pfeffer, a Jewish scholar widely regarded at that time as the leading scholar of American church–state relations, maintained that Baptists in America were "the denomination by far most vigorous in the struggle for religious freedom and separation of church and state" (Pfeffer 1953: 90). "This contribution," former Chief Justice Charles Evans Hughes of the US Supreme Court, declared "is the glory of the Baptist heritage, more distinctive than any other characteristic of belief or practice. To this militant leadership all sects and faiths are debtors. . . ." (Weaver 1944: 13).

Although religious liberty is readily conceded to be one of the cardinal principles of Baptists, the principle all too often today appears obscure to, or at best taken for granted by, many modern-day Baptists in many areas of the United States. Writing more than 70 years ago, John M. Mecklin declared, "The great Baptist church in large sections of this country [USA], where it practically dominates the religious life of the masses, is utterly oblivious of its noble traditions of liberty formulated by Baptist heroes of the past" (Mecklin 1934: 34). In his definitive study of American church–state relations more than a half-century ago,

Anson Phelps Stokes paid glowing tribute to the historic role of Baptists
to the cause of religious liberty: "No denomination has its roots more
firmly planted in the soil of religious freedom and Church-State separation than the Baptists" (Stokes 1950, 3: 485). Nevertheless, Stokes
observed, the principle of religious liberty has been less descriptive of
Baptists in recent times than their early espousal of the principle might
suggest. He wrote:

> The Baptists today are typical of those groups who have fought heroi-
> cally to secure their own freedom from State interference and would
> fight again to maintain it; but in freedom of thought and teaching [i.e., in
> their own denomination], or even freedom for certain other groups, such
> as Roman Catholics on the one hand, and liberal theologians on the
> other, their record has not been uniformly good.
>
> *(Stokes 1950, 1: 762)*

To be sure, the status of Baptists in twenty-first-century North America,
particularly in the United States, is radically different from their status
in England, Europe, Africa, Asia, Latin America, or colonial America.
In approximately two hundred and thirty years, Baptists have moved
from the position of a persecuted and disinherited sect to the largest
Protestant denomination in the United States, comprising a little less
than one-eighth of the total population. As a denomination in the
United States and Canada, Baptists have become affluent, politically
influential, and in certain sections of the countries, socially established
as the dominant and largest single religious community. In this social
transformation, many Baptists have become extremely conservative and
authoritarian, in contrast to the Baptists of seventeenth-century England and the United States. Many Baptists in North America increasingly show more concern for doctrinal uniformity and denominational
or "convention" authority over both its individual members and its
churches than with the great social and moral issues of the day that
bear upon all societies.

History attests that religious liberty has been the concern primarily
of the persecuted and disinherited, not the religious communities of the
powerful and privileged. Massive institutional growth and elaborate
denominational structure encourage uniformity, not diversity, and ecclesiastical authority, not soul freedom. In reviewing the Baptist principle
of religious liberty and the separation of church and state, certain
questions inevitably arise. Can the primacy of the Free Church tradition be preserved when the church becomes favored and socially established? How are the traditions of dissent and the competency of the

individual under God maintained within a burgeoning ecclesiastical structure accompanied by an expanded denominational authority? How is liberty of conscience or religious liberty addressed within the denomination in the face of demands for "orthodoxy" or "denominational authority"? There are, to be sure, no easy answers to these questions, but they at least deserve some serious reflection. The danger for Baptists is that their changed status, today powerful and privileged, may so separate them, both culturally and socially, from the circumstances of their early history as to alienate them from some of their noblest and most distinguishing principles, such as religious liberty and the separation of church and state.

This volume presents a fair and impartial account of Baptists in North America, focusing on the history of Baptists in the United States and Canada. Particular attention is given to the pattern of dissent which has been a recurring theme of Baptists, both in Canada and the United States. The author has chosen to be largely descriptive of the many divisions of Baptists without passing any theological judgment in recounting the denominational divisions among Baptists of North America. While continuing to give witness to the principle of separation of church and state in spite of denominational schisms, which, from time to time, many would consider to be based on relatively minor doctrinal issues, the author notes in some detail the phenomenal growth of Baptists, particularly in the United States. Strong supporters of the American Revolution, Baptists moved from the smallest and weakest of all mainline Protestant groups at the time of America's founding, to become by far the largest of all the Protestant communions in the United States today. This is an important chapter in the history of American Christianity.

James E. Wood, Jr.
Simon and Ethel Bunn Distinguished Professor Emeritus of Church-State Studies at Baylor University and former Executive Director, The Baptist Joint Committee on Public Affairs

Preface

This book arose from two different expressed needs: one for a thematic, analytical history of Baptists in America, the other the desire to have an up-to-date chronological essay on Baptist history in the United States. I have combined the two for the series that Blackwell is launching. In addition, I have added nuances of my own, including the interweaving of Baptist life in Canada with that in the United States, to provide a "North American" picture of a denominational tradition. Chapters 1 through 7 provide the chronological flow, each with a "legacy" section, and my overall conclusion. I hope this will serve to highlight what I think were the major determinative characteristics of the respective eras. Chapters 8 through 11 are thematic discussions of categories I think are absolutely essential to the making of Baptist identity in North America: the come-outer tradition, the uniqueness of African American Baptists, the missionary impulse, the social concerns and mores of an evangelical tradition, and my conclusion.

Anyone who takes on this task is indebted to everyone who has gone before. I am dependent upon classics like Morgan Edwards, Isaac Backus, David Benedict, A. H. Newman, Henry C. Vedder, and W. W. Barnes, as well as to a long list of state Baptist historians who have rendered a unique service. In the modern era, I was much influenced by my close friend, Robert G. Torbet, whose library I inherited; by my own teacher of 'things Baptist', Norman H. Maring; by friends and colleagues in the American Baptist Historical Society: C. C. Goen, Robert Handy, Winthrop Hudson, and Ellis E. O'Neal, Jr.; by outstanding Southern Baptist historians, Robert A. Baker, H. Leon McBeth, James Leo Garrett, Robert Gardner, and most of all, Walter Shurden. My Canadian Baptist orientation has been shaped by Murray J. S. Ford, T. T. Gibson, J. Daniel Gibson, John Irwin, Walter Ellis, George Rawlyk, Leslie Tarr,

Stanley Fowler, and especially Jarold K. Zeman. In some ways, this book is an attempt to carry Robert Torbet's work to the next generation: a careful, balanced, accurate accounting that also breaks some new ground in light of contemporary research.

There are some "angels" in the life of an historian who provide guidance and direction of just the right kind. These include Dr. Louise Barber, a scholar who labored over this manuscript line by line for its infelicities and Canadian nuances; C. Wallace Christian, an historical theologian who read it all for content and interpretation. Having been where the archivist sits, I am indebted to these very good scholars, librarians, and researchers: Diana Yount and Cindy Bolshaw at Andover Newton, the Rochester and Valley Forge staffs of the American Baptist Historical Society; the Library of the International Mission Board, Richmond, Virginia; Tyler Gillespie at the Baptist Joint Committee for Religious Liberty; the reference and interlibrary loan staffs of Jones Library, Baylor University, especially John Robinson and Jeff Taylor. My experience in Baptist congregations as diverse as Tripp Baptist Church and Blueridge Baptist Church in Texas, First Baptist, Brantford, and New Minas Baptist Church in Canada, plus the Landover Hills Baptist Church and First Baptist Church in Riverdale, Maryland, have been personally instructive for me in Baptist life and practice.

Finally, I wish to express deep gratitude to my former honors student and now colleague, Dr. Douglas M. Strong at Wesley Theological Seminary, for recommending me for this project; to Rebecca Harkin and Hannah Berry who have overseen this work at Blackwell with care; to Jenny Roberts whose expertise and timeliness in editing and sorting out important details is unmatched. At the last, Erin Brackney, my daughter, energetically assisted in the preparation of the index.

William H. Brackney
Eastertide, 2005

Introduction:
What Are the Baptists?
or Who Are Baptists?

Contemporary Baptists are a denomination of Christian believers that have their origins in the English Reformation at the turn of the sixteenth century. They emerged on the stage of religious history as part of the Puritan movement in Elizabethan England with characteristics that resemble the earlier sixteenth-century Radical Reformers of western and central Europe. That in itself begins to define Baptist identity. Puritans were part of a reform that placed the authority of Scripture over against all church traditions. The true church, they believed, would be drawn apart from the episcopal establishment and "popish superstitions." Some of the Puritans became Separatists, further refining their understanding of the church from scriptural warrant. Baptists also exhibited a lively ardor for religious liberty, congregational government of their churches, and believer's baptism, earmarks of Swiss and Dutch Anabaptists.

Among the English Separatists of the seventeenth century, Baptists bore a close kinship to Quakers, Seekers, Ranters, Muggletonians, Fifth Monarchists, and Sabbatarians. They were antiestablishment, solicitous of others about their faith, and many held to a belief in the literal return of Christ. What these sects all had in common was the opportunity to interpret Scripture for themselves in matters of faith and life. The new-found availability of the English Scriptures and increased literacy among the middle and even lower classes gave liberties to dissenters in general and Baptists in particular. Scripture, then, becomes a first priority mark of Baptists. As the article on Scripture put it in the first published Baptist confession of faith, "The Rule of this Knowledge, Faith, and Obedience, concerning the worship and service of God, and other Christian duties, is not mans inventions, opinions, devices, lawes, constitutions, or traditions unwritten, whatsoever, but onely the word of God contained in the Canonicall Scriptures."[1]

Interpreting Scripture, however, can create a new set of difficulties. Left alone, one might arrive at a "free-willer" position on understanding the atonement of Christ that emphasizes human response, or antinomianism,[2] or a requirement to continue to keep the Sabbath, or a conviction that Christ's return to earth is imminent, or a subversive understanding of the sacraments that requires a new baptism by full immersion in water for all adult professing members of the church. So much of the agenda of seventeenth-century dissenters like Baptists was so contrary to the *Book of Common Prayer* and the *Thirty-nine Articles*, that the Church of England could not, and did not, allow the tendencies of dissent to go unchecked. For Baptists, this led to imprisonment, confiscation of property, fines, and sometimes banishment. The record of Baptist losses for their beliefs is clearly told in works like Thomas Helwys's *A Mistery of Iniquity* (1612), John Murton's *Objections Answered . . . That No Man Ought to Be Persecuted for His Religion* (1615), Roger Williams's *Bloudy Tenent of Persecution* (1644), and John Clarke's *Ill Newes from New England* (1652). Because of the intolerance and outright harassment and persecution they suffered, Baptists naturally arrived at a position advocating toleration, if not full religious liberty, early in the seventeenth century. What made their position unique is that they espoused religious liberty without boundaries.

The doctrine of Christ is also of paramount importance to Baptists. Christ is certainly understood to be an historical figure, as affirmed in the creeds. But Baptists understand Christ to be a living presence in their midst. Lacking a human pope or archbishop, Baptists conclude that Christ dwells among his people. The church is understood to be the Body of Christ, made up of all true believers of all times and most vividly seen in faithful congregations. Baptists also understand Christ as redeemer with headship and full Crown rights in the church: "This office of Mediator between God and man, is proper onely to Christ, who is the Prophet, Priest, and King of the Church of God; and may not be either in whole, or any part thereof transfer'ed from him to any other."[3]

In their understanding of human beings, Baptists respond to the idea of spiritual independence under God. It begins with the assumption that human beings are created in God's image and that among their greatest attributes is God-given freedom to make choices. Baptists are quintessential religious voluntarists and the voluntary principle permeates every facet of their lives. What follows naturally is the assumption that individuals are accountable directly to God without any mediator for their choices. The theological principle continues with congregations that are free of external ecclesiastical or political control and are held mutually accountable under God. Finally, it reaches to Baptists in the social order, where they see themselves as advocates of freedom and spiritual independence. Historically this can take the form of "dissent." Far removed from religious establishments, Baptists offer alternatives, criticize mainstream patterns, and take unpopular stances.

Another of the defining character traits of Baptists is their penchant for interdependence. Evident throughout the English Baptist phase of development in the seventeenth century was the need to communicate and cooperate with congregations of like mind. Matters of polity such as the choice of a pastor, the proper mode of administering the sacraments or ordinances, discipline of members, theological interpretation, and a desire to be visibly something of the Body of Christ or the Kingdom of God led Baptists to seek each other out. From time to time they also sought relationships beyond their own ranks in the wider Christian community, such as with Mennonites or the Three Dissenting Denominations in England.[4] This particular facet of Baptist identity created a tension with independent congregations. Early in the North American colonial experience, Baptists sought each other out and met in councils and associations.

No one can follow Baptist history very far without appreciating the importance of religious experience. Religious experience involves a behavioral response to the reality of God. In contemplating God, Baptists experience feelings of awe, humility, unworthiness, assurance, joy, and gratitude, and their hymnology and worship demonstrate this. Baptists hold the relationship with God to be personal, in the same way as a relationship with another human is experienced. Prayer is a conversation with God where Baptists expect answers and interpret experience as responses from God. The sacraments/ordinances also provide Baptists with a deep religious experience. Generally Baptists observe two sacraments (more often referred to as ordinances): believer's baptism and the Lord's Supper. In believer's baptism Baptists have the opportunity to respond to God by a prescribed physical activity, namely being immersed in water in obedience to the command of Christ. Some Baptists make this even more vivid by a triune immersion that is symbolic of the triune Godhead. In celebrating the Lord's Supper, Baptists re-enact the meal and imagine themselves present as the living Christ passes the bread and cup. Far from this being the "mere memorialism" so often claimed by critics, in the Lord's Supper at its best Baptists experience the communion meal as *anamnesis*, a kind of re-enacted drama in which one personally participates. In less sacramental practices,

Baptists use the laying on of hands upon the head of candidates for ordination, as well as the continued practice with newly baptized persons who experience the prayers of deacons or elders by the laying on of hands. And there are several kinds of Baptists who continue the experience of footwashing before the Lord's Supper, demonstrating an intimate moment among true disciples. It is not inaccurate to argue that religious experience is constantly at work throughout Baptist believers' lives, as they interpret doctrine in light of experience and understand events as part of God's purposes for their lives.

To be fair to those Baptists who raise Scripture to a supremely important role, religious experience is problematic. Partly in response to European theology in the nineteenth century that overemphasized the importance of experience in writers like the German Friedrich Schleiermacher, and also the runaway influence of revivalism, many confessional Baptists retreat from much appreciation of religious experience. For them Scripture is a sure, unchanging authority in contrast with human experience that is variegated, capricious, and undependable. Most of these Baptists are heavily indebted to a Calvinistic influence in Baptist life. General Atonement or Arminian Baptists tend to create a balance between the authority of Scripture, the sovereignty of God, and human experience.

Rounding out the traits of Baptists, one finds a tendency toward separation of church and state, founded on their own experience in England, New England, and Virginia, where Baptists among other dissenters suffered greatly at the hands of a state-supported church. First in the Church of England context, severe laws were passed by Parliament intended to obliterate dissenting groups. From the pursuits of Archbishop Laud in the 1630s to the Clarendon Code of the 1660s, Baptists were hunted, fined, imprisoned, and banished. Out of their bleak prospects emerged a vision for a separation of ecclesiastical authority from that of the state. Once in the colonies, again Baptists (and their predecessor antipaedobaptists) were coerced to conform to unwanted baptisms and taxes supporting Congregationalist Standing Order churches. In the southern colonies, Baptist preachers were silenced by civil authorities acting in collusion with Anglican priests. Little wonder that in the Revolutionary Era, Baptists moved ahead of all other dissenters in championing separation of church and state.

Baptists in the United States easily became part of the multidenominational Protestant advance to establish a Christian nation. As historian Robert Handy has argued, this involved three dimensions: religion, morality, and education. Baptists joined other evangelical Protestants in promoting a theological interpretation of America as a nation under God, a nation that enjoyed peculiar blessings of God for its faithfulness, and a nation whose ultimate destiny lay in the eschatological purposes of God. The highest form of government under God was deemed to be democratic, and true religion was entirely voluntary. Baptists achieved high marks in both areas. Further, it was assumed that an evangelical moral code should pervade the United States, the chief spokesmen of which were preachers. America was supposed to behave like a Christian country and Baptists laid out their version of that in a literalistic biblical mandate. Baptists produced leading moral philosophers like Francis Wayland, whose textbook was widely used in colleges until well after the Civil War. Finally, Baptists joined other evangelical Protestants in placing a very high priority upon education. Education was enlightenment, born of God and a chief responsibility of the churches. Baptists planted colleges in every state and offered an opportunity to all citizens to earn college degrees. Colleges were second only in missionary import behind church planting, in helping to establish a Christian America.[5]

The relationship between Baptists and national aspirations was also evident in the Canadian experience. Shortly after the Dominion of Canada was proclaimed in 1867 a Methodist politician from New Brunswick, Leonard Tilley, recalled the words of Psalm 72: 8: "He shall have dominion from sea to sea." Although there was no concerted effort to celebrate the creation of a new nation among the churches, the "His Dominion" movement did illustrate an interest in not only uniting Canada by a railroad, but also by claiming the country from sea to sea for the Kingdom of Christ. While disestablishment and the secularization process had been set in motion earlier in the century, what took up the Protestant agenda was a congeries of voluntary associations, missionary organizations, benevolent and educational projects, in particular to win the West for Christ. Although in declining percentages as a part of the total population (from 6.7 percent in 1871 to 5.3 percent in 1911),[6] Canadian Baptists were counted among the groups that joined the organizational and evangelical effort.

Finally, one turns to the question of "Who are the Baptists?" socioeconomically. In England Baptists could be found at all levels of society: some were among the well-to-do, such as the Seventh Day Baptist, Dr. Peter Chamberlyn, who was royal physician to three Stuart monarchs, or Francis Bampfield, brother to a prominent member of Parliament during the Restoration, or William Kiffin, a wealthy woolen merchant and "sometime" brewer who loaned funds to Charles II to pay off his gambling debts. But for the most part, Baptists were laborers or farmers, and not of the managerial class. Michael Watts's definition of dissenters is probably valid for Baptists: "persons of devotion, discipline, individualists, and humble people."[7] In the North American scene, Baptists seized upon new opportunities. Early Baptists were farmers, village dwellers, craft workers in trades as diverse as wagon making and bricklaying, and shopkeepers. In New England, one source had it that Baptists were honest, hardworking plowmen, artisans, mechanics, and day-laborers. In a 1795 list of Welsh Baptists who desired to settle in the United States there were farmers, carpenters, coopers, tailors, shoemakers, and masons.[8] But colonial Baptists also included presidents of colleges, members of colonial legislatures, and prominent commercial entrepreneurs. Canadian historian John Webster Grant claimed that well into the nineteenth century Baptists in central Canada were congregations of farmers closely hugging the shorelines of the Great Lakes, served by part-time ministers.[9] Probably their most illustrious leaders among the denomination were their pastors.

In another work,[10] I have dealt with the question of whether Baptists are a movement, a denomination, or a tradition. They are all three. In their earliest development, they behaved like a new religious movement, possessed of charismatic leaders, a clear theological self-understanding, and a targeted constituency. They were fairly aggressive and achieved permanency across regions, oceans, and social classes. By the eighteenth century in Britain and North America, Baptists were at least a series of denominational groups confidently nudging their way into mainstream Protestantism, somewhere between Presbyterians and Congregationalists and with more variety than either of the other two. They worked in the midst of other "denominations" of Christians and recognized their commonalities when it suited them. Each of the parts of the Baptist family grew to maturity in the nineteenth century to be recognized in tables and encyclopedias of religious groups as having several traits in common as Baptists: a congregational church government; symbolic ordinances, notably believer's baptism by immersion; a passion for evangelism and mission; sturdy independence and a commitment to religious liberty; and an epistemological lodgment in the Scriptures. As analysts sorted out the contrasting distinctive features of essentially Protestant categories, Baptists, however organizationally diverse, represented a permanent religious tradition.

Notes

1   *The Confession of Faith, Of those Churches which are commonly (though falsly) called Anabaptists* (London: Matthew Simmons, 1644), Art. VII.

2 Literally, "beyond the law," antinomianism was a serious accusation against seventeenth-century Baptists and Separatists because many laid greater stress upon grace, soul liberty, freedom in Christ or the Holy Spirit to the exclusion of laws, social obligations, and religious duties. Compare Alan Simpson, *Puritanism in Old and New England* (Chicago: University of Chicago Press, 1972), 54–5, with Darrett B. Rutman, *American Puritanism* (New York: W.W. Norton, 1977), 106–7, and Allen Carden, *Puritan Christianity in America: Religion and Life in Seventeenth-Century Massachusetts* (Grand Rapids, MI: Baker Book House, 1990), 200–1.

3 *Confession of Faith Put Forth by the Elders and Brethren Of many Congregations Of Christians (baptized upon Profession of their Faith) in London and the Country* (London: n.p., 1677), Art. VIII, sect. 9.

4 This was the eighteenth-century forerunner to the Dissenting Deputies. Originally this included Independents (Congregationalists), Presbyterians, and Calvinistic Baptists.

5 See Robert T. Handy, *A Christian America: Protestant Hopes and Historical Realities* (New York: Oxford University Press, 1984), 27–56.

6 Census data quoted in George Rawlyk (ed.), *The Canadian Protestant Experience 1760–1990* (Burlington, ON: G. R. Welch, 1990), 104.

7 Michael Watts, *The Dissenters: From the Reformation to the French Revolution* (Oxford: Clarendon Press, 1978), 5.

8 "Welsh Artisans to Samuel Jones" (Irving R. McKesson Papers, Jones Section, Historical Society of Pennsylvania); quoted in Hywel Davies, *Transatlantic Brethren: Rev. Samuel Jones (1735–1814) and His Friends: Baptists in Wales, Pennsylvania and Beyond* (Bethlehem, PA: Lehigh University Press, 1995), 198.

9 John Webster Grant, *A Profusion of Spires: Religion in Nineteenth Century Ontario* (Toronto, ON: University of Toronto Press, 1988), 44–5.

10 William H. Brackney, *Historical Dictionary of the Baptists* (Lanham, MD: The Scarecrow Press, 1999), xxv–xxx.

Chapter 1
Coming to America

Foundations

Anyone investigating the origins of Baptists in North America must take a further step into the past and locate the first Baptists in England. The first people to be called Baptists, and who held to principles that can be unmistakably identified as baptistic, are found in a northeastern London district known as "Spitalfields." Spitalfields had long been inhabited by mostly poor persons, offering substandard accommodation to an impoverished and partly criminal population, where "the lanes were deep, dirty, and unfrequented" in Daniel Defoe's words. It was here that Thomas Helwys and his company of 20 or more friends arrived in 1610 from Amsterdam to take up residence again in their native land. These English nonconformists shared views of the church similar to continental Anabaptists, particularly Dutch Mennonites in Amsterdam. They could well have been influenced by Anabaptist tracts or associations through trading ventures. Radical Congregationalists called "Independents" were all around them. They were part of a second English reformation that would surpass all of the changes of monarch and reformers in the Tudor period. Whatever their immediate theological influences were, they gathered the first Baptist congregation in history.

Thomas Helwys was part of the forced emigration of hundreds of dissenters under the threat of imprisonment and/or loss of property under Elizabeth I and James I after James's accession to the English throne in 1603. The term "separatist" applied to many because of their initiative to separate from the Church of England, which they considered corrupt. Separatists were a branch of the Puritan tradition that emerged in the late 1560s, mostly small groups of believers who were scandalized by the changes in the 1559 English *Book of Common*

Prayer and who were increasingly pursued by the authorities to cease their nonconformity. To the alarm of Queen Elizabeth their numbers increased in the 1590s and they were nurtured by theologians at Cambridge University. Among those who imbibed the theology of non-conformity at Cambridge was John Smyth. Smyth became a teaching elder in Gainsborough in Lincolnshire at the turn of the seventeenth century and eventually gathered a congregation that searched the Scriptures to ascertain the will of God for their lives. Helwys, a devoted member of Smyth's congregation, urged Smyth and about 40 others to flee to The Netherlands to wait out the difficult period in England.[1] In Amsterdam, Smyth pursued closer ties with Mennonites, while Helwys and others became disillusioned with the direction that Smyth pursued, and returned to England.

From Helwys and the congregations in the area around Spitalfields, the General Baptists emerged. Their theological orientation was in the greater Reformed tradition, with the exception that they understood Christ's death or atonement was applicable to all persons. Helwys himself had written treatises on free will and the universal redemption of Christ, and others like John Murton followed with similar emphases. Edward Barber, a merchant tailor of Threadneedle Street in London, published the earliest known Baptist tract on baptism, *A Small Treatise of Baptisme or Dipping* (1642) in which he acknowledged that the scriptural mode of baptism was dipping or immersion. Another distinctive of the General Baptists came to be the laying on of hands. This ordinance, based upon the fourth principle of Hebrews 6: 1–2, was practiced following a candidate's baptism to signify the coming of the Holy Spirit into the life of a believer as the elders of the congregation physically laid hands upon the head of the individual. The rite became a requirement of the Particular Baptists in the United States for a time, but was more characteristic of General Baptists in England and America in the seventeenth century.

The General Baptists grew to prominence in seventeenth-century England through starting churches in the greater London area. They met as a general assembly in 1660 and created several forms of confessions of faith or statements of their beliefs. Among their theologians was Thomas Grantham of Lincolnshire who published his work under the title, *Christianismus Primitivus* (1678). It was the first comprehensive doctrinal treatise in the Baptist tradition. The General Baptists stressed clear principles of connectional church government, and yet there was a tendency toward deep theological divisions characteristic of Arminian groups. With the aging of their movement, the General Baptists lost many of their leaders; they had limited financial resources to modernize buildings; they did not grow geographically beyond London and the Home Counties, and Lincolnshire and Somerset; and they experienced intermarriage outside their ranks. Even more importantly, some of their ecclesiastical leaders adopted antitrinitarian positions and they were excluded from the fund set up by a prominent London Baptist to train ministers.[2] By 1715 many General Baptist congregations had dwindled in numbers and had wandered toward theologically unitarian and universalist positions.

A second stream of Baptists came from another evolved congregation of English separatists. At the turn of the century, some opted to leave for the continent, while most remained in England. Among the numerous separatist communities, Henry Jacob, an Oxford graduate, in about 1616 founded a congregation in Southwark, a poor, isolated urban area urban area south of the Thames from the City of London known for its overcrowded housing, breweries, and unemployment. Jacob had been a Puritan refugee in Leyden where he came under the influence of John Robinson of Pilgrim Fathers fame. Jacob served as pastor of the church until he left for Virginia in 1624. John Lathrop, another separatist who had been imprisoned for two years, followed Jacob as pastor of the Southwark church until he too fled for New Hampshire in 1634. After Lathrop, the Southwark congregation apparently divided initially into two factions, one led by Praise-God Barbon, a leather seller, and the other by Henry Jessey, a graduate of Cambridge. That division concerned the size and makeup of the congregation and the question of who should be baptized. In the mid-1630s Samuel Eaton became leader of one division in the Jessey congregation that proved to be mixed in its acceptance of believer's baptism. Those who were apparently more decisive about the matter organized themselves yet again in 1638 under the ministry of John Spilsbury, and adopted believer's baptism as a key tenet. The Spilsbury congregation is credited with being the first of the Calvinistic Baptist congregations in history, also known as "Particular" Baptists because of their belief that Christ died for a particular group, the Elect. Spilsbury himself published in 1643 the first treatise on believer's baptism among the Particular Baptists.[3] In 1644 the aggregate of former separatists who had formed themselves in the vicinity of London as Calvinistic Baptists published a confession of faith and included Hanserd Knollys, who had fled to New Hampshire as a persecuted separatist, William Kiffin, a wealthy merchant and brewer, Praise-God Barbon, and Henry Jessey himself. The Particular Baptists would become numerically the leading group of Baptists in England, Wales, and Scotland by the end of the sixteenth century.

Yet a third variety of Baptists were known by their Seventh Day beliefs. One of the questions that arose among many nonconformists was the relation of the Old Testament Law to grace. Many held that certain parts of the Law remained valid, notably the keeping of the Sabbath (Saturday) holy. Yet another issue that energized nonconformists at the time of the Puritan Revolution was the Second Coming of Christ. Some of these who held that Jesus's return was imminent were called Fifth Monarchists because they yearned for the establishment of Christ's kingdom on earth. Both of these positions were incorporated into the formation of the Seventh Day Baptist movement whose earliest congregation was at Mill Yard in London from about 1651. Other congregations were organized at Pinner's Hall and Bell Lane in London and at Colchester in Essex. Theologically, Seventh Day pastors exhibited diversity on other doctrinal matters, for instance some being general and others being Calvinistic on the atonement of Christ. Some even preached at both Sabbath and Lord's Day meetings, such as Joseph Stennett at Mill Yard (Seventh Day) and Little Wild Street Church (Particular) in London.

There was at least one additional type of seventeenth-century English Baptist, the Leg of Mutton Baptists. In 1709 Marius D'Asigny, a Presbyterian observer of dissent, noted that in Lambert Street, Whitechapel, there was a congregation that celebrated the Lord's Supper by supplementing the bread and wine with a sumptuous selection of legs of mutton and other meats. Presumably they were in some manner acknowledging the roots of the Supper in the Passover Feast. D'Asigny called them "Leg of Mutton" Baptists and noted there was but one congregation of them. What this obscure type of English Baptist represented was a variety of interpretations of the ordinal/sacramental rites of the Church, from those who were close to their Anglican roots to those who took literally every relevant passage in both testaments.

The Westward Flow of People and Convictions

The question remains: how did these disparate believers of an emerging tradition reach the American shores? Unlike some religious groups, they did not come *en masse*. One historian put it aptly, "Those who came to the Colonies were neither numerous or unduly prominent."[4] Certainly, some came as individuals in the ships' companies that established communities along the Atlantic coast. The first doubtless came to the colonies of Massachusetts and later to East New Jersey. Some of the early people to hold baptistic views held them in part or were unaware of any articulated system. They were merely "anti-paedobaptists" or persons who did not practice the baptism of infants and children. As time went on, some of these folk would develop a sophisticated understanding of several related theological ideas like the believer's church, soul freedom, religious liberty, congregational governance, and a radical biblicism. Among those we can clearly identify in this group were Henry Dunster, an early president of Harvard College, and Thomas Goold, an articulate leader in the Charlestown community.

Henry Dunster was an important precursor of the Baptist persuasion. Born in England and educated at Cambridge University, he was ordained to the Anglican priesthood. Under Stuart auspices, he came to dislike equally King Charles I and the Presbyterians. Dunster emigrated to Massachusetts in 1639. His educational attainments were impressive in the colony and he was asked to be president of the new college at Cambridge. He served Harvard for a decade, but ran afoul of both ecclesiastical and civil authorities in 1652 when he refused to have his child baptized. His steadfast position led to admonishment and then a celebrated trial 1653–55. He was found guilty of "being unsound in the faith" and sentenced to a public admonition, giving bond for his future good behavior, and resignation from his position. His removal from Harvard, against the pleas of his friends, also meant the forfeiture of his home, for which he was later compensated. Dunster moved to the Plymouth Colony where he hoped for greater toleration, but apparently did not accept a full baptistic identity, for they would not have tolerated a rejection of infant baptism either. Continuing to travel in the Bay Colony, his saga became a *cause célèbre* in the pursuit of religious liberty that many Baptists subsequently adopted. Dunster's incomplete pilgrimage toward Baptist principles, however, clearly demarcated him from others of his era.[5]

While some were struggling with the meaning of baptism, others moved to form congregations on entirely new bases. The first congregation of Baptists in America was formed at Providence, Rhode Island in 1638 by Ezekiel Holliman, Roger Williams, and a handful of others. Williams had fled from Massachusetts Bay and was probably persuaded by a female friend, Mrs Richard Scott,[6] to accept believer's baptism. He wrote of his acceptance of a new community, "I believe their practice comes nearer the first practice of our great Founder Christ Jesus, than other practices of religion do, and yet I have not satisfaction neither in the authority by which it is done, nor in the manner...."[7] While he was convinced of certain Baptist principles, apparently the other tenets of the Providence congregation did not hold Williams, for he dissociated himself from the Baptists in Rhode Island and did not join with them in England in 1643–44 and 1651–54 or upon his return to Rhode Island from 1655 onward. The first decade and a half is a silent period in the life of this initial congregation, in which it likely ceased meeting for a time and was reconstituted about 1650. First Baptist in Providence thereafter leaned toward a General Baptist theology and the practice of the laying on of hands was debated, ultimately leading to a schism in 1652. As late as 1711 Providence was formally identified as a "Six Principle Church" and this remained the case until 1771 when James Manning moved the congregation toward a mainstream Calvinistic posture and full membership in the Warren Baptist Association of churches.

Baptist identity was greatly reinforced elsewhere in Rhode Island by John Clarke who started a church at Newport sometime around 1639 or 1640.[8] Shortly after its formation a split, led by Robert Lenthall, a Baptist from England, occurred in 1641 over antinomianism. The early church was remarkably open on many matters, not least of which was the role of a pastor – Clarke preferred the designation of teacher and probably was never ordained. Personally he opposed doctrinal rigidity and this led to what was apparently an open and diverse congregation. During his tenure, for instance, prophesying among members was encouraged. With the counsel of Mark Lucar, recently arrived from England, Clarke in 1651 led in the practice of believer's baptism by immersion. In this second Baptist congregation in the colonies, a third type of American Baptist emerged over a division of opinion about the Sabbath: the Seventh Day Baptists. Stephen Mumford, an English Sabbatarian and Baptist, arrived in Newport in 1664 and led other families to consider the importance of the Sabbath. Lucar and Obadiah Holmes joined Clarke in opposing the Sabbatarians in the church and, after a protracted dispute, the Sabbatarians formed their own congregation in Newport in 1671. The main Newport Baptist congregation suffered further doctrinal upset in conversation with the Quakers and in the 1670s over a denial by some of the full humanity of Christ.

Another important beginning was the regathering of a Baptist congregation at Swansea, Massachusetts. John Myles, an Oxford graduate, joined the Baptists in London and conducted preaching in Wales. For a time he served as a "tryer" or government assessor of religious orthodoxy for the Cromwell Protectorate. In 1649 he gathered a congregation at Ilston, near Swansea on the Gower Peninsula in south Wales, and this congregation struggled along through the 1650s. In 1663 Myles and most of the congregation determined to move to America and they transplanted to Rehoboth, Massachusetts. On the voyage to

New England the Welsh-speaking congregation ceased keeping records in that language and began a new chapter of their life in English. Myles became a leader among the Baptists in eastern Massachusetts, settling essentially as the only minister in his town of Swansea (named for their hometown in Wales) and serving from time to time as an interim pastor at Boston. He practiced "mixed communion," meaning he allowed the benefits of full membership in his congregation to those who had been baptized as believers as well as paedobaptists.

Third in importance in the New England Baptist story was the beginning of First Baptist, Boston. Here the chief figure was Thomas Goold, a wagon maker and well-established freeman of the colony since 1641. Between 1640 and 1655 Goold was a cooperating member of the Charlestown Church, accepting with enthusiasm its sacramental traditions. In 1655 however, he refused to allow his child to be baptized and the following year he was suspended from communion. His frequent association with Henry Dunster suggests that he might have been influenced toward an antipaedobaptist position by Dunster's banishment from Harvard, and influenced further to a Baptist understanding by English Baptists known to be in the colony. For the next nine years Goold was involved in a complex and protracted debate with church and civil authorities over ecclesiastical authority. He was charged with not having his child baptized, nonattendance at public worship, and conducting "schismatical" religious services.[9] In 1663 Thomas and Hannah Goold, Thomas Osborne and his wife, and five others gathered at the Goold home in Charlestown to create a Baptist congregation. According to John Eliot, the Congregationalist apostle to the Indians who was then a pastor at Roxbury, for a time they also conducted a lecture at the home of one of the couples. Eventually, it is thought that either John Myles or John Clarke of Rhode Island baptized them and Goold composed the confession of faith. On June 7, 1665 the first Baptist church in Boston was organized, the second of the tradition in the Bay Colony after the church begun by Myles at Swansea. Goold was fined in 1656 and imprisoned intermittently until his death in 1675. The 1665 congregation that began with nine members and doubled by 1671, continued to meet either at Goold's home or on Noddle's Island in Boston Harbor when persecution was unrelenting. The original band of Boston Baptists included landowners like Goold and Osborne, Edward Drinker, a potter, and John George, a chimney sweep. To these original members were added Richard Goodall, a shipmaster of the colonial carrying trade who had been a member of William Kiffin's congregation at Southwark, and William Turner and Robert Lambert, former members of Mr Stead's congregation in Dartmouth, England. Also notable were two women: Mary Goodall and Mary Newell, both of whom had been Baptists in England.

An important outgrowth of the Boston congregation was the establishment of a related congregation in Kittery, Maine. When authorities in Massachusetts who controlled the District of Maine pressed William Screven, a merchant in the coastal trade, to abide by laws requiring the baptism of children, he refused, and was accused of blasphemy. A trial ensued, and he was jailed and fined. The court ordered him to attend worship services and to cease his nonconformist activities. Instead, Screven sought the advice of the Baptists in Boston where he was baptized in 1681. The next year the Boston church licensed Screven to the ministry. When the little band of Kittery Baptists was organized as a church, they used the model confession and polity of the Boston congregation.[10] Doubtless as an outgrowth of his business pursuits, Screven settled for part of the year at what became Charleston in southern Carolina Colony, perhaps as early as 1684. He remained in the Kittery area for part of each year until 1695–96, when he departed Maine permanently for Carolina. American and Southern Baptist historians have recognized his church planting efforts as the first Baptist congregations in Maine and the American South.

Baptists settled in Connecticut, Long Island, and the Jerseys between 1680 and 1710. Valentine Wightman, a descendant of Edward Wightman, an English Baptist minister who was burned at the stake, planted a church at Groton in the southeastern part of the province, the first congregation in Connecticut. Some Baptists from Massachusetts had moved as individuals to lands in East Jersey, notably Monmouth and Elizabeth townships, as early as 1665. Still others moved to West Jersey, joining some emigrants from England who were Baptists in the 1670s. The oldest Baptist congregations in the Jerseys were at Middletown, Piscataway, and Cohansey from 1688–90. When William Penn opened settlement of "Penn's Woods" in 1681, Baptists were among the first to move there. An initial church at Cold Spring, composed of perhaps 20 people, including a transplanted Irishman from Rhode Island named Thomas Dongan, was established in 1684 near present day Bristol, Pennsylvania. Later, in 1687 the Pennypack Church, the oldest surviving congregation, was started in Lower Dublin Township, north of Philadelphia. Among the Old World connections that continued was the recognition of Elias Keach, son of the illustrious Benjamin Keach of London.[11] Elias had fled his father's Baptist faith to colonial Pennsylvania, only to find himself destitute and in need of a community of support. Attempting to preach under false pretenses, he saw the error of his ways and surrendered to the will of the congregation to be their pastor.

A remarkable story of long-term witness to Baptist principles is involved in the settlement of New Hampshire. According to Isaac Backus,[12] in about 1720 a pious woman named Rachel Thurber Scammon moved from her home in Rehoboth, Massachusetts, to Stratham, New Hampshire, in the southeast of the colony. She was imbued with a missionary spirit, and against strong prejudices, she witnessed to her neighbors with little apparent success, save one convert. She became convinced of Baptist principles and traveled to Boston, where Ephraim Bound, a New Light pastor at Second Baptist Church, baptized her. Perhaps upon the suggestion of Bound, she secured and read John Norcott's *Baptism Discovered Plainly and Faithfully, According to the Word of God* (1674). Much impressed with Norcott's presentation, she purchased a hundred copies for gifts to her friends and acquaintances. She predicted that as a result of her efforts a Baptist church would be formed in the area. This did happen, but long after her death. The eminent physician, Dr Samuel Shepard, as a young man found one of the copies Mrs Scammon had distributed at a patient's house and switched to Baptist affiliation about 1770. He was ordained in First Baptist, Boston and over the next decade gathered a congregation at Brentwood that stretched forth branches to four adjacent towns.

As witnessed in some unusual developments in Pennsylvania, Baptists in colonial North America were multiethnic. Baptists from Wales established a beachhead in southeastern Pennsylvania in the early eighteenth century, as did Germans with a baptistic orientation. In the 1680s Welsh settlers purchased considerable lands in the Welsh Tract along the Schuylkill River, west of Philadelphia. They had come with dreams of substantially improving their economic prospects over those in the old country. Most of these emigrants were Presbyterian, with a few Baptists settling in the western Schuylkill valley. In 1701 the first Baptist settlers from Wales – Rhydwilym, in southwest Wales to be precise – arrived in Philadelphia and for a time joined the Pennepack church at Lower Dublin. Desirous of having Welsh services in Welsh and being served by Welsh pastors, the Welsh Baptists separated themselves and fanned out in a geographical arc beyond the settled limits of Philadelphia. Some followed Thomas Griffith to Newcastle County where 30,000 acres were purchased and became known as a second Welsh Tract. In 1703 they erected a meetinghouse on Iron Brook at Pencader Hundred, known thereafter as the Welsh Tract Baptist Church.

Another congregation settled at Montgomery in Lower Bucks County, and another in the Great Valley, 30 miles west of Philadelphia. According to their historians, they originated from the Teifi Valley in Wales, rural areas of Pembrokeshire, Carmarthenshire, and Cardiganshire, close-knit communities that remained so in America.[13] In 1712 a new congregation was added at Cape May in New Jersey, and, in 1737, 48 members of the Welsh Tract Church relocated to the Pee Dee River in southern Carolina to extend their arable lands. They became the Welsh Neck Baptist Church with continuing connections to Pennsylvania. Another important part of the Welsh Baptist story entailed the itinerant mission of Morgan John Rhees in 1796–97 who penetrated Cambria County, central Pennsylvania, and at the confluence of the Blacklick and Connemaugh Rivers, formed a Baptist colony he called "Beulah." On two hundred acres he built a community that he referred to as a "Christian Church," an attempt to recover the life and spirit of the apostles. Although a bit of a maverick Baptist, Rhees remained in contact with the other Welsh Baptist congregations in the United States and Wales.[14] The principal influences of the Welsh on Baptists in colonial America were in the areas of polity and practice, they being concerned for discipline and order and confessional statements, the laying on of hands, closed communion, and good record-keeping.

Like the Welsh, German immigrants found William Penn's real estate inducements attractive as well. Among them were the spiritual descendents of Alexander Mack of Schwarzenau, Germany. In 1719 the first 20 families arrived in Philadelphia and settled in the Wissahickon area. The English-speaking community referred to them as "Dunkers," "Tunkers," and "Dunkards," though they preferred the name "Brethren." They practiced believer's baptism by triune immersion, footwashing, and the Love Feast or Agape Meal, a fellowship meal that accompanied the Lord's Supper. In 1721 Conrad Beissel, a baker from Germany who had joined the Brethren, separated in 1728 to form his own colony, first at Mill Creek and later at Ephrata in central Pennsylvania. Beissel recognized the Sabbath and soon the group became known as the German Seventh Day Baptists. Further, Beissel's group was strictly communitarian in keeping with apostolic patterns in Acts 2 and built a semimonastic community at Tunkerstown called "The Cloister." When Morgan Edwards of the Philadelphia Association visited them in the 1770s he reckoned that they were General Baptists in their interpretation of Christ's atonement and it is also known that they were pacifists during the American Revolution. Another leading Baptist, Elhanan Winchester, also visited the Tunkers in 1790 and thought they shared a universalist position similar to his own.

In the southern colonies, the earliest Baptist congregational presence was at Charleston, as noted above. At the beginning of the eighteenth century, however, a separate story commenced. Some accounts indicate that Baptists were in the vicinity of Isle of Wight County and Prince George County, Virginia, and along the coast of Carolina, perhaps as early as 1700. Actual records place a meeting of "Annabaptists" (sic) at Martins Brandon Parish in Prince George County in 1714. Presumably these were of the General Baptist family from England who had been dispatched from London on a church-planting mission under the leadership of Robert Norden, a Messenger among the General Baptists from Sussex. The southern Virginia planters appealed to their brethren in England for funds and books. This group was poor and had come to little consequence by 1725 when Norden died. Many of the congregation apparently relocated back to Carolina in another settlement at Chowan. In a renewed phase of that work, Paul Palmer of Maryland settled in the region of Albemarle Sound at Pasquotank. After some evangelistic effort, Palmer gathered a church in 1727, the first on record in North Carolina. In the next three decades Palmer and other leaders passed from the scene and the churches were again isolated and destitute. Through correspondence, the Philadelphia Association heard of the Carolina situation and sent missionary pastors to work among the churches, including John Gano of Scotch Plains, New Jersey, and Peter P. Van Horn of Pennepack Church. The result was a transformation of the formerly General Baptist congregations to the Calvinistic position, the establishment in 1755 of the Kehukee Baptist Association, and an ongoing tie to the Philadelphia Baptist Association.

With respect to Baptists in North America, then, the English Baptist heritage provided definite genetic traces. First, Baptists as a religious tradition among Protestants were originally an English phenomenon. Second, the original types of Baptists found in seventeenth-century England provided the basic varieties in the colonial context: General, Calvinistic, and Seventh Day. Third, many examples may be adduced of cross-involvement of Baptist personalities reinforcing the English heritage: John Clarke, Mark Lucar, Hanserd Knollys, Elias Keach, and John Norden to mention a few. Fourth, the principles that made English Baptist identity clear among other dissenters were carried forth in colonial America: Bible-centered Christianity, the Lordship of Christ, congregational governance, and religious liberty.

At the conclusion of the "planting" phase of Baptist life in America, then, there was variety and expanse of congregations. Baptists in colonial America were not well organized and possessed virtually little unity among the various types. The General Six Principle Baptists of

New England held a rudimentary association meeting as early as 1670. Seventh Day Baptists in Rhode Island and Connecticut conferred with each other. The needs of the half dozen or so Calvinistic congregations in the Delaware River Valley led eventually to cooperation in the 1680s and a permanent meeting was formed by 1707 known as the Philadelphia Association, with the Quaker city at its heart, but with most of the congregations in adjoining New Jersey.

Baptist beginnings in America, then, must be understood as one of multiple origins.

Philadelphia: The First Capital of Baptist America

Although Baptists settled in New England initially and spread early in their history to the South, it was in the Middle Colonies, particularly the Delaware Valley, where they organized a significant regional presence with far-reaching influence. The small cluster of congregations on both sides of the Delaware River began meeting together for consultation in matters of polity and ministry as early as 1689. By 1707 this "yearly meeting" became "an association of messengers authorized . . . to meditate and execute designs of public good."[15] This was the beginning of the Philadelphia Baptist Association, the oldest continuing cooperative body among Baptists in North America. Its original members consisted of Lower Dublin and Welsh Tract in Pennsylvania, and Piscataway, Middletown, and Cohansey in New Jersey.

The privileged position of Philadelphia Baptists was due in part to Philadelphia itself. The city was situated at the confluence of two navigable rivers and in the midst of a prosperous farming and trading community. When William Penn and the Society of Friends founded the city in 1681, the religious atmosphere was free and open, beckoning to many kinds of dissenters. Eventually, of course, the city's juxtaposition between the New England colonies and the South gave it an import in the Revolution as the seat of government. Philadelphia became the market town and social center for both eastern Pennsylvania and the hinterlands of South Jersey, to which highway markers were directed. But, beyond the advantages of the "City of Brotherly Love," the Baptist community possessed important assets. First was the connection with English and Welsh Baptists. As much as anywhere in the colonial Baptist community, Philadelphia Baptists confirmed the transatlantic connections among Baptists. The pastors of the early congregations were an unusually gifted group of men: Abel Morgan (Middletown), David Jones (Upper Freehold, Great Valley), Samuel Jones (Southampton and Lower Dublin), Benjamin Griffith (Montgomery), and Stephen Van Horn (Lower Dublin).

In the mid-eighteenth century, the Philadelphia Association took an important set of steps that cast it as a capital of the Baptist movement. In 1742 the Association adopted the Second London Confession of Faith as its doctrinal basis. In 1746 the Association commissioned Benjamin Griffith to write an essay on "The Power and Duty of an Association of Churches." Along with the Confession of Faith, the essay became a landmark document for Baptists in the United States. Third, in the 1760s a pivotal figure, the Rev. Morgan Edwards of Wales, arrived in Philadelphia to chart a course of mission and ministry that became synonymous with the "Philadelphia Tradition." Edwards was a graduate of Bristol Baptist Academy and carried the approbation of the eminent John Gill and other leading English Baptists. He was a scholar and perceptive observer of Baptist life, producing a series of notes on Baptist life in the colonies that would constitute the first history of the denomination in North America. As a commissioned evangelist of the Philadelphia Association in 1771, Edwards traveled amongst the churches and became one of the best-known Baptists of the American Revolutionary era.

Later in its development the Baptist community welcomed William Staughton, another English Baptist. Staughton made his mark in Philadelphia by establishing the first theological school among Baptists in North America. As the nineteenth century moved forward, several of the congregations in the Association became leaders in the Baptist cause, including First Baptist, First African Baptist, Fifth Baptist, Grace (Baptist Temple), First Italian, Spruce Street, Falls of Schuylkill, Roxborough, Fleischmann Memorial, Second, Germantown, Great Valley, Lower Merion, and Second Wilmington, Delaware. The associational model that the Philadelphia Baptist Association forged became a paradigm of unity and mission cooperation for much of the rest of the Baptists in the United States, including churches in New York, New England, Kentucky, Virginia, and the Carolinas. Morgan Edwards, one of its chief architects, early envisioned "a plan for uniting all the Baptists on the Continent in one body politic, by having the Association of Philadelphia (the center) incorporated by charter, and by taking one delegate out of each Association into the corporation."[16] Obviously Edwards's plan was most energetic and too centralized for American Baptists of the eighteenth century, but it did signal the future. The later American Baptist Churches in the USA trace their organizational heritage to the Philadelphia Baptist Association.

Legacy: Religious Toleration

One cannot narrate the early American history of Baptists without reference to the challenges and obstacles they faced with respect to the free exercise of their religious convictions. Baptists and other dissenters, notably Quakers, were not allowed legal recognition in most of New England. They were expected to pay taxes to support clergy and churches of the Standing Order, and they were subject to fines and capricious judgments when they sought converts or preached publicly. There were numerous laws in the Bay Colony against blasphemy, heresy, and disturbing the peace. These same laws allowed the suppression of Anabaptists. This led to Baptists being natural champions of religious toleration, if not religious freedom. Outside New England, their numbers were small and altercations with the law or the prevailing churches in New York, New Jersey, and Pennsylvania were rare.

Legends grew up around Baptists in America and religious toleration in the seventeenth century. It began with reports that traveled back to England in the persons of Roger Williams and John Clarke. In 1636 Williams incurred the wrath of Massachusetts Bay Colony and was banished from the colony. He repaired to Narragansett Country to the southwest and made a pact with the Indians who received him cordially. Williams looked at several possibilities for a settlement and selected a site at a bubbling spring of water that he subsequently called Providence Plantations. In 1652 he engaged in a literary debate with John Cotton over religious intolerance. Williams published his best-known tracts as a result: *The Bloudy Tenent of Persecution for the Cause of Conscience, Discuss'd in a Conference Between Truth and Peace* (1644) and *The Bloudy Tenent Yet More Bloody, By Mr. Cotton's Endeavour to Wash It White in the Blood of the Lambe* (1652). Although Williams remained a Baptist for only a short time, his understanding of religious liberty became canonical among Baptists.

John Clarke's *Ill Newes From New England* (1652) opened the case against religious dissenters for all to see. He told the vivid story of his trip to Lynn, Massachusetts, in 1651 to preach at the house of William Witter, a blind man. Clarke and his two companions, John Crandall and Obadiah Holmes, were apprehended while on their evangelical errand and coerced to attend a Congregationalist meeting. Ever defiant, Clarke put his hat on and pretended to be reading during the discourse. The magistrate, Robert Bridges, was outraged and had the threesome imprisoned at Boston under charges of conducting an unlawful meeting, making slanderous remarks about the church at Lynn, disturbing the peace, and rebaptizing persons. Against his protests, Clarke's fine was paid and he remonstrated against the authorities in support of his principles. Obadiah Holmes was sentenced to public whipping and Clarke's telling of that event made Holmes an instant hero of the cause of religious freedom. Having been brutally lashed 30 times with a three-corded whip, Holmes responded, "You have struck me as with roses," and he accepted the mantle of Christ's sufferings upon himself and forgave the magistrates and the whipper.[17]

The outlook for Baptists was not altogether bleak, however. Elisha Callendar, son of the seventeenth-century Baptist minister Ellis Callendar, graduated from Harvard College in 1710, the first colonial Baptist to receive a college education in North America. He was called to succeed his father as pastor of First Baptist, Boston and the venerable Increase Mather, president of Harvard, preached at his ordination. The recognition given to young Callendar not only produced much goodwill toward Baptists in New England, but also a gift from the Thomas Hollis family of London establishing Harvard's first endowed chair in divinity. As the seventeenth century closed, there were 27 Baptist congregations in the English colonies of North America. Scattered and isolated, but gaining in respect, their chief characteristic was a stubbornness for liberty.

Notes

1 He later wrote that the basis of his decision was Matthew 10: 23: "When they persecute you in one town, flee to the next."

2 Raymond Brown, *The English Baptists of the Eighteenth Century* (London: The Baptist Historical Society, 1986), 25–30.

3 John Spilsbury, *A Treatise Concerning the Lawful Subject of Baptism* (London: Henry Hills, 1643). Available on line at <http://victorian.fortunecity.com/dadd/464/Spilsbury.html>.

4 Robert G. Torbet, *A Social History of the Philadelphia Baptist Association 1707–1940* (Philadelphia, PA: Westbrook Publishing Co., 1945), 11.

5 A view of Dunster favorable to the college and the colonial Massachusetts authorities is found in Samuel Eliot Morison, *Harvard College in the Seventeenth Century*, 2 vols. (Cambridge, MA: Harvard University Press, 1936), I: 305–19. Morison argued that Dunster was treated exceptionally fairly and that the heroic labels of martyr, persecution, and banishment were unfounded.

6 Mrs Scott was a sister of Anne Hutchinson, the Puritan religious leader who emigrated to Rhode Island after being expelled from Massachusetts Bay.

7   Quoted in Champlin Burrage, *The Early English Dissenters in the Light of Recent Research (1550–1641)*, 2 vols. (Cambridge, UK: Cambridge University Press, 1912), I: 356.

8   There is much debate over the centuries as to whether the Providence or Newport church deserved the place of "first" Baptist congregation in America. Exact records for both congregations are lacking.

9   Nathan E. Wood, *The History of the First Baptist Church of Boston (1665–1899)* (Philadelphia, PA: American Baptist Publication Society, 1899), 39–82.

10 Details on Screven are originally noted in the Church Book of First Baptist, Boston and published in Wood, 179–180.

11 Benjamin Keach's revision of the Second London Confession became the basis of the Philadelphia Confession of Faith, published in 1742. It is likely his son urged its use in the Delaware Valley churches.

12 Isaac Backus, *A History of New England with Particular Reference to the Denomination of Christians called Baptists*, 2 vols. (Newton Centre, MA: Backus Historical Society, 1871), II: 167–8.

13 Hywel M. Davies, *Transatlantic Brethren: Rev. Samuel Jones (1735–1814) and His Friends: Baptists in Wales, Pennsylvania, and Beyond* (Bethlehem, PA: Associated University Presses, 1995), 43–53, 61, 67.

14 Ibid., 69, 106–36. This historian uses the term "Baptist Atlantic" to describe the transatlantic nature of Welsh connections.

15 Source: Morgan Edwards, "Origin of the Philadelphia Baptist Association." In William Williams Keen (ed.), *The Bi-Centennial Celebration of the Founding of the First Baptist Church of the City of Philadelphia 1698–1898* (Philadelphia, PA: American Baptist Publication Society, 1899), 461.

16 *Minutes of the Philadelphia Baptist Association 1707–1807*, edited by A. D. Gillette (Philadelphia, PA: American Baptist Publication Society, 1851), 371.

17 The saga was recounted in John Clarke, *Ill Newes from New England* (London: Henry Hills, 1652; repr. New York: Arno Press, 1980), 51.

Chapter 2
Revivalism and a Fondness for Liberty

A movement that had a huge impact upon Baptist growth and identity in North America was the Great Awakening. Beginning in the 1720s, spiritual renewal broke forth in local churches and villages throughout the colonies across confessional lines and political and social categories. It lasted over four decades. Among its chief characteristics were itinerant preaching; dramatic conversion, often accompanied by religious excitement; increased lay participation; and finally realignment of ministers and congregations.[1] The impact upon Baptists can be seen in its statistics: in 1700 there were only 14 Baptist congregations in North America with about 1,500 members; in 1800 there were 1,200 congregations and about one hundred thousand church members.

Revivalism and Separatism

Baptists were the chief religious heirs of the Awakening and it is fair to observe that the fledgling denomination of fewer than 20 congregations, mostly in New England and the Middle Colonies, was transformed during this period. In New England entire Separate congregations shifted to Baptist principles, for example, Sturbridge and Attleborough, Massachusetts, and Montville and West Woodstock, Connecticut. Yet another shift occurred among mixed-communion parishes like Middleborough, Massachusetts, and South Kingston, Rhode Island. The outstanding figure of this part of the Awakening was Isaac Backus who went through his own personal pilgrimage at Middleborough. A third kind of Baptist church was born as prorevival forces (also called New Lights) left older Baptist congregations. Like many Calvinistic Congregationalists, the older Baptist churches of New England opposed many aspects of the revival, especially the emotional excesses and breaches of Calvinist theology that they labeled "Arminianism." This was the case in First Baptist, Boston where a split in the 1740s led to the establishment of Second Baptist Church. In the General Six Principle Baptist community of Rhode Island where David Sprague at North Kingston was swept into the revival by the Calvinist evangelist George Whitefield, and with other New Lights in western Rhode Island, he organized a new congregation at Exeter on Calvinistic lines.[2] In New England alone, of 98 congregations that left the Congregationalist Standing Order and became Separatist during the Awakening, 19 became Baptist and 130 new Baptist congregations were formed.

The flames of revivalism were kindled among urban and village Baptists across their entire geography. At the beginning of his long and illustrious career, John Leland of Connecticut was heavily engaged in revival preaching. In 1781 he sold his horse, and with a pair of new shoes that pinched his feet, he set out to preach in central Virginia. In a field that extended in that colony 120 miles from Orange to York, he baptized 130 converts in a two-year period. As he noted in his memoir, the experience was transforming: "Souls appeared very precious to me, and my heart was drawn out in prayer for their salvation. Now for the first time, I knew what it was to travail in birth for the conversion of sinners. The words of Rachel to Jacob were the words of my heart to God: Give me children or else I die."[3] Among the singular successes Leland claimed were adherents among the imprisoned troops of British Lord Cornwallis, several of whom subsequently became Baptist preachers. Later in 1784 Leland did a six-week stint in Philadelphia speaking to three hundred at one time and twice that number on a second occasion. One of his hearers there recalled heavenly singing attendant upon Leland's preaching that produced his immediate conversion and membership in a Baptist church.[4]

The revival was not confined to any one section. Exponents of the New England experience, now formally known as "Separates," moved in the 1740s to Carolina where they carried forth the revival ethos. One of the young Awakener-preachers was John Gano of New York, who in 1755 found himself nervously preaching before a crowd in Charleston, South Carolina, that included the celebrated George Whitefield.[5] Shubal Stearns, a native of Stonington, Connecticut, was caught up among the Whitefield New Light Separates, with whom he united in 1745. Six years later he joined the Baptists and was ordained. In 1754 Stearns left Connecticut for Virginia where he settled at Opekon Creek. He was soon joined by his brother-in-law, Daniel Marshall, also a convert of Whitefield who had joined the Baptists. Stearns and

Marshall itinerated as evangelists in Berkeley and Hampshire Counties for a time, encountering a good deal of criticism for their evangelical preaching. They moved in 1755 to Guildford (later Randolph) County in central North Carolina where they settled at Sandy Creek. The church, under the pastoral leadership of Stearns, was the epicenter of a wide region of mission effort; its churches linked to Sandy Creek as far as one hundred miles from the mother congregation. One of the features of the Stearns-Marshall ministry was Martha Stearns Marshall, a woman of "good sense, singular piety, and surprising elocution,"[6] who preached frequently among the congregations and planted churches herself.

Gradually the Sandy Creek phenomenon spread back into Virginia. One of the preachers "raised up" in the Sandy Creek tradition was Samuel Harriss. Harriss preached for 10 years before he was ordained and dedicated his new house in Pittsylvania County to public worship. His church became an epicenter for others of the Separate persuasion and he became a leading evangelist and suffered intense persecution from the Virginia authorities. The decade of the 1760s witnessed remarkable efforts and gains for the Separates in Virginia. Several Baptist preachers dated their conversions to George Whitefield's visits to the Colony, like Reuben Ford, the apostle to the Baptist churches in Goochland County. Against stiff persecution from Anglicans, Separate preachers reached large numbers of everyday Virginians, sometimes preaching to over a thousand hearers while enduring much litigation and imprisonment. James Ireland, for instance, in 1769 preached publicly at Culpeper and was incarcerated for not being commissioned by the ecclesiastical authorities. The jail itself was a despicable place, made worse for Ireland by an unchecked raging fever, attempts to poison and suffocate him, and verbal abuse against his preaching from what he referred to as "my Palace in Culpepper." Robert B. Semple, historian of Virginia Baptists in the early nineteenth century, noted there were over 1,300 members in 11 congregations comprising the first Separate association in the colony in 1771.[7] To other non-Baptist observers, the Separates seemed strange indeed. The historian David Benedict recalled one woman's candid description that "hardly any of them looked like other people . . . hair-lipped, clump-footed, blear-eyed, bow-legged, and humpbacked . . . they were all for plunging and let the poor, ignorant children run wild. . . ."[8]

Another remarkable outgrowth of the Separate movement was the foundation of the African American or black Baptist tradition, discussed here in chapter 8. The experiential tone of the Separate Baptists in the black context can be readily seen in the conversion of David

George. George, who heard George Leile preach, remembered the impact on his experience:

> His sermon was very suitable, on *Come unto me all ye that labour and are heavy laden, and I will give you rest*. When it was ended, I went to him and told him I was so; That I was weary and heavy laden; and that the grace of God had given me rest. Indeed this whole discourse seemed for me.[9]

David George in many respects became a connecting link to the on-going revivalistic tradition, with Baptists in Canada and overseas as discussed later in the context of African American Baptists.

Given their overall essentially Calvinistic theological outlook, it is not surprising that the Separates would eventually gravitate toward the Calvinistic or Regular Baptists. In Connecticut this occurred most vividly in the Stonington (Union) Association. Formed in 1772, it was a Separate Baptist association whose churches practiced strict communion and adopted the Second London Confession (or its equivalent) as their doctrinal guide. Gradually in the 1780s Regular Baptist congregations in the vicinity dropped mixed communion and were accepted into the Stonington Association. This in turn led to the Association's establishing a wider fellowship with older Regular associations that also had reached rapprochement with Separate principles: Warren, Philadelphia, Danbury, New York, and Charleston. In 1817 a merger was consummated even with the Groton Union Conference, founded upon mixed communion principles. Similarly in Virginia in 1783 the General Association of Separate Baptists began to consider the possibility of expansion across the state. The earlier Arminian tendencies had apparently disappeared and it was agreed to adopt the Philadelphia Confession of Faith, liable to alterations. Most of the churches had given up their Separate practices like weekly communion, love feasts, laying on of hands, and footwashing, although many, the historian A. H. Newman noted, continued to dress plainly. In Virginia in 1787, the United Baptist Churches of Christ was created "on a permanent and happy basis."[10]

Revivalism, as manifested in the Separate Baptist movement of the eighteenth century, had long-lasting impact upon Baptist identity. First, it laid an emphasis upon religious experience as a priority over confessionalism. While Separates were not unconcerned about doctrinal orthodoxy, they wanted to see doctrine mediated in life experience. There was a stress upon human response; this was the basis of charges of "Arminianism" among the Separates. Another area of religious experience pertained to matters of lifestyle. Most Separates denounced intermarriage, maintained rigorously biblical rules of conduct, and disciplined members who departed from the norms. Third, Separates were growth-oriented. They were conscious of the rapid increase in numbers of congregations sympathetic to their practices and they took note of the large crowds attracted by their preaching. Another feature of revivalism's effect upon Baptist identity was to create an irenic spirit among dissenters. John Gano, the peripatetic preacher from New York and New Jersey, studied divinity under a Connecticut Presbyterian, and was a close friend of Aaron Burr, Sr., the president of Princeton College, who frequently attempted to recruit Gano to the school.[11] Finally, early Baptist historians noted that it was the revivalistic style that moved westward on the frontier with Baptists of the next century. One estimate had it that a quarter of the Baptists in Virginia migrated to Kentucky between 1790 and 1810, just as Separates made their associational peace with Regulars. Because of their experientially directed theology and practices, Separates were in actuality a liberalizing force among Baptists who were previously much bound to their confessional traditions. In the next chapter we shall see how influential these factors were in the westward advance of the Baptists.

Baptists and the American Revolution

As numerous historians have shown, there was a direct connection between revivalism in the Great Awakening and the fervor of the Revolution. The preaching of evangelical doctrines led people to become "a vital communion of kindred spirits," as the historian Alan Heimert has put it. The Calvinistic foundation of evangelicals produced sermons that were not vindications of actions already taken but an encouragement to further endeavor on the part of the populace, a quickening of their wills as well as informing their minds. Evangelist George Whitefield warned John Wesley, "the work of God is carried on here by doctrines quite opposite to those you hold."[12] Clearly the majority of Baptists in pre-Revolutionary America could identify both with the prevailing Calvinistic ethos as well as an activistic experience in which words like "liberty" were often heard. The evangelical ministry of the mid-eighteenth century New Lights offered Americans new commitments in the political, moral, and ethical realms.

Baptists were engaged in the issues of the Revolution at several points. First, there were those ardently devoted to the Patriot cause. In New Jersey, John Hart was a leader during the period of resistance leading up to armed rebellion. A prominent miller and member of the Hopewell church, he took an interest in politics and was elected to the New Jersey legislature in 1761. He voted against approval of the Stamp Act in 1765 and supported an address to King George III asserting that the Crown had no right to levy taxes without representation. Marking his course deliberately, in 1770 he voted in favor of a measure that prohibited any further supply of the King's troops in the colony. When pressed by the colonial governor to rescind this action, Hart stood his ground in 1775. The following year when New Jersey selected its representatives to the Second Continental Congress, Hart was among them and became a signer of the Declaration of Independence, the only Baptist to do so. When he returned to New Jersey he was elected Speaker of the House, which meant that he and the legislature were obliged to move constantly to avoid capture by the British. Upon returning to his home, he found it in ruins, his crops were destroyed, his wife had died and his children had fled to the safety of the hills in northern Jersey. His health broken, Hart died a Patriot hero in 1779. Another example of Patriotic gallantry was Richard Furman of South Carolina. Upon the issuance of the Declaration of Independence, Furman declared himself in support of the Revolution and preached in that vein until threats against his family were apparent. In 1776 and 1777 he even visited Tory settlements to rally the cause; with his ministerial colleagues, Oliver Hart and Edmund Botsford, he fled South Carolina to southern backcountry Virginia as the British invasion of the colony progressed. It is said a British bounty was upon his head and several times he narrowly escaped capture. Finally, the eminent preacher in Boston, Samuel Stillman, became an outstanding "Patriot orator" and was forced to leave his city in 1776. He and his family stayed in exile for a time in Philadelphia, where he advocated the Patriot cause and preached before the Continental Congress.

Baptists served in large numbers and with distinction in various regiments of the Army. Laymen served as soldiers, frequently fading in and out of service as the conflict moved out of their regions. Reune Runyan and Recompense Stansbury in New Jersey served on committees of correspondence and in military conflict. General James Cox, Colonel Asher Moore, and Colonel Joab Houghton were well known. In North Carolina, where Baptist preachers were considered "a unit" for independence, Jesse Cobb at New Bern constructed a magazine to preserve military supplies for the Continental Army. Many Baptist pastors aided the cause of independence and none so nobly as those who served as chaplains. Nicholas Cox, pastor at Wantage in Sussex County, and William Worth from Pittsgrove, Salem County, served for the entire four years. William Rogers, pastor of First Baptist, Philadelphia, was a friend of George Washington and of Benjamin Rush, who became a brigade chaplain. Another later minister of that church, Henry Holcombe, a southerner, preached his first sermon on horseback in the 1770s to his regimental troops. David Jones, pastor at Upper Freehold, New Jersey, fled to Pennsylvania and joined the regiment of Brig. Gen. Anthony Wayne. Jones preached a sermon that was widely circulated in print form and fueled the fires of Patriotism. The title was "Defensive War in a Just Cause Blameless" and its author urged his fellow citizens to recognize that God has a people reserved for himself and "Our present dispute is just, our cause is good. A martial spirit from God has spread throughout the land." He went on, "Surely, if this is not a heavy judgment, it is a presage of Success."[13] For his rhetoric, he merited a reward on his head from General Howe. John Gano left First Baptist, New York and served as a chaplain to Washington and later with the notorious Sullivan-Clinton Expedition in western and central New York State; Hezekiah Smith was appointed chaplain to the Continental Army and served in several campaigns in the New York and New Jersey regions. Smith interpreted the war as "America's salvation." James Manning showed his support for American independence by arranging for the public reading in 1776 of the Declaration of Independence from the steps of his church, First Baptist, Providence, Rhode Island.

There were also those Baptists who remained loyal to the British sovereign. Historian Norman Maring found members in Morristown, Cohansey, and Piscataway churches that went over to the other side and eventually emigrated to Nova Scotia.[14] In Philadelphia, the most illustrious Baptist to declare Loyalist sympathies was Morgan Edwards. Edwards was a stiff, outspoken Tory accused by his detractors of "rash and imprudent expressions." In 1775 he was forced by peers to recant:

> for the future I will conduct myself in such a manner as to avoid giving offense, and at the same time, in justice to myself, declare that I am a friend to the present measures pursued by the friends to American liberty, and do hereby approve of them, and as far as in my power, will endeavor to promote them.[15]

Others like Matthew Moore and George Leile in Georgia, fled that colony for the West Indies. In Anson County, North Carolina, James Childs, a New Light Baptist preacher, refused to take the oath of allegiance and would not bear arms, a position that he claimed was a commitment to his denominational principles. A unique case of Baptist disengagement in the Revolution occurred in the German Baptist or Tunker community west of Philadelphia that refused to supply the Patriot (or any other) Army, upon which refusal the colonial government laid a fine of two pounds, ten shillings upon them.

Many of the state historians among Baptists note the damage done to Baptist facilities as a result of the war. When British troops landed at Newport, Rhode Island, they burned the Baptist meetinghouse and parsonage. Likewise, when General Howe landed in Boston in 1776, he ordered the meetinghouse of Second Baptist Church torn down for firewood for his troops. Some congregations were spared destruction, but not dislocation. First Baptist, Boston was converted to a British barracks and used for a hospital, as was Morristown, New Jersey; at Middletown, New Jersey, pastor Abel Morgan and his flock had to meet in his barn. The landmark "old yellow meetinghouse" at Upper Freehold was much damaged. The general impression from the wartime minutes of both congregations and associations was that services were frequently suspended, the religious and moral climate was low, and attendance was in some cases half what it was previously. In Pennsylvania several congregations suffered constant turmoil due to the passage of both armies through their villages. Brandywine Baptist Church at Chadd's Ford found itself in the midst of a major battle for the defense of Philadelphia and the Church in the Great Valley (near Valley Forge) was ransacked and looted by General Howe's men. In New York City, John Gano's building was used as a British stable and he found only 37 members out of two hundred to greet his return after the war. The sole building of the Rhode Island College was used as a hospital facility for wounded French and American soldiers during the war. In 1777 the minutes of the Philadelphia Association simply recorded "no meeting this year."

The Beginnings of a Liberal Tradition

An important new direction was taken among Baptists in New England in the Revolutionary epoch. Not all Baptists remained in the deterministic Reformed theological stream. In 1770 Benjamin Randal, a tailor and sailmaker, heard George Whitefield preach and he experienced a conversion. Within a year young Randal became active in the local Congregational church and took up preaching as a sideline. Following a stint in the Patriot Army, he became a Baptist and joined the church at Berwick. He continued preaching and moved to New Durham in central New Hampshire where he purchased a farm on a prominent ridge. Here in the up-country of the colony he found more receptivity for his New Light style, in a region where frontiersmen were "impatient of law, religion, and morality," as Timothy Dwight recalled.[16] It is known that Randal consulted with Edward Lock of London-Canterbury and Tozier Lord of Barrington and a handful of other freewill preachers who held the principle of "common grace." After rumors circulated about the unorthodox nature of his preaching, the Regular or Calvinistic Baptists called Randal to account. At a ministerial meeting at Gilmanton in 1779 he revealed his extreme distaste for Calvinistic doctrine. This drew the ire of the Baptists and forced Randal to set another course for his emphases of "free grace, free will, and free communion." Eventually, Randal's following would openly reject the doctrines of the imputation of Adam's sin to the human race, eternal security, and the incapability of the human will.

In 1780 Randal formed a Freewill Baptist congregation in a covenant meeting at the home of Zechariah Boody in New Durham, and within a year he and a small congregation erected a meetinghouse on the ridge near the Randal farm. From that epicenter Randal preached on itinerant tours of northern New England, organizing congregations and recruiting other freewill preachers. In the next two decades he gave shape to a unique polity of monthly, quarterly, and yearly meetings over which he presided across northern New England. The system, eclectic in its origins, looked more like an amalgam of Quaker and Methodist usage than anything associated with the Regular Baptists. However, it became a highly effective organizational scheme on the frontiers of New England and New York. Like many Baptist preachers of his era, Randal was self-taught and built his theology out of his own experience, positive and negative, rather than rigid adherence to a doctrinal confession. He was Baptist because the Scriptures taught baptism; every other doctrine had to pass the same test. Similarly Freewillers required that worship involve believers only, and strict discipline of un-Christian conduct and "disorderly walking" was meted out according to literal readings of the Bible. Ultimately, Benjamin Randal and his following broke with the rigid determinism and elitism of both the Standing Order and older Baptists of New England, exhibiting the raw courage of a dissenter: "I do not believe them," he retorted of Calvinistic doctrines. "The more they disputed with me on these points, the stronger I grew in my sentiments; for it drove me to searching the Scriptures with greater diligence and pray more earnestly to God for a correct understanding of their meaning." But, as a less than perfect person himself, Randal told a brother whom he had offended, "As a man I have sinned, as a Christian, I'll confess it."[17]

Randal's movement spread throughout New England and with the expansion of that section into western New York, Ohio's Western Reserve, and Michigan Territory, on the moving frontier as well. The Freewill Connexion drew to itself some gifted leaders who, like Randal, were weary of the old systems: Pelatiah Tingley, a graduate in divinity from Yale College, Hosea Quinby, an educator and author of the formal doctrinal treatise of Freewill Baptists in 1834, and John Buzzell who gave shape to the General Conference of Freewill Baptists (organized in 1827) and many of its publishing ventures. In New England and on the New York frontier, the Freewill Baptists formed a shadow Baptist presence to the Regular Baptists, often building meetinghouses in the same villages with Calvinistic Baptists, as in Fairport, New York, where the two meetinghouses almost faced each other. To its credit as an open and tolerant Baptist tradition, the Freewill Baptists were able to weather difficult leadership contests and transitions in their pilgrimage to develop an alternative Baptist movement. Major interruptions of their progress occurred in 1783, 1786–92, and again in 1808 when Benjamin Randal died. In each case substantial revivals subsequently broke forth among their churches in New England, bringing new life to the movement.

Eventually, the Freewill Baptists would follow the typical organizing path of the Regular or Calvinistic Baptists. They started schools like Parsonfield Seminary in southern Maine and the Bible School at Whitestown, New York. The Bible school reflected a long-standing disinclination among some Freewill Baptists toward an educated ministry. Later secondary academies flourished in Vermont, New Hampshire, Ohio, and Iowa; collegiate level schools included Bates College in Maine, Hillsdale College in Michigan, Keuka College in New York, Rio Grande College in Ohio, Storer College in West Virginia, and Parker College in Minnesota. They created a network of societies to conduct foreign missions (1833) and home missions (1834), publish educational materials (1846), and pursue a modest social concerns agenda in the Freewill Baptist Antislavery Society (1842). In 1828 and again in 1832, the General Conference became in essence a national temperance society, urging all of its related quarterly meetings to organize themselves as abstinence societies in the model of the Washingtonian Movement.

Other Baptists reacted negatively to the Old Calvinist theology as well. In South Carolina, a young pastor near Charleston, Elhanan Winchester (1751–97) who gained a reputation as a gifted pulpit orator, moved toward universalism. He was much influenced by Paul Siegvolk's work *The Everlasting Gospel* (1753) and openly taught universal restoration. As he confided to his memoir on the reading of Revelation 7: 9:

> I became fully persuaded that the number of the finally saved would equal if not exceed the number of the lost. And I was so forcibly impressed with this new and very joyful discovery, that I not only conversed in that strain privately, but boldly preached it in the congregation, which generally consisted of nearly a thousand persons upon Sundays.[18]

When called to the vacant pulpit of First Baptist, Philadelphia in 1780, Winchester commenced preaching universal restoration and this offended the congregation's leadership. Although a majority of the church enthusiastically supported Winchester's preaching, the trustees of the church locked Winchester out of the building in March 1781. He subsequently went to a lecture hall at the University of Pennsylvania with a portion of the congregation that remained loyal to his teachings. He enjoyed the support of numerous prominent Philadelphians, including Benjamin Rush. The inquiry was held within the Association and involved Baptist luminaries like Samuel Jones, William Van Horn, and Oliver Hart. They determined that Winchester was beyond the Philadelphia Confession of Faith in his position and they ruled in favor of conformity with the Confession. Winchester had so galvanized the Philadelphia Baptist community that anyone connected with him was suspect. Young John Leland, who had been converted earlier under Winchester's ministry in Grafton, Connecticut, attempted to reconnect with Winchester but was shut out of the First Baptist Church for fear he too was a universalist. He did join Winchester in preaching to about 200 at University Hall, but found that ultimately unacceptable.[19] As for Winchester himself, he traveled to England where he mingled with John Murray, a Methodist, and William Vidler, a Baptist, both popular universalists.

Close to the positions of Winchester was Jonathan Maxcy, second president of Rhode Island College. He was accused by prominent New England Baptist pastors, including the venerable Isaac Backus, of holding universalist views. Maxcy was able to deflect the accusation successfully, but it was clear that universalism had a vivid impact upon the growing Baptist movement. Universalists were in general credited with bringing down the Standing Order and its Calvinist stranglehold in New England and they were often ahead of the Baptists in pressing for an end to compulsory religious taxes. There were not a few instances where, in the face of limited worship facilities in small villages, Freewill and Regular Baptists shared church buildings for a time with local Universalists.

Denominational Connectedness

Although the Baptist movement was relatively small by comparison with Congregationalists in New England or the Church of England in the South, the pastors of congregations interacted in several creative and important ways. One of these was the pastoral ministry itself and the other was in the area of higher education. Hardly an obscurantist collection of unlettered religious enthusiasts, Baptists at the end of the Revolutionary era gave evidence of a full-fledged transcolonial religious tradition.

Baptist ministers in the colonies were a remarkably resourceful lot. Often emerging from modest to poor family backgrounds, they sought education from mentors and later from collegiate institutions. This meant that one could originate in one colony, be trained in another, and serve yet elsewhere. For instance, Samuel Stillman, who in the later century would be the outstanding Baptist in Boston, was born in Philadelphia, studied under Oliver Hart in South Carolina, and served the church at Upper Freehold in New Jersey in the 1760s. He was recognized with an MA by both the College of Philadelphia and by Harvard. Oliver Hart, considered by some to be the best read of the mid-century Baptists, was pastor in Charleston and moved to serve the Hopewell church in New Jersey in 1781. Hezekiah Smith hailed from Long Island and moved to Morristown, New Jersey where he was converted under the celebrated John Gano. Smith graduated from the College at Princeton and went south where in Charleston he was ordained an evangelist. In the early 1760s he preached frequently to crowds of 15 hundred to two thousand hearers. He considered remaining in New Jersey or New York, but accepted the pastorate at Haverhill, Massachusetts that he served for four decades. Being resourceful also meant for some staying alive in hostile conditions. In 1782, John Corbley, pastor at Goshen Church near Garrad's Fort in western Pennsylvania, was en route to the meetinghouse when his family was attacked by Indians; four of his children and his wife were scalped and left for dead.

John Gano was perhaps the most widely circulated of the colonial Baptist clergy. He first united with the Hopewell, New Jersey church, then toured the South and returned to be pastor at Scotch Plains, New

Jersey. He was the founding minister at First Baptist, New York, and during the Revolution served in Washington's Army as a chaplain in the Hudson Valley and upstate campaigns. After the Revolution, Gano went West where he pioneered congregations in Cincinnati, Ohio, and northern Kentucky. One could also mention Morgan Edwards and William Staughton in this regard. Both emigrated from England, were graduates of Bristol Baptist Academy, and both for a time served in the South, only to move north to the Middle Colonies. Henry Holcombe, mentioned earlier in connection with service in the Revolution, was born in Virginia, reared in South Carolina, where he was baptized, and ordained at Euhaw. While serving in South Carolina he was a member of that state's constitutional convention. Later he went to Savannah for the unheard-of salary of $2,000 per year. He was there until 1811 when he received the call to Philadelphia. Rounding out this distinguished list was James Manning, who was an outstanding graduate of Isaac Eaton's academy at Hopewell, then a standout student at Princeton College, and later pastor at Warren and Providence, Rhode Island. He was, of course, the first president of the College of Rhode Island.

The successful attempt to establish a denominational college in Rhode Island illustrated just how connected the Baptists of the eighteenth century were. Morgan Edwards, the moving force behind the idea, recognized the opportunity for the Baptists in Rhode Island, by 1760 the last colony without an institution of higher education. He proposed the idea to leaders of the Philadelphia Association who in turn delegated James Manning to survey the possibilities. Manning visited Newport and associated towns and met with prominent Baptists: Samuel Ward, John Gardner, Job Bennet, and Josias Lyndon, all of whom encouraged the project. Even Ezra Stiles, a Congregationalist pastor in Newport, responded favorably and lent his hand to writing a draft of the charter. Stiles proved to be more limiting to Baptist interests than was desirable, and the Philadelphia Association dispatched Samuel Jones and R. S. Jones to aid in the final drafting process. When the charter was passed in a legislature dominated by Baptists, it revealed how interconnected was the entire Baptist community in the American colonies. Among the Baptist trustees and fellows of the Rhode Island College were: Samuel Ward (Rhode Island governor, supreme court justice, and congressman), Daniel Jenckes (chief justice of Rhode Island), Josias Lyndon (governor of Rhode Island), Nicholas Brown, Job Bennet, Joshua Babcock, Samuel Stillman, John Gano, and Hezekiah Smith. To launch the institution successfully, Morgan Edwards visited the English Baptist community and drew up a list of possible candidates for honorary degrees, and Hezekiah Smith toured the southern colonies raising support. In the last three decades of the eighteenth century the College was both a rallying point and proud achievement of the Baptist community in North America.

Observers of Baptist congregational life at the conclusion of the Revolutionary era in the United States noticed a maturity and solidity across the denomination. Pastors were called and regularly installed, churches grew in membership and nurture and gained social acceptance in most communities. Beyond the local churches, there was a healthy associational life where disputes were resolved, questions of polity and praxis were queried and satisfied, and a mutually supportive, interactive network was emerging. This was not by accident. Leaders like Samuel Jones of Lower Dublin Church in Philadelphia worked hard over decades to "regularize" Baptist life. Jones, a tall and robust man of Welsh parentage, was educated at Isaac Eaton's Academy and the Academy of Philadelphia (later the University of Pennsylvania) under Francis Alison, an Enlightenment devotee. Never inclined toward the Awakening, Jones was a measured preacher, a scholarly thinker with a Calvinistic orientation. He was the quintessential long-term pastor, being informed in 1765 that his church would not discharge him to accept a call to Boston, expecting him to remain permanently in their employ. He frequently traveled on behalf of the Association, for instance to Boston or Rhode Island on business of the College, and much about the Delaware Valley representing the churches. He was a leading writer for the Association, penning much correspondence and the official published letters. This allowed him the privilege of virtually defining the purpose of associations in America, "a threefold cord is not easily broken," and serving as a de facto bishop among his peers. Typical of his attitude and advice were his prefatory words in his *Treatise on Church Discipline* reflecting over 40 years of pastoral ministry and associational leadership:

> I will only add, That you be particularly careful, to maintain and preserve temper, coolness, and impartiality, in your meetings of business. To be rigid, obstinate, partial, passionate, and overbearing, in administering the concerns of the house of God: how unlike the followers of the meek and lowly Jesus! How unworthy of office under their divine Master.[20]

By the end of the eighteenth century, Baptists in North America had laid the foundation for a substantial contribution to American and eventually Canadian religious life. Not only were there growing numbers of converts and congregations, but there was a college and recognized clergy to be reckoned with. In the popular mind Baptists were also the leading advocates of religious liberty and in particular the separation of church and state.

Beyond US Borders

An important part of the eighteenth-century saga of Baptists in North America concerns their plantation in British North America. At the end of the Great War for Empire between France and Great Britain (1756–63, also known as the Seven Years' War and the French and Indian War), the French largely withdrew from their colony of Acadia, leaving an attractive opportunity for British colonization. The first Baptists to journey to what is now Canada were part of the New England planter community that sought lands under the offer of the British government to resettle in what became Nova Scotia, New Brunswick, and Prince Edward Island in the 1760s. Between 1760 and 1763 about 5,000 immigrants left New England for the Atlantic colonies to the North. Along with Anglicans, Congregationalists, and a few Presbyterians, Baptists joined the shoreside settlements of Yarmouth, Barrington, and Horton in Nova Scotia. One of the settlers was Ebenezer Moulton, formerly of South Brimfield, Massachusetts. Moulton had been active in the campaign to exempt dissenters from colonial taxes in Massachusetts and was involved in a mercantile business that prospered during the French and Indian War. When the war ended, however, Moulton's business sagged into insolvency and he fled his creditors and family to Nova Scotia. In 1760–61 he worked as a surveyor of lands and a traveling preacher. One of the settlements he visited frequently was at the head of the Bay of Fundy, Horton's Landing. There, about 1763–65, he gathered a small congregation. The congregation languished after Moulton departed for the US in 1767, and almost ceased. In 1778 it was regathered and has had a continuous history since as a mother congregation to Baptists in the Maritimes, the first college in the region, and a strong missionary outreach.

Another part of the Maritime Baptist story transpired in Halifax between 1823 and 1827. Halifax, which had assumed the role of a colonial capital for the Maritimes, included both strong Anglican and Nonconformist religious communities. There was a split at St Paul's Anglican Church (the oldest Anglican parish) from which emerged leadership for a congregation that started up on nearby Granville Street. The Granville Street church moved in the direction of a Baptist orientation. In its search for a permanent pastor, advice was sought from the

New England Baptist community and the answer was to send a young graduate of Brown University, Alexis Caswell, to Halifax. Caswell was ordained in 1828 and remained long enough to establish firmly the congregation. He was followed by Henry K. Green, a graduate of Union College and Andover Seminary, who had taught at Columbian College with Caswell in the 1820s. One of the leaders of the Granville Street Baptist Church was Edmund Crawley, who would later become a pioneer in Baptist higher education in the Maritimes.

Farther to the West in the British provinces, the first Baptists were American missionaries from Vermont, Massachusetts, Connecticut, and Maine. In 1794 Vermont missionaries John Hebbard and Arial Kendrick, planted congregations at Caldwell's Manor in the eastern townships of Quebec, and later other congregations sprang forth at Stanstead, Hatley, Sutton Flats, and Eaton (1797) and Abbott's Corner (1799). Still farther inland, missionaries from New York and Vermont helped to plant congregations around the edge of Lake Ontario: Hallowell (1795), Thurlow (1796), and Beamsville (1796). An association grew up around three churches at Thurlow in 1803. A similar fellowship emerged among the Eastern Township churches in 1805, nurtured by the associational life in the United States. Suggestive of ties across great distances, the Charlotteville Church near Lake Erie in Upper Canada, applied for membership in the Shaftsbury, Vermont, Association in 1804, from whence their pioneering missionaries Obed Warren and Lemuel Covell had come. To offset the American influence in the Canadas, Scottish and English Baptist missionaries were sent out in the 1820s to plant churches and eventually begin a college. The first congregations were at Lochiel Township (1817), Clarence (1822), and Montreal (1830). The British influence was especially strong in the Ottawa Valley. In these scattered efforts, Baptists would build a foundation in Canada that primarily resembled that in the United States, with certain nuances of a British and uniquely Canadian kind.

Legacy: Baptists and the Separation of Church and State

The challenge of the revolutionary era brought growth and internal conflicts to the community of Baptist congregations. The newer churches in New England were shunned by older Baptists and misunderstood by Congregationalists. Often Baptists became unwitting objects of derision, unwarranted taxation, and complex litigation. In Virginia a similar fate prevailed, albeit with a different antagonist, the Church of England. Only in the Middle Colonies and the Deep South were Baptists free to plant congregations and propagate their values.

The situations in New England and Virginia led to Baptist identification with the position of separation of church and state, soon to evolve as a liberalizing position. As historian Robert Handy has observed, the basic principle at stake was religious liberty. What Baptists have called the separation of church and state is a way to protect and extend that principle.[21] In New England, as we have seen in the earliest period of Baptist development in North America, there was a deep antagonism toward the intermingling of religious and political institutions. By the eighteenth century, this became a concert of action from within the Baptist community. Its leading proponents were Ebenezer Moulton (who would later take the Baptist tradition to Canada), Thomas Greene, Isaac Backus, John Leland, and Hezekiah Smith.

In Massachusetts, the General Court passed legislation in 1728 and again in 1747 exempting Baptists and Quakers from payment of the tax if they supported a church of their own denomination within five miles of their home. This gave limited relief from the burdensome Standing Order tax, but it rankled Baptists because it meant that they must register their congregations in order to qualify for the exemption. It left the Congregationalists in the position of being able to determine the legitimacy of an application for exemption. Further, in 1753 the Court passed an amendment to the original law, obviously in response to the recent growth of "new" Baptists in the colony, that required the testimony of three other "Anabaptist" churches that the applicant congregation was an acceptable "Anabaptist." This, of course, brought further contretemps between the Old Baptists of the colony and the Separates. Matters worsened by 1757 when the law was renewed and strictly required all Baptists to be listed on a roster. Baptists wavered on whether to pursue the matter through the provincial jurisdictions or bypass the General Court and go directly to the Privy Council in England. The newly organized Warren Baptist Association, under the leadership of James Manning, John Gano, and Isaac Backus collected letters of grievances from the churches and created a committee to prepare petitions for the legislatures of Massachusetts and Connecticut. With the combined threat of redressing the grievances in England, and the growing unity of Massachusetts Baptists with their colleagues in Philadelphia, the General Court of Massachusetts passed another act that allowed Baptists tax exemptions provided they had certificates of good standing from their congregations.

The exemption process was too little, too late, and a committee headed by Isaac Backus in 1774 took a petition to the Continental

Congress. En route he weighed the importance of the persecuted Baptists for conscience's sake versus support for a united Patriot effort with the Standing Order. In Philadelphia the Warren Association of Baptists joined forces with Baptists from the Middle Colonies and met with prominent members of the Congress, including John and Samuel Adams. Both the Adamses assured the Baptists that their request was unfounded and reflected the position of fanatics. After four hours in conference at Carpenter's Hall, Backus and his Baptist colleagues were informed there was as much chance of expecting a change in the solar system as to expect that Massachusetts would give up the Standing Order. While temporarily this appeared to be a serious defeat for the Baptist cause for making religious liberty a national issue, all was not lost. On December 9, 1774, the Continental Congress's meeting in Cambridge, Massachusetts under the presidency of John Hancock, resolved that the establishment of civil and religious liberty to each denomination was the wish of the Congress. Lacking any civil authority, however, it referred the matter to a general assembly at the provincial level that would care for such matters under a new constitution. That became a protracted process for New England that was not resolved fully until 1833.

In Virginia, Samuel Harriss of Culpeper and John Waller of Lower Spotsylvania led a host of preachers who would not be silenced by religious intolerance and overzealous magistrates. Their tenacity, expressed through the General Committee of Baptists in Virginia, paid dividends through associations with leading politicians like Patrick Henry, Thomas Jefferson, and James Madison. In 1779 Jefferson introduced his bill for religious freedom to the Virginia Assembly, drawing official support from Virginia Baptists. It became a charter for religious liberty in the American experience. Later, in 1785, Madison introduced another bill for the same purpose and it was passed. Eventually in that stronghold of Anglican supremacy, the Incorporation Act was repealed and religious liberty was won.

What Baptists meant by separation of church and state was that the state had no inherent right to prosecute persons for matters of conscience and it was no worthy adjudicator between denominations of Christians, legitimating some and dismissing others. "Consistently with the principles of Christianity," Backus wrote, "we claim and expect the liberty of worshipping God according to our consciences, not obliged to support a ministry we cannot attend. . . ."[22] Government, leading Baptists contended, was to refrain from interference in matters of the spiritual realm. Leland was more direct than Backus: "Government has no more to do with the religious opinions of men, than it has with the principles of mathematics."[23] This was to have enormous theological and organizational implications both for the United States and Canada, and for Baptists themselves.

Ironically, however, modern writers are surprised to learn, Baptists did not cease from interposing their opinions upon the civil order. Some held forth that America was destined to be a Christian nation, and others supported government chaplaincies and urged interpretations of Scripture upon lawmakers and persons of influence. At the conclusion of the eighteenth century, Baptists had assumed the mantle of religious libertarians and nursed a distinguished institution of higher education and a theological pluralism that ranged from primitivism to universalism. At times they were the most direct beneficiaries of their separationism.

If the Standing Order/Establishment position on the merged interests of church and state are understood to be a conservative position, politically and theologically, the Baptists were clearly the libertarians of their era. Their understanding of religious liberty for all persons, regardless of creed or no profession, placed them high above the theological differentiations of biblical literalism and Reformed thought. That, together with the practical experience of groups like the Freewill Baptists and Universalist-Baptists, plus the educated elite graduates of the College of Rhode Island, assured the Baptists of the eighteenth century a legacy of liberal proportions. As well, many urban centers in both the North and South had multiracial Baptist congregations.

Notes

1   For a useful set of criteria, see C. C. Goen, *Revivalism and Separatism in New England 1740–1800: Strict Congregationalists and Separate Baptists in the Great Awakening* (New Haven, CT: Yale University Press, 1962), 8–35.

2   Ibid., 239–41.

3   L. F. Greene, *The Writings of the late Elder John Leland, including Some Events in His Life, Written by Himself, with Additional Sketches, etc.* (New York: G. W. Wood, 1845), 20–1.

4   Ibid., 24.

5   John Gano, *Biographical Memoirs of the Late Rev. John Gano of Frankfort (Kentucky) formerly of the City of New York* (New York: Southwick and Hardcastle, 1806; repr. Particular Baptist Press, 1998), 60.

6   Robert B. Semple, *History of the Rise and Progress of the Baptists in Virginia* (Richmond, VA: n.p., 1810), 374.

7   Robert B. Semple, *History of the Rise and Progress of the Baptists in Virginia* (Richmond, VA: c), 70.

8   David Benedict, *Fifty Years Among the Baptists* (New York: Sheldon and Co., 1860; repr. Glen Rose, TX: Newman and Collins, 1913), 71.

9   Journal of David George quoted in Mechal Sobel, *Trabelin' On: The Slave Journey to an Afro-Baptist Faith* (Princeton, NJ: Princeton University Press, 1979), 106.

10 A. H. Newman, *A History of the Baptist Churches in the United States* (Philadelphia, PA: American Baptist Publication Society, 1898), 300–2.

11 Gano, *Life and Ministry of John Gano*, 38, 39.

12 Alan Heimert, *Religion and the American Mind, from the Great Awakening to the Revolution* (Cambridge, MA: Harvard University Press, 1966), 4, 14, 18–19.

13 Norman H. Maring, *Baptists in New Jersey: A Study in Transition* (Valley Forge, PA: The Judson Press, 1964), 72.

14 Ibid., 74–5.

15 Quoted in Henry C. Vedder, *Baptists in the Middle States* (Philadelphia, PA: American Baptist Publication Society, 1898), 78–9.

16 Quoted in Norman Allan Baxter, *History of the Freewill Baptists: A Study in New England Separatism* (Rochester, NY: American Baptist Historical Society, 1957), 19.

17 Quoted in Baxter, *Freewill Baptists*, 50.

18 Edward Martin Stone, *Biography of Rev. Elhanan Winchester* (Boston: H. R. Brewster, 1836), 37.

19 Greene, *Writings of Elder John Leland*, 24.

20 Samuel Jones, *A Treatise of Church Discipline and a Directory Done by Appointment of the Philadelphia Baptist Association* (Lexington, KY: T. Anderson, 1805), iv.

21 Robert T. Handy, "The Principle of Religious Liberty and the Dynamics of Baptist History," *Perspectives in Religious Studies* 13/4 (December 1986): 32.

22 Quoted in Edwin S. Gaustad, "The Backus-Leland Tradition," *Foundations* 2/2 (April 1959): 147.

23 John Leland, "The Rights of Conscience Inalienable," Ibid., 184.

Chapter 3
Growth and Diversification

The early nineteenth century was for the Baptist community in North America a period of growth, diversification, and identity formation. Baptists were a part of what historians refer to as the "Protestant quest for a Christian America."[1] At the commencement of the century there were five types of Baptists in the United States in a rapidly growing community of congregations.[2] By 1900, there were 12 types of Baptists and an aggregate membership in excess of 4.2 million members in 43,000 churches. In Canada, the numbers included three basic varieties with almost 97,000 members in 930 congregations.[3] What brought about this proliferation from a dissenter sect to a major North American denominational tradition?

Baptists on the Moving Frontier

It is important to draw an accurate picture of the Baptist movement beginning with the local congregation. There were significant congregations in all of the urban centers in the United States by 1800. These churches took their place in the communities alongside other denominations like the Lutherans, Congregationalists, Methodists, and Episcopalians. They were typically named "First Baptist," "Second Baptist," "First African Baptist," and so forth. Beyond the eastern seaboard, in the interior Baptists grew exponentially. Baptist congregations were often gathered in the log cabin homes of settlers on the frontier. They were family churches, mostly 20–30 in membership. The father of Abraham Lincoln, for instance, helped to construct the meetinghouse on Pigeon Creek in southern Indiana; it was 26 by 30 ft. (8 by 9 m.) with a brick fireplace.[4] Owing to the importance of the ordinance of baptism, they took their names from a nearby stream or creek: Sandy Creek, Fourteen Mile Creek, Otter Creek, Raccoon Creek, Big Crossing, Forks of the Elk, and Buck Run, to name a few. Often these isolated congregations could enjoy the presence of a regular preacher only infrequently. Itinerant preachers were typical of rural Baptist America:

> John Lee was a very unique man; nobody disliked him. Born and reared in England, uneducated in the school sense, with much of the Yorkshire accent and a large share of inherited devotion, he came to America when quite a young man and entered the ministry. His natural abilities were fine. His inspirations all centered in the gospel. The Bible was his whole library, and it is astonishing how thoroughly conversant he was in it. He seemed to have no inclination to the pastorate. He was not an evangelist, not a revivalist, in the modern sense of the word. He was an itinerant, always floating from place to place. A good, safe, sound, earnest preacher, thoroughly Baptistic . . . He would visit all parts of Southern Missouri and Southwestern Illinois, with a little bundle tied up in a handkerchief swung on his shoulders, a walking stick in hand . . . He never married, but lived and died an unmarried man. How he managed to have bread to live on, but few knew. He never would allow a church to pay him for his labors, nor would he accept missionary money. The facts were that a few benevolent friends in St. Louis maintained him in the work to which he gave up his life.[5]

The revivalist tradition was strong in the frontier regions. Of the first two dozen Baptist preachers in Kentucky, 20 were known to have been Separate Baptists in Virginia.[6] The fires of evangelical fervor spread as far as Nova Scotia and Upper Canada. As evangelicals understood it, a revival was a spiritual awakening that brought new converts into the churches and quickened the religious consciences of those already in the faith. It was attended often by emotional, physical, and communal manifestations like singing, shouting, weeping, and self-declarations of various kinds. Some held that revivals were entirely works of a sovereign God, while others recognized human efforts and agency. The New Light itinerant Henry Alline recorded in his diary that at Yarmouth he preached two sermons after which there was a "cry" by a number of hearers seeking salvation for about two hours. Likewise, John Gilmour, the church planter in the Ottawa Valley and Lower Canada, recalled:

> The people come thirty or forty miles to attend our meetings. Their anxiety about salvation becomes so intense that we are obliged to protract our services for days; and on such occasions we have to preach three or four sermons in succession. On one occasion I dismissed the

congregation by pronouncing the blessing four times. In other words, I had to preach four sermons before I could satisfy the insatiable spirit of hearing; and one of my brethren had to do the same no less than six times before they would leave the place. This is surely of the Lord![7]

Those who served the frontier Baptist congregations were farmer-preachers. They came from among the people they served. As Daniel Parker in Illinois put it, "I had until this time been altogether raised and traditionized to the backwoods, or frontier country, having no learning, and being rough and coarse in my language and manners. I made but a poor appearance as a preacher. . . ."[8] Stories abound of the hardships that preachers endured attempting to meet their families' needs through subsistence farming and itinerating among several congregations. To help with the supply of clergy, a licensing process evolved to provide preachers from within the congregations. Generally, these men were not yet ready for all the spiritual direction of a congregation, particularly the administration of the ordinances. Several licensed preachers could serve within a single congregation. Once a preacher had proved his gifts through experience, he might be ordained. There were few opportunities for education and many frontier churches were opposed to an educated ministry. Payment for their services was minimal and often not in specie: John Shackleford at South Elkhorn in 1798 accepted a subscription from his congregation consisting of salt, corn, wheat, pork, flour, sugar, tallow, and whiskey, and a small amount of cash.[9] Zacharias N. Morrell, a Texas Baptist pioneer who preached his first Texas sermon in December, 1835, settled near the Falls of the Brazos River with about six other families. His biographer wrote that:

> he staked out land and planted a crop, took his turn at guard duty, and preached as he had opportunity. The immediate danger was Commanches. The crops had to be worked under armed guard, and the settlers learned to dread the full moons of summer . . . Morrell traveled constantly, preaching wherever he found people. By his account he carried two weapons: his "Jerusalem blade" (Bible) in his saddlebag, and his "carnal weapon" (a Tennessee long rifle) in his hands across the saddle. Morrell knew how to use both weapons, and was not loath to do so . . . At church services armed guards patrolled outside the building, and men inside kept their rifles across their laps even during worship.[10]

Perhaps the most significant organizational manifestation among Baptists to grow out of the western revivals was the General Baptist movement.[11] While the prevailing theological sentiments among the scattered Baptist communities in Kentucky and the Ohio Valley were closed communion and Calvinistic, there were notable exceptions. One association, the South Kentucky, was said to be strongly Arminian in tone, while holding fast to the traditional Calvinistic principle of the perseverance of the saints. The United Baptists of Kentucky, who formed a regional confessional body in 1801 that brought together the Separates and the Regulars, produced a confession that allowed the preaching of those who held that "Christ tasted death for every man," a phrase that signaled a general understanding of the atonement of Christ.

Into that open ethos the family of Benoni Stinson (1798–1869), an emigrant from Georgia moved about 1819. Stinson was baptized in 1820 and, self-taught, began to preach in Kentucky and southern Indiana. He was ordained and called to serve the Liberty Baptist Church in Wayne County, Kentucky, but moved again to Evansville, Indiana, where he planted a new congregation that he called "New Hope." Barely 22 years old, Stinson moved away from the United Baptists and pursued a course imitating Arminian thought. Like a second Benjamin Randal of the Freewill Baptists in the eighteenth century, Stinson's theology was hard to trace, whether from his father's family that may have encountered General Baptists in the southeastern US, or some awareness of the English General Baptists whom he may have read about in published accounts. He was connected with yet another congregation in southern Indiana that he called "Liberty," to signal his freedom from Calvinistic oppression, and began his leadership in a new Baptist subgroup: "I then felt like the Calvinistic yoke was off my neck, and I was determined never to wear it anymore, even if I lived and died in this church, connected with no other."[12]

Stinson's Arminian progeny emerged from his itinerant preaching journeys on behalf of the Liberty Church. By 1824 Stinson and two other elders had started four churches that in October 1824 became the Liberty Association of General Baptists, centered in southern Indiana. At the core of their doctrine was the principle that Christ died for all and that repentance was an act of human beings towards God. Stinson campaigned against open communion and eventually the article on "perseverance of the saints" was removed from General Baptist articles of faith, to be supplanted by a statement that affirmed the possibility of falling from grace. The movement itself grew to over 1,200 members in three associations by 1850, though much inhibited by both finances and unpaid leadership. A paper, *The General Baptist Herald*, commenced in 1845, but was short-lived due to inadequate subscriptions. Overtures were made in the 1830s to join forces with the Freewill Baptists and receive assistance from their home mission society, but this reached an impasse. The Freewill Baptists declined to allow the General Baptists to continue to use the name "General Baptists" and their associational polity. Moreover, several of the Freewill Baptist congregations in the Midwest included black members and a clear antislavery stance that was unacceptable to the General Baptists. Most importantly, the founder of the General Baptists, Benoni Stinson, weighed in against "entanglements" and recognized that his following lacked the educational interests of the larger Arminian body. Another overture that was made to the Free Communion Baptists in New York State in 1844 failed as well, creating a solitary path for the General Baptists until after the Civil War.[13]

New Measures for a New Era

The revivals recorded among the frontier Baptist congregations and the acceptability of blatant Arminian tendencies among Baptists signaled a subtle long-term change among Baptists across the continent akin to what Congregationalists and Presbyterians experienced at the same time. Theologically it had its roots in the late eighteenth-century writings of Robert Hall, Sr. and Andrew Fuller, two English Baptist pastors whose writings were well-circulated among Baptists in North America. Their titles suggest the new directions: Hall's *Help to Zion's Travelers* (1781) and Fuller's *Gospel Worthy of All Acceptation* (1785). Added to their contributions were the short-term evangelical schools that James and Robert Haldane operated in Scotland that sent forth numbers of missionary-church planters to British provinces from 1797 to 1808. Another influence was certainly the case Robert Hall, Jr. and others made for ending closed communion and accepting the work of other evangelical ministers.

The most far-reaching evangelical changes were those introduced by Charles G. Finney. Finney, a lawyer who turned to ministry, was a Presbyterian who from 1824 swept across New York State, then New England, the Middle States, and the Midwest, holding a new kind of meeting for sinners of all kinds: the churched and the truly heathen. Finney's methods, dubbed the "New Measures," assumed the correctness of Nathaniel W. Taylor's theological case for "Arminianized" Calvinism in which human response and responsibility were emphasized as much as God's sovereignty in converting individuals and reforming society. Finney introduced the "New Measures" to the conduct of revivals. These strategies and devices included protracted meetings (up to two weeks in a city), itinerant evangelists, meetings held in tents, a sawdust trail up the middle aisle between the benches that those under conviction would use to reach the bench in front where "anxious" persons could express their feelings, and hymns of decision conducive to repentance and sanctification. Sawdust was used to dry up the often muddy floors under the tents. These practices became the "means" of the new revivalism, called by some a "Second Great Awakening."

Unsurprisingly, these methods caught on among America's most evangelistic group, the mainstream Baptists. Also to no one's surprise, the two proponents of Finney's work, Jabez Swan and Jacob Knapp, both hailed from upstate New York and were graduates of the Hamilton Literary and Theological Institution, known for its missionary emphases. At Hamilton, both had been exposed to changes in Baptist thought suggested in the writings of Fuller and both preached extensively in small congregations in the region. Swan was tall and gaunt like Finney and had great success in the smaller towns that Finney's efforts did not reach. Labeled the "chief protracted meeting engineer of the Chenango Valley," Swan used Finney's techniques and aroused "animal excitement" like fainting, shrieking, and groaning in his hearers. Sometimes he used the laying on of hands to conduct faith-healings in meetings that lasted all night and went on for up to 12 weeks. Swan's sense of humor was a great asset: he referred to dancing as "kickups of the Devil," and the Universalist Church as a Fire Insurance Company because of its assured place in Hell. Sinners were "iron-clad and copper fastened . . . upon whom arrows of gospel truth would rattle like shot on the scales of an alligator."[14]

Jacob Knapp, less good-humored, deadly serious, and clever in his techniques, broke out of the Burned-Over District in western New York and preached to great crowds in the cities of New England and along the East Coast. He held forth in the late 1830s and 1840s and is said to have converted 100,000 persons by 1874, a record nearly as impressive as Finney's. He would conduct research on local persons in order to call them out in meetings, and refer to Old Calvinists as "old fogies." W. G. McLoughlin noted that Knapp was the first to run into trouble as an evangelist who made great sums of money from his ministry. In 1842 Knapp was led to clear his reputation of charges that he misrepresented his poverty and family in order to obtain large charity offerings.[15] The New Measures made their way gradually through the Baptist family and became a staple of both churches and institutions. Part of the annual program at Wake Forest Institute and Mercer University in the 1830s was the student revival, essentially a protracted meeting to quicken student morality. Likewise, pastors of urban and village congregations felt obliged to bring new life into their midst regularly and the church revivals became commonplace from New England to Philadelphia to Kentucky and Tennessee.

A remarkable aspect of the New Measures leaders was their advocacy of social reform. Finney had led in the expectation that America could be reformed from its intemperate, enslaved state and he became an ardent promoter of antislavery, antimasonry, temperance, and peace causes. Jabez Swan with great fervor attacked the strange emerging sects like Swedenborgians, Mormons, and Odd Fellows. He was against Freemasonry and for temperance as well. Knapp went after gambling, dancing, and alcohol, joining the Washingtonian Movement of extreme temperance advocates in the 1840s. In Washington and Baltimore he drew the wrath of pro-Southerners by inveighing against slaveholding. This clear investment in social reform had its impact upon Baptist life. Coalitions of Baptists, already keen on mission efforts, turned their reforming tendencies toward associations within and without the denomination to extirpate Freemasonry, slavery, and the sale of intoxicating liquor.

The Power and Reach of Voluntary Associations

It was mission that produced the organization vehicle of the voluntary association so important to Baptist development. Protestant missions had been conducted from the mid-seventeenth century when the New England Company, established in 1649, sent the Rev. John Eliot to preach to New England Indians. In part, Baptists imitated the Company and other Anglican societies in the establishment of the Particular Baptist Society for Propagating the Gospel Among the Heathen, formed in 1792. Baptists watched with much interest the subsequent formation by English Congregationalists and others of the London Missionary Society in 1793 and the multidenominational Religious Tract Society in 1799.

In the American seaboard colonies, Baptist missions had been conducted as preaching tours of pastors. In the 1790s this had become more intentionally missionary as the first Baptist missionaries for a stated term were appointed along the frontiers in western New York and New England. The New York Baptist Missionary Society assumed the support of Elkanah Holmes in 1801 in his evangelistic tours in western New York and Upper Canada. In 1800 Baptist and Congregationalist women of Boston formed the Boston Female Society for Missionary Purposes under the able leadership of Mary Webb, a person confined to a wheelchair but a genius at organization. She was much encouraged by her pastor, Thomas Baldwin, at Second Baptist, Boston. Two years later he and other Boston pastors Samuel Stillman, Daniel Sharp, Lucius Bolles, and Hezekiah Smith shaped the Massachusetts Baptist Missionary Society (MBMS) that was to be the harbinger of a full-blown missionary movement among Baptists in the United States.

The stated purpose of the Society was to furnish occasional preaching and promote knowledge of evangelistic truth in the new settlements of the United States. Baptists were in fact following the pattern laid out by the Congregationalists of New England who formed the Massachusetts Missionary Society three years earlier. In the two decades after 1789 nine Congregational and 11 Baptist missionary organizations were started to evangelize western New York. Gifts ranged from 75 cents to $258.00 in support of full-time and part-time itinerants who spent three to six months a year preaching and gathering congregations from the Finger Lakes to the Niagara frontier. Each missionary received at least $5.00 per week and had to supply his own horse to reach the isolated settlements. David Irish, a native New Yorker who for a long while was the only Baptist clergyman west of Utica after the Revolution, wrote:

> I set out and made my way through Ontario and Genesee counties, preaching as I went. After I had crossed the Genesee River I went to the town of Caledonia and in the evening I preached to a crowded assembly of Baptists, Methodists, Universalists, Deists, and Nothingarians. The season was solemn: Some rejoiced, others complained, and seemed to think their "craft was in danger."[16]

Another MBMS missionary, Peter P. Roots, who ventured as far as Upper Canada, preached 170 times in 150 days.

By the 1820s MBMS appointees were ranging as far as Illinois Country, the Maritime Provinces, Upper Canada, and Michigan. The itinerants like John Mason Peck in the Mississippi Valley often worked for more than one voluntary society at a time, making an annual salary from piecemeal appointments. As settlements became stable and congregations were permanently organized, associations, state conventions, and institutions resulted. The founders of the Massachusetts Baptist Missionary Society themselves were the founders of the Massachusetts State Convention and Newton Theological Institution, while their employees were the pastors who formed the New York State Baptist Convention and trustees of Hamilton Literary and Theological Institution. When the Society merged its efforts in 1835 with the Massachusetts

Baptist Convention, it had successfully pioneered a threefold pattern of home missions that the national American Baptist Home Mission Society would adopt for the next century: short-tem evangelistic preaching tours, funding for stated preaching in new congregations, and support for ongoing state conventions.[17]

The British and New England voluntary association pattern found its way to other regions and kinds of Baptist work. In 1812, behind the leadership of William Staughton, a transplant from the West of England through the American South, Baptists in Pennsylvania formed the Baptist Education Society of the Middle States. This second foray into voluntarism led to the prominence of Staughton on the national scene. Pastor of First Baptist, Philadelphia and later Sansom Street Church in that city, Staughton brought a clear perception of organized effort. He had witnessed personally the formation of the Baptist Missionary Society at Kettering, in Northamptonshire in England, in 1792. He trained several of the first missionaries in the first Baptist theological school in his home: John Mason Peck, James Welch, and Samuel Wait. His concept of a unified Baptist movement resembled what he had known in England: an integrated series of single-purpose voluntary societies.

In careful steps to expand the Baptist witness in the United States, William Staughton was joined by Richard Furman, pastor at First Baptist Charleston, South Carolina, who was clearly the leading Baptist of the South. Together, they launched the most ambitious voluntary society of all. By 1814, virtually all far-sighted Baptist leaders agreed that a comprehensive, national effort was needed to meet the challenges of missions at home and overseas. Methodists and Congregationalists were already engaged. In the interests of his region, Furman vigorously pursued cooperation for mission and education. The third member of the emerging nationalist triumvirate of Baptists was Luther Rice, a recent convert from Congregationalism who was one of America's original overseas missionaries to India in 1813. Rice, a peripatetic preacher who had seen the foreign situation firsthand and made a compelling case on behalf of the American Baptist missionaries Adoniram and Ann Judson, was joined to Staughton's impressive financial development skills and Furman's recognition as a Patriot and towering pulpit orator. Together they created the General Baptist Missionary Convention in the United States of America for Foreign Missions in 1814 (GMC).

The GMC, or "Triennial Convention," as it was also known because it met every three years, was the triumph of the national spirit among Baptists in the United States. This representative body, inspired by other great conventions of partisans like the Federal Constitutional Convention or the Hartford Convention, drew delegates from each section of the new nation, the preponderance at first coming from New England and the Middle States. Luther Rice may be credited with the structure of an integrated regional and national plan of voluntary societies: he said it came to him during a stagecoach ride from Richmond to Petersburg, Virginia in early 1814. His models were the Baptist Missionary Society in England, for its general and local connectedness, and the American Board of Commissioners for Foreign Missions that had appointed him and the Judsons in 1812, for its administrative board accountability. Within three years the outreach of the GMC included domestic missionaries to work among Indian tribes in the Northwest and Mississippi Valley, and within its first six years it took on the responsibilities of operating a college and theological studies program.

The heart of the General Missionary Convention was its overseas mission work. Between meetings of the triennial assembly, the Convention created a Baptist Board for Foreign Missions and an executive committee to administer its policies. Its first actions pertained to the appointment of missionaries to the Burma field, Adoniram and Ann Judson, in 1814. Luther Rice, who fully expected to return to Burma, was retained as agent for the Convention. Within three years the overseas personnel were expanded to include Africa with the appointments of Colin Teague and Lott Carey, two free black preachers from Virginia. They sailed in 1820 under joint sponsorship of the GMC and the American Colonization Society and established a base at Monrovia in Liberia. By 1826, Calvin Holton of Waterville College in Maine was the first Caucasian appointed to the African Mission. The next field was Europe and this interest grew from Irah Chase of Newton Theological Institution and Barnas Sears of Hamilton Literary and Theological Institution in New York. Sears promoted the establishment of a mission in France and one in Germany, respectively. He baptized a colporteur, Johann G. Oncken, in 1834 who subsequently became the Baptist apostle to the Germans and an advocate of religious liberty. Later in the 1830s, American Baptists extended their missionary reach even farther, to Bangkok in 1835, Haiti in 1837, and before 1840 among the Telugus, Karens, and the Assamese in Asia. The mission at Bangkok opened a door to establishing a mission among the Chinese that William Dean followed on behalf of the Board. As much as any other factor, missionary endeavor united Baptists in North America as they met to review and plan missions and collected ever-increasing sums of money to support both the overseas effort and a modest administrative structure at home. Because missionary outreach was such an important extension of Baptist culture in North America, it will be discussed in a separate chapter below.

The lofty objectives of the GMC were much debated. There were those who felt the sole purpose of the Convention should be overseas mission. Still others thought it should be the making of a comprehensive denominational body, marking the maturation of Baptists in the life of the nation. The latter, led by Rice, Staughton, and Furman, favored Washington DC as a logical base of operations and sought to establish Columbian College and a national periodical, *The Latter Day Luminary*, there. By 1822, however, reality struck the Convention harshly in the form of financial insufficiency and internal bickering over control. Two Philadelphia pastors, William White and Henry Holcomb, bitterly opposed the extension of the Convention as well as the Washington scheme. They were joined by Baron Stow, Heman Lincoln, and Francis Wayland from Boston who organized an effort to investigate Rice's conduct as a fundraiser and possibly discredit his efforts. In 1826, in what was called the "great reversal," the General Convention was reduced to a missionary society, its support was withdrawn from the Columbian College project and the base of operations was shifted to Boston where most of the executive committee resided. While not directly culpable, Rice was thereafter reduced to raising money for Columbian College in the southern states where he laid the groundwork for a regional body a decade before his untimely death in 1836. The Triennial Meetings, held in Philadelphia, Richmond, New York, and Baltimore, continued through 1844 to be a symbol of national unity for mainstream Baptists, though the national vision organizationally was divided between the other two national societies, the American Baptist Publication Society in Philadelphia, and the American Baptist Home Mission Society in New York.

Diversification in Polity

As more Baptist congregations sprang up in virtually all sections of the United States, a wide variety of styles and structures emerged to characterize Baptist life and ministry. Some were confident socially in their urban contexts, while others drew careful boundaries around their fellowship. Some kept simple worship styles and lacked music or even regular preaching. Some were isolated either by location or by intention as close-knit families. The sweep of cultural expectations and internationalism that came with a new century in 1800 and was reinforced in the War of 1812 separated Baptists from each other in long-lasting ways.

For instance, not all Baptists cared to join the great missionary thrust. Some held tenaciously to the theological and polity views of the great eighteenth-century English Baptist pastor and theologian, John Gill, that "the principal end and use of the public ministry of the word, to which all others tend, is the glory of God, which ought to be chiefly in view in the performance of it."[18] Resentment was also strong against the fund-raising techniques of "agents" like Luther Rice. Rice was accused at one point of preying upon widows who mended his socks. The opponents soon voiced their concerns through pamphlets and sermons, becoming known as "Old School" Baptists, their theory of the "old" school being:

> That portion of Baptists who have not departed from the faith and order of Baptists of a hundred years ago, to say nothing of the Apostolic Age, must be the true church of Christ. It was unto the true church of Christ that the keys of the kingdom of Heaven were committed, with which to bind or loose, as she thought proper. And by virtue of this Divine authority, she has loosed, withdrawn from and excommunicated these disorderly brethren, and therefore has no fellowship for them.[19]

"New Order" or "New School" Baptists, in contrast, practiced missionary system "innovations" like Sunday schools, Bible societies, tract societies, theological seminaries, the reading and preaching of freewill sermons, and "money-hunting," as their critics dubbed fundraising. Old Schoolers demonstrated that prior to the eighteenth century all of these efforts were unknown among the Baptists and they blamed Adoniram Judson and Luther Rice for introducing them among the churches and associations. Their high Calvinism earned them the name "Hard Shell" and the movement in general eventually came to be called "Primitive" Baptists after the overall distinction to emulate the primitive or New Testament churches. As Gilbert Beebe, the leader of the Old School movement in the Middle States who denounced the wickedness of unscriptural Christianity for over four decades in his newspaper, *Signs of the Times*, put it, "To our feeble mind the conclusion is unavoidable, that the predestination of God either controls all things or nothing."[20]

There were five geographical foci of Old Schoolism clustered around spokesmen for its principles: New England, south central New York and central New Jersey, northern and eastern Maryland, the Ohio Valley including Kentucky and Illinois Territory, and Georgia/Alabama. This radical form of dissenting behavior within Baptist ranks would place the overall Baptist movement in permanent jeopardy of ever being unified in any practical sense like other denominations in North America.

Some of the earliest manifestations of antimissionism are to be found in Elias Smith and John Leland. New England's eighteenth-century frontiers in Maine, New Hampshire, Vermont, and western Massachusetts produced a distinctively individualistic form of Baptist life, much inclined toward local church protectionism. Elias Smith (1769–1846), raised in upstate Vermont, was typical of the pattern. Early in his ministry among Massachusetts Baptists, he turned on the prevailing Calvinism, pomp, and circumstance of the urban ministers. He approached the faith in a simple, biblicist manner: if he could not locate the idea or practice in a clear statement of Scripture, he did not follow it. He therefore opposed college-trained ministers, associationalism, and catechisms. He concluded that voluntary societies, except for Bible societies, were agents to deprive Americans of their liberties. Characterized as the "champion of reviling, railing, and slander," Smith left controversy everywhere he went.[21] As many of the voluntary societies got underway after 1815 in New England, Smith inveighed against them as "religious manufactories." "In one place you will see a manufactory for making ministers," he wrote, "at another . . . where a solitary workman is employed in manufacturing what is called 'Bodies of Divinity.' In another place may be found a manufactory for abridging bodies of divinity. . . ."[22] For him, seminaries produced ministers in search of large salaries and nonscriptural missionary work. His autobiography, *The Life, Conversion, Preaching, Travels, and Sufferings of Elias Smith* (1816), still in print,[23] provided generations of like-minded Baptists with a bedrock of antiestablishment thinking.

A second New England example of proto-antimissionism can be seen in John Leland. Much of his thinking stemmed from his Jeffersonian egalitarian mechanistic views of American society. Leland disliked government intensely and was equally antagonistic to any form of ecclesiastical hierarchy. He lumped the Federalist Party with the Congregationalist Standing Order, Roman Catholicism, and even the voluntary societies. A thoroughly committed Calvinist, he was also a pure individualist and anything that came between God and humans was anathema. Observing the dramatic rise of voluntary associations for numerous purposes, "Father" Leland wrote in 1818 what has been called the first antimission document in Baptist history. His main argument was that the societies lacked the character and quality of Jesus and the disciples, and were energized by money, not the Holy Spirit. He wrote, "It is a vain thing to hold up a man to whom God has given no legs. The law, the sword, and the college, first linked to the Church under Constantine, has ever after corrupted it."[24]

In Leland's wake and tradition was John Taylor (1752–1835). Raised in Virginia, Taylor remained all of his life in Kentucky and on the Ohio River frontier, mingling amongst small churches. He knew John Leland, Luther Rice, Daniel Parker and most of the others in the antimission cause. His tract, *Thoughts on Missions*, written amidst the Panic of 1819, was profoundly influential among the Baptist churches and associations. His theme text came from Proverbs 30: 15, "The horse-leech hath two daughters, crying, Give, give." His metaphor against the mission promoters was not to be missed: "I have taken some little notice of the horse-leech. It is said of that creature, that it has a forked tongue, with two branches that are called its daughters, with both of which it sucks blood with great vigor. Thus missionaries, with many strings to their bow, cry mightily for money."[25] Taylor circulated stories particularly about Luther Rice, that he ate sumptuously while traveling, consuming large amounts of coffee and tea, and that he used unethical fund-raising methods not sanctioned in the Bible. In his later years, Taylor seems to have mollified his antimissionism as indicated by the domestic missionary James Welch who claimed that Taylor repented of having written his influential tract.

Daniel Parker (1781–1844) was among the most vituperative exponents of the Old School. Parker was born in Culpepper, Virginia, a scene of colonial persecution of Baptist preachers, and later reared on the Georgia frontier. Baptized at Nail's Creek Baptist Church in Franklin County, Georgia, Parker moved to Tennessee, Kentucky, and then Illinois, where he served small, rural churches. At the peak of his career he was recalled as a short, thin and poorly dressed man with a belligerent attitude: ". . . with what I called my *Jerusalem Blade* which had two edges, and cut every way, I laboured to cut off everything that was aiming to touch the crown on the Redeemer's head, or remove the rights and foundation of the church of God."[26] First he confronted Methodist Arminianism, then Luther Rice, and ultimately his chief missionary nemeses in the West, Isaac McCoy and John Mason Peck. Working through the Baptist associational structure Parker attempted to defeat the support of missionary societies. He even sponsored a bill in the Illinois legislature in 1828 that forbade begging money in the territory for missionary societies on pain of $15.00 fine.[27] Through his tracts like *A Public Address to the Baptist Society* (1820) he launched an anti-intellectual attack upon a learned clergy and gospel means. Further, he articulated a backwoods theological understanding of "two-seedism" that suggested two kinds of spiritual offspring in the church, the Devil's seed and those of Adam's son, Seth, including Christ. Not all Old School Baptists concurred with Parker's ideas, and his new opponents included John Taylor, Alexander Campbell, and numerous antimission associations.

In 1833 Parker organized in Illinois a traveling congregation that he called "The Pilgrim Church of Predestinarian Regular Baptists" and the group (including several members of the Parker clan) floated down the Ohio and Mississippi Rivers and trudged across Louisiana to Texas. Parker thus started what became the first Baptist church in Texas and a progenitor of the rugged, individualistic, Calvinistic stream of Texas Baptists. His "Union Association" of congregations stretched from Louisiana to the Panhandle and the Sabine River, literally hundreds of miles of territory, much under his teaching and episcopacy. This brought about the first major split in the Baptist family of the new century, that contemporaries cast as a denial of classic Christian doctrines like bodily resurrection, combined with ancient Persian dualism.[28] Parker's beliefs led to the beginnings of a small group known as the Two Seed in the Spirit Double Predestinarian Baptists. Their numbers climbed to about 13,000 in 24 states at the end of the nineteenth century.[29]

In noteworthy ways the Primitive Baptist movement came to assume some general institutional characteristics of its own in the 1830s. Following a regular meeting of the Baltimore Baptist Association in 1832, ministers sympathetic to the Old School cause met at Black Rock meetinghouse near the Pennsylvania state line to discuss the crisis over missions. Twenty-two elders and lay leaders from five states and Washington, DC, convened as a "convention" and heard a sermon from Samuel Trott of Delaware's Welsh Tract Church. Trott's message was contemporary and apocalyptic: it identified those supporting missions with the image of Babylon in Daniel 2: 34–5. Trott was appointed to chair a committee to write an address and invite churches across the United States to join the cause. What became known as the "Black Rock Address" vitiated targets on the Old School agenda: mission societies, colleges, revivals, and any attempt to create a national Sabbath. Protracted meetings, the writers claimed, stirred up "animal feelings" rather than the Holy Spirit. Inherent in the document was also opposition to hireling ministers and women preachers.[30] Theologically, a simplistic, strict Calvinism undergirded the Black Rock Address. The convention itself carried forth on an annual basis, repeating the same pattern each year and consciously using the Black Rock formula and the sobriquets "Old School Cause" and "Primitives." About the same time, Gilbert Beebe of New Vernon, New York, began publishing *Signs of the Times*, a general newspaper for the Old Schoolers in which meetings, church lists, and addresses were regularly published. Samuel

Trott assumed the role of unofficial historian and theologian for a movement overall that numbered 58,000 in 1860 and reached a peak of about 100,000 in 1880. The exodus of Old School churches, reflecting the first major polity schism among Baptists in the United States, had a serious impact upon Baptist unity, with three-fifths of the Baptists in Illinois becoming antimission, only one association in Georgia remaining true to the missionary cause, the state convention of Alabama existing in name only, and the debilitating effect upon church life extending from the northeast to Texas.[31] Perhaps the most damaging aspect of the era was the tendency toward slanderous name-calling among Baptists, the Old Schoolers using against the "missionary pests" names like: Hopkinsians, "florid professors of religion," synergists, the effort party, "workmongers," apostates, idolaters, "bloodsuckers," passion-exciting, and mesmerizing "do-and-livers." Not to be outdone, mainstream Baptists responded with terms like "Black-Rockers," "Kehukeeites," "Lawrenceans," "Osburnites," "Do-Nothingites," "Straightjackets," "Hard Shells," antinomians, and ignoramuses.[32]

The missionary impulse of mainstream Baptists continued unabated and took its domestic course in new directions in the 1820s. In support of the overseas mission, the need for evangelical literature for churches at home led to the creation in 1824 of the Baptist General Tract Society. Again the redoubtable Luther Rice was the originator of the idea, joined by Obadiah Brown a postmaster and pastor in Washington, DC, and Noah Davis, a worker from Eastern Shore, Maryland. With a small office in the Nation's Capital, they produced tracts on Baptist practices and beliefs and eventually commissioned editions of the works of John Bunyan, Andrew Fuller, and others. It seemed natural in 1841 to include Sunday school work in the Tract Society's mission, and it became known as the American Baptist Publication and Sunday School Society. Its genius came to be the teams of colporteurs or Bible salesmen it sent forth to distribute tracts and encourage Sunday schools.

Literature distribution led to planting congregations. As we have noted, the work of short-term missionaries of the Massachusetts Baptist Missionary Society and those appointed by the General Missionary Convention produced a sense of urgency in the Mississippi Valley to focus organizational interests on domestic missions. One of the leading voices in the Illinois Country was John Mason Peck (1789–1852) who warned that the whole West could be lost to the paedobaptists, by which he meant Methodists and Presbyterians. A scouting expedition led by Jonathan Going, pastor at First Baptist Worcester, Massachusetts, was sent out to assess the situation, visiting churches, associations, camp meetings, pious ministers and laypeople, consulting, praying, weeping and rejoicing together, and he reported favorably on the prospects for Baptists. Peck wrote to Going of the urgency of acting promptly: "You MUST devote yourself to the cause in the West – Now is the crisis – tomorrow will be too late." At a recessed meeting of the Triennial Convention in New York in 1832, the American Baptist Home Mission Society (ABHMS) was formed much as Going and Peck had conceived it in Kentucky.[33] It quickly organized its resources to focus on church planting, Indian missions, and witness to the new immigrants pouring into eastern coast ports. Prominent in support of the ABHMS were Jonathan Going, Archibald Maclay, pastor of Mulberry Street Baptist Church, New York, and Spencer H. Cone, pastor of Oliver Street Baptist Church in New York, and his illustrious deacon, William Colgate. Colgate, a soap maker and entrepreneur, was to provide funds for many projects during his long and generous career. With the formation of the ABHMS, the semblance of a national Baptist denomination came into focus in the three separate but interfacing societies – the General Missionary Convention, the Baptist General Tract Society, and the ABHMS – and their annual or "anniversary" meetings.

Alongside the mainstream of missionary cooperative missionary Baptists, a unique example of Baptist diversity according to the accepted polity of the early nineteenth century was witnessed in the evolution of the Sabbathkeeping Baptists. It will be recalled that Seventh Day Baptists differed chiefly on the matter of recognizing Saturday as the legitimate Sabbath, to be kept inviolably. As it was to evolve, their polity was a creative combination of the three emerging structures of Baptist life in the United States, the association, the society, and the conference. In 1802 a General Conference was formed, largely as a response to the missionary impulse among Seventh Day Baptists. In this regard they presaged the structure of Freewill Baptists. Historian Don Sanford has pointed out five functions of this body, namely: denominational identity, definition of doctrine, communications, education, and program initiation.[34] In the first few years, ordination was also cared for at the conference level of activity. The associational life of the nascent denomination developed according to the westward and southern migration of Sabbathkeepers, so that four associations coalesced before 1860, each sending 12 delegates to meet with the General Conference. The society model, fostered by the Baptists of the North, also flourished among Seventh Day Baptists. In 1828, the first missionary society was formed and three years later the Seventh Day Baptist General Tract Society commenced, in 1840 to become the American Sabbath Tract Society. Education societies became the foundations of Seventh

Day schools (10 academies and three colleges), as well as a general society to promote educational interests in 1849. From time to time Seventh Day Baptists interacted with and imitated their First Day brothers and sisters, while at other times they were far advanced in pursuing the Baptist principle. Altogether, there were approximately 1,100 Sabbathkeeping members in eight congregations located in four states at the beginning of the nineteenth century. After a century of work with the General Conference, it is estimated there were 100 congregations in 23 states with an aggregate membership of over nine thousand.[35]

Diversification Along Lines of Ethnicity and Race

A significant amount of energy that the American Baptist Home Mission Society expended was among the new emigrants to the United States. At the outset, mission with the language groups was supposed to eventuate in English-speaking churches that would join the regular associations. However, the individual languages and cultures were reinforced through continued services and fellowship in German, Swedish, Danish, and so forth. Permanent ethnic language associations were the result. Foremost among the groups was the German community. Estimates are that almost 700,000 emigrants from Germany arrived in the US between 1789 and 1860. One of the principal centers of the German community was Philadelphia and it was in that German Lutheran context that the first German Baptist church was born in 1843 under the ministry of Konrad A. Fleischmann. Called the "German Church of the Lord that Meets on Poplar Street" or "The Meeting House of the Baptized Church," five years later that congregation joined the Philadelphia Baptist Association and it became the launching place for other missions to German Americans.[36] Strong German communities developed in upstate New York, Illinois, Wisconsin, Missouri, and Texas. In Canada, German Baptists were later found in Upper Canada (Ontario), Manitoba, Saskatechewan, and Alberta.

Similarly, missionary witness to the Swedes reaped benefits. The initial Swedish witness was among sailors in seamen's Bethel ministries in New York City. Capt. Gustavus Shroeder steered many of his countrymen toward Baptist affiliations, while retaining his membership in the English-speaking Baptist community. Gustave Palmquist, a Pietistic singer and teacher, was baptized in 1852 and immediately set out for Rock Island, Illinois where he began a ministry among Swedes with the support of the American Baptist Home Mission Society. The third major group was the Norwegians who began to emigrate to the US in the 1830s and settled in colonies in the Great Lakes region. Several were baptized in the Ottawa, Illinois, Baptist church and soon thereafter Hans Valder, a recent immigrant from Norway, joined the colony and began to evangelize his countrymen and organize Norwegian-speaking Baptist congregations in the area. Each of these ethnic groups formed language associations that provided a distinctive witness while maintaining cooperation with English-speaking Baptists: German Baptist Conference (1851), Rock Island Conference of Swedish Baptists (1856), Danish-Norwegian Conference (1883).

Though not nearly as energetically as Methodists and Congregationalists, Baptists did exercise an interest in missions to various tribes of aboriginal Americans. The earliest recorded work came about on Martha's Vineyard where Thomas Mayhew, the Proprietor of Nantucket and Martha's Vineyard, employed Peter Foulger as a teacher to the Indians.[37] Later in that mission John Tackamason, a Baptist, became the first Indian pastor. By 1694 there were two Indian Baptist congregations in Massachusetts, one at Martha's Vineyard, the other on Nantucket Island. There are scant references to Indian members of Baptist congregations in New York, Georgia, and New Jersey in the eighteenth century, but this was a rare circumstance. As we have seen, the first concerted outreach was made in 1796 in the New York Missionary Society when an ecumenical body supported Elkanah Holmes, a Baptist minister, in a mission that Baptists in New York later assumed. Holmes preached on both sides of the Niagara River and was highly affirmed among the Six Nations. His example, plus the military strife in the Great Lakes region, focused the need of a witness to the tribes and this won limited support in the Massachusetts Baptist Missionary Society in the first decade of the nineteenth century.

Native Americans were an early focus of the domestic mission movement. In the first triennium (1814–17) the General Missionary Convention approved work among the tribes of the Old Northwest, primarily in Indiana and Michigan territories. Isaac McCoy, James Welch, and John Mason Peck were all authorized to conduct missions among the Northwest Tribes; the Miamis, Kickapoos, and Potowatomies were the recipients of this effort. Success attended the missions; however the financial insufficiency of the Convention led to spasmodic Indian mission efforts until the 1830s, when McCoy's urgings were influential in the policy making of the General Missionary Convention. Work was pursued in evangelism, industrial education, and church planting among Creeks, Choctaws, Ottawas, Ojibwas, and Delawares, largely at the behest of McCoy, Humphrey Posey, and Evan Jones, the leading missionaries.

Isaac McCoy, who actually helped to develop the reservation system and church responsibilities for relating to that arrangement, formed the independent American Indian Mission Association (AIMA) in 1842 to focus attention on the missions. With the creation of the Southern Baptist Convention in 1845, McCoy and the AIMA elected to affiliate with the Southern Baptist Domestic Mission Board, and the American Baptist Missionary Union continued the Indian mission work of the General Missionary Convention with the support of the Baptist churches in the northern states. Following the Civil War, new treaties with Indian nations were concluded and the work of the Missionary Union was transferred to the Home Mission Society. ABHMS and the Woman's American Baptist Home Mission Society thereafter concentrated efforts in Oklahoma, New York State, and later in New Mexico and Arizona territories. By 1860, the various efforts of the conventions and associations resulted in over 60 commissioned missionaries and in excess of two thousand baptisms in the Native American communities.

Regional Diversification

The amount of missionary activity that American Baptist pastors and organizational missionaries expended in the British provinces north of the American border could easily have been permanently related to churches and conventions in the United States. This was, in fact, what happened to the later German, Swedish, and Danish congregations in Canada who continued to relate to their respective US conferences. In the English-speaking communities, political realities and cultural differences, however, proved otherwise.

In 1800 the first association of churches in Canada was formed in Nova Scotia and New Brunswick. Mostly gathered around the coastlines, this maritime collection of congregations used the plan of the Danbury, Connecticut, Association as its model since in both situations diverse Baptist communities came together to cooperate. What they had in common was a Calvinistic theological perspective based upon the Second London Confession of Faith, a self-awareness of nonconformity, and the practice of believer's baptism. Shortly thereafter, a second association was formed in Upper Canada in 1803 around the northern shores of Lake Ontario. The Baptists who settled in the Upper Canada regions were a diverse lot: some from Scotland, some from England, others from New England and New York; some were open communion, others closed communion. The Canadian churches were located within a band not more than one hundred miles inland from the US border and reliance upon the US churches was evident. The pastoral candidates who could afford an education, more often than not, went to Hamilton Literary and Theological Institution (New York), Brown University, or Newton Theological Institution (Massachusetts) and returned to serve Canadian churches. Robert A. Fyfe in Upper Canada and Alexis Caswell in Halifax, respectively, exemplified this pattern. After the English Baptist experiment at a college in Montreal failed in 1849, faculty for the continuing institution at what became Acadia College were trained primarily in US institutions. Newton was a first choice, owing to its proximity to the Maritimes and encouragement of a learned clergy. As the American Baptist Missionary Union overseas mission program grew, Canadian churches contributed and even formed an auxiliary in 1866 to the US organization.

The realities of the War of 1812 resulted in permanent separation between American and Canadian Baptists. To start with, fewer American missionaries went to Canada after 1813. Canadian congregations and missionary organizations assumed their own responsibility for church planting and missions, the first one of which was founded at Aylmer, Upper Canada in 1816. Emulating the associational principle of the Americans, central Canadians and Maritimers formed seven associations by 1868, three conventions by 1858, and two schools to provide pastors, Acadia University in Wolfville (1838) and the Canadian Literary Institute in Woodstock (1861). Fraternal relations continued on both sides of the border and when two visitors from Britain, Francis A. Cox and James Hoby, toured the US Baptist community in 1836, they also included Montreal on their itinerary. The Baptist population grew steadily in the first half of the nineteenth century, reaching 23,000 members in 330 churches from the Maritimes to Upper Canada in 1850.[38]

By far the major form of diversification in the North American Baptist family came in the establishment of the Southern Baptist Convention (SBC). Several factors were involved in the birth of what has become the largest organization of Baptists in denominational history. First was a disagreement about the role of socioeconomic issues in the administration of programs of the General Missionary Convention. As a region, New England was a tight-knit community in which Baptists cooperated as congregations in associations. Individual Baptists, especially pastors in the Boston vicinity, also joined voluntary societies that handled mission concerns. The single purpose independence of these societies was quite acceptable, given the interlocking directorates that the boards exhibited. However, in the South, distance was a problem, as was a strong spirit of antimissionism. Southerners wanted a strong unified organization that administered its work through accountable boards. The business would thus be conducted by a few key leaders meeting with less frequency than in the North and with greater oversight. This difference between regions became greater as division between north and south was more likely and eventually it became the more compelling explanation for a Southern Baptist Convention in Southern Baptist historiography.[39]

The leading issue was, of course, slavery, and both the Baptist Board of Foreign Missions and the ABHMS officers refused after 1844 to appoint missionaries who were known slaveholders or who countenanced the peculiar institution. For decades Baptists had owned slaves on their plantations and in households from Virginia to Mississippi and Texas. This posed little problem among the local associations, but when the southern delegates to the national societies cooperated in domestic and foreign missionary work, problems arose among an increasingly sensitive minority of the Baptist delegates from the North. The initial volley was shot in a communication from the American Baptist Antislavery Convention in 1840 to southern Baptists that they would not continue to tolerate fellowship with slaveholders: "If you should . . . remain deaf to the voice of warning and entreaty . . . we cannot and we dare not recognize you as consistent brethren in Christ; we cannot hear preaching which makes God the author and approver of human misery and vassalage. . . ."[40] This brought about an action by the Alabama Baptist State Convention that withheld funds for the Triennial Convention until clarity had been established on the matter. In 1840 the General Missionary Convention met in Baltimore (considered a "southern" city) and reached the famous "Baltimore Compromise," that evaded the issue by pointing out that the Convention had taken no action on the issue of slavery and concentrated its efforts on "sending the glad tidings of salvation to the heathen." Four years later the Convention again affirmed its position "disclaiming all sanction of slavery or antislavery."

The slavery question, seemingly dodged in the Convention, resurfaced in the Home Mission Society. There the Georgia Baptist Convention proposed a test case whereby they would guarantee the expenses of a missionary to the Cherokees, James Reeves of Villa Rica, Georgia if the Board would appoint him. Reeves was a known slaveholder and no effort was made to obscure his practices. Following five meetings of at least three hours' each, a vote was taken that split on regional lines, with the majority against appointing Reeves. From the Georgia point of view, the ABHMS board had failed the test. Later in 1844 the Alabama Baptists offered another test case, this time to the Baptist

Board of Foreign Missions of the General Missionary Convention, requesting the legitimate rights and privileges to which slaveholders and nonslaveholders alike were entitled under the constitution of the Convention. Solomon Peck, the foreign secretary of the Convention, responded on behalf of the Acting Board that the Board had never appointed any slaveholding missionaries and would not do so at that time. "One thing is certain," Peck wrote, "We can never be party to any arrangement which would imply approbation of slavery." Peck knew the anguish of the members of the Board, as well as the inevitability of the withdrawal of southern delegates from the united work of the Convention. While southern delegates protested the lack of authority in the Acting Board of Missions that had reached this conclusion, plans were laid to create a new organization in harmony with southern realities. Jesse Mercer, a leading Georgia Baptist, observed, "Our abolition brethren, are exceedingly mistaken in the case they have undertaken to remedy; and therefore, their measures can only operate *a bad influence, and the tendency will inevitably be to break up all our united operations, and I seriously fear our civil Union also.*"[41]

With a sectional crisis inevitable there was widespread feeling among many southerners in favor of a purely sectional identity. Many felt the need in the South for a more highly integrated form of organization than the society model then being pursued through the Triennial Convention and its affiliates. Arguments in favor of a southern home mission society and also for separate conventions for the West and South surfaced in the late 1830s. In the heat of the debate over slavery, James B. Taylor, president of the Virginia Baptist Foreign Mission Society and a strong proponent of a new national organization, wrote that "we wish not to have a merely *sectional* Convention . . ." and he invited brethren from all quarters to attend a planning meeting. Further, Taylor urged the union of Bible and publication organizations and the establishment of a southern theological seminary.[42] Finally, it is now evident that key pastors in the south were supportive of a uniquely southern convention as early as the 1830s, among whom were William Bullein Johnson, William T. Brantly, Jeremiah B. Jeter, Jesse Hartwell, and Richard Fuller.[43] The last meeting of the General Missionary Convention or its Board, in which Baptist delegates north and south participated, was held in the historic First Baptist Church in Providence, Rhode Island, April 18, 1845.

The new Southern Baptist Convention set about its work with vigor. The constitution of the SBC allowed any Baptist body or brethren one delegate for every $250 contributed to the work of the Convention, plus one representative of each district association that cooperated with the SBC. The benevolent work of the Convention was carried forth by boards that were directly accountable to the Convention and its executive committee. Great plenary powers were retained by the Convention itself, a response to the supposed interference of the executive committee of the former General Missionary Convention. A strong executive committee led by J. B. Jeter and W. B. Johnson, organized two boards, one for foreign missions and one for domestic missions. With limited funds, the Foreign Mission Board assumed the work of two General Missionary Convention personnel, J. Lewis Shuck and Issachar J. Roberts, both assigned to China. Roberts became quite influential in China during the Taiping Rebellion that in turn gave Southern Baptists a strong position of influence. Southern Baptists further opened missions in Africa in Liberia and Sierra Leone that were short-lived for missionary health reasons, and later in Yoruba Land (Nigeria) in 1849. Southern Europe followed on the SBC roster, as did South America, Mexico, and Cuba.

In 1855 the Domestic Mission Board assumed the work – and the debt – of the American Indian Mission Association of Isaac McCoy, becoming the Domestic and Indian Mission Board of the SBC. Educational leaders in Charleston also believed the Convention should engage in publishing and founded the Southern Baptist Publication Society in 1847. The Publication Society was only "endorsed" by the Convention and suffered secondary status and intense competition from the Bible Board formed in 1857 and a Sunday School Convention in 1857 that were both dominated by James R. Graves, a strong-opinioned Tennessee Baptist editor. None of the publishing efforts ultimately succeeded until after the Civil War when the Sunday School Board, founded in 1863, was resuscitated within the Convention structure. Almost unnoticed on the eve of the war was the founding in 1859 of the Southern Baptist Theological Seminary in Greenville, South Carolina. Its founders were James P. Boyce and Basil Manly, Jr., both graduates of Princeton Theological Seminary, who envisioned a unique ministerial training institution for the whole convention.

The Baptist churches of the northern states did not tarry long in search of a new form of cooperation after the exodus of the southern delegates. The General Missionary (Triennial) Convention reduced its scope for a second time and became essentially the foreign mission enterprise of northern Baptists. The American Baptist Board of Foreign Missions (incorporated as the American Baptist Foreign Mission Society in Massachusetts) became the American Baptist Missionary Union (ABMU). This organization continued to oversee the foreign program of the northern churches plus the stations of the American Indian tribes. Any regular Baptist church that contributed at least one hundred dollars to the Union earned a delegate and any individual who contributed the same sum in one year was entitled to honorary life membership. Continuing the tradition of the General Missionary Convention, its fully empowered Board of Managers (and *ad interim* executive committee) met each year in May along with the boards of the American Baptist Home Mission Society, and the American Baptist Publication and Sunday School Society (formerly the Baptist General Tract Society) in the "anniversary meetings" held in the same cities each year for the convenience and coordination of delegates, some of whom served more than one board. This "society" model of denominational organization continued among the northern churches until the organization of the Northern Baptist Convention in 1907.

Political Division and the Era of the Civil War

The era of the Civil War was an opportunity for many Baptist groups and a retardant factor for others. For those who had been part of the antislavery crusade or abolitionism, the war provided an opportunity to seize the moral high ground. Thousands of Baptists joined the Union army and many served as chaplains. There were many stories of heroism, notably that of Eliza N. Aiken, known as "Aunt Lizzie," who enlisted as a nurse in the US Army in the place of her invalid husband. She ministered to hundreds of wounded Union soldiers, earning the title "Angel of the Battlefield." During the war, the ABHMS laid plans for a southern strategy in two directions. First, the Society asked the War Department for permission to take over all Baptist church buildings in the South where there was no loyal minister. Ostensibly, this was to protect the properties involved, but it soon appeared to be a reassertion of northern Baptist hegemony in the South. Second, support was widely enlisted for missions among the former slave populations for church planting, human development, and education. Donors came forth from New England, New York, and Pennsylvania to provide the capital funds for buildings and salaries for teachers of schools, colleges, and seminaries for freedmen.

Southern Baptists forged ahead under extremely challenging circumstances. The seminary at Greenville closed in 1862, the Bible Board was discontinued after Nashville fell in 1863, the Home Mission Board lost most of its staff to the Confederate Army, and many pastors joined the cause as sometime chaplains. Enthusiasts for the cause wrote of thousands of profane and reckless young men who became trembling enquirers on the battlefield; such was the inducement to churches to allow pastors to travel and preach to the troops. It was estimated that 2,000 soldiers in Lee's Army professed religion following the disaster at Gettysburg.[44] George B. Taylor, the lone staff member of the Foreign Mission Board who was frequently in harm's way, recalled the make-shift religious services he put together:

> While I was in the field we were always moving and nothing better than the ground was ever used by either preacher or people, and when I preached at night, some brother would hold a torch or candle while I read hymn or chapter. But here I found a large amphitheatre of log-seats, with a pulpit in the centre, covered with an arbor, and flanked on either hand by a platform, whose blazing lightwood illuminated every face in the vast congregation. The sea of upturned earnest faces, and the songs swelling from hundreds of manly voices and making the forests resound, I was, from the accounts received, prepared for. But they were nonetheless impressive, and I felt it a luxury to preach under such circumstances.[45]

Robert Ryland, the president of Richmond College, regularly visited soldiers' hospitals in the Richmond area distributing religious tracts, Bibles in English, German and French, and religious newspapers not only from the Baptists, but Presbyterians and Methodists as well.[46]

Following the military hostilities, southern churches found their numbers depleted from the loss of slaves who now formed their own congregations, the shifts in population of many from the Old South to the southwest, and finally new political affiliations like western Virginia's churches separating with West Virginia portrayed numerical losses.[47] On the positive side, new churches were organized, new state conventions were formed, and statistical growth occurred in Arkansas, Texas, New Mexico, and Indian Territory. Following the Civil War, 15 of the state conventions formed the foundation of the future Southern Baptist Convention.[48] The reopening of Southern Baptist Theological Seminary in the fall of 1865 became an important symbol for the future of Southern Baptists.

Southern Baptists passed another milestone in their maturing process in the 1890s. From its founding and especially during the Reconstruction era, the American Baptist Home Mission Society had exercised a mission responsibility for the southern states. This brought much resentment and expressed antagonism between the ABHMS and the Domestic (after 1873 "Home") Mission Board of the Southern Convention. Much of that antagonism was focused upon Baptist development in New Mexico, Missouri, Oklahoma, Arizona, and California, in effect the western frontier of Southern Baptists. The northern society claimed these territories as its field by virtue of its longstanding Indian effort (Oklahoma and Arizona), and by the settlement of northern Baptists in these territories. Southern Baptists likewise claimed that the presence of southern missions gave the field to them. At length, a series of "comity" meetings resolved the issues and essentially redefined the mainstream Baptist territories in the United States. The first was held at Fortress Monroe in Virginia in 1894 where representatives of ABHMS and the Southern Baptist Convention agreed to cooperate on behalf of the "colored" race. Expenses were to be shared among the Society, the Home Mission Board, and the white and black state conventions. A second comity meeting was held at Old Point Comfort, Virginia, in 1911 to consider the issue of New Mexico. It was agreed that the ABHMS would withdraw from New Mexico, but the southern delegates held that any Baptist congregation anywhere could choose its alignment. This latter position virtually nullified the second round of agreements for the ABHMS. A third meeting occurred at Hot Springs, Arkansas, the following year at which three principles emerged: the autonomy of local congregations, the moral interdependence of Baptist life, and the advisory nature of all denominational organizations. Practically, the delegates agreed to respect a sister organization's mission work, support from a denominational board should not impair a local congregation, and one Baptist group should avoid injuring the work of another. The result of the discussions was the virtual withdrawal from the south of the ABHMS, except for its educational institutions, the withdrawal of the ABHMS from New Mexico, and the recognition that both Northern and Southern Baptists would work together in Oklahoma, Arizona, and California. Southern Baptists thus achieved recognition of their status as at least a pan-southern, if not national, organization of Baptists.

Legacy: The Associational Principle at Work Amidst Diversity

One might well enquire what the factors were that worked toward Baptist unity in the midst of such great diversification. The answer is the associational principle. Here we find the organizational tendency among all religious groups to combine for mutual benefit and seek common ground where consensus of principles can be established.

As far back as the 1620s, English Baptists exhibited a tendency to consult each other and to be in dialogue with other Christians of similar faith. By the mid-seventeenth century, all three major types of Baptists – General, Particular, and Seventh Day – held regular meetings, produced minutes of their proceedings and agreed upon common projects and communications. This characteristic passed over to Baptists in the colonies as early as the 1680s in the Middle Colonies and New England. In 1707 the Philadelphia Baptists organized the oldest continuing associational body in North America and it was replicated throughout Baptist history, regardless of theological or socioethical orientation. In the South there were five associations formed before the Revolution: Charleston, South Carolina (1751); Sandy Creek (1758) and Kehukee (1765), both in North Carolina; Ketockton (1776) and Strawberry (1776), both in Virginia. Likewise in the New England colonies there were three: Warren, Rhode Island (1767), Stonington Union, Connecticut (1772), Shaftesbury, Vermont (1780), and in the West, Redstone (1776) and Chemung, both in Pennsylvania (1796). As the older associations grew beyond practical limits, new associations were constantly being formed to reproduce the facility of local cooperation.

The idea of an association has roots in biblical accounts of the early churches. In Acts 15 Baptists found support to disown erroneous teaching, to send delegates to support the position of a congregation, to deliver decrees to congregations, and to share aid and leadership when requested. To discerning Baptist pastors like Benjamin Griffith in Pennsylvania, there appeared to be an important theological basis for associating with other churches. First, when gathered for prayer and consultation, the congregations were looked upon as one church, because of the unity of faith and conformity of practice that obtained among the churches of Christ. Reminiscent of the Second London Confession, Morgan Edwards had mused in the 1770s, "the chief advantage of this Association [Philadelphia] is that it introduces into the visible Church what are called joints and bonds whereby the whole body is knit together and compacted for increase by that which every joint supplieth."[49] Here was a clear doctrine of the church inclusive of several congregations. Such congregations of course had previously agreed upon a common confession of faith. Second, churches voluntarily consenting to mutual communion were capable of determining the mind of the Holy Spirit and declaring the proper sense of Scripture concerning things in dispute among them. Third, for practical reasons it seemed appropriate to eighteenth-century Baptists in North America that defections in doctrine and order were best handled in the consensual association of churches that still carefully guarded the independence of each congregation. Again, Acts 15 was the model.

From the mid-eighteenth century to the first two decades of the nineteenth century the association of about 25 or fewer congregations was the leading collective expression of Baptists. The Philadelphia Association, that once included congregations from New England to the Carolinas, was reduced in geography to the southeastern Pennsylvania region, and with the growth of churches just in the city of Philadelphia and suburbs, to its named area and about 50 churches. In 1814, as we have seen, an expansion of the association was legitimated among most Baptists in the United States in the General Missionary Convention. It became a kind of grand association of cooperative Baptists that drew upon congregations, associations, societies, and individuals. Noticeably, when the ethnically defined congregations looked for cooperative opportunities, they formed associations within their own language groups. Even those who were most vehemently opposed to missionary Baptists, the Hard Shells or Old Schoolers and the extreme Separates like Daniel Parker and Gilbert Beebe, sought a kind of associationalism in their newspapers, other publications, and infrequent meetings. When the Southern Baptist Convention was born in 1845 and the black Baptists coalesced into national movements, each honored the need for associations.

Baptist historians like Winthrop S. Hudson have referred to this idea of the importance of associations being formed in Baptist life as the "associational principle."[50] The principle is really at the heart of being Baptist and certainly the fiber of what it means for Baptists to be an identifiable denomination. Each major definition of the association in early Baptist history stressed the importance of the independence of each congregation. This could easily lead to isolationism and obscurantism. What therefore must be held in tension for Baptists is their equal desire to associate, to consult, cooperate, be mutually taught and informed, and to be disciplined by each other. The key to the associational principle is voluntarism, whereby like members of a congregation, and member congregations of an association, voluntarily consent to associate with each other. For this reason, no associational body is a superior adjudicatory over the congregation, but the congregations together form a pact of mutuality. When the factors producing the mutuality are most evident, such as theological consensus, mission needs, persecution, or personnel identification, the association is strongest. Likewise, when any of these factors is diminished or erodes, the mutuality is lost and the association loses strength. As we shall see in the narrative ahead, this legacy of Baptists from the earliest stages of Baptist history, brought to fullness in the early nineteenth century, continued to work well for Baptists, even under extremely trying circumstances.

Notes

1 Baptist church historian Robert Handy introduced this terminology in his seminal article, "The Protestant Quest for a Christian America," *Church History* 22/1 (March, 1953): 8–20.
2 Regular or Calvinistic, Black Baptists, Freewill, Separates, and Seventh Day.
3 *American Baptist Yearbook, 1900*, ed. J. G. Walker, DD (Philadelphia, PA: American Baptist Publication Society, 1900), 223.
4 William Warren Sweet, *Religion on the American Frontier: The Baptists 1783–1830* (New York: Henry Holt, 1931), 54.
5 Quoted in Justin A. Smith, *A History of the Baptists in the Western States East of the Mississippi* (Philadelphia, PA: American Baptist Publication Society, 1896), 84.
6 J. H. Spencer, *History of Kentucky Baptists*, 2 vols. (Cincinnati, OH: J. R. Baumes, 1885), I: 107.
7 Quoted in William Brackney (ed.), *Baptist Life and Thought: A Sourcebook* (Valley Forge, PA: Judson Press, 1999), 480.
8 *The Church Advocate*, ed. Daniel Parker (Vincennes, IN: Elihu Stout, 1831), II, 270.
9 Ibid., 37.
10 Harry Leon McBeth, *Texas Baptists: A Sesquicentennial History* (Dallas, TX: Baptistway Press, 1998), 17.
11 Early General Baptist historians attempt to connect various strands of general atonement Baptists into a kind of succession from the earliest Baptists in England to the Six Principle and Carolina types in the colonial period. There is no evidence for the connection of these isolated outcroppings of non-Calvinistic Baptists. The term is here used to denote those Baptists who followed Benoni Stinson. More recently, Randy Mills, *Christ Tasted Death for Every Man: The Story of America's General Baptists* (Poplar Bluff, MO: Stinson Press, 2000), 61, has argued that originally Stinson may have chosen the term "general" for practical rather than theological reasons in a pocket region in Indiana.
12 Quoted in Ollie Latch, *History of the General Baptists* (Poplar Bluff, MO: The General Baptist Press, 1954), 128.
13 Ibid., 166–73.
14 Quoted in McLoughlin, *Modern Revivalism: Charles Grandison Finney to Billy Graham* (New York: Ronald Press, 1959), 139.
15 Ibid., 142–4.

16   William H. Brackney, "Yankee Benevolence in Yorker Lands: Origins of the Baptist Home Missions Movement," *Foundations* 24/4 (October 1981): 301.

17   Ibid., 305–6.

18   John Gill, *A Complete Body of Doctrinal and Practical Divinity or, A System of Evangelical Truths Deduced from the Holy Scriptures* (London: 1770), 952.

19   Cushing Biggs Hassell, *History of the Church of God, from the Creation to A.D. 1885; Including Especially the History of the Kehukee Primitive Baptist Association* (Middletown, NY: Gilbert Beebe's Sons, 1886), 751–2.

20   Elder Gilbert Beebe, "Absolute Predestination of All Things," in Hassell, *History of the Church of God*, 949.

21   Elias Smith, *The Clergyman's Looking-Glass, No. III* (Portsmouth, ME: John E. Palmer, 1804), 3.

22   *Herald of Gospel Liberty* Vol. III, No. 66 (March 1811): 263.

23   It is also available online at <http://www.mun.ca/rels/hrollmann/restmov/texts/esmith/es1.html>.

24   L. F. Greene, *The Writings of the late Elder John Leland, including Some Events in His Life, Written by Himself, with Additional Sketches, etc.* (New York: G. W. Wood, 1845), 531.

25   John Taylor, *Thoughts on Missions* (Franklin County, KY, 1820), 24. Available online at <http://www.geocities.com/baptist_documents/j.taylor.miss.html>.

26   *The Church Advocate*, ed. Daniel Parker (Vincennes, IN: Elihu Stout, 1831), II: 12 (September 1831), 272.

27   Prominent among its supporters were Peter Cartwright the Methodist and James Lemen, a prominent friend of John Mason Peck. See Byron Cecil Lambert, *The Rise of the Anti-Mission Baptists: Sources and Leaders, 1800–1840* (New York: Arno Press, 1980), 270.

28   Hassell, *History of the Church of God*, 636. Later historians would associate this with Manicheism

29   Robert G. Torbet, *History of the Baptists* (Valley Forge, PA: Judson Press, 1963), 262.

30   The address is available online at <http://www.pb.org/pbdocs/blakrock.html>.

31   See the assessment in Lambert, *Rise of the Antimission Baptists*, 391–2.

32   Ibid.

33   *Forty Years of Pioneer Life: Memoir of John Mason Peck D.D.*, ed. from his journals and correspondence by Rufus Babcock (Carbondale, IL: Southern Illinois University Press, 1965), 244; Brackney, *Baptist Life and Thought*, 188–9.

34   Don A. Sanford, *A Choosing People: The History of Seventh Day Baptists* (Nashville, TN: Broadman Press, 1992), 148–9.

35   Ibid., 148.

36 Frank H. Woyke, *Heritage and Ministry of the North American Baptist Conference* (Oakbrook Terrace, IL: North American Baptist Conference, 1979), 29.

37 Foulger was a member of the Newport Church and a grandfather of Benjamin Franklin.

38 *American Baptist Register*, 1852 (Philadelphia, PA: American Baptist Publication Society, 1853), 467.

39 Compare William W. Barnes, "Why the Southern Baptist Convention Was Formed," *The Review and Expositor* 51/1 (January 1944): 5–6 with H. Leon McBeth, *The Baptist Heritage: Four Centuries of Baptist Witness* (Nashville, TN: Broadman Press, 1988), 347, 381.

40 Quoted in Robert Gardner, *A Decade of Debate and Division: Georgia Baptists and the Formation of the Southern Baptist Convention* (Macon, GA: Mercer University Press, 1995), 4.

41 Ibid., 6.

42 *Religious Herald*, April 10, 1845.

43 On the establishment of the Southern Convention, compare Jesse C. Fletcher, *The Southern Baptist Convention: A Sequicentennial History* (Nashville: Broadman Press, 1904), 43–49 with William W. Barnes, *The Southern Baptist Convention 1845–1953* (Nashville, TN: Broadman Press, 1954), 10–18.

44 A. Broaddus, "Messrs Editors," in J. William Jones, *Christ in the Camp Or, Religion in Lee's Army* (Richmond, VA: B. F. Johnson, 1887), 347.

45 "Brethren Editors," in Jones, *Christ in the Camp*, 333.

46 "Letter from R. Ryland," in Jones, *Christ in the Camp*, 212.

47 The associations in western counties of Virginia formed the West Virginia Baptist Convention in 1864, politically and socially inclined to the North and associated with the American Baptist societies.

48 The "states" were Virginia, North Carolina, South Carolina, Georgia, Florida, Alabama, Tennessee, Mississippi, Louisiana, Texas, Maryland, Kentucky, Arkansas, Missouri, and the District of Columbia.

49 Morgan Edwards, *Materials Towards A History of the Baptists in Pennsylvania* (Philadelphia, PA: Joseph Crukshank, 1770), i.

50 Winthrop S. Hudson, "The Associational Principle Among Baptists" *Foundations* 1:1 (January 1958): 10–23.

Chapter 4
The Institutionalization of a Tradition

The latter half of the nineteenth century was a period of steady growth among churches, the creation of associations and conventions, and the establishment of an impressive number of colleges and theological schools. Given the mainstream conventions and various ethnic associations, Baptists in North America enjoyed a remarkable degree of unity. It is accurate to say that a subtle process of institutionalization was taking place among Baptists at the congregational level in this period in congregational life and in the establishment of educational institutions. As a "denomination," Baptists emerged to take their place among American and Canadian religious categories.

A More Sophisticated Ministry

One of the most important signs of the institutional maturity of Baptists was the rise in formal education and experience of pastoral ministers. Essentially Baptists followed a twofold order of ministry: elders (or pastors) and deacons. Originally in North America, both grew out of the laity, with elders assuming the leadership of congregations and deacons providing care for the membership and support for sacramental services. Pastors generally remained in a given location for most, if not all, of their ministry until well into the nineteenth century.

In the early development of the Baptist ministry before 1740, ministers were raised up within a congregation whose responsibility it was to recognize gifts of preaching, interpretation of Scripture, pastoral discernment, and personal discipline. An opening in a church led to a "search" for a suitable candidate who emerged with the approbation of his senior minister and those in surrounding congregations of the association. After examination by either a local church council or an associational council, candidates for ministry were ordained by a service of the laying on of hands. The "education" of a minister consisted of learning by observation and reading selected (and available) theological works. Ministerial libraries were limited to sermons, theological tomes like John Gill's *Body of Divinity* or the *Works of John Bunyan*, and commentaries. The selection of authors was quite eclectic, comprising Presbyterian, Congregational, and Anglican writers.

Then came the Great Awakening. Scores of new congregations switched to Baptist principles in New England and many new churches were planted in the southern colonies. The demand for more ministers increased sharply. There were not enough "senior" ministers to mentor the candidates and the phenomenon of the self-taught pastor met the need. This led to poor exposition of Scriptures, idiosyncratic theological positions, and reliance upon confessional statements adopted by associations. One was considered orthodox if judged by the London, Philadelphia, or New Hampshire Confessions of Faith. Religious experience in the revivalist tradition became the *sine qua non* of many preachers. By these standards, not all candidates passed muster: at Beamsville in Upper Canada in 1808 Christopher Overholt displayed his gifts for ministry, only to have the local church council report back that they did not think he had profitable gifts, so "they desired him to stop and he likewise did."[1]

Two factors changed the course of preparation for ministry. First, there was the concern of other Christian leaders for the seeming ignorance and lack of talent of Baptists. They were often shunned and ridiculed in their communities. For decades in the seventeenth century, Baptists were shut out of the existing academies and colleges in the colonies as practical embarrassments. Second, there were those who took it upon themselves to create opportunities to train ministers. The process began as mentoring in parsonages, and grew to courses of study under the tutelage of recognized pastor-theologians. Samuel Stillman and Thomas Baldwin in Boston were among the first of these in New England. William Staughton and William Rogers in Philadelphia were major catalysts in the Middle States, and Richard Furman and Jesse Mercer were proponents in the South. This in turn led to voluntary societies that set up schools, colleges, and later theological seminaries for training pastors.

The urban congregations were the first to seek an improved ministry. Pulpit oratory was absolutely essential to building a Baptist congregation. In fact it was the standard by which the effectiveness of Baptist ministers was judged. Preachers needed to be students of the content of

Scripture and all of the emerging scholarship in biblical, linguistic, and historical backgrounds, but also well versed in their cultural settings. They were leading critics and generalists who aided the popular understanding of events and circumstances. Next was requisite experience in managing a congregation of 200–300 members or more. This entailed pastoral care and services, execution of quality weekly worship services (sometimes numbering five or six sermons per week), oversight of an educational program, care of the physical facilities, representing the congregation in community events and associations, and leadership in the conduct of the business life of the church. Finally, stature was an important component whereby sophisticated congregations of laypersons who led the industry and commerce of their communities demanded that the Baptist pastor be a figure of import and presence of equal status. Baptist churches expected their pastors to hold their own intellectually and socially with lawyers, physicians, schoolteachers, professors, well-read laity, and other clergy in their communities. For these heightened expectations, urban pastors were paid in excess of one thousand dollars per year from the 1820s. Those who enjoyed long tenures were sometimes unusually feted: Rollin Heber Neale, pastor at First Baptist, Boston 1837–77, was presented with a commemorative communion set crafted from silver dollars contributed by the congregation. When Samuel Stillman died in 1807, businesses in the City of Boston closed in honor of his ministry.

The process of locating the appropriate pastor for a sizeable church in the 1850s entailed searching through the Baptist communities for outstanding pastors in smaller or emerging congregations who had earned a reputation as speakers at associational events or in applied Christian endeavor organizations. Alumni of various institutions recommended their fellows to churches and certain schools became signatures of particular theological orientations. Francis Wayland, an alumnus of Union College and Newton, was called to First Baptist Boston in 1821. His ordination council proceedings may be the largest in North American Baptist history, entailing eight hundred congregants including three college presidents and all the prominent clergy of the city, plus eight marshals, and four constables. Afterwards, there was a private dinner catered at one dollar per head. J. Newton Brown, a distinguished alumnus of Madison University was called to Exeter, New Hampshire in 1829, as was William N. Clarke of a later class in 1863 to Keene, New Hampshire. Cyrus Pitt Grosvenor, who went on to serve First Baptist Hartford, Connecticut, graduated from Dartmouth College, after which he administered an academy and took a year at Princeton Seminary. Licensed by the Congregationalists, his views on baptism changed and he was baptized by Richard Fuller in Charleston,

South Carolina, and ordained an evangelist. Academic work at Princeton was highly prized in the southern Baptist congregations, as illustrated in James P. Boyce, whose undergraduate degree was from Brown, but his theology was determined under Charles Hodge at Princeton. Even the office of evangelist, that some assumed to themselves without any special training or recognition in the previous century, fell to Madison University graduates like Jacob Knapp and Jabez Swann in the 1830s.

Maturing Congregations

The average size of Baptist congregations in North America in 1850 was 80 members.[2] If one surveys the evolution of local congregations in the period 1840–90, several features of growing sophistication are apparent. First, the early town and city churches founded in the seventeenth and eighteenth centuries became pillars of urban Protestantism and religious culture in the East coast cities and in the Midwest. First Baptist, Providence, Rhode Island, whose building was constructed in 1774, remains a magnificent landmark of the Baptist denomination in the capital of Rhode Island. However, other equally impressive church edifices were to rise in major cities of the northern and midwestern states. First Baptist, Boston, Philadelphia, New York, Rochester, Syracuse, and Second Baptist, Boston dreamed of new impressive edifices to mark their community presence and raised vast sums of money in the Gilded Age to erect their churches. First Church, Boston, that had erected three previous buildings marked by great names and events within their walls, built an elaborate Gothic church in 1854 that contained 158 pews and was lighted by gas. Its steeple on Beacon Hill was a city landmark and acclaimed by sailors as a navigational aid at sea. Similarly, the fortunes of First Baptist, Hartford, Connecticut, rose sharply in its history: in 1798 members solicited funds for a "plain, workmanlike" meetinghouse, with a 14 ft (4.3 m.) square spire; in 1856 during the pastorate of Robert Turnbull, a striking "rigidly Romanesque cruciform" church was built at a cost of $75,000, half of which was paid by 12 men. The seating capacity of the sanctuary was 1,100 (largest in the city), and the overall structure featured a vestibule and pastor's study.[3] One of the most ostentatious building projects was at Newark, New Jersey where in 1890 the Peddie Memorial (First Baptist) Church erected a $355,000 sanctuary furnished with pews and organ that resembled the Hagia Sophia in Istanbul with a spire.

In the southern cities, a similar progress was noticed in bold Baptist undertakings. The construction of a new church in Charleston, South Carolina, led the way for Southern Baptists into a position of prominence both in the city and, given its status in the region, for the denomination in general. Under the distinguished pulpit ministry of Richard Furman, in 1822 the members of First Baptist, Charleston erected their classic Greek Temple edifice, described by Robert Mills as "simply grand in its proportions and beautiful in its detail." It included a solid mahogany pulpit from the West Indies and a baptistery in the floor in front of the pulpit.[4] R. B. C. Howell arrived in Nashville, Tennessee in 1835 to find a racially mixed congregation, no building, no Sunday school, and meager financial resources. His preaching spurred growth, and in 1841, according to John Mason Peck, "a splendid building in Gothic style surmounted by two circular towers" with a gallery for the choir and basement space for education and prayer meetings, was constructed at a cost of $27,000. Four decades later, the congregation moved to Broad Street and erected an American Gothic masterpiece at a sum of three times the former structure.[5] First Baptist, Richmond, Virginia, erected a new building in 1841 because the old building was too small for the congregation, it served mixed racial groups, and its architecture was "far behind the times." In Louisville, Kentucky, the members of First and Second Baptist Churches in 1849 called the same pastor to a new combined congregation, Walnut Street Baptist Church. The merger prospered and the 800-seat church building dedicated in 1854 was among the handsomest elaborate Gothic structures in the country. It had multiple pinnacles atop buttresses and a 240 ft (73 m.) steeple. In the southwest, Baptists grew strong and First Baptist Dallas, Texas, became a symbol of their coming of age. The congregation was formed in 1868 in the Masonic lodge hall, a familiar saga for Baptists in the state. Within just a few decades, the congregation was assured of its role in the growing city and proceeded with plans for a sanctuary of nearly $100,000 at the corner of Ervay and Patterson Streets in the heart of Dallas. The commodious stone and brick edifice had a gallery and magnificent pipe organ. Under pastor George W. Truett's ever-increasing ministry, the auditorium was enlarged to provide seating for 4,000 worshippers and in 1925 a four-storey educational building was built, bringing the space to 282 rooms and the value of the property to over a million and a half dollars.[6]

Some Baptist congregations like Mulberry Street in New York, Sansom Street in Philadelphia, and Calvary Baptist in Washington, DC began with magnificent houses of worship. Mulberry Street Church (also known as Tabernacle Baptist) built a perpendicular Gothic structure, seating one thousand, for the ministry of preachers like Archibald Maclay, a Scotsman who led the city in voluntary Christian endeavors. It boasted three front entrances and one of the finest organs in the city.

A split occurred in the congregation of First Baptist, Philadelphia in 1811, prompting the friends and supporters of William Staughton to move with him to Sansom Street, where a new church building was constructed according to plans laid by the celebrated US Capitol architect, Robert Mills. The chief feature of this unique meetinghouse was its circular seating pattern with the baptistery located in the center. Unfortunately, the church project incurred a huge debt, and after Staughton's departure in 1823, it went into insolvency and the building was used for industrial purposes. Amos Kendall, a leading newspaper publisher and US postmaster general under Andrew Jackson, twice single-handedly financed the red brick sanctuary of Calvary Baptist in Washington, DC, one of his many philanthropic projects, although he was not a member of the congregation. Another striking example of Baptist architectural achievement was the Judson Memorial Church in New York. Completed in 1914, the church on historic Washington Square was designed as a memorial to pastor Edward Judson's father, Adoniram Judson, the first American overseas missionary. It featured classrooms, a gymnasium, library, an apartment house, and sanctuary with memorial windows. The original concept included the creation of a missionary institution to the city, a workshop for Christian education, and a revenue-bearing property, in addition to a worship center. The impressive exterior followed a unique Italian Renaissance pattern, including a tower that became a neighborhood landmark.

There was much that pertained to the "institutional" church that went far beyond architectural and financial dimensions. The term itself was coined by William Jewett Tucker, president of Dartmouth College (1893–1909), when he described Berkeley Temple as an institutional church. Judson contextualized the idea in New York City where immigrants lived in abundance:

> The streets swarm with children like a rabbit-warren. There is a saloon on every corner. These people outvote us at every election. We catch their diseases. The miasma from this social swamp steals upward and infects our whole municipal life, and our cities determine the character and destiny of our country. We must be either hammer or anvil – either subdue these people with the gospel or in the end be assimilated by them.[7]

Judson and other urban pastors had something much different in mind for the church of their future. As Judson put it, "Church institutionalization is nothing more than organized kindness, which conciliates the hostile and indifferent, alluring them within reach, and softening their hearts for the reception of the word of life."[8] In his best-selling book,

The Institutional Church (1899), Judson focused the church's ministry on the poor and alienated. For children he proposed kindergartens and for young people gymnasia; during winter cold spells, he proposed using church space as a shelter out of the cold; for little children and the indigent, he created fresh air opportunities in the country; for girls there were sewing classes and stenography lessons, and for both boys and girls there were English language classes. The outstanding symbol of the institutional church was Judson's neighborhood water fountain that pumped thousands of gallons of filtered water through two tons of ice to produce water at a precise range of temperatures the summer through. One observer commented that the crowds around the fountain were so great as to cause a blockage for passers-by at the street corner. Another saw a child carrying buckets of fresh water home to her family tenement.[9]

As one might expect, the institutional church concept had its critics. Amzi C. Dixon, a conservative Baptist pastor in Brooklyn, New York, studied the relative success of institutional churches and concluded that the program was no substitute for traditional evangelism. "We must confess that as a means to an end, it is often a dismal failure," he asserted. "Institutional churches lose about as many as they gain by their philanthropic work." Dixon knew of a pastor of an institutional church in New York who declared that after 12 years of philanthropic work, which involved the expenditure of thousands of dollars, he could not recall a single person who had been made a Christian and become a permanent, useful member of the church through receiving material assistance. Instead, Dixon reported that after receiving lucrative employment such persons disappeared from the church as a reminder of their bleak beginnings.[10]

Gradually, the older frame and brick meetinghouses on urban side streets had given way to impressive neo-Gothic sanctuaries, accompanied with educational facilities, and situated on main streets near similar Methodist, Presbyterian, and Episcopal churches. This signaled maturity for urban congregations and the prosperous memberships wanted the beauty of worship space, great choirs accompanied by pipe organs, and distinguished pulpiteers holding forth in Baptist oratory. If music can be an appropriate indicator, Baptists in city churches moved from revivalistic songs and Isaac Watts hymns to a serious repertoire of classical religious music. The centennial celebrations of First Baptist, Richmond, in 1880 featured a choir of seven trained vocalists who performed works by Fauré, Handel, Mendelssohn, and Mozart.[11] Some churches built galleries just for the acoustical improvements that a choir needed; ironically some of the choirs that sang in Baptist churches were not part of the congregational membership. As the young Joseph Smith found out when he was reflecting upon the four churches at the main intersection in Palmyra, New York in 1819, there was no distinguishable difference between Baptists and other denominations. Even smaller congregations added new facilities or rebuilt on more advantageous sites, imitating their urban cousins. Perhaps the most outstanding example of the socioeconomic maturation of Baptists came in 1931 when Riverside Church in Morningside Heights, New York City was dedicated. It was the result of the transformation of Fifth Avenue Baptist Church (later Park Avenue) into an interdenominational Upper West Side Protestant church under the leadership of founding pastor, Harry Emerson Fosdick. John D. Rockefeller bankrolled the project, contributing eight million dollars for the property alone and millions more for the carillon tower. Riverside included apartments, offices, a community kitchen and restaurant, educational and community rooms, and worship space meant to imitate the cathedrals of Europe. American Baptist in its basic orientation, it has become at once an institutional church and the national cathedral of mainstream Protestantism, valued in the hundreds of millions of dollars.[12]

A unique movement among Baptists in the United States was the "temple" church. Following the great Methodist halls of Britain and the United States, these were vast auditoria with velvet seats rather than pews, wrap-around balconies of several tiers, massive pipe organs and choir lofts. In many cases, the temples were built in the heart of the business districts in buildings devoted to office space unrelated to the congregations. The temples were a concession to rising corporate America and its urban planning, while they carried a veneer of Old Testament application as large gathering places of God's people. The most impressive in the United States was Russell Conwell's Baptist Temple on North Broad Street in Philadelphia that was built to imitate the Metropolitan Tabernacle of Charles H. Spurgeon in London. Of equal stature in their cities were Tremont Temple in Boston, Akron, Ohio Baptist Temple, and Baptist Temple, Rochester, New York. The temples became the showplace of great Baptist preaching.

Among Canadian Baptists this same architectural upgrading and institutionalization trend may be noticed as the Baptist denomination there matured from the nineteenth century. Elmore Harris, an heir to the Massey Harris farm machinery company, built up a congregation at Walmer Road Baptist Church in downtown Toronto on the reputation of his expository preaching that in 1889 constructed a sanctuary seating 500 persons. Three years later it was replaced by one that seated 14 hundred worshipers. Senator William McMaster, a banker and philanthropist who constructed and endowed the university that bears his name, built a matching pink granite Gothic church on Jarvis Street for the congregation of which he was a member. Before the fundamentalists assumed control of the congregation, it was the first among equals in the city in the 1880s and 1890s. The flagship of Toronto Baptists came to be the combined congregations of Park Road and Bloor Street Churches (later Yorkminster Park) that in 1928 built an imitation of York Cathedral in England on north Yonge Street, the longest main street in the world. Under pastor-designer, W. A. Cameron, Yorkminster featured an unobstructed view of the preacher for every worshiper, and the first split chancel in a Baptist church in Canada. Outside Toronto, impressive building projects include Brunswick Street Baptist Church in Fredericton; First Baptist, Halifax, which built an edifice in an Anglican style in 1950 with a seating capacity of six hundred; and Westmount in Montreal, which recreated a Greek Revival temple in brown brick in an affluent English-speaking section. In the West, First Baptist Calgary became a leading congregation on the Prairies; the congregation rapidly expanded and built three edifices from 1891 to 1911, the last one a corner Gothic sanctuary with a commodious balcony and a pipe organ. On the Pacific Coast, First Baptist, Vancouver, obtained its initial property from the Canadian Pacific Railroad in 1881, later moving to a more central location for a new edifice in 1887 that seated 800 worshipers. When the architect of McMaster Divinity College designed an elaborately carved communion table, pulpit, and altar in a split chancel form for the university chapel in 1960, it was thought to be indicative of the future liturgical tastes of most Canadian Baptists.

The Kingdom in the States and Cities

One of the most remarkable developments in the maturing Baptist communities of North America were the state, provincial, and city organizations that naturally evolved. Baptists paralleled Methodist, Presbyterian, Congregationalist, and Lutheran organizations of the same period in this regard. Some were new forms of cooperation with larger Baptist interests in view, others were outgrowths of earlier Baptist mission societies, still others were the results of denominational mission work in rural areas and cities, and finally a type of state convention reflected the political growth of their regions. In this regional development of Baptist polity, Canadian Baptists emulated closely the patterns set in the United States.

State conventions were the logical response to the enlargement of the field of cooperative endeavor to a reasonable geographical unit. Associations were often awkwardly drawn and limited to churches in close proximity. Moreover, some associations were sharply defined theologically, resulting in alternative associations serving overlapping regions. As laws were enacted, taxes collected, political representation and public works were conducted within states, religious groups identified with that political unit. More importantly, the proliferation of Baptist congregations in virtually every section of the country demanded a larger unit of organization that would bridge the relationships between associations and the national organizations. The first Baptist state organizations were in Massachusetts, New York, and South Carolina. Richard Furman, the leading Baptist in his state, first president of the General Missionary Convention, and promoter of Columbian College as the national Baptist experiment in higher education, was the architect and president of the first state convention. He and a small group of South Carolina pastors including William Bullein Johnson, Lee Compere, and William Dossey, arranged for a meeting at Columbia in December 1821 to form a larger body than their associations represented. Three associations were present through "delegates": Charleston, Edgefield, and Savannah River, with the hope that the others, Bethel, Saluda, Reedy River, and Twelve Mile River would eventually be added.[13] The grand designs of the "State Convention of the Baptist Denomination in South Carolina" were to form a bond of union, a center of intelligence, a means of vigorous, united exertion in the cause of God, and the promotion of truth and righteousness. Specifically, the Convention planned to start a seminary of learning, to promote Baptist missions, to provide religious education for children, and to collect funds through charity sermons, donations, and bequests. Among the agreed-upon principles were the recognition of the independence of local congregations, properly elected officers, a board of agents for the recess business of the Convention, and a published constitution. The membership of the Convention was identified as delegates from the associations in South Carolina; later, representatives of missionary and benevolent societies were added. The identity of this model of state convention for the South revealed dependence upon ideas of Baptist polity extending back to Benjamin Griffith and Morgan Edwards in the Philadelphia context, plus the achievements of the General Missionary Convention of the previous seven years. The terminology in the official name, probably attributable to Furman, indicated a complete sequence of Baptist organizations: congregations, associations, state conventions, and the national convention.

Elsewhere, state conventions were essentially enlarged missionary societies that conducted church planting, evangelistic tours, and raised consciousness about national and overseas Baptist mission efforts, in other words, promotional organizations. At the state levels, substantial sums of money could be raised and budgets planned for the next year's work. Thus state staff persons were hired by the conventions, first as corresponding secretaries, then additional positions as editors of the state papers, and administrators for church development, financial management, and educational programs such as Sunday schools. Indicative of this type of state convention, characteristic of the northeast, was New Hampshire (1826):

> The object of this Convention shall be to promote union and coopera-
> tion among the churches of the Convention, the cultivation of Christian
> acquaintanceship, to communicate intelligence respecting the state of
> religion in the churches, to inculcate an interest in education and evange-
> lism among the people of New Hampshire, to render assistance to needy
> Baptist and Free Baptist churches in the State, and to help sustain preach-
> ing of the gospel in neglected regions of the State.[14]

A third type of state convention was the apex of missionary work in the state. Baptist presence in Minnesota commenced in 1847 with the arrival in St Paul of Harriet E. Bishop, a schoolteacher from Vermont, who founded a Sunday school. With territorial organization and the arrival of a Home Mission Society appointee in 1849, the First Baptist Church in St Paul was organized. Soon thereafter a statewide association was formed and at the insistence of a Minneapolis pastor, Amory Gale, the Minnesota Baptist State Convention was organized in 1859, essentially to continue the planting of churches more directly under local auspices. This pattern was adopted as a primary strategy of the American Baptist Home Mission Society as it appointed missionaries in each of the western territories: Wisconsin, Iowa, Nebraska, Wyoming, North Dakota, South Dakota, Colorado, Oregon, and Montana. The small number of churches in Utah mandated that it be connected with Nevada; conversely, the great distances in California necessitated two conventions, and the mountainous divide in Washington led to two conventions there, the eastern one of which was connected with Baptist churches in Idaho. In New Mexico, Arizona, and Oklahoma, the Home Mission Society invested great efforts to organize at the state level, only to retreat in the face of Southern Baptist growth.

A significant challenge to the growth of state conventions that represented all or most of the Baptist congregations was the advent of ethnic associations. In Minnesota, Wisconsin, Nebraska, and Iowa Danish and Norwegian Baptist churches created associations. In North Dakota, where numerous Germans, Swedes, and Norwegians settled, the ethnic factor was very significant: a Norwegian Baptist Conference for the Dakotas was founded in 1894, a Swedish Conference was formed in 1900, and a German Conference that included congregations in Montana was chartered in 1907. The Swedes related to the Baptist General Conference and the Germans joined the North American Baptist Conference (NABC), while the Norwegians merged into the American Baptist Convention. By 1970, the North Dakota Baptist State Convention had dwindled to only 19 churches and was linked to the American Baptist work in South Dakota.

Another type of regional organization that was founded in most cities of the North was the city mission society or association. Evidence of the enlargement of city associations is seen in New York in the 1790s when the City Mission Society commissioned a missionary to upstate New York to plant churches and preach among the Indians of the Six Nations. In the next decade a city society was instituted in Boston to minister to new immigrant groups and seamen. Gradually in the nineteenth and early twentieth centuries, these mission organizations became an urban feature of Northern Baptist life focused upon immigrants, the urban poor, and the black population that had gravitated toward the cities of the North. Approved City Societies were found in Los Angeles, New York, Boston, Philadelphia, Pittsburgh, Detroit, Chicago, Cleveland, Buffalo, and Indianapolis.

In Canada, where the geographical expanses were huge, regional conventions were built around strong association of churches gathered about the urban centers and stretching to political boundaries. In Ontario, for instance, the main body of churches was situated within a hundred miles of the US border from Montreal to Detroit, with Ottawa, Kingston, Toronto, Hamilton, and London as the epicenters. Mission work was conducted in northern Ontario, Quebec, and in the cities as new immigrants arrived. Several attempts were made between 1833 and 1850 to unite congregations in a common purpose: the Upper Canada Baptist Missionary Society, the Baptist Canada Missionary Society, and the Canada Baptist Union. Ultimately, it was the Union Act of 1840 that merged Upper and Lower Canada into a single province of Canada West and Canada East. The Regular Baptist Missionary Convention of Canada West was formed in 1854 and four years later a similar convention for Canada East was created, largely as a home mission agency for evangelism, assisting feeble churches, and education. Eventually these two organizations, plus the Baptist Foreign Mission

Society of Ontario and Quebec, the Church Edifice Society, and the Superannuated Ministers' Fund, would be united in 1888 as the Baptist Convention of Ontario and Quebec.

The West proved to be a formidable challenge to Baptist regional organization. Early missionaries from Ontario had gathered congregations across the prairies mostly along the rail lines. In Vancouver the impetus to commence Baptist life was an influx of railroad employees for the Canadian Pacific plus a gold rush that made real estate in Vancouver a second only to Toronto. The Vancouver church became a forerunner of much of the work related to the British Columbia Baptist Convention.

Other Baptist groups in the United States also followed a pattern of state or regional organization. Freewill Baptists developed a unique terminology early in the nineteenth century to describe their state organizations: the "yearly meetings." In tandem with the quarterly meetings that were equivalents to associations, and monthly meetings that behaved like congregations, yearly meetings were constituent parts of the General Conference. Generally, the purpose of these organizations was to provide program support and mission direction at the state or regional level, while also fundraising and promoting the overall ideals of the denomination. Most other smaller Baptist groups used an expanded geography of the associations to meet the regional needs of the churches.

General or National Organizations

One of the noticeable trends among Baptists of most kinds in the last quarter of the nineteenth century was that toward general or national organizations. This followed a pattern among other American denominations. One of the prime examples of this was among the General Baptists, who as we have seen, were largely scattered from the Ohio Valley through Illinois to Missouri, and were rebuffed in several attempts to join with the Freewill Baptist General Conference from the 1830s to the 1860s. Steps were taken to "comprise all the annual associations in the General Baptist denomination, to complete the organization of the connection, to consolidate the body by harmonizing its different parts, to concentrate its strength in a common cause, and to promote a growth in grace and a knowledge of the gospel truth."[15] The General Association of General Baptists thus came into being November 2, 1870. In an attempt to identify with Free(will) Baptists and other non-Calvinistic Baptists, the constitution of the Association sought to promote fraternal relations with "Liberal Baptists." Membership in the Association was based upon a minimum of one voting representative, plus additional representatives for every one hundred members. Eight associations comprising 143 congregations and over 6,200 members made up the General Association at its second meeting.

Institutionally, the new General Association promised real progress for General Baptists. In 1871, a General Home Mission Board was established, vigorously promoting church extension. In 1883 a College Board was started that two years later laid the groundwork for the denominational school, Oakland City College (Ind.). In 1903 a Foreign Mission Board commenced. Within a decade of the founding of the General Association, a paper, *The General Baptist Messenger*, began publication in Evansville, Indiana. There were opponents to this move toward general organization, but General Baptists forged ahead of their times among smaller Baptist bodies.

Similarly, the infrastructure of national boards and agencies reflected growth in programs and support staffs of the northern societies and the Southern Baptist Convention. A review of northern Baptist denominational agencies in the 1880s reveals 50–60 staff in northern Baptist national boards in three cities, 20–30 staff in Southern Baptist organizations in three cities, and about the same among black Baptists mainly in Nashville. Each of the Baptist subdenominations had publishing concerns, many of which maintained their own printing operations, employing 20–25 persons in the trades and sales.

The final quarter of the nineteenth century was decisive for Southern Baptists. As was the case in other Protestant groups that had divided before the war over slavery, there was some hope that reunification might take place. Richard Fuller, a pastor in Baltimore with extensive service in the South, held out that North and South would again join hands. The American Baptist Home Mission Society redoubled its efforts in the South, openly courting both black and white congregations. And the American Baptist Publication Society engineered new ways to produce literature and literacy among the former slaves and new southwestern regions. In the end, southern perseverance prevailed.

Perhaps the cleverest strategy that was ever devised to conduct home missions appeared in the post-Civil War application of technology to evangelism. In 1891 Wayland Hoyt and Boston W. Smith, the latter a secretary of the American Baptist Publication Society, designed a program of chapel car evangelism; it was actually an extension of the colporteurs and wagons of the 1840s. In conjunction with the ABHMS, and later the American Baptist Missionary Union, the Publication Society commissioned a series of railroad chapel cars to be used for evangelism and church planting in the West and South. Eventually seven of the cars were built through a Chapel Car Syndicate on Wall Street. The routes covered the regions from Texas and Arkansas to the Dakotas, Montana, the Northwest and Southwest. An agreement with railroad executives allowed for free transport of the chapel cars from one location to another. So successful were the railroad missionaries that, as opportunities overseas, in Alaska, and in the Great Plains continued to open, chapel boats and chapel automobiles were placed in service of the American Baptist mission societies.

The issue of competing home mission efforts in the South was a thorny one. During the war, the ABHMS had applied to the Federal government for oversight of the Baptist church properties left vacant by military maneuvers. This was most onerous to local southern Baptists who saw it as an occupation strategy not unlike military Reconstruction. As the Society began to open schools for blacks in every southern state, Southern sensitivities were awakened. Despite some comity conversations in 1868, the Southern Baptist Convention, behind the esteemed seminary professor John A. Broadus, rejected any closer cooperation with the American Baptist Home Mission Society. Broadus represented the educational symbol of the South, the reopened Southern Baptist Theological Seminary that eventually relocated from Greenville, South Carolina, to Louisville, Kentucky.

Problems with other weak national agencies were also resolved. The Foreign Mission Board, that had retained its fragile work in China, forged ahead with strengthened work in the Far East, and new stations in Europe, Africa, and Mexico. Its architects were James B. Taylor and J. B. Jeter. An auxiliary body, the Women's Missionary Union, was created in 1888. Against efforts of the American Baptist Publication Society and grassroots Landmarkism (see below), proponents like James B. Gambrell and B. H. Carroll of a revitalized Sunday School Board, won the day in 1891 when the Board began business in Nashville as what would be the largest publisher of Christian literature in the world. Schism with the northern churches and an independent international strategy would insure the survival of a Southern Baptist Convention.

The largest accomplishment of Southern Baptists in this era was territorial growth. Historically, the Convention built upon its congregations in Virginia, North and South Carolina, Georgia, Florida, Alabama, Mississippi, Louisiana, plus Kentucky, Texas, Arkansas, and Missouri. Tennessee Baptists, long divided by geography and dissension, united in a statewide convention in 1875. Two years later, Baptists in the District of Columbia hived off from both Maryland and Virginia and formed a convention, though it was historically related to both northern and southern Baptists. Right after the turn of the century, Southern Baptist missionary work from the 1880s paid dividends in organizing new state conventions in Oklahoma, New Mexico, and Illinois. This would consolidate the old South and the southwest into a Southern Baptist foundation that became the basis of Southern Baptist identity for the next hundred years.

Rise of Educational Institutions

One of the most impressive accomplishments of the Baptist community in the nineteenth century was in the area of higher education. Academies, colleges, seminaries, and, later, universities, were the first extraparish institutions of the Baptist community in North America. It was important to Baptists to create institutions of learning for several reasons. First, as discussed earlier, was the need for a learned ministry. From the late seventeenth century, English Baptists imitated other nonconformists in starting academies that evolved into colleges. Several graduates of English Baptist schools emigrated to the colonies and served with distinction, including for instance, Morgan Edwards, William Staughton, and graduates of the Haldane seminaries in Scotland. Secondly, Baptists viewed institutions as status symbols for their principles. Often labeled uneducated "farmer-preachers," many Baptists were eager to achieve greater recognition among other clergy. This could be seen in Boston, New York, Philadelphia, and, later, Charleston. Third, Baptist institutions became centers of specialization for Bible scholarship, theological reflection, religious education, missionary training, and publishing.

At the beginning of this era, there was one Baptist college in Rhode Island. In 1900 there were over 15 schools, 50 colleges, and five theological seminaries under the auspices of Baptist leaders, conventions, and associations. In the first quarter of the century, it was New England and the Middle Atlantic states that promoted higher education. William Staughton brought his idea of a theological school from his Bristol experience to Philadelphia in 1812. It was the first of its kind. In Maine, a new model emerged in the literary and theological (L&T) school at Waterville in 1813. It was a mixture of arts and theological students in its first generation. Close on the heels of Waterville came Hamilton Literary and Theological Institution (later Colgate University), and similar L&Ts in Ohio (1831) and Michigan (1833). An impressive effort was put into securing a national charter from the US Congress for the Columbian College, established at Washington, DC in 1821. The first stage concluded when Massachusetts Baptists created Newton Theological Institution outside Boston, the first postgraduate theological seminary in the denomination. It was an imitation of Andover Theological Seminary operated by the Congregationalists.

Various parts of the Baptist constituency founded even more institutions from 1825 to 1850. In the South and West, a second model, the manual labor school, was used widely. It allowed students of modest means to work on a farm in support of their tuition and expenses while also learning a trade. Such colleges were started at Richmond, Virginia (1832), Kalamazoo, Michigan (1833), Penfield, Georgia (eventually Mercer University) (1833), Wake Forest, North Carolina (1834), and Franklin, Indiana (1834). Theological institutions were founded at Rochester, New York, and Covington, Kentucky. Baptists in Canada, drawing upon both personnel and curricula from British and American Baptists founded two institutions in this era, Canada Baptist College at Montreal and Acadia University in Wolfville, Nova Scotia.

Already noted are the schools founded by the ABHMS for the Freedmen community after the Civil War. In the last four decades of the century more institutions were founded in the western states and several of a special kind in the East. Perhaps the most energetic educational project was the revival of the foundering University of Chicago in 1892. William Rainey Harper sought the generous assistance of Baptist oil millionaire John D. Rockefeller to build a thoroughly modern research university based upon German universities and Johns Hopkins University. The new university had a divinity school which would eventually become a primary center for doctoral-level religious research. Other examples of specialized schools that Baptists founded were Vassar College, Colby Sawyer College, and Freewill Baptist Keuka College in New York (1891) for women, and Indian University (1880), later Bacone College in Oklahoma. Missionary training needs were foremost at Baptist Missionary Training School in Chicago (1877); the Baptist Institute in Philadelphia (1892) founded by the missionary to the Shan people, Ellen Cushing; and Boston Missionary Training School (1881) fostered by A. J. Gordon and the Clarendon Street Church in Boston. Other states had lofty plans for schools that never reached the collegiate level, but prospered as academies: Parsonfield Academy, Maine (1832), Suffield Academy, Connecticut (1833), New Jersey Classical and Scientific Institution (1869), New Hampton Institute, New Hampshire (1853), New Hampton, Vermont (1853). Lastly, Seventh Day Baptists founded Salem College in West Virginia in 1888. One analyst noted at the turn of the twentieth century that Baptists had more money invested in property and endowments for educational interests than any other religious body in North America.[16]

The richness of ethnic diversity in the growing Baptist family provided new opportunities for Christian education as well. Shortly after its opening in 1850, Rochester Seminary took an interest in the area German Baptist churches and eventually hired a German professor, Karl August Rauschenbusch, to teach in the school. By 1871, a second professor was added and an endowment secured for the establishment of a "German Department." In the late 1890s, an eminent New York pastor, Walter Rauschenbusch, Karl August's son, went to Rochester and took up the responsibilities in the German Department that eventually built its own facilities. Ironically, it was Walter Rauschenbusch who developed the social gospel emphases of the Seminary, giving it much of its reputation, while distancing his German constituency who thought his teachings too liberal (see below). What became the German Baptist Seminary at Rochester in the 1920s, in 1949 decided to relocate from Rochester to Sioux Falls, South Dakota, preserving both its ethnic identity and its theological conservatism. The new institution became North American Baptist Seminary, reflecting the new name adopted by the German Conference in 1942.

A similar story unfolded among Scandinavian Baptists in North America. The Rev. J. A. Edgren, a Swedish Baptist pastor in Chicago, determined to offer theological education for young Scandinavians, and the Baptist Union Theological Seminary at Morgan Park offered him space in their buildings in 1857 to open classes. In the early years, Swedish, Danish, and Norwegian students studied in the school. In 1884 the Danes and Norwegians formed their own seminary, when the Swedes moved their classes first to Minneapolis and then to Stromberg, Nebraska, to be more central to their church populations. In 1892 when the newly reorganized University of Chicago opened, both the Swedes and the Danish-Norwegian programs became departments of the University, reaping great benefits from interaction with the English-speaking faculty. N. P. Jensen, a Dane, and Carl Gustaf Lagergren, a Swede, gave outstanding direction to these efforts. Eventually a combination of factors – financial, theological conservatism, and the desire to maintain an ethnic identity – led to closure of the Scandinavian work at Chicago. In 1913 the Swedes moved their seminary to St Paul, Minnesota, where it became Bethel College and Seminary and the Danish-Norwegian program closed with many of its prospects assumed by the new Northern Baptist Theological Seminary, affiliated with the Northern Baptist Convention.

As the century of expansion and differentiation closed, Baptists had earned their place among the major denominational traditions of North

America, still divided between two basic families. Yet the seeds for more division and ongoing disintegrative forces were already sown.

Landmarkism

Landmarkism is essentially a southern version of what has been called "local church protectionism," which is evident in every region of Baptist life in North America. The Landmarkist movement had its origins in the ministry and writings of James Robinson Graves, a Vermonter who made his way to Tennessee and built a lifelong following across the upper South and Southwest. Essentially Graves and his followers taught that the heart of the true church was the local congregation, beyond which there was no recognized authority in the Body of Christ. As one classic text put it, "The church is the local and visible judiciary and executive of the kingdom of Christ. It consists of such members of the kingdom as have voluntarily associated together for the maintenance of the public worship of God, the observance of Christ's ordinances, and the execution of his laws."[17] Pulpit affiliation with other denominations, recognition of "alien" baptisms, and cooperation with other religious "societies," as other churches were characterized, was anathema.

Constituting a "Great Triumvirate" of Landmarkism, James M. Pendleton and Amos Cooper Dayton joined J. R. Graves. Pendleton was a faculty member at Union University in Tennessee, then a member of Graves's editorial staff at the *Tennessee Baptist*, and after the Civil War a pastor in Pennsylvania where he also lectured at Crozer Theological Seminary. Dayton was a dentist from New Jersey who went South and contributed to various Baptist papers, eventually becoming editor of the *Baptist Banner* in Atlanta. Dayton unequivocally proclaimed the role of the Baptists in Christian history: "The Baptists may be considered as the only Christian community which has stood since the days of the Apostles, and as a Christian Society which has preserved pure the doctrine of the Gospel through all ages."[18] While Pendleton agreed with Graves and Dayton on most points, he never lost the idea of the universal church, he refused the more limited understanding of the Kingdom of God, and he rejected the idea of church successionism.

As the movement gained strength, other articles of Landmarkism took definite shape. A kind of successionist view of church history came forth from Dayton's writings whereby he and Graves identified the local churches together with the Kingdom of God. Graves added the notion that the true church (and the Kingdom of God) had been in existence since the days of John the Baptist. Graves maintained that this kingdom had never been broken in pieces and would never cease until Christ returned personally to reign over it. All true churches had all the landmark characteristics and if any one congregation were found to be lacking one, it would be disqualified. Graves drew upon the work of mid-nineteenth century Southern Baptist historian, G. H. Orchard, who noted the presence of groups like Novationists, Paulicians, Albigenses, Lollards, and Mennonites in a chronological lineage with the early modern Baptists. All of the Landmarkists dismiss the Protestant Reformers as not being part of the true churches. Further, all non-Baptist churches of modern times are not true churches.

Some Landmarkists went a further step towards what they called "unanimity." In his tract, "Thoughts on Church Government," T. P. Crawford, author of the Gospel Mission movement (discussed in chapter 9 below) denounced "party rule of the majority that had become the rule of nearly all of our churches." Instead, he suggested restoring the time-honored principle among many Baptists in the South that the rule of the whole body for the edification or upbuilding of itself should be in love and good works. Unanimity is the only kind of self-government possible to a Christian church or to any other organized body. He thought unanimity would remove all fears of defeat and oppression and place every member in the best possible mood for the transaction of business. Every congregation needed to approve a resolution as followed:

> This Christian church desires as a body, under the guidance of the Holy Spirit, to reach a unanimous and proper decision on all cases coming before it. To this end the Moderator of the church will show respect for the rights and opinions of every member thereof by passing any question which fails to secure the approval of all through a second and even a third consideration and vote, at the request of any member present in the business session. Failing thus to secure a unity, the proposition is lost. This church desires to govern itself as the executive body of Christ without fear or partiality, in accord with the teachings of his word.[19]

Landmarkists made their influence felt through various means. First, as the state Baptist papers were the major informational resource to the Baptist communities, the Landmarkist editorials and news about events like debates were very influential. Second, throughout his long life, Graves was a constant debater and a spellbinding speaker. His most famous debate was held at Cotton Grove, Tennessee, in June 1851.

This debate actually marked the formal beginning of the movement and publicly concluded, "Can we consistently address as brethren those professing Christianity who not only have not the doctrines of Christ and walk not according to his commandments, but are arrayed in direct and bitter opposition to them?"[20] Third, Graves started a rival Southern Publication Society that produced Sunday school materials and other publications from the Southwestern Publishing House, the Southern Baptist Sunday School Union, and Graves, Marks, Company (later Graves, Jones & Co.), that were widely used in the churches. Graves chose Nashville as the base of his operations, the city where the mainstream Sunday School Board was also located.

As a number of historians have shown, the Landmarkist Movement may well have been the most important influence upon the developing nineteenth-century identity of Baptists in the South and later.[21] Whole groups of associations and congregations were part of the Landmarkist tradition. The Whitsett Controversy illustrates just how the movement gained political clout. In 1895 William H. Whitsett, a faculty member at Southern Baptist Theological Seminary in Louisville, soon to become president of that institution, wrote an entry for a religious encyclopedia that claimed Baptists had adopted immersion as the proper form of baptism in 1641, about three decades after their establishment. With its obvious implications about Baptist identity from their beginning and in succession with apostolic churches, Whitsett created a firestorm of editorial controversy that raged for three years across the South. While most of the Seminary community supported President Whitsett and the trustees declined to terminate him, he tendered his resignation in 1898 believing that no useful purpose was served by his continuing role and the strife it generated. Whitsett was followed by Edgar Y. Mullins, who steered a careful course around the controversy, always cognizant of local church protectionism. Perhaps more importantly, Landmarkism was firmly planted in the churches of the Southwest, where a new school, Southwestern Baptist Theological Seminary, behind the strong leadership of B. H. Carroll of Texas, emerged from Baylor University to rival Southern Baptist Seminary. At the same time, those with very ardent Landmarkist tendencies bolted from the Convention and followed leaders like Benjamin Bogard in an "anti-Convention" stance described below.

Landmarkism would drive a permanent wedge among Baptists, especially in the South, but also far beyond. As its founder claimed, it gave many Baptists a means of discerning authentic Christianity from other forms:

This then, is the infallible test by which genuine Christianity may be tested and known; it places blood before water; it teaches that we come to the church *through* Christ, to the water of its baptism through his *blood*; while all human and counterfeit religions reverse this and teach that we come to Christ through the church, and to the blood of Christ through the water of baptism.[22]

Urbanization and the Gospel of Wealth

In the Northeast and Great Lakes regions, plus select cities in the South like Richmond, Charleston, Atlanta, Louisville, and Nashville, the dominant congregations in the Baptist family were urban and included some of the most illustrious persons in their communities. Earlier in the century, this was illustrated in the active Christian careers of Nicholas Brown, Gardner Colby, William Colgate, Amos Kendall, William Peddie, Dr Nathaniel Shurtleff, Dr William H. Brisbane, and John Nuveen. Other examples of successful Baptist capitalists were John Price Crozer of Upland, Pennsylvania, who was in textiles, and his son-in-law William Bucknell, who designed public works projects in Philadelphia; Matthew Vassar, a brewer from Poughkeepsie, New York; and a cluster of Baptist worthies in Rochester, New York that included Alvah Strong, newspaper publisher, Hiram Sibley and John Wilder, merchants, William Sage and Edwin Pancost, who manufactured shoes, and David Barton, who designed edge tools. Later, in the new century, their successors in Baptist philanthropy were William Montgomery, a manufacturer of automobile parts; William Howard Doane, a toolmaker and lumber magnate from Cincinnati; John J. Jones, a Rochester brewer; John B. Stetson, a hatter in Philadelphia who purchased land for a Florida school; Dr William W. Keen, a world-renowned surgeon who operated on President Grover Cleveland; and J. L. Kraft, a Canadian cheesemaker who emigrated to Wisconsin and funded numerous Northern Baptist projects. Oil tycoon John D. Rockefeller, pre-eminent among this group, taught Sunday school at First Baptist, Providence, Rhode Island as a student at Brown University, and was an active layman at Euclid Avenue in Cleveland Ohio, and later in congregations in New York City.

The urban congregations displayed their wealth and success. This proved to be a problem for some, while very useful to others. Some Baptists associated wealth with ill-gotten gain. In the writings of social critics, the barons of industry fared poorly for their disregard of women and children in the labor force and for the living conditions of working classes, Baptists being no exception. Many Baptist philanthropists donated to schools where capital projects bore their names, most notably the chapels or the institutions themselves like Bucknell University and Rockefeller Chapel at the University of Chicago. The earliest colleges and universities were anxious for an initial generous gift, often to chart the identity of the school from a rather perfunctory classification. Thus Maine Literary and Theological Institution became Colby University, DeLand College became Stetson University, and Rock Spring High School and Seminary became Shurtleff College. It was often the pastor of the Baptist congregation where the industrialist was a member who served as the gate to generosity and the defender of the donor's reputation. Noteworthy in this regard were Augustus Strong who was Rockefeller's minister at Euclid Avenue in Cleveland, Ohio and Pharcellus Church who in one pastorate protected the likes of the Colgate Family and later ministered to the Baptist elite in Rochester, New York.

Most agree that Russell H. Conwell was the best exemplar of the gospel of wealth among Baptists. Conwell, a lawyer/preacher from Massachusetts accepted a call to Grace Baptist Church in North Philadelphia in 1882. His preaching style and emphases soon won him great crowds of hearers. He built up the membership dramatically and created the Baptist Temple; he also ventured into dental education and medical care, creating Good Samaritan Hospital and related professional schools. In 1887 Conwell started his great monument, Temple University, completing his triad objective: preaching, teaching and healing. To raise the requisite funds for the Temple enterprises he lectured all over the United States, using his most popular lecture, "Acres of Diamonds," raising in excess of eight million dollars.

Conwell built upon a Calvinistic/capitalistic foundation that asserted that God was the source of wealth and those who worked hard, and faithfully served God, should expect material blessings. ". . . wealthy men are usually men of economy – men who have worked hard year after year to secure property, and it is a good thing for the world that they have it."[23] He held firmly to an economic aristocracy that would become the Christian stewards of society. It was the competition of the marketplace that determined who would attain the wealth God promised. So, he urged, "Every good man ought to be rich. Every good man would be rich if he had as much common sense as goodness. I say, Get rich, get rich! But get money honestly or it will be a withering curse. Money being power, it ought to be in the hands of good men and women."[24] John D. Rockefeller, the best example of what Conwell taught, told the first graduating class of the University of Chicago that "The good Lord gave me my money." Herein was a fulfillment of the nineteenth century dictum that one holds wealth that one acquires as a steward of the Lord.[25]

Some of Conwell's hearers were critical of what appeared to them to be crass materialism. The urged him to "preach the gospel" instead of telling people how to make money. In the latter part of his career, Conwell responded by discountenancing the inheritance of money, dismissing luxurious lifestyles, preaching against exploitation of labor and stock watering,[26] and encouraging the endowment of colleges and Christian institutions. In 1915 he even went so far as to approve the classless society of the socialists, an obvious concession to the rise of the social gospel.

The Challenge of New Theology

American Protestants began to absorb and interact with new theological developments in the second half of the nineteenth century. Many of the trends originated in German universities, notably higher criticism of the Scriptures, the evolutionary nature of Christian doctrine, and the primacy of religious experience. By 1850 leading seminaries in other denominations like Harvard, Yale, and Andover among the Congregationalists; Union, Auburn, and Pittsburgh among the Presbyterians; and the Lutheran institutions at Gettysburg and Philadelphia were teaching new ideas about the atonement, the dynamic inspiration of Scripture and the progress of Christian civilization. Gradually as Baptist faculty spent sabbatical leaves in Europe and took degrees at German universities like Leipzig and Berlin, Baptists were on record with changed theological perspectives.

The initial changes were noticeable at Newton Theological Institution and Colgate Theological Seminary. At Newton, there was a growing interest in German theological trends. Irah Chase, the president and leading theologian, had worked closely with William Staughton in Washington and steered a course close to his esteemed counterpart at Andover Theological Seminary, Moses Stuart. Chase attended lectures in three German universities in 1823 and returned to design the curriculum of Newton around the new results of biblical criticism. His colleague in theology, Barnas Sears, followed in his adoption of German scholarship and clearly set Newton on the course of a biblical theology that was methodologically critical in the first decade of its existence. At what would become Colgate University, the revivalist tradition opened the door for yet another interest in the New Theology. Nathaniel Kendrick, Colgate's first theologian and president, brought a strong commitment to revivals in the Second Great Awakening regionally from New England to the New York frontier. As time went on, the chief characteristic of Kendrick's version of the New Theology was an emphasis upon understanding religious experience in the ratification of doctrine, seen clearly in the work of Ebenezer Dodge and William Newton Clarke.

Before long, signs of accommodation to the New Theology were seen at Rochester Theological Seminary and Southern Baptist Theological Seminary. Ezekiel G. Robinson trained at Brown and Newton and was schooled in German theologians. Although Robinson wanted to avoid any hint of heterodoxy, he was equally averse to old orthodoxy, such as seen in the Princeton School, that he dubbed "a series of legal fictions."[27] He saw the nature of theology as a progressive science, and read and quoted a wide variety of writers from Romanticists to Hegelians. What Robinson began at Rochester was a pursuit of a theological system that bridged tradition with modern ideas and expressions. Even the stalwart, much-quoted A. H. Strong, Robinson's student and successor, thought one of his highest achievements was his monistic speculation that he derived from philosophic discussions in the University of Rochester and blended with evangelical terminology.

At Southern Baptist Seminary, Edgar Y. Mullins became the bellwether of the new trends. Mullins came from a secular university background and was a theological inquirer all of his life. He imbibed the new scientific thought at Johns Hopkins University while he was a pastor at Lee Street Baptist Church in Baltimore and as a local pastor adjoining Newton Theological Institution, he knew and learned from Newton's outstanding biblical scholars and theologians. One of his close friends was William Newton Clarke. When Mullins became president at Southern Seminary in 1899, he steered a cautious course between the Landmarkists of the Southwest and the learned community of the northeast. Time and again in editorials and forums where he could speak freely, Mullins behaved much like a selective advocate of the New Theology. He used terms slightly different from Walter Rauschenbusch and even developed a vocabulary of his own with words like "soul competency" and "autonomy of the local church." His later career suggests how he lost some favor among many Southern Baptists, but became the chief advocate of religious liberty across the Baptist world.

Numerous writers have shown how important the University of Chicago was in advancing the New Theology. With few boundaries on "untrammeled research," William Rainey Harper, Shailer Mathews,

Shirley Jackson Case, and George Burman Foster led the Baptist community and, it is fair to say, much of the American Protestant tradition, in an embrace of modernistic theology. Chicago theologians eschewed "authority religion" and, influenced by major German thinkers, stressed the essentially historical basis of religion. Social science methods were employed to ascertain contemporary Christian character and much effort was expended in demonstrating the changing contexts of theology through the centuries. Some Chicago theologians, like Douglas C. MacIntosh, attempted to quantify religious experience as a basis of theological understanding.

In all, the Baptist community was among the leading Protestant denominations in North America to address and incarnate the ideas associated with the New Theology. The leading seminaries – Newton, Colgate, Rochester, Crozer, Chicago – all responded creatively to the new possibilities. The longevity of four seminary presidents – at Rochester, Newton, Crozer, and Southern – across four decades at the turn of the twentieth century made many of the changes more palatable because of the personal trustworthiness of Strong, Hovey, Weston, and Mullins, respectively. In addressing the New Theology, the Baptist community was not without its exponents of a conservative bent. Local church pastors generally withstood the teachings of theological school-teachers and some built large constituencies opposed to the modernistic tendencies. As the twentieth century will demonstrate, the legacy of theological ferment from the 1880s laid the foundation for a multi-faceted family under the name Baptist.

Legacy: The Social Gospel

If the gospel of wealth reflects a major trend among urban congregations, its reactive element may be seen in the social gospel, which was diametrically opposed in perspective to the gospel of wealth. Some Baptists concluded that the historic Baptist understanding of individualism was inadequate and looked to more communal understandings. Baptists were not the first to understand that the gospel had social as well as communal implications; Josiah Strong and Washington Gladden among the Congregationalists had written about such themes in the 1870s and 1880s. The scientific community and the social sciences combined with economics and politics to produce new intersections of sociology and religion and an appreciation for "Christian socialism," often defined as a veiled attack upon uncontrolled capitalism. The most powerful, popular, and articulate version of the social gospel was to be found in Walter Rauschenbusch, a minister in the German Baptist Conference of America. Rauschenbusch (1861–1918), a pastor in Kentucky and New York's "Hell's Kitchen," arrived at his convictions while serving the needs of an immigrant community that was characterized by overcrowded housing and poor sanitation, the exploitation of women and children in the labor force, and insensitive capitalist barons bent upon commercial profitability. Rauschenbusch was influenced himself by study in Germany under Albert Ritschl and Adolf von Harnack, and by social theorists in New York and elsewhere like Jacob Riis, Leighton Williams, George D. Herron, Henry George, and Richard T. Ely.

For Rauchenbusch, there was nothing less than a growing social crisis. He interpreted Christian history to assert that the essential purpose of Christianity was to transform human society into the kingdom of God by regenerating all human relations and reconstituting them in accordance with the will of God. But he strongly believed the Christian Church had backed away from this purpose. The result in the late nineteenth century had been to create a socioeconomic crisis involving two classes: the powerful employers and the wage-earners who lacked power or the means to transform their circumstances for the better. He held the churches to be the most potentially influential institutions in society to meet the social crisis.[28] In his 12 books, the social gospel could be summed up thus: the righteous rule of God in human affairs.

Within his own Baptist family, the German Conference, Rauschenbusch received some of his most searching critique. E. Anschuetz, German Baptist minister in West Hoboken, New Jersey, engaged the young pastor on New York's East Side in a series of editorial debates and exchanges in the Conference paper, *Der Sendbote*, beginning in 1890 and continuing for over a decade. As Rauschenbusch stressed the immediacy of the Kingdom of God, his friend Anschuetz reminded him that the Kingdom of Christ was to be established, not through gradual evolution, but through the Lord at his return. The importance of the millennium as the time of the righteous rule of Christ must not be neglected. Rauschenbusch responded by asserting that the social order required radical change and this change was not to be postponed to the future. "The victory over the world is ours," Rauschenbusch retorted, "the worst distortion of Christianity occurs when the renewal of life is put off until a future life and is not demanded or expected in the present."[29] Rauschenbusch and Anschuetz both recognized some basic differences in outlook on the social question, namely, that ordinary Christianity emphasized renewal of the individual, while social Christians preferred to concentrate on the renewal of society. Also there had to be a distinction between the socialist movement that stressed materialistic reforms, and the Church that must not ignore the reality of "Christ in us" as the greatest power on earth. A later German Baptist theologian observed, "The German Baptists were those who heeded Rauschenbusch least. For the most part they steadfastly refused to listen to his message of the social responsibility of the church."[30]

In his long service as professor of church history at Rochester Theological Seminary, Rauschenbusch became a national figure and lecturer, and influenced countless Baptist and black thinkers with his social Christianity. First were pastors and denominational leaders who carried forth his theories, like Dores R. Sharpe, Edwin Dalglish, and Samuel Zane Batten. Next were the black students who imbibed his work even after his death: Mordecai Johnson, Howard Thurman, Benjamin Mays, and Martin Luther King, Jr. As a seminal thinker, Rauschenbusch lay dormant for decades until the mid-twentieth century, when he was rediscovered by historical studies of the Progressive Era and American intellectual thought. At Colgate Rochester, his work was repristinated in a lecture series; at Crozer Seminary social ethicists picked up his themes; and in the South, the pastor and writer Carlyle Marney and Henlee Barnette of the Southern Baptist Theological Seminary developed an affection for his work. Gradually, the social gospel became respectable even amongst the most ardent evangelicals who came to refer to the "social dimensions" of the gospel. Perhaps no one made a greater contribution than Rauschenbusch to the Baptist family of his era and beyond.

Notes

1 Minutes of the Beamsville Baptist Church, 1808 (Mss. Canadian Baptist Archives, McMaster Divinity College).

2 *American Baptist Register*, ed. Lansing Burrows (Philadelphia, PA: American Baptist Publication Society, 1853), 410.

3 *Centennial Memorial of the First Baptist Church of Hartford, Connecticut, March 23rd and 24th 1890* (Hartford, CT: Office of Christian Secretary, 1890), 205–13.

4 *Two Centuries of the First Baptist Church of South Carolina 1683–1883*, ed. H. A. Tupper (Baltimore, MD: R. H. Woodward and Co., 1889), 121, 305–6. Prior to this, baptisms were held at a font in the adjacent cemetery.

5 Lynn E. May, Jr., *The First Baptist Church of Nashville, Tennessee, 1820–1970* (Nashville, TN: First Baptist Church, 1970), 55–8; 147–9.

6 *The First Century of the First Baptist Church of Richmond, Virginia* (Richmond, VA: Carlton McCarthy, 1880), 247; Leon McBeth, *The First*

Baptist Church of Dallas: Centennial History (1868–1968) (Grand Rapids, MI: Zondervan Publishers, 1968), 162–7.

7   Charles Hatch Sears, *Edward Judson: Interpreter of God* (Philadelphia, PA: Griffith and Rowland Press, 1917), 90.

8   Ibid., 92–3.

9   Edward Judson, *The Institutional Church* (New York: Lentilhon & Co., 1899), 160–9.

10   Amzi C. Dixon, *Evangelism Old and New: God's Search for Man in All Ages* (New York: American Tract Society, 1905), 16.

11   *First Century of First Baptist, Richmond*, 25–6.

12   Peter J. Paris et al., *The History of the Riverside Church in the City of New York* (New York: New York University Press, 2004), 18–24.

13   The minutes of the first meeting indicate an *ad hoc* nature of delegates rather than the official authorizations of the associations to form what could be understood as a superior body.

14   Quoted in Frank W. Padelford, *The Kingdom in the States* (Philadelphia, PA: Judson Press, 1928), 19.

15   Ollie Latch, *History of the General Baptists* (Poplar Bluff, MO: The General Baptist Press, 1972), 204.

16   George C. Lorimer, *The Baptists in History* (Boston, MA: Silver Burdette, 1893), 106.

17   A. C. Dayton, *Theodosia Ernest*, vol. II (Nashville, TN: Graves, Marks and Rutland, 1856), 168.

18   Ibid., vol. I, 173.

19   T. P. Crawford, "Thoughts on Church Government." In *Evolution in My Mission Views, or Growth of Gospel Mission Principles in My Own Mind* (Fulton, KY: J. A. Scarboro, 1903), 157–9.

20   J. R. Graves, *Old Landmarkism: What Is It?*, 2nd edn. (Texarkana, TX: Baptist Sunday School Committee, 1880), xii.

21   W. Morgan Patterson, *Baptist Successionism: A Critical View* (Valley Forge, PA: Judson Press, 1969); James E. Tull, *High Church Baptists in the South: The Origin, Nature, and Influence of Landmarkism* (Macon, GA: Mercer University Press, 2000); H. Leon McBeth, *The Baptist Heritage: Four Centuries of Baptist Witness* (Nashville, TN: Broadman Press, 1988).

22   Graves, *Old Landmarkism*, 245.

23   Russell H. Conwell, "Kept From Evil," *Temple Review* March 3, 1899: 594.

24   Russell H. Conwell, *Acres of Diamonds* (Philadelphia, PA: Columbian Advertising and Distributing Co., 1892), 19.

25   Quoted in Ralph H. Gabriel, *The Course of American Democratic Thought: An Intellectual History Since 1815* (New York: The Ronald Press Co., 1940), 149.

26   Stock watering refers to the common practice in the 1870s and 1880s of bloating the value of railroad common stock value without comparable

investment in money. It was widely considered an unscrupulous practice. See Edward Chase Kirkland, *Industry Comes of Age: Business, Labor, and Public Policy, 1860–1897* (Chicago, IL: Quadrangle Books, 1967), 55–7.

27 Ezekiel G. Robinson, *Christian Theology* (Rochester, NY: E. B. Andrews, 1894), 61.

28 Walter Rauschenbusch, *Christianity and the Social Crisis* (New York: Harper, 1907), xxiii, 216, 341.

29 Quoted in Frank H. Woyke, *Heritage and Ministry of the North American Baptist Conference* (Oakbrook Terrace, IL: North American Baptist Conference, 1979), 277.

30 Woyke, *Heritage and Ministry*, 273–81. The theologian was Klaus Juergen Jaehn, a German Baptist pastor.

Chapter 5
A Tradition of Several Families

As the twentieth century dawned, Baptists in North America took stock of themselves and were generally pleased with the prospects. Within a decade, there would be a major merger among Baptists in the northern United States: all the major groups would join an international body, the Baptist World Alliance, and a strong sense of denominational identity was articulated in the press. Yet there were clouds on the horizon coming in particular from the British Baptist family, where schism among Baptists had been legitimated in the closing decade of the last century. That would become a major characteristic of Baptists in North America in the next one hundred years as well.

Northern Baptists: Independence and Interdependence

Perhaps the most logical and yet boldest step among Baptists in North America at the dawn of the twentieth century was the unification of the historic American Baptist national organizations into the Northern Baptist Convention. Baptist congregations were found in every state and territory outside the traditional South, with the highest number of Northern Baptists located in New York State: 150,000 members in 937 churches.[1] After three-quarters of a century of categorical ministries such as the American Baptist Missionary Union (American Baptist Foreign Mission Society), the American Baptist Home Mission Society, the American Baptist Publication Society, the American Baptist Education Society and the Woman's American Baptist Foreign Mission Society and Woman's American Baptist Home Mission Society, improved coordination became a watchword. In 1896 a Commission on Systematic

Beneficence unified fundraising efforts for the churches. Then the women's organizations took a logical step and urged coordination in publications. As a result, the first general denominational meeting among northern Baptist churches since 1844 occurred in 1901 in Springfield, Massachusetts. In the ensuing five years, halting progress was made as executives of the societies and regional leaders debated the merits of a national organization. In 1906 the Baptist Congress, representing important congregational and institutional leaders, petitioned the executives of the American Baptist societies to renew their quest for greater unity. A final persuasive expression of desired cooperation came from the Chicago Baptist Association, over the signatures of Dean Shailer Mathews at the University and J. Spencer Dickerson, editor of the *Standard*, that brought about a provisional organizational meeting on May 17, 1907 at Calvary Baptist Church in Washington, DC.

Historians agree that what transpired at Calvary Church was a significant development. Baptists in the northern states, not unlike their southern brothers and sisters, had a long history of local church protectionism; some expressed outright disinclination towards central organization. The first affirmation of the provisional body was to declare belief in the independence of the local church and the advisory and representative nature of the local and state associations. So as to leave no component out, the work of the missionary and education societies was also affirmed. The second was a resolution that, in view of the growth of the country and the denomination, a general body to serve the interests of all Baptists was necessary. The Northern Baptist Convention (NBC) was thus organized with careful terminology and organizational boundaries, avoiding the language of "national" in favor of "general." Becoming like Presbyterians was always a fear, as University of Chicago president Harry Pratt Judson put it:

> Individualism is at the heart of Baptist polity, individualism of the local church – democracy, and of the member in the church – soul liberty. A Baptist church is a complete unit in itself, and it would not be a Baptist church if it recognized any ecclesiastical superior. It is not surprising, therefore, that any attempt at a very large organization should be looked at askance. An association is a neighborhood. A State Convention is in reach. A grouping of states for organization purposes looks too much like the General Assembly of the Presbyterian Church not to win sharp scrutiny from Baptist churches.[2]

The Northern Baptist Convention brought with it three profound changes in Baptist outlook. First, there was a growing sense of corporate ministry: national boards and agencies, national budgets, national officers, and a national annual meeting. In addition to the five national societies and 36 state conventions,[3] the Convention created two boards – the Ministers and Missionaries Benefit Board and the Board of Education – and 37 committees encompassing executive decisions, finance, stewardship, affiliating organizations, nominations, and missionary work. Later, a Board of Promotion (Missionary Cooperation) was added. The first presidents of the NBC included Chief Justice Charles Evans Hughes, Harry Pratt Judson, Shailer Mathews, and Clarence A. Barbour. In 1920 the first woman president of any American Protestant denomination, Helen Barrett Montgomery, was elected president of the NBC. To counter what appeared to be a centralizing tendency, the basis of membership and voting in the NBC was to be among delegates from each church on a proportional membership scale. This differed from the old General Missionary Convention that was based upon financial contributions of individuals, and the Southern Convention that utilized a financial basis in conjunction with membership statistics for its church "messengers." Further, the executive committee was composed mostly of laypersons, no salaried employee had the right to vote, the legal independence of each cooperating organization was guaranteed, and the financial records of all bodies were subject to review by the Convention Finance Committee.

Next, the corporate nature of the NBC easily, and desirably for many, folded into the newly formed Federal Council of Churches of Christ in the United States. The Council was driven by Congregationalist and Methodist dreams of "one flock" of American Christians and at its inception in 1908 sought to express the fellowship and catholic unity of the churches. Operating on a federal model of denominations, the Council wanted to unite Americans in Christian service, to increase American Christian involvement in the world, and to encourage mutual counsel concerning the religious life of the churches. Its only requirement was recognition of Jesus Christ as "Divine Lord and Savior."[4] Unashamedly, the Council displayed a heightened social interest that was directly attributable to the social gospel. Here Baptists like Walter Rauschenbusch, Shailer Mathews, and Samuel Zane Batten were especially influential and wanted Northern Baptists to join the Council. By 1910, 31 US denominations had joined, major holdouts being Southern Baptists, Lutherans, and the Protestant Episcopal Church. With the entry of the NBC into membership of the Federal Council, Baptists formally engaged other aspects of the ecumenical movement, notably the international Faith and Order, and Life and Work movements. During the remainder of the century, American Baptists, Seventh Day Baptists,[5] and National Baptists (incorporated) would be formally involved in the ecumenical movement, while Southern Baptists for a time would send observers to official meetings.

It was not long before Northern Baptist leaders expressed openness to merger with other Baptist groups. One sees in the annual papers presented at the Baptist Congress a concerted interest in cooperating with other denominations. The first respondent was the Free Baptist General Conference, successor to the Freewill Baptists, discussed earlier. A dialogue between representatives of the NBC and Free Baptists began in earnest in 1904 and culminated with a denominational merger in 1911. For many local churches and regional organizations, this was a surprising move and the response was mixed.

Merger with Free(will) Baptists addressed some important historical aspects of Baptist history in North America. It will be recalled that in 1781 Benjamin Randal had given impetus to an Arminian, open evangelical Baptist witness in response to overwhelming determinism in the New England Baptist community. His followers had organized well and the movement spread across the northern states, the Great Plains, and the Southeast. At the time of merger, there were over 1,500 congregations in 291 yearly meetings, two associations, 10 educational institutions, and eight societies clustered under the organization of a national general conference. Additionally, there were several hundred congregations in eastern North Carolina and Tennessee, not directly connected to the main movement.[6] The Conference encompassed 87,000 members with an aggregate property value of $3.1 million. Interpreters of the merger argued that over the course of the nineteenth century, the theological differences between Calvinistic and Freewill Baptists had diminished, both being essentially evangelicals. Agents for the Northern Convention took to the road after 1911 to positively interpret the merger, but found mixed responses. In the urban areas, merger appeared acceptable. But in many rural areas, such as the Genesee Valley in New York, and Nebraska, several congregations left the merged denomination over perceptions that it was theologically liberal. In many ways, a "great reversal" had occurred where the once liberal Freewillers had evolved to a conservative orientation, and the once closed communion Calvinistic Baptist community had adopted much of the New Theology, including biblical criticism, the social gospel, and inclusiveness. One of the outcomes of the merger was the emerging reputation of the Northern Baptist community that it was theologically nondescript. That would become painfully obvious to conservative evangelicals.

Predictably, the increased institutional development in Northern Baptist work required dramatic new funding from the churches. World War I reminded leaders of the possibility of retrenchments in missions and education; several schools were perilously close to closure in 1918. On the positive side, there was an abiding optimism among Baptists that a new world order was appearing: "Poverty in a Christian land must not be tolerated. Industrial warfare among Christian men should be unthinkable. War between Christian nations is treason against the kingdom of God. The so-called Christian nations must stop war or stop claiming allegiance to Christ. The world will no longer accept excuses for these things," wrote Samuel Zane Batten.[7] Other Protestant denominations had similar dreams and faced similar crises, and the Foreign Missions Board of the Presbyterian Church, South, suggested a united effort called the Interchurch World Movement (IWM). They all agreed that the churches must bring forward the idea of the kingdom of God; this translated into a large, comprehensive program of social reconstruction.[8] The objectives of IWM were evangelism, education, and social betterment, imitating to a large degree the agenda of the Federal Council of Churches. An initial Conference in 1920 established a plan for meeting mission needs on a cross-denominational basis that was specified in budgetary lines. The combined budgets constituted the basis for a massive stewardship campaign that was guaranteed by bank loans. The Northern Baptists agreed to participate and in 1919 the NBC approved its most energetic fundraising scheme ever, calling it the "New World Movement." From 1920 to 1924 all fundraising for NBC agencies came under the aegis of a Board of Promotion to raise $100 million. Based on strategies the US government had used in Liberty Loan drives, each congregation was solicited.

The governing committee of the Interchurch World Movement had decided to respond to the crippling steel strike of 1919 and the report came out in sympathy with the workers. This produced widespread promanagement, antiunion agitation and severe criticism of the Movement. I. M. Haldeman, pastor of First Baptist, New York, led a crusade against the Movement that reached across the country and rallied antiecumenical leaders in the NBC. As a result, only slightly more than half of the goal of the New World Movement was reached through the gifts of 86 percent of NBC churches. Further, many pledges were not honored, causing the NBC mission societies to exceed their program limits in the 1920s. Overall, the ecumenical venture went into receivership with the Protestant mission boards having to repay $50 million in bank loans and irreparable public relations damage achieved as the fundamentalist campaign erupted across Protestantism. While historians sympathetic to the NBC claimed that the New World Movement phase had firmly established the principle of unified fundraising and that over $50 million had been raised,[9] a more serious result was

evident. Within five years of the conclusion of the New World Movement, contributions from all sources to Northern Baptist work de-
creased by almost 50 percent. The Foreign Mission Society, long the
pride of Northern Baptist outreach, reduced its appointed overseas
staff from a peak of 313 in 1923 to 179 15 years later. In retrospect,
the failure of the New World Movement campaign and the ensuing
theological strife in the NBC were major signals of the eclipse of the
Northern Baptist Convention as the leading family of Baptists in North
America. Its membership would slip from 1.5 percent of the US population in 1900 to 1 percent in 1950. At the same time, American
Baptist *influence* as a Free Church contributor to the ecumenical movement, would increase dramatically.[10]

Southern Baptists Assert their Identity and Unity

While much more highly integrated for half a century before Northern
Baptists, Southern Baptists in the new century pursued a corporate
model of national ministry, as well as establishing a new sense of denominational consciousness. As far back as the comity agreements of
the 1890s, Southern Baptists had been careful to define their identity
and territory of mission. In 1900, Georgia claimed the highest number
of Baptists (405,000), while Texas had the largest number of Baptist
congregations (4,364) of any state related to the SBC.[11] With the establishment of the Baptist World Alliance (1905), the Northern Baptist
Convention (1907), the Federal Council of Churches (1908), and International Mission Conferences and Faith and Order meetings (1910–),
there was a window of opportunity for Southern Baptists to rejoin the
efforts of mainstream Baptists in the United States, if not internationally. However, due to factors of regional competition and continuing
Landmarkism, Southern Baptists turned inward. In 1914 the Convention adopted a position urging the continuity of Southern Baptist
independence:

> By preserving a complete loyalty at home and abroad, unembarrassed by
> entangling alliances with other bodies holding to different standards of
> doctrine and different views of church life and church order ... by de-
> voting our energies and resources with singleness of heart to fostering
> and multiplying denominational schools and other agencies at home and
> abroad in full denominational control and in full harmony with the spirit
> and doctrine of the churches contributing funds to our Boards ... by
> placing renewed and greatly increased emphasis on the education, train-
> ing and enlisting of all our people to the end that they may intelligently

and joyfully participate in all the work of the denomination . . . by sending out a loud, insistent and persistent call to the Baptists of the South to enter whole-heartedly into greatly enlarged plans for progress, with higher standards of consecration and giving . . .[12]

In fact, the leadership of the SBC in full awareness of the value of free discussion of all intradenominational questions that would be "brotherly and illuminating," believed that the "main emphasis upon the main things" required strategies that would conserve and not injure approved denominational agencies. The result of this concentration upon Southern Baptist self-identity was a growth from 2 percent of the US population in 1900 to 5 percent in 1950, outdistancing Northern/American Baptists fivefold in total membership.

At the same time that Northern Baptists engaged in the New World Movement campaign, Southern Baptists declined to be part of the Interchurch World Movement and commenced a national crusade to celebrate the 75th anniversary of the SBC, the "Seventy Five Million Campaign." Launched in October 1919 under Texans J. B. Gambrell and Lee R. Scarborough, the drive sought to eliminate Convention debt and begin a bold postwar initiative. By year's end, over $92 million had been pledged and the celebration in Washington DC the following May was one of great jubilation. The only sobering elements of the Seventy Five Million Campaign were that total pledges paid amounted to a little over $58 million, and some important congregations followed the lead of J. Frank Norris at First Baptist, Fort Worth in canceling their pledge as a protest against what Norris called "rampant liberalism" in the SBC, a sign of the fundamentalist revolt to come.

Many historians view the adoption of recommendations on "denominational efficiency" in 1914 to be the beginning of a new confessionalism among Southern Baptists that culminated in 1925 with the adoption of the *Baptist Faith and Message* and the establishment of the Cooperative Program. That confessionalism, combined with connectionalism and consensus, led to widespread cooperation, all-important words in the alliterative twentieth-century Southern Baptist vocabulary, according to its recent historian.[13]

The Cooperative Program is undoubtedly the most successful stewardship effort ever launched and sustained among Baptists anywhere in the world. Convention leadership had learned important lessons from the less than stellar results of the Seventy Five Million Campaign. First, they put in place a system of centralized fund collection that demonstrated national coordination. Second, by eliminating solicitation agents, each church basically made one contribution that was in turn distributed in several directions. Third, the idea of a unified denominational program emerged, helping the average church member to feel deeply about being "Southern Baptist." The Cooperative Program, in conjunction with the Lottie Moon Offering (see chapter 10), would become the engine of the world's largest Baptist organization, with proceeds by 1990 in excess of one billion dollars annually.

Less noticed among the congregations was the creation in 1917 of the Executive Committee of the Southern Baptist Convention. With little recall of the extreme antagonism to convention founders in the 1840s of the executive committee of the General Missionary Convention that ruled against slaveholding, a second report on efficiency led to the creation of an executive committee and a unified budget. It was George W. Truett, the pastor of First Baptist, Dallas, Texas, as president in 1927, who pushed the Convention to approve a larger role for its executive committee that involved coordination of all boards and agencies, implementation of program strategies, and expenditure of the Cooperative Program receipts. After a brief survey of the possibilities, the home of the Executive Committee, and in essence the SBC, became Nashville, Tennessee, already the address of the Convention's Sunday School Board.

The Baptist World Alliance: Uncommon Unity

The Baptist World Alliance is the official, international body of Baptists that parallels other ecumenical fellowships like the Anglican World Communion, the World Methodist Council, and the Lutheran World Federation. Its origins lie in experimental intradenominational fellowships within the North American Baptist community. In the last decades of the nineteenth century, there was a concerted effort among Protestant communities to recover their common heritages. Several different kinds of Methodists, for instance, from holiness bodies like Wesleyan Methodists and Free Methodists to the Methodist Episcopals and African Methodists, sought to recover the heritage of John Wesley on the centennial anniversary, in 1884, of the organization of American Methodism. Work overseas in India, China, and Africa often seemed duplicated and this was a powerful impetus to find partners of like heritage for cooperative missions. Some Protestant bodies looked earnestly toward reunion of the schisms caused over slavery before the Civil War. Among Baptists in the 1890s, there was a decided interest in building a "national" consciousness, if not a united witness, to the world of Baptist principles.

Since the Civil War, many Baptists in North America had yearned for a forum to exchange ideas and have fellowship across regional and denominational boundary lines. The first successful venture to achieve this worthy goal was the Baptist Congress. The Congress was an annual meeting of scholars, pastors, and denominational leaders, from the North, South, and Canada, who convened from 1881 to 1913 in various cities east of the Mississippi. Their stated purpose was to discuss current questions and to promote a healthful sentiment among Baptists. Its founders included John Peddie, an educator from New Jersey; pastors Robert S. MacArthur, Norman Fox, Wayland Hoyt, and George Dana Boardman, Jr.; A. J. Rowland, a denominational worker; Elias H. Johnson, a seminary professor. Among the timely issues they discussed through presented (and later published) papers were labor questions, immigration policy, temperance, family relations and church-state relationships. The Congress over the years had a category for "troubling issues" and there they faced liturgical procedures, Roman Catholicism, urbanization, the tactics of evangelists, biblical criticism, and the implications of the social gospel. Topics that surfaced repeatedly on the agenda were the ordinances, church architecture, worship, eschatology, Christology, and the nature of the New Testament church. A frontier of Baptist tolerance, the papers of the Congress reveal a vibrant interactive community at the turn of the twentieth century.

The Baptist Congress was largely eclipsed by those in Great Britain and North America who wanted to join the ranks of international denominationalism. The British Baptists, behind the leadership of J. H. Shakespeare and James Rushbrooke, joined forces with Congregationalists, Quakers, Presbyterians, and others in the Council of Free Churches. Many in North America wanted to connect with their British roots and as correspondence indicates, looked for the opportune moment, such as in 1904 when the editor of the Kentucky *Baptist Argus*, J. N. Prestridge, issued a call for an alliance of international Baptists. Baptists from across Europe and the Americas met in London under the presidency of John Clifford to establish the BWA. Meeting every five years in a general Conference, the Alliance has carried out its major agenda of promoting religious liberty, study and research, evangelism and education, and Baptist World Aid each year in its general council meetings. In the 1920s, in the wake of World War I, president E. Y. Mullins traveled throughout Europe as an ambassador of religious freedom and Baptist unity, and did much to establish the credibility of the Alliance. One of the most far-reaching tasks of the Alliance has been a series of theological conversations with other Christian bodies, including the World Alliance of Reformed Churches, the Lutheran World Federation, Roman Catholics, the Anglican World Communion, and the Mennonite World Conference.

The BWA has enjoyed the leadership of prominent Baptists from around the world including William Tolbert of Liberia, Duke McCall of the US, G. Noel Vose of Australia, Billy Kim of Korea, and Nilson Fannini of Argentina. Its general secretaries have included Josef Nordenhaug of Norway, Robert S. Denny and Denton Lotz of the US, and Gerhard Claas of Germany. The three largest contributing members of the Alliance have been the Southern Baptist Convention, the Baptist Union of Great Britain, and the American Baptist Churches, USA. A crisis in the evolution of the BWA occurred in 2004 when the Southern Baptists, one of the founding denominations, withdrew from the Alliance under pressure from fundamentalist factions that had taken control of the Convention. They were especially upset with BWA recognition of the Cooperative Baptist Fellowship, a doctrinally moderate splinter group of the SBC, and what they perceived were definite theologically liberal directions of the world group. In response to this reality, the Alliance changed its basis of membership to include contributing congregations and regional bodies.

Deep Rifts Develop

The third major rift among mainstream Baptists (after the Old School and Southern Baptist schisms) in the United States and Canada occurred in the period 1915–25. Largely as a response to the theological position of Prof. George Burman Foster at the University of Chicago, millionaire brothers Lyman and Milton Stewart, Californian Presbyterian laymen, published *Fundamentals of the Faith*, in 12 pamphlets between 1910 and 1915 (edited version in 1917) and sent copies to every Protestant pastor, theological student, theological professor, evangelist, missionary, and YMCA/YWCA worker in the United States – three million recipients in all. The *Fundamentals* were an attempt to stem the tide of Baptists (and others) toward the New Theology and drew a vocal response from both conservatives and progressives. Suspicions had been raised around the ministry of Charles Haddon Spurgeon in London during the 1890s "Down Grade Controversy."[14] His concerns began to manifest themselves in North America with the curricular reorganizations in four Northern Baptist seminaries and the retirements of seminary presidents like Henry G. Weston at Crozer, A. H. Strong at Rochester, and Alvah Hovey at Newton. New appointments at Brown and McMaster Universities 1910–1920 were especially troubling to the "conservatives" as they came to be called. Most flagrant among the progressive and liberal theologians was William H. P. Faunce, president at Brown, the oldest Baptist school, who openly taught that science substantiated Christianity, rather than repudiating it, and that there ought to be reconciliation among the world's religions. In his 1912 Cole Lectures at Vanderbilt University, Faunce defined Christianity as "purpose." "It is the revelation of the persistent loving purpose of the eternal God," he wrote, "and the implanting of that same purpose in the life of men."[15] At the insistence of Faunce and his successors, Brown left denominational affiliation in 1922, holding fast to its position of not allowing any form of religious tests.

Theological labels became popular ways of identifying the various theological camps among North American Baptists. For many the term "conservative" was too reactionary in all walks of life. "Premillennialist" was too closely aligned with a single doctrine to be broadly applicable. "Landmarkist" was southern in scope and had a particular association with a party of radical conservatives. The term "fundamentals" meaning the irreducible minimum of the faith, had long been in usage among Baptists, perhaps as early as the eighteenth century. But the term took on new meaning with the publication of The Fundamentals in which one prominent Baptist, President E. Y. Mullins of Southern Baptist Seminary, had a contribution.[16] It suggested a new movement or party of advocates for traditional evangelical doctrines and biblical interpretation. The writer who coined the term "Fundamentalist," Curtis Lee Laws, the editor of the Watchman-Examiner weekly newspaper, defined it this way: "Baptist fundamentalism is a spontaneous movement within our beloved denomination which seeks to reaffirm and reemphasize the age-long principles for which our fathers suffered and died. It seeks to unite our denomination rather than to divide it." Laws was willing to be called a "fundamentalist" in 1921 and he saw it not disparagingly, but as a compliment.[17]

Perhaps no other American denominational family was as deeply affected by fundamentalism as were the Baptists. The apex of the fundamentalist crusade among Baptists occurred between 1920 and 1925. Baptists had played a prominent role in the meeting of the World's Christian Fundamentals Association (WCFA) that was organized in Philadelphia in 1919. In fact, fundamentalists in other denominations complained that Baptists like William Bell Riley, J. Frank Norris, J. C. Massee, and John Roach Straton dominated the programs. Riley was the kingpin of the WCFA and raised in excess of $200,000 in its support during its heyday before 1927. Yet, he lamented the extreme individualism of the coalition that he described as a kind of "guerilla warfare."[18] As the annual Northern Baptist Convention meeting in Buffalo, New York, approached in 1920, scores of NBC pastors and laypeople expressed loyal concern over the theological direction of the Convention. Uppermost was the impact of the Interchurch World Movement and the primary role the NBC played in its promotion. Many met in a pre-Convention meeting at Delaware Ave. Baptist Church, June 20–21, to hear speeches and formulate some response. The numbers present overcrowded the facilities and the meetings shifted to the Civic Auditorium where 3,000 attended. The strategy that emerged was directed at stemming the tide of liberalism and rationalism in the NBC and resulted in a committee selected to investigate charges leveled against seminaries and colleges. Politically the battle raged on into 1922 where at the annual NBC meeting in Indianapolis an historic vote was taken affirming the New Testament as the all-sufficient ground of faith and practice. The ballot pitted William Bell Riley Of Minnesota against Cornelius Woelfkin of New York in a personal confrontation. The result was 1,264 in favor of Woelfkin and 637 against.[19] While the Woelfkin faction won the day in keeping the Convention free of confessional requirements, Riley hammered the Northern Convention between 1924 and 1926 with unsuccessful motions seeking to impose a doctrinal test upon missionaries, another to rescind the denomination's membership in the Federal Council of Churches, and yet another to require baptism by immersion for members in Convention churches.

One of the most outstanding concerns for fundamentalists was unsound teaching in denominational schools. College biology classes were suspected of teaching Darwinian evolution. Bible classes had imbibed too much German higher criticism. College administrators often honored outstanding liberals with honorary degrees, as though to be complicit in what they advocated. In the seminaries, troubling questions were heard from students about denial of Mosaic authorship of the Pentateuch, the veracity of the virgin birth of Christ and his miracles, and the validity of the substitutionary theory of the atonement. Under scrutiny of dispensationalists, some professors denied a literal second coming of Christ. This suggested the need for a full-scale investigation of schools related to the Northern Baptist Convention, and if need be, removal of the problematic professors or withdrawal of financial support. John Roach Straton, pastor of Calvary Baptist Church in New York City, led the charge against the institutions as well as social vices from gambling to dancing. In 1922 he formed the Fundamentalist League of Greater New York City and Vicinity for Ministers and Laymen, and rallied the Baptist community and others to support his charges. At a mass meeting in 1923, Straton and J. Frank Norris castigated Episcopalians and Unitarians as being "wealthy but empty churches." This eventuated in a series of public debates in 1923–24 between Straton, representing the fundamentalists, and Charles Francis Potter, a Unitarian pastor, representing the liberals, adjudicated by a distinguished panel of judges. After exchanging textual and moral arguments in the midst of musical theatrics first in Straton's church and later at Carnegie Hall, the judges ruled split verdicts, with Straton receiving a majority overall. Upwards of three thousand hearers per debate, plus radio and extensive newspaper coverage, gave broad vent to fundamentalism as well as unexpected limelight to the liberal cause.

The attempt to investigate schools met with universal disdain, if not opposition, among the schools, and the process failed within Northern Baptist Convention circles by 1925. Frustrated within the Convention, the radicals moved ahead. Pastor-theologians took up verbal arms against the professional theologians of the denomination, and it was they who led in the formation of new organizations. Chief among them were William Bell Riley, J. Frank Norris, and John Roach Straton in the United States, and Thomas Todhunter Shields and William Aberhart in Canada. This new coalition of radical fundamentalists began meeting and eventually formed the Baptist Bible Union of North America (BBU). An international body born in 1923, it was made up of individual pastors in the Northern and Southern Baptist Conventions in the US and the Baptist Convention of Ontario and Quebec in Canada. The Union declared its unqualified opposition to this "God-dishonouring, Bible denying, man-degrading doctrine of evolution,"[20] and they appealed to the boards of governors of denominational schools to investigate and discover who had adopted evolutionary teaching and remove every such professor from his chair. The BBU became the principal channel through which Baptist fundamentalists advocated their agenda through the late 1920s.

The moderate fundamentalists in the Northern Baptist Convention, led by J. C. Massee, Curtis Lee Laws, and Frank W. Goodchild, remained in the Convention and reminded their hearers of the historic differences among Baptists between creeds and confessions of faith. As Massee put it, "The ministry to which we are committed . . . is a ministry of reconciliation not of denunciation or condemnation. . . ."[21] When Massee called for a temporary truce in the battle in the late 1920s, Riley retorted, "It is a war from which there is no discharge."[22] The moderate fundamentalists sought means within the Convention and placed their support squarely behind new confessionally based schools that they trusted would raise up a new generation of faithful pastors for the denomination. Northern Baptist Theological Seminary in Chicago (1913) benefited in the Midwest and divided the constituency between the University of Chicago and fundamentalists. The Eastern Baptist Theological Seminary in Philadelphia opened in 1925 with a doctrinal statement written by either Laws or Frank W. Goodchild and eventually with Austen K. DeBlois, a Canadian/American warrior against the "Chicago School," as president. Eastern Seminary effectively divided the Philadelphia Baptist community that had long given its support to Crozer Theological Seminary, but was now clearly antifundamentalist. Gordon College in Massachusetts also took up recruiting evangelicals among the New England conventions, since it appeared Newton Theological Institution was moving closer to the Andover Theological Seminary liberal tradition.

The fundamentalist movement also affected smaller Baptist groups. The Seventh Day Baptists were able to manage the challenges from within and avoid major disruption. As early as 1908 Seventh Day writers joined the inquiry between the Bible and science. Two groups clearly emerged around the issues. The denomination's primary institution of higher education, Alfred University in New York State, took the moderate to liberal perspective through its dean, A. E. Main. Main was a distinguished scholar who favored the view of the Bible as essentially a wonderful piece of religious literature. Alfred earned a negative reputation among many conservatives as the decade of the 1920s evolved. The conservatives behind the Seventh Day Baptist pastor Elston Dunn propagated a position that held biblical criticism was ultimately destructive. For about a decade the *Sabbath Recorder* printed the ongoing debates, and at meetings of the General Conference both positions were frequently aired. In 1922 Alfred University Dean Main shocked many with his assertion that revelation was sometimes stated in the form of myth or legend. This led to conservative reaction in the formation in 1925 of the Bible Defense League. The League, a group of pastors, maintained strict loyalty to Seventh Day Baptists and sought ways and means of conciliating both sides around a fully authoritative Bible. Commencing in 1927–28, the *Sabbath Recorder* printed a page for each "side." Ultimately, the moderates took a lead among educated pastors and the fundamentalist page closed publication in 1931. Denominational historians believe that a major rift had been avoided by an exercise of freedom of thought and an affirmation of real scholarship.[23] While the denomination's schools began to decline seriously after the 1940s, Seventh Day Baptists had demonstrated that they could meet challenges to their unity better than other branches of the Baptist family. Evidence of this victory over schism came in the adoption of a

Statement of Belief in 1937 wherein SDBs "cherished liberty of thought" and refused any binding creed.

After the tumultuous decade of the 1920s, fundamentalism settled down into permanent patterns. The new Baptist coalitions were actually subgroups of the old consensus. In 1932 the General Association of Regular Baptist Churches (GARBC) was cobbled together from the Baptist Bible Union in the Northern Baptist Convention. It became radically fundamentalist. Related to the GARBC were the mission groups, Baptist Mid-Missions and the Association of Baptists for World Evangelism (ABWE). Baptist Mid-Missions was formed in 1920 to offset the appointment of theologically liberal missionaries by the American Baptist Foreign Mission Society and came quickly to cater to the overseas needs of the radical fundamentalist churches in the US and Canada. Within just 15 years, yet another seemingly loyal group of moderates appeared among Northern Baptist churches in response to the continued inclusivism of the American Baptist Foreign Mission Society. This group, the Conservative Baptist Fellowship, failed in its attempts to control mission policy and left the Convention to become a new family in its own right, the Conservative Baptist Association (CBA) in 1944. At the time of the formation of the CBA, overtures were made to both the German Baptists and Swedish Baptists in the United States to join ranks with the CBA, but both declined and pursued separate family paths of their own.

The German Baptist Conference evolved into the North American Baptist Conference (NABC) with congregations in the US and Canada. Following World War I, the Conference also struggled with issues of theology and social identity. Much of this struggle came to be focused in the evolution of its theological program in Rochester, New York, and the Conference's overall relationship to other Baptist bodies. In the first matter, the strong wave of anti-German feelings in Canada and the United States led Conference leaders to wonder if students would be well-served studying at a "German" institution. In 1940 the name was changed to "Rochester Baptist Seminary" and the program continued its relationship with Colgate Rochester Divinity School, then a theologically liberal seminary of the Northern Baptist Convention. Many pastors in the Conference felt that the seminary was out of touch theologically with most of its constituency and this came to focus in the 1940s upon the teaching of Prof. Arthur A. Schade in biblical studies. Schade, who had taught at the seminary since 1932, was forced to resign in 1943, and plans were made to relocate the school from Rochester. In the midst of the Conservative Baptist revolt in the Northern Baptist Convention, Conference officials conferred with the administration of Bethel College and Seminary (Swedish Baptist) in St Paul about a possible merger, but Bethel rejected the overture. This led to acceptance of an offer from the Dakota Conference (NABC) to move the school to Sioux Falls where it could operate in relationship with Sioux Falls College, a Northern Baptist-related school. In 1949 the theological program became the North American Baptist Seminary in Sioux Falls. Earlier provision had been made for Canadian students where in 1940 the Conference lent its enthusiastic support to establish the Christian Training Institute in Edmonton, Alberta.

Gradually in many of the Conference churches the German language gave way to services in English. An important step toward independence was taken in 1920 when the Conference Mission Society no longer received financial assistance from outside sources. The primary tie with the Northern Baptist Convention continued as the latter listed the conferences as one of several "foreign language" groups related to it. Moreover, the Rochester Theological Seminary continued its subsidies to the German Department into the 1940s. The NBC, however, took the first step toward potential amalgamation in 1938 when one of its regional executives, Henry C. Gleiss of Detroit, proposed an "associated" status for the foreign language groups. Gleiss suggested that this could be acceptable if the group had a national organization and if it would endorse the objectives of the NBC. After a two-year study, the German Conference found the idea impractical because its territory overlapped with not only Northern Baptists, but also Southern Baptists and two Canadian conventions as well. An underlying suspicion also prevailed that the Conference wanted to distance itself from the emerging theologically liberal reputation of the Northern Baptists. While many German congregations continued to work with Northern Baptist associations and conventions, the tie was severed graciously. Signaling overall a new life for German American Baptists the name was changed in 1942 to North American Baptist General Conference and in 1946 a full time executive secretary, Dr William Kuhn, was authorized.[24]

The Swedish Baptists who had organized themselves as the Baptist General Conference faced declining immigration from Sweden at the turn of the twentieth century and this called for a new sense of identity. Serious discussion of the use of the Swedish language in the churches ensued. Beginning in 1930, Swedish was dropped as the language of instruction at Bethel College. The Conference minutes were published in English, beginning in 1933. Even more important to the inevitable cultural transition, the denominational paper, *Svenska Standaret*, became the *Standard* in 1940. Signaling a new era, the Swedish Baptist General Conference of America in 1945 became the Baptist General

Conference of America, or popularly "Conference Baptists." Many Conference leaders were also concerned with the growing trend toward a more liberal theology in the Northern Baptist Convention. Of special concern was the New World Movement and its potential to be a part of the international ecumenical movement. Thus began the first steps toward an independent organizational identity. After 1940, important decisions were taken against incorporation into the NBC or merger with either the German Baptists or the Conservative Baptist Association, both of which made overtures in the 1940s. In 1951 the Conference dedicated its headquarters building in Chicago, one year before the celebration of the Conference Centennial. The Conference would eventually join the Baptist World Alliance and the Baptist Joint Committee on Public Affairs, along with the larger bodies of Baptists in the United States. What were really at stake were the common history, life, and purpose of the language conferences, which continued to have personal meaning for many families.

Counter to their European coreligionists, however, the Danish-Norwegian Conference did not experience the statistical or territorial growth of its German and Swedish counterparts and it came to a different conclusion. In 1956, Conference leaders decided that a separate organization was unnecessary and the Conference was dissolved and the assets and congregations distributed within the American Baptist Convention. Its churches were largely concentrated in the Midwest and Upper Plains states and they eventually lost much of their ethnic recognition in the associational and regional life of American Baptists.

Resurgent Confessionalism and American Influences

In the 1960s and 1970s the impact of neo-orthodox thinking was seen in many parts of the Baptist family in both the United States and Canada. This in turn produced a resurgence of theological confessionalism. Theological works by Karl Barth and Emil Brunner were used widely as textbooks in seminaries like Andover Newton and Eastern Baptist Seminary. Among Southern Baptists, Dale Moody at Southern Baptist Theological Seminary was a leading proponent of neo-orthodoxy, as was John W. Eddins at Southeastern Seminary in Wake Forest, North Carolina. By the 1970s entire Southern Baptist seminaries at Kansas City and San Francisco were suspected of being beyond the acceptable traditional conservative doctrinal teaching of the SBC churches. Dale Moody studied with both Barth and Brunner and was a decisive influence in the revision of the *Baptist Faith and Message* of 1963; significant numbers of Southern Baptist doctoral candidates were choosing to study outside the United States.

Canadian Baptists developed their own organizational patterns in the twentieth century, but suffered some of the same fates as their US coreligionists. On the positive side, after a century of attempts to unite Baptists across Canada, Watson Kirkconnell of McMaster University led a coalition of unity-minded Baptists to form the Baptist Federation of Canada in 1944, the same year the Canadian Council of Churches was formed. The Federation brought together the three primary conventions of English-speaking Baptists plus the French Union of Churches. In the Canadian regionalized tradition, there was a good deal of autonomy left to the provincial/regional conventions, while the Federation concentrated upon national and international issues. An identifiable minority of Baptists remained aloof from such efforts, however, and formed a major new type of Baptist in Canada, the Fellowship of Evangelical Baptist Churches.

The fundamentalist controversy was deep, sustained, and bitter in Canada. In 1909–10 and later in 1925, serious charges of theological liberalism were made against McMaster University, the premier Baptist institution in Canada. After several investigations and floor debates in the Baptist Convention of Ontario and Quebec (BCOQ), the University won the right to make its faculty appointments through academic processes, but it lost valuable support from its constituency. About one hundred churches (or about one seventh of the membership) left the convention relationship in the provinces of Ontario and Quebec to join the Union of Regular Baptist Churches. Over the next several decades, ironically, the University's reputation among convention Baptists slowly withered until it severed its ties with the BCOQ in 1957 in favor of an arrangement for a continuing theological college related to a provincial university. McMaster Divinity College, the new institution, inherited the university's theological reputation and by the 1970s only a minority of ministerial candidates attended McMaster. A majority of Baptists in central Canada turned to Bible college educational training and a theological definition forged in the context of the Evangelical Fellowship of Canada.[25]

During the early years of the century, Maritime Baptists had not been split over the issue of theological fundamentalism, but extreme conservatism eventually took its toll in that region as well. The Kingston Parsonage Case (1935) illustrated a shift in the evangelical/revivalistic orientation of Maritime Baptists, in exposing progressive to liberal trends at Acadia University's theology program.[26] When called to testify on behalf of the Maritime Baptist Convention's theological orthodoxy, Dean Simeon Spidle was evasive and noncommittal and gave fuel to the accusations of fundamentalists that Acadia had become unsound in the faith. Spidle was a graduate of Newton Theological Institution during the years of its shift toward the New Theology and earned his doctorate in psychology and theology at Clark University. Few understood his directions and he earned for himself and the university a reputation as a harbinger of modernism among Canadian Baptists. As Acadia University fell from full acceptance in Nova Scotia and especially New Brunswick, many Baptists looked to independent fundamentalist New Brunswick Bible Training Institute in Woodstock or to Gordon College and Divinity School in Massachusetts for training of ministry candidates.

In the West, the influence of McMaster's ministerial troubles was felt across the lower Prairies to Vancouver. Many of the churches in the Baptist Union of Western Canada were isolated and lacked permanent pastoral leadership; this led to a local solution for leadership. Beginning in the 1930s Bible colleges sprang up. These were of a non-denominational kind that provided pastors for many of the Baptist congregations. Faculty in these institutions were often trained in the fundamentalist schools of the United States and England and this left an indelible stamp of biblical inerrancy and dispensationalism upon the Baptist community. William Aberhart, a Calgary, Alberta, Baptist minister was greatly influential in winning converts to the fundamentalist agenda through his radio broadcasts and Bible conferences. By the 1970s, when mainstream Baptists had caught up with the educational needs of their Union, the theological die was cast toward conservative evangelicalism and a new western institution, Carey Hall in Vancouver (later Carey Theological College), was permanently linked with Regent College, a Calvinistic, consciously evangelical institution with roots in the Brethren tradition.

Baptist influence from the United States continued to have an important effect among Canadian Baptists in the second half of the century. In the 1960s the Baptist Convention of Ontario and Quebec contracted with personnel of the American Baptist Home Mission Society to do congregational analyses of churches in order to determine the strategies for church development and renewal. This followed a well-known program in the American Baptist Convention. One of the results of this process was the restyling of conventions and associations into regions and areas identical to that of the American Baptists. Even the titles changed from "executive secretaries" to "executive ministers" and "area ministers." In Ontario, Nathaniel Parker, a Mississippi Baptist, taught at McMaster University and was dean of theology and first principal of the McMaster Divinity College. Following Parker at McMaster were other professors drawn from American and Southern Baptist circles of influence. In the Maritimes, Southern Baptist influence was felt keenly. Rather than planting SBC missions in the Maritime Provinces, an arrangement was struck between the Southern Baptist Home Mission Board and the Maritime Convention, and in the 1980s Acadia University's Divinity College employed Southern Baptist personnel under Maritime Baptist auspices. The *Atlantic Baptist*, official organ of the Maritime Convention, began to use journalistic content prepared by Baptist Press in Nashville. Finally, leadership in theological education reflected American influences as Millard Cherry, a Louisville-trained theologian from Kentucky, was invited to take the chair in theology at Acadia, eventually becoming principal of the institution. In the West, where many southerners had relocated to work in the Alberta oilfields, Southern Baptists moved in boldly to start churches and create associations across the Prairie Provinces. In 1987 Canadian Southern Baptist Theological Seminary opened at Cochrane, Alberta. Finally, a significant number of Canadian ministry students sought theological education among Baptist schools in the United States, including Southern Baptist Seminary, Southwestern Baptist Seminary, and Trinity Evangelical Divinity School in Illinois. They would earn a wide range of degrees from the basic theological degree to advanced degrees in ministry and theology.

The smaller Baptist groups in Canada also reflected a decidedly American influence. German Baptists had planted churches in immigrant communities, first in Ontario, and later in Alberta and Saskatchewan. At first these congregations received aid from the American Baptist Home Mission Society and later small amounts from the mission board of Canadian Baptists. As the need for pastors rose in the postwar period, the German Conference began a school at Edmonton, Alberta as an outgrowth of North American Seminary in Sioux Falls, South Dakota. Within time it evolved into both Edmonton Baptist Seminary and Taylor College, many of whose faculty members were educated in the United States. Likewise, Swedish Baptists, originating from St Paul, Minnesota, spread their witness across the Prairies toward Vancouver. They too required a school for their tradition and began a Bible school at Wetaskiwin, Ontario, in 1925. What became Canadian Baptist Seminary, related to the Baptist General Conference of Canada, was born in 1988. Fellowship Baptists, the strongest of the nonconvention Baptists, drew heavily upon leadership from Dallas Theological Seminary and Trinity Evangelical Divinity School in the US.

Legacy: A Growing Sense of Ecumenism
and its Effects

As much as any other factor in the first half of the twentieth century, ecumenism was the defining relationship that energized Baptists in North America. It either brought a larger picture of the Kingdom of God into view or caused new isolationism to surface in smaller Baptist groups.

Beginning in the 1880s many Baptists looked for opportunities to unite their denomination and to reach out to other Christian communions. This could be seen in the intra-Baptist fellowships like the autumnal meetings of the Baptist Congress and among Free Baptists, Disciples, and regular Baptists. The Baptist theological schools in the North exchanged faculty among themselves and shared faculty in their cities. The rise of academic professional societies led Baptists to interact with other theologians in organizations like the American Society of Church History and the American Theological Society. Baptist theologians traveled on sabbaticals and read widely the books of other Christian writers. Baptist newspapers carried book reviews of Christian literature and editorials from a wide variety of writers. Likewise, teachers and administrators of colleges and universities interacted with other Christian educators and with government officials who were developing the rudimentary standards of accreditation.

As we have seen, Baptist response to the formation of the Baptist World Alliance in 1905 was enthusiastic. The three major branches of the denominational family in the United States sent representatives and helped to fund the new enterprise. This same spirit was manifested in Baptist responses to the Federal Council of Churches, the International Missionary Council, and the advance of regional and local cooperative Christian organizations. In Canada, Baptists sent representatives to the major ecumenical meetings, formed their own Council of Churches in 1944, and were in constant dialogue with the United Church of Canada, the most successful venture in Protestant Christian organic union on the continent. At the tables of ecumenical Christianity, Baptists had the clearest articulation of Free Church values and plainly felt the tide was turning toward their understanding of church and society. A kind of Baptist triumphalism can be seen in the literature of the era, whether in the sermons of Baptist delegates to general church meetings or in the growing reluctance of Southern Baptists to water down their sense of identity as their numbers and influence increased.

On the other side ecumenism had manifold negatives effects on Baptists. Landmarkers in the South were intolerant of any other forms of Christianity back to the time of Christ. They allowed no pulpit exchanges or involvement in ecumenical organizations. Likewise, Primitive Baptists were unengaged in any of the denominational relations with other Christians. In a context where socialism and communism loomed, and fear of European nationalism brought out Baptist prejudices against Germans and Italians, discussions and cooperation with other Christians conflicted with Baptist plans to evangelize the world. Mentioned repeatedly in the fundamentalist tracts and sermons was the specter of combinations with non-Baptist and non-Christian movements that seemed to fulfill prophecies about the rise of evil at the end of the age. The Interchurch World Movement, the New World Movement, and the councils of churches were for many Baptists the very essence of modernism. Thus the antidote for "come-outer" Baptists of this generation, we shall see, was a reaffirmation of the local church as the central feature of Baptist polity, and only loose associations allowed beyond the congregations. So serious was the ecumenical movement's impact upon the denomination, that some parts of the family, like Northern Baptists, National Baptists, and convention Baptists in Canada defined themselves by their relationships, while others like Southern Baptists and fundamentalist Baptists defined themselves by not having such connections.

Notes

1 *1900 American Baptist Yearbook*, ed. J. G. Walker (Philadelphia, PA: American Baptist Publication Society, 1900), 100.
2 Harry Pratt Judson, "Introduction." In *A Manual of the Northern Baptist Convention, Prepared by Request of The Executive Committee to Commemorate The Completion of Ten Years of Service to the Kingdom of God 1908–1918*, ed. W. C. Bitting (Philadelphia, PA: American Baptist Publication Society, 1918), 13–14.
3 The state conventions affiliating with the NBC were: Arizona, California (N&S), Colorado, Connecticut, Delaware, District of Columbia (dual with SBC), Idaho, Illinois, Indiana, Iowa, Kansas, Maine, Massachusetts, Michigan, Minnesota, Missouri, Montana, Nebraska, Nevada, New Hampshire, New Jersey, New York, North Dakota, Ohio, Oregon, Pennsylvania, Rhode Island, South Dakota, Utah, Vermont, Washington (E&W), West Virginia, Wisconsin, and Wyoming.
4 Ruth Rouse and Stephen Charles Neill (eds), *A History of the Ecumenical Movement*, 3rd edn (Geneva: World Council of Churches, 1986), vol. I, 620–1.

5   Seventh Day Baptists were members of the Federal Council from 1908 to 1973.
6   In 1916 the Carolina Freewill Baptists and many of the churches in the Southwest joined to form the Cooperative General Association of Freewill Baptists that evolved into the National Association of Freewill Baptists in 1935. Another cluster of churches, originally formed as the Cape Fear Conference in 1855, interacted with the post-Civil War holiness movement and later the Azusa Street Revival in 1906, adopting Pentecostal characteristics. This group in 1959 was constituted as the Pentecostal Freewill Baptist Church, headquartered in Dunn, North Carolina.
7   Samuel Z. Batten, *The New World Order* (Philadelphia, PA: American Baptist Publication Society, 1919), 147, 150.
8   Ibid., 33.
9   Robert G. Torbet, *History of the Baptists* (Valley Forge, PA: Judson Press, 1963), 394.
10 Although the Interchurch World Movement disbanded in 1921, much of its vision was recovered in the National Council of Churches in the 1950s, in which the American Baptist Convention (successor to the NBC) again played a major role.
11 *1900 American Baptist Yearbook*, 100.
12 "Report of the Committee on Denominational Efficiency." In *Annual of the Southern Baptist Convention 1914* (Nashville, TN: Marshall and Bruce, 1914), 77–8.
13 Jesse Fletcher, *The Southern Baptist Convention: A Sesquicentennial History* (Nashville, TN: Broadman Press, 1994), 144. See also William R. Estep, *Whole Gospel, Whole World: The Foreign Mission Board of the Southern Baptist Convention 1845–1995* (Nashville, TN: Broadman and Holman Publishers, 1994), 196–7.
14 Spurgeon was concerned about liberal thinking within the Baptist church. See chapter 7 for a discussion of the controversy.
15 William Herbert Perry Faunce, *What Does Christianity Mean?* (New York: Fleming H. Revell, 1912), 39.
16 Mullins wrote the article on "The Testimony of Christian Experience" in vol. IV.
17 Curtis Laws, "Fundamentalism is Very Much Alive," *Watchman-Examiner* (July 28, 1921): 941 and "Convention Sidelights," *Watchman-Examiner* (July 1, 1920): 834.
18 Quoted in C. Allyn Russell, *Voices of Fundamentalism: Seven Biographical Studies* (Philadelphia, PA: Westminster Press, 1976), 100.
19 Quoted in William H. Brackney (ed.), *Baptist Life and Thought: A Sourcebook* (Valley Forge, PA: Judson Press, 1999), 357–8.
20 *A Call to Arms!* (1924), quoted in Brackney, *Baptist Life and Thought*, 357.
21 Quoted in Russell, *Voices of Fundamentalism*, 113.
22 Quoted in Russell, *Voices of Fundamentalism*, 97.

23 Don A. Sanford, *A Choosing People: The History of Seventh Day Baptists* (Nashville, TN: Broadman Press, 1992), 347–53.
24 The story, with documentation, is told in Frank H. Woyke, *Heritage and Ministry of the North American Baptist Conference* (Oakbrook Terrace, IL: North American Baptist Conference, 1979), 360–2.
25 A summary of this evolution in theological distinctives is found in William H. Brackney, *A Genetic History of Baptist Thought* (Macon, GA: Mercer University Press, 2004), 472–3.
26 The Kingston Parsonage Case involved a dispute over the rightful owners of the Baptist parsonage in Kingston, Nova Scotia, when part of the congregation wanted to break fellowship and retain the property. The court hearings revealed the deepening rift between fundamentalists and mainstream Convention Baptists. See George Rawlyk, "Fundamentalism, Modernism, and the Maritime Baptists in the 1920s and 1930s" *Acadiensis* 17/1 (Autumn 1987): 24–7.

Chapter 6
The Pinnacle of Baptist Denominationalism

Most denominations went into World War II financially strapped and uncertain of their future goals. They had just survived what historian Robert Handy dubbed the "American Religious Depression."[1] After the war, there was a new spirit of witness and service, bolstered by a commitment to work together. The ecumenical spirit that had its roots in the 1920s touched both Canada and the United States deeply. At the same time the forces of modernity, seen in corporate structures, headquarters buildings, national executive officers, and unified budgets, had a profound impact upon all of Baptist life in North America. If one counted success by these forms, then the second half of the twentieth century was a series of pinnacles for Baptist denominations across the continent.

Things Pertaining to a Mainline Denomination

In the second half of the twentieth century the major Baptist groups in North America entered a new phase of institutionalization. Historians now see a definite cycle of rise and decline, however. Two of the main denominational streams in the United States, American Baptists and Southern Baptists, developed full-blown ecclesiocratic machinery that imitated corporate structures. In Canada, Convention Baptists followed the same trends. Most remarkable, perhaps, were the emergent patterns of new Baptists, born out of discontent with the mainstream, but pursuing their own directions of institutionalization.

Northern Baptists

Northern Baptists determined to recover their national prominence following World War II. In 1932, on the centennial anniversary of the founding of the American Baptist Home Mission Society, a covered wagon caravan carrying the executives of the Society made a five thousand mile trek from Brockton, Massachusetts, to West Union, Oregon, holding 63 celebration meetings in 17 states. True, the family had weathered painful schism over conservative thrusts in theology and mission, but new leaders desired to signal a new era. The Northern Baptist Convention, composed of five major boards and numerous regional associations, conventions, and societies, in 1950 became the American Baptist Convention (ABC). The ABC held the name "in trust" for other Baptists in the hope that some form of reunification might take place among Baptists as had been the case among American Methodists in 1939. Eventually, however, only one affiliated organization responded to the invitation: the Danish-Norwegian Baptist Conference merged with the ABC in 1957. Another direction the ABC pursued was one of organizational consolidation. The office of general secretary was created in 1950. The executives of each of the boards were linked to the general secretary in a new management structure. Urban corporate models beckoned and one of the more attractive possibilities for a new denominational headquarters site was the Interchurch Center in New York City, a project fostered by American Baptist financial leaders. The Center was constructed in 1958 with Rockefeller Fund gifts and came to symbolize the strength of ecumenical Christianity in the United States, with several Protestant denominational headquarters housed there. Nearby was Riverside Church, related to both American Baptists and the United Church of Christ. Another plan involved a move to the Midway in Chicago, more in the center of the country and adjacent to the University of Chicago. The winning proposal was Philadelphia, or rather rural Valley Forge, Pennsylvania, where the Home Mission Society had long owned property. The new headquarters building, designed by nationally prominent architect, Vincent Kling, was a careful "statement in stone," comprising three stories but circular in structure, reflecting the cooperative polity of American Baptist life for over a century and a half. The site also included a manufacturing plant for Judson Press, which by the 1970s became one of the leading union shop printers in the Delaware Valley. A denominational presence in New York City at the Interchurch Center was maintained by the Ministers and

Missionaries Benefit Board in order to interact daily with the investment community on Wall Street.

To accompany the corporate model American Baptists had pursued, a new theology emerged in the denomination. Young theologians like Harvey Cox at Andover Newton and later Harvard Divinity School, wrote of the influences of secularization upon religious and spiritual life. Cox argued that inherent in the urbanization process is a loss of traditional religious categories and beliefs. What was needed, he wrote in *The Secular City* (1965), was a theology of social change. For Cox, "the church is first of all a responding community, a people whose task it is to discern the action of God in the world and join his work."[2] Even more critical of traditional Protestant systems were radical theologians like William Hamilton, who held the William Newton Clarke chair in theology at Colgate Rochester Divinity School. Hamilton joined others in proclaiming the "death of God" as the church had understood transcendence.

The application of the new theological thinking was taken up in the national life of American Baptists by executives like Jitsuo Morikawa of the Home Mission Society. Morikawa, the son of Japanese detainees in Los Angeles during World War II, was educated at Biola College and Southern Baptist Seminary; this background suggested a personal evangelical orientation to mission. Instead, Morikawa taught that it was the evil in systems that American Baptists needed to address. He worked out of a Rauschenbuschian formulation that called for corporate evangelism to root out social evils. Critics of Morikawa saw the reduction of personal evangelism and new church development just as other Baptists, notably the Southern Baptists, were surging ahead numerically. The election in 1972 of Robert C. Campbell, an evangelical dean from California Baptist Seminary, as General Secretary, was to check the shift from "soul salvation" to "social salvation," an equation many evangelicals observed in ABC life. During Campbell's tenure as general secretary there were signs of an evangelical renaissance, particularly in the confessional seminaries like Eastern and Northern, plus the denominational programs for new church development and increasing mission awareness – "Grow by Caring" and "Alive In Mission" – designed to add 500 new congregations to the ABC from 1984 to 1989. Among the prominent voices in the evangelical wing of the ABC in the 1980s were Emmett Johnson, a former Swedish Conference executive from Minnesota; Anthony Campolo, a professor of sociology at Eastern Baptist College; Roger Frederickson, a pastor from Sioux Falls, South Dakota; and Daniel Weiss, a former professor of homiletics from Gordon Conwell Theological Seminary. Weiss, who followed

Campbell, had led Eastern Baptist Seminary and Eastern College, and later became executive director of the ABC Board of Educational Ministries. Weiss oversaw the initial downsizing of Educational Ministries and was quite enamored of ecumenical relationships. Much polarization took place under his 12 years as general secretary and noticeable decline set in among both the national and regional organizations of ABC. Significant amounts of money were spent on realizing a democratic election district process that replaced the older convention delegate process, and more internal restructuring. Perhaps the most obvious change in American Baptist polity was the transition in 1973 from annual Convention meetings, where debates over actual policy matters dominated the agenda, to biennial meetings whose main function was information and celebration. Both Campbell and Weiss tried to stress the role of American Baptists as a bridge denomination between evangelicals and the ecumenical community, but the constituency of the era had questions about the sincerity of ABC's evangelical witness.

Southern Baptists adopted a more regionally diffuse, but nevertheless corporate identity in the same period. The Foreign Mission Board, at its peak employing over 400 staff and 5,000 missionaries, was rooted in Richmond, Virginia. The Home Mission Board was headquartered in Atlanta, Georgia, and the Sunday School Board, largest publisher of Christian education materials in the Baptist world, was in Nashville, Tennessee. The Southern Baptist Annuity Board was located in Dallas, a city that symbolized the economic prominence of the developing Southwest. Multimillions of dollars of capital improvements were made on the campuses of Southern Baptist universities like University of Richmond, Furman University, Wake Forest University (entirely new campuses), and Baylor University. Among theological schools, Southern Baptist Seminary and Southwestern Baptist Seminary registered record enrollments in the thousands during the 1970s, as new seminaries opened at Wake Forest, North Carolina (Southeastern), Kansas City, Missouri (Midwestern), and Mill Valley, California (Golden Gate). The former Baptist Bible Institute in New Orleans became a major seminary in the Deep South. Most state conventions in the SBC had affiliated Baptist hospitals, the most impressive of which became the Baylor Health Care System in Texas in the 1980s.

However, the tide turned on the Baptist communities of the 1980s and serious downturns or internecine struggles tore asunder many of the accomplishments of the earlier three decades. American Baptists engaged in yet another reorganization following a Study Commission on Denominational Structures (SCODS), a second on Administrative Areas and Relationships (SAAR), and a third, the Study Commission on Regions (SCOR). In 1973 the Convention renamed itself the American Baptist Churches in the USA to symbolize its recovery of local church autonomy. What was really at stake was a funding crisis among the regional, state convention, and urban organizations that charged that too much of the unified American Baptist Mission Budget was being retained at the national level while the states and cities were starved for program and salary funds. It took over a decade of negotiations between the national boards and regions to ratify a Budget Covenant that allowed for roughly half of all funds collected to remain in the regions. Still, many of the regional organizations suffered financially and by the conclusion of the 1990s, consolidation of state conventions had taken place in New England, New York State, and the Dakotas. Generally, the historic city societies that had carried the urban mission portfolio for the denomination became dependent upon declining national funds and their relations with the state organizations. Boston, Pittsburgh, Buffalo, Detroit, San Francisco, and Long Island all merged into their respective state regions. New York City, Philadelphia, Chicago, Indianapolis, and Los Angeles all continued as smaller reshaped regional organizations.

Like much of mainstream American and Canadian Protestantism, the ABC had developed a diversified theological identity that many attributed to its involvement in ecumenical life and, within its seminaries, an adoption of neo-orthodox and liberal theologies. The works of Emil Brunner and Karl Barth were common textbooks in the 1970s in the confessional seminaries, while at Colgate Rochester a prominent professor of theology and ethics, William Hamilton, was terminated for teaching beyond the boundaries of historic liberalism. Andover Newton appointed a new dean in 1966: George Peck, an Australian Baptist missionary and an avowed devotee of Karl Barth. In response, significant numbers of evangelical candidates for the American Baptist ministry sought training at schools like Fuller Theological Seminary in the West, Trinity Evangelical Divinity School, North American Baptist Seminary and Bethel Theological Seminary in the Midwest, and Gordon Conwell Theological Seminary and Westminster Theological Seminary in the Northeast and mid-Atlantic region – all confessional schools and ironically, most with American Baptists on their faculties. In the 1990s, the national programs had to contend with declining congregational receipts coupled with unclear denominational identity issues. The stock market plunges also depleted the financial capabilities of the once well-funded Northern/American Baptist societies. Further internal galvanization occurred over social concerns, for instance between those who favored recognition of gays and lesbians, the "Welcoming and Affirming" congregations, and the traditionalists who wanted a confessional style of evangelicalism restored and a more conservative social agenda, the "American Baptist Evangelicals."

American Baptists reached a crisis point in 2002 when the General Board of the denomination voted to close down the debt-ridden Board of Educational Ministries and the overseas missionary force was greatly curtailed. Some analysts observed that while ABC leaders were realizing their goals of racial/ethnic diversity, the older, mostly Caucasian congregations were dying and leaving a smaller financial pool for American Baptist missions to draw from. The once long list of American Baptist-related colleges and seminaries was pared down to six theological schools and seven colleges in relationship.[3] Notable among those who withdrew from full denominational relationship were Bucknell University, Colby College, University of Redlands, Denison University, and Colby Sawyer College. Colorado Women's College, Bishop College, Baptist Missionary Training School, and Ellen Cushing College for Women closed. Two former Freewill Baptist colleges, Bates in Maine and Hillsdale in Michigan, severed ties with the denomination. Crozer Theological Seminary merged with Colgate Rochester Divinity School (which had taken on a partnership with a Roman Catholic seminary and an Episcopalian school); California Baptist Seminary merged with Berkeley Baptist Divinity School to become the American Baptist Seminary of the West; the Divinity School of the University of Chicago became officially nondenominational, and every other theological school related to the denomination has so extensively "ecumenized" that American Baptist students are a significant minority in most seminaries remaining affiliated with the denomination. Marking the diminution of the corporate model, the Valley Forge national headquarters had by the late 1990s leased much of its adjacent land and office space, reduced its office staff, and was renamed a "National Mission Center" to capture a new focus. As of the new millennium, American Baptists claimed to be the most diverse of all Baptist groups: in 1995 General Secretary Daniel E. Weiss characterized the ABC as "no longer a majority denomination."[4]

Southern Baptists

In the second half of the twentieth century, Southern Baptists were a stark contrast to American Baptists. The SBC expanded well beyond its native region in the United States and developed entirely new global horizons for their witness. This came at least in part from the unilateral action of the Northern Baptist Convention in assuming the name "American Baptist Convention" in 1950, and also in response to American Baptist negotiations with the Disciples of Christ. In 1949 the SBC messengers approved a resolution that:

> no compact or agreement be formed with any organization, convention, or religious body that would place Southern Baptists in a compromising position, or would appear to be a step toward organic union with religious bodies that do not believe in or practice the aforesaid New Testament Baptist principles as set out in this report.[5]

And further in 1951:

> We recommend that whereas the Southern Baptist Convention has defined its territorial position in reports to the Convention in 1944 and in 1949 by removing territorial limitations and whereas the Northern Baptist Convention has changed its name so that it is continental in scope, the Home Mission Board and all other Southern Baptist Convention boards and agencies be free to serve as a source of blessing to any community or to any people anywhere in the United States.[6]

With resolve, what has been referred to as the "Southern Baptist Invasion" commenced. Churches in California and Kansas had already petitioned for SBC recognition in the 1940s, and in 1948 the Baptist General Convention of Oregon and Washington was fully accepted into the SBC. In the 1950s, the first SBC congregations were planted in the Delaware Valley in Pennsylvania leading to the Penn Jersey Association. In the same period, Maryland Baptists, related to the SBC, provided a base for expansion into New York City and Massachusetts that led to the Greater New York Association and the New England Baptist Convention. The latter organization is housed in the renovated eighteenth-century homestead of Luther Rice at Northborough, Massachusetts, a recapturing of history not lost on American Baptists in the region. Elsewhere Southern Baptists built in Chicago out of strengths in the Illinois Convention of Southern Baptists and in Utah, Idaho, North Dakota, South Dakota, Nevada, Colorado, and Montana, new associations or conventions were organized and would later become part of the Home Mission Board's program, "Bold Mission Thrust."[7]

Launched officially in 1978, Bold Mission Thrust was an entirely new, aggressive, and comprehensive effort to ensure that "every person in the world shall have the opportunity to hear the Gospel of Christ in the next 25 years." It was the result of several factors. In the 1950s a gradual shift in the relationship between the Home Mission Board and the state conventions evolved whereby instead of conducting missions directly as it had from the Reconstruction era, the Home Mission Board began a cooperative effort with and through the state conventions. The Southern Baptist Convention officially sanctioned the new paradigm in 1959: directors of missions in each state would develop a strategy specifically to evangelize key areas and plant new congregations with funding provided by the Home Mission Board. The field became all of North America. Another factor leading to Bold Mission Thrust was the intense stewardship campaigns that the SBC conducted in the late 1950s and 1960s. As one observer has noted, Southern Baptists had more to say about stewardship in this era than anything else.[8] The Baptist Jubilee Advance in 1964, that celebrated Baptist life in the United States and beyond on the occasion of the 150th anniversary of the establishment of the General Missionary Convention, was another catalyst for Southern Baptists to forge ahead as the clear numerical leaders of the Baptist movement in the United States at that time.

Beyond North America, changes in US foreign policy and increased American military presence overseas beckoned the Southern Baptist Foreign Mission Board to redouble its energies as well. Through dramatically increasing its missionary personnel and partnership programs involving short-term lay volunteers, Southern Baptists pushed ahead on every continent. R. Keith Parks, head of the Foreign Mission Board during this era, is credited with emancipating missions from older syndromes and stereotypes and building bridges with other world mission bodies. Among his singular achievements was the hiring of widely acclaimed missiological scholar, David Barrett, to the Board team. Evangelism took priority over institutional development and missionaries were appointed irrespective of a particular theological stance. These two emphases would become problematic on the home front in the Southern Baptist communities of the 1990s, despite the triumphalism and euphoria that many felt with the romantic challenges of Bold Mission Thrust. On the basis of Matthew 24:14 many Southern Baptist postmillennialists predicted the nearness of Christ's return as the gospel of the kingdom was indeed preached in all the world.

In spite of the efforts of Bold Mission Thrust, however, dark clouds appeared on the Southern Baptist horizon. For the first time in Convention history, commitment to missions did not overcome theological or political strife. Southern Baptist growth was checked by clashing forces of polity and theological confessionalism. As Southern Seminary proudly exhibited neo-orthodox tendencies in professors like Dale Moody and Glenn Hinson, and Broadman Press published work from a variety of

Baptist authors, conservative groups within the family began to organize the ultimate takeover. Judge Paul Pressler of Houston and Paige Patterson of Dallas, carrying an agenda set by W. A. Criswell, pastor of First Baptist Church in Dallas, plotted a takeover of key SBC posts to restore the theological integrity of the Convention's agencies and institutions. Fueled by a coterie of younger theologians trained outside the SBC, the conservatives took control of the convention presidency and through them the Committee on Committees. Pastors of prominent congregations came to the fore, such as Bailey Smith (Arkansas), Charles Stanley (Georgia), Ed Young (Texas), and Jerry Vines (Florida). Year after year, the presidency went to a conservative/fundamentalist candidate. When it became obvious that the moderate faction was unable to mount sufficient floor votes to recover their leadership, moderates formed the Cooperative Baptist Fellowship and the Alliance of Baptists. At first these groups seemed to continue their identity as Southern Baptists, but as time wore on and the conservative resurgence captured control of each of the national agencies and the six seminaries, the Alliance and Fellowship became permanent new families of Baptists.

As the millennium turned, Southern Baptists seemed destined for permanent reorganization. The first target of the resurgent confessionalists was to gain control of the Convention boards and agencies. One by one the transition was total: at the Home Mission Board, Larry Lewis, a small college president, replaced William Tanner (1987); James Draper, a Euless, Texas, pastor and protégé of W. A. Criswell, replaced another Texan at the Sunday School Board, Lloyd Elder, who had been forced into retirement (1991); Jerry A. Rankin, a career missionary and administrator, succeeded Keith Parks at the Foreign Mission Board (1993); Foy Valentine, a long time social activist, retired to be succeeded eventually by Richard Land, a Princeton and Oxford-educated historian and Republican Party afficionado, at the Christian Life Commission; Morris Chapman, pastor at Wichita Falls, Texas, succeeded the venerable Harold Bennett (1990) as president of the executive committee, a position roughly equal to that of general secretary. Beyond the control of the Southern Baptist hegemony, but very much in the orbit of SBC funding and influence were the Baptist Joint Committee on Public Affairs and the Baptist World Alliance. The Joint Committee, which opposed the confessional resurgent position on prayer in public schools among other issues, and was led by vocal James Dunn, was defunded in 1989. Under accusations of theological liberalism, lukewarm commitments to evangelism, and allegations of openness to homosexuality, the Convention severed its ties to the BWA in 2004.

Another primary strategy of the SBC resurgent confessionalists was to reverse the trend toward critical biblical scholarship and the classical disciplines in the seminaries toward more practical, evangelical training. Succeeding Roy Honeycutt at Southern Seminary was R. Albert Mohler, a former state Baptist editor and enthusiast for Reformed theology in the Baptist tradition. Anticipating the changes his presidency would mandate, most moderate professors left Southern quickly. Likewise at Southeastern Seminary, considered the most progressive-to-liberal of the six schools, Randall Lolley was replaced by Lewis Drummond. At both institutions enrollment in the masters' programs plummeted while new undergraduate degrees were instituted. Russell Dilday, president of Southwestern Seminary was fired in 1994, soon thereafter to be elected president of the Association of Theological Schools in the United States and Canada. Paige Patterson, one of the overall architects of the conservative resurgence, assumed the presidency of Southeastern Seminary and later Southwestern Seminary, one of only two in Southern Baptist history to serve as president of two seminaries. By 2004 all of the Southern Baptist seminaries were under the control of presidents committed to implementing the Baptist Faith and Message 2000. In the midst of the battle for the hearts of Southern Baptists, a Peace Committee was formed in 1985 of prominent leaders from across the Convention. It failed to reflect the legitimate concerns of the Moderates and became a tacit victory for the resurgent confessionalists and their biblical inerrancy agenda. Twenty years into the "reorientation" process of the Southern Baptist Convention, in 2003 it claimed 16 million members in over 40,000 congregations in the United States, collecting over $9.6 billion from all sources.

Other Baptist groups in the US and Canada

Imitating the Northern/American Baptist national organizational evolutions, significant denominational progress occurred among the former German and Swedish Baptist conferences. In the wake of establishing general secretariat offices before World War II, North American Conference Baptists built an office center in Forest Park, Illinois. In 1961, with the staff doubled in size, a new building was erected. Subsequently, an NABC Board of Missions was created and the associations replaced the older conference regional structure. The national missions and publication work became cooperating societies, again imitative of NBC terminology. In 1975 a further reorganization occurred, bringing more coordination to national and regional programs, fully embracing a smaller brand of Baptist denominationalism. The following year, with further expansion of the North American Baptist Conference, a move was made to Oakbrook Park, Illinois, near the major airport facilities for Chicago. Similarly, among Swedish Baptists, beginning in the late 1960s with a Special Committee on Organizational Relationship (SCOR),[9] the Conference was thoroughly reorganized to allow for a greater integration of districts, churches, and the Conference. A new corporate headquarters building in Evanston that had been occupied in 1970 was sold and a smaller "Conference Service Center" facility was dedicated at Arlington Heights, Illinois in 1980.

Smaller Baptist groups, now national in scope, were not immune to pursuing the corporate model of ministry. Seventh Day Baptists moved to adopt a national institutional presence in building what amounted to a headquarters site between 1917 and 1929. The Tract Society long needed a structure for printing, executive meetings, and a denominational library. In 1922 after two years of studying various locations, the first denominational building was constructed in Plainfield, New Jersey; the second choice had been Battle Creek, Michigan. The first stage entailed the publishing operation, and in 1929 a second stage was completed housing executive offices and "serving as a fitting memorial to a worthy past."[10] For the next half century, the Plainfield building was a symbol of Seventh Day Baptists and the General Conference in particular. As the work of the Conference moved through the mid-century decades, appropriate adjustments in budget and board cooperation were made with the important advancement of the incorporation of the General Conference. Yet another set of studies and corporate decisions were made in the 1970s over concerns of utility costs, convenience, security, the western movement of related churches, and a more modern structure. The new denominational headquarters was established at Janesville, Wisconsin, near the former Milton College campus. In recognition of this move, Janesville renamed two streets "Newport" and "Plainfield" in recognition of Seventh Day Baptist heritage. On the down side, Seventh Day Baptists lost their educational institutions during the mid to later twentieth century. Alfred University in New York severed its ties in 1945, Milton College in Wisconsin closed in 1982, and Salem College in West Virginia evolved into a nonsectarian school in 1989.

General Baptists made strides toward a national denominational identity in the twentieth century. Having achieved a national comprehensive organization three decades before Northern Baptists, the General Baptists added to their denominational agenda. A Women's Mission Board started up in 1911, following the growth of women's work among northern and southern Baptists. In 1914 a General Board began to function as a coordinating body of the other boards. Gradually, this body became a policy-making group for General Baptists. To manage the publishing interests of the denomination, a Board of Publications was added in 1921 and a Board of Religious Education in 1925. Finally, a Ministers' Aid Board was created in 1953 to handle endowments and superannuated clergy. The newly achieved infrastructure inevitably led to the creation of a unified denominational budget. In 1916 the General Association of General Baptists recommended to the local associations an apportioned budget for all of the agencies; at first it was very meagerly supported. In 1920, as other Baptists in the United States were gearing up for major financial campaigns, General Baptists authorized a Centenary Campaign of $250,000. Unfortunately, overly visionary planners distantly associated the Campaign with the Inter-Church World Movement and this practically scuttled the entire effort as local churches expressed great alarm at the amounts of money requested and the entanglements with the ecumenical movement. Not until 1996 would the General Association of General Baptists be restructured to provide a fully integrated and unified denominational program.[11]

General Baptists also suffered their share of schisms, though not linked directly to the fundamentalist crusade. At the turn of the twentieth century, a move to incorporate the General Association brought deep divisions between eastern and western associations. Another problem arose in 1903 over the articles of faith with several Missouri associations dropping out of the General Association. At counterpoint with the General Association, a Missouri State Association of General Baptists was organized to defend the alternative doctrinal articles. In 1903–4 Josephus Lee, an elder in Indiana intensely loyal to General Baptist teaching and opposed to the conversations with the Separate Baptists of Indiana, proffered an unorthodox interpretation of the Parable of the Lost Sheep and the Parable of the Prodigal Son in which he argued that there are persons who do not rebel against God and some sheep who never stray from the fold. His views, in support of changing the third article of faith on "perseverance," were articulated in a book, *Where Is My Baby?* (1903). Lee drew the ire of many in the General Association and he joined forces with the Missouri Association. He remained a bitter partisan and caused many to be suspicious of the authority of the General Association. Well into the last century, the historian of the General Baptists reported that local church folk mocked those in the ministry of the General Association in the style of Lee by referring to the officers as "they" and with pejorative epithets like "big bugs" and "dudes."[12]

Not to be untouched by organizational evolution, the General Association of Regular Baptists and the Conservative Baptist Association built corporate centers to administer their family interests. The GARBC has continued its operations at Schaumburg, Illinois, that includes Regular Baptist Press and other program offices, employs 70 staff, and is collectively known as the International Ministry Resource Center. Formerly located in Wheaton, Illinois, Conservative Baptists in 2001 underwent a decentralizing process that closed the national CB Center and placed various operations for CB America, and Home and International Ministries in regional centers in the Pacific Northwest, Colorado, and the Southwest. The national executive is located in Littleton, Colorado.

Also imitative of the modified corporate model of Baptist denominationalism were the mainstream Baptists in Canada. Although in statistical decline across the century, the sophistication of organizational structure and work progressed. In 1944, after a century of aborted attempts, Canadian Baptists united their efforts in the Baptist Federation of Canada, formed at Yorkminster Park Baptist Church in Toronto. This included the Baptist Convention of Ontario and Quebec, the United Baptist Convention of the Maritimes, the Baptist Union of Western Canada, and the Union des Eglises Evangéliques aux Français. The Baptists in Ontario and Quebec purchased an office space in downtown Toronto in 1952, later to be known as "Church House"; those in the Maritimes built a convention office center at St John, New Brunswick; the French Union headquartered in Montreal, and the Western Union built its headquarters in Calgary, Alberta, in 1973. For a time the Federation joined in a corporate facility with the Canadian Baptist Overseas Mission Board in Mississauga, Ontario. Executive staff terminology and a board structure for missions and education accompanied the architectural progress.

In the last two decades of the twentieth century, Baptists in Canada have moved through a transitional period. In central Canada, the strong congregations in urban centers have failed to maintain their earlier numerical strength and some congregations have succumbed to age. In Toronto, for instance, once prominent churches like Walmer Road, Olivet, Calvary, and Emmanuel have declined appreciably. Yorkminster Park, often reflecting the British tradition, remains strong. Montreal congregations, First Baptist and Westmount, have declined due to the emigration of English-speaking members from Quebec in the 1980s. Likewise in Hamilton, James Street, Trinity, and MacNeill churches have lost significant parts of their congregations and the dominant

Baptists in that city are Fellowship congregations. Ancaster Baptist and Park Church, Brantford, have closed in the same region. On the other hand, Baptist membership remains static among the small city and town congregations, while the Chinese Baptist community in Toronto has increased exponentially in the same period, adding 6,300 members in 17 congregations from 1968 to 2004. Among the French-speaking union, Baptist work is still fragile, after several attempts to plant churches and create in 1982 a local ministerial school, the Centre d'Etudes Théologiques Evangéliques.

Among the Maritime Baptist churches, strong, but transitional congregations remain in Halifax, Dartmouth, Charlottetown, St John, Fredericton, Woodstock, and most of the smaller cities and towns of Nova Scotia and New Brunswick, but the number of very small congregations near closure is high. In the upper Annapolis Valley, for instance, where much of the early Baptist movement originated, over 20 churches are below 50 members. Across the Prairies, large buildings with decreasing congregations dot the landscape of the old railroad cities, Winnipeg, Brandon, Edmonton, Calgary, Regina, Saskatoon, and Medicine Hat.

Legacy: The Baptist Jubilee Advance

The year 1964 marked the sesquicentennial of the founding of the General Missionary Convention of the Baptist Denomination of the United States of America for Foreign Missions, commonly called the Triennial Convention. As the date approached, a surge of unusual cooperation and good will abounded among mainstream Baptists in the United States and reached even to Canada. Baptists who had been in recent competition with each other planned joint celebrations and agreed to further strategies for a united witness to North America and the world.

The Baptist Jubilee Advance was the joint brainchild of the American, Southern, and National Baptist Conventions in 1955. At a meeting in Chicago, representatives of the groups resolved to begin a six-year program of witness and work, culminating in a worthy third jubilee celebration in 1964. The stages involved evangelism, 1959; Bible teaching and Baptist witness, 1960; stewardship and enlistment, 1961; church extension and leadership training, 1962; world missions, 1963; and Third Jubilee Celebration, 1964. Invitations to participate went to all major Baptist bodies in the United States and Canada. By 1956 a coordinating committee of representatives was created from among 13 Baptist organizations including the Baptist Federation of Canada. They approved an agenda, a slogan, "For Liberty and Light," and a logo involving a torch and bell over the words, "Baptist Jubilee Advance."

There were tangible results to the Advance that were more, and less, than one might have expected. First, there was a book published at the end of the five years that was intended to be distributed to every congregation, institution, and agency in a relationship with the effort. The book contained essays on the history of Baptist groups, statistical analyses since 1814, thematic essays on religious liberty, ecclesiology, ecumenism, and theological topics characteristic of Baptists, all grouped together under the theme, "Baptist Contributions to America." There was also a selection of photographs of institutions and church buildings that illustrated the growth of Baptists in tangible ways. The volume was well received, and over the years since has been a useful reference tool. Next, the Advance gave the leaders of many Baptist organizations the opportunity to discuss matters that were held in common. This led to a consensus about the common faith and common heritage, along with the missionary evangelistic motives that all the groups shared. From the consensus came a remarkable sense of cooperation that was realized in the continuation of meetings and cooperative efforts such as the North American Baptist Fellowship in the Baptist World Alliance.

What the Baptist Jubilee Advance did not produce was any step toward actual organizational cooperation, let alone merger. The invitation of the American Baptist Convention of 1950 to other Baptist groups in the United States to join a larger family, went unheeded and, after 1964, died. During the five years 1959–64, a major rift occurred in the National Baptist Convention USA, that spawned a new black Baptist group, the Progressive National Baptist Convention. Southern Baptists moved aggressively into the Northwest, Midwest, and Northwest, planting new congregations and starting new conventions in American Baptist territory. The same thing could be witnessed as Southern Baptists went ahead with plans to enter Canada. Further, no greater cooperation was undertaken among the ethnically defined subgroups (the Baptist General Conference did not participate over the entire quinquennium), and no visible desegregation of either the American Baptists or Southern Baptists took place.

The important legacy of the period was that historians of all mainstream Baptist groups in the US and Canada would thereafter find unavoidable the common roots of Baptist life in North America. That in itself was worth the effort in a fragmented tradition.

Notes

1 Robert T. Handy, "The American Religious Depression, 1925–1935" *Church History* 29/1 (March 1960): 3–16.
2 Harvey Cox, *The Secular City: Secularization and Urbanization in Theological Perspective* (New York: MacMillan, 1965), 91.
3 The theological schools are: Andover Newton, Colgate Rochester, Eastern Baptist, Northern Baptist, American Baptist Seminary of the West, and Central Baptist. The colleges are: Judson College, Ottawa University, Alderson Broadus College, ABC directories also list dually affiliated Shaw University, Virginia Union, Morehouse School of Religion, and Evangelical Seminary in Puerto Rico as "partner schools."
4 The statistics demonstrate a preponderance of African American over Caucasian churches, 52 percent to 43 percent; cf. William H. Brackney (ed.), *Baptist Life and Thought: A Sourcebook* (Valley Forge, PA: Judson Press, 1999), 467–8.
5 *Annual*, Southern Baptist Convention, 1949, 53.
6 *Annual*, Southern Baptist Convention, 1951, 36.
7 See Robert G. Torbet's essay, "Historical Background of the Southern Baptist 'Invasion'," *Foundations* 2/4 (October, 1959): 314–19.
8 Jesse C. Fletcher, *The Southern Baptist Convention: A Sesquicentennial History* (Nashville, TN: Broadman & Holman Publishers, 1994), 192–3.
9 Not to be confused with the SCODS and SCOR discussed above in connection with the American Baptist Connection.
10 Don A. Sanford, *A Choosing People: The History of Seventh Day Baptists* (Nashville, TN: Broadman Press, 1992), 278–85.
11 Leland Duncan and Edwin Runyan, *The Journey with General Baptists* (Poplar Bluff, MO: Stinson Press, 2005), 100–34.
12 Ollie Latch, *History of the General Baptists* (Poplar Bluff, MO: General Baptist Press, 1972), 230.

Chapter 7
The Come-outer Tradition

St Paul's quotation of the ancient injunction, "Therefore come out from them, and be separate from them, says the Lord" (II Cor. 6: 17) justifies the schismatic tendency for many Christians, and Baptists have surely exhibited the pattern. Here they have followed a path that significant groups of Methodists, Presbyterians, Lutherans, Episcopalians, and even Mormons have trod in the saga of American religious history. Separating from the mainstream, the norm, a predominant group, is in fact a timeworn nonconformist trait that characterized the earliest English Baptists. John Smyth found himself among Separates and left the established church in 1606. He believed it was part of a true believer's covenant with God "to forsake every evil way whither in opinion or practice that shalbe manifested unto us at anytime. . . ."[1] His famous book, *Principles and Inferences Concerning the Visible Church* (1607) was a clear statement of discontinuity with uniform practices. He wrote without equivocation,

> . . . if the church will not reforme open knowne corruptions after due proceeding, separation must be made from it til reformation come. Therefore separation may be made from true churches for incorrigible corruptions, and to separate from a defiled church that is incorrigible, is not to forsake the communion of holy things, but the pollution and prophanation of holy things.[2]

Surviving documentation indicates that the first split among Baptists occurred in 1610–11, within a few years of the formation of the first congregation.[3] Smyth and his most devoted follower, Thomas Helwys, parted company, Smyth remaining in Amsterdam among the Mennonites, and Helwys returning to England. In the 1620s Mennonites in Holland

noticed this schismatic tendency among Baptists in their early development and advised them to achieve unity within their own family as a
condition for fellowship on a broader scale. The English General Baptists either could not or would not resolve their internal difficulties,
because their first attempt at cooperation with other Christians went
silent for three centuries.

The come-outer tradition manifested itself early among Baptists in
the United States. Separate Baptists in the eighteenth century eschewed
any cooperation with Regular Baptists and this could be explained by
"come-outerism." Likewise, the Old School/New School split was a
form of the same tendency, as was the Abolitionist decision to organize
apart from the General Missionary Convention. And, of course, the
pilgrimage involving the separation of the Southern Baptist Convention
in 1845 and the National Baptist Convention of America in 1915
could be interpreted as come-outer ecclesiastical politics. In Canada,
schisms over open versus closed communion and American/British cultural clashes had the same nuance. Several groups more purely demonstrate the come-outer tendency even more than these examples and are
worth discussion.

Mountain People and Wiregrass Baptists

As the Trans-Virginia frontier opened to the mid-Appalachians and
Kentucky, numerous Baptist families located in the valley hollows, and
small congregations emerged, beginning in the 1790s. Many of these
isolated churches fell under the influence of the antimissionary movement described above. Still others persevered in maintaining what they
considered to be the "regular" tenets of the Baptist faith. This term
hearkened back to the Regular Baptist movement that defined itself by
the Philadelphia Baptist Confession of 1742. Some also eventually joined
either the Virginia or Kentucky Baptist associations.

Old Regulars are very much defined by their regional locations.
Isolation produced both firmly entrenched doctrinal positions and
rigid ethical norms. But it also has produced a deep sense of fellowship
within associational life. Typically associational meetings last for three
days, include preaching, footwashings, tactile encounters like embracing and handshaking, common meals, construction and handcraft work,
and religious discussions in an atmosphere of extended family, symbolized best in the annual memorial services. A genuine sense of intimacy
among families grows over years and, despite the distance over mountains and rough terrain, Old Regulars know each other by name from

congregation to congregation. Howard Dorgan, the principal historian of the movement in the 1980s, underscored the importance of "homegoing" and a sense of place. "Homegoing" referred to the annual association meetings; when Old Regulars move outside the region, powerful attitudes of dislocation create magnetic forces drawing them back to the "lodestones."[4]

Theological matters have been defining issues among Mountain Baptists. Those congregations of the early nineteenth century that adhered to a rigid understanding of the atonement of Christ and were predestinarian, came to be the Primitive Baptists. At the other end of the theological spectrum were the southern Freewill Baptists who penetrated western North Carolina and Tennessee with an open view of Christ's death for all, "whosoever will might be saved." Very gradually from the 1850s through the 1890s, a third or middle way of understanding evolved among many congregations whereby it was taught that humans ultimately did not control their salvation as Arminians taught, but that they needed to respond to God's call and by so doing became part of God's elect, and that no one was automatically particularly damned or saved. In 1891 the New Salem Association in Kentucky was the first group of congregations to use the term "Old Regular" which charted their unique position.

As time went on, the Old Regulars distanced themselves from Primitives as well as the Philadelphia Confession. The Old Regular movement was located in northwestern North Carolina, southwestern Virginia, West Virginia, western Pennsylvania, and Maryland. Their ethical principles included opposition to membership for divorced persons, inappropriate dress for women, pulpits open to non-Regular preachers, and female leadership in worship. A related faction in the same region, calling themselves simply "Regulars," differed from Old Regulars in their allowance of Sunday schools, and music in worship. Old Regulars were steadfast in holding Sabbath school as "extra-gospel" and allowing no musical instruments or note-singing in services.

Historians of Old Regularism have noted its relatively static numerical reports in the latter half of the twentieth century. From about 5,000 members in 1900, the movement might now comprise six to seven thousand adherents and members. Old Regularism continues to be organizationally volatile, having experienced faith and order schism mostly over differing understandings of human action in salvation, and lifestyle concerns like whether women should "bob" their hair.[5]

Similar in tenor to the Mountain Baptists are clusters of "Wiregrass Baptists" who live in the Piedmont and tidewater regions of southeastern Georgia, northern Florida, and southern Alabama.[6] Like the mountain region, this was a wilderness area isolated by swamps, thickets, and the sea. In the 1820s and 1830s, missionary Baptists behind strong leaders like Jesse Mercer vied with Arminian Baptists on the one hand and hyper-Calvinist congregations on the other. The typical antimissionary proclivities emerged as elsewhere and accounted for a significant number of Georgia Baptist congregations in the Primitive relationship. Come-outerism was rife among all of the groups. The first evidence was seen among the Columbus Association in 1829 when Cyrus White published a tract advocating universal atonement. Two associations of churches eventually followed White in his strong position against primitivism. In 1835 the "mother" primitive Ochlocknee Association was divided over the missionary leanings of William Blewett – a pastor in Randolph County, Georgia – and his "hetridose" sentiments.[7]

The come-outer tendency continued among the Wiregrass Baptists. Here, largely in the Primitive Baptist context, harsh, rigid declarations of doctrine were accompanied with vituperative exclamations and associations with the demonic against those whose practices were unacceptable on either side of an issue. In the early 1870s, centered in Effingham County, Georgia, opposition to the Georgia Homestead Act (1868) broke out, whereby Elder Reuben Crawford of Pierce County, Georgia, contended with Elder Richard Bennett of Appling County, essentially over the rights of creditors to withhold a certain portion of their property from foreclosure. "Crawfordites" supported the legislation, while "Bennettites" opposed it in keeping with what they thought Primitive Baptist ethics required. Bennettites eventually joined forces with the Primitives, but the Crawfordites became a permanent schism in new associations across the region, surviving on the basis of strict discipline and doctrine. Another rupture occurred in the 1870s over the Two Seed doctrine associated with Daniel Parker in Illinois; Elder Isaac Coon at Bethlehem Church in the Altabaha River Association took an allegorical interpretation of Scripture, denied a bodily resurrection, positing a spiritual body that awaited the child of God in heaven, and denounced the Calvinistic theory of election. His followers, known locally as "Coonites," persevered until the 1920s when the last leaders died. In 1875 controversy ensued in a regional convention in the Brushy Creek, Georgia, area over election and fatalism. Jacob Young in Georgia's Union Association and the "Youngites," advocates of openness to Arminian-style doctrine, remained in "discouraged isolation" for years.[8] To complicate matters further, the "Jackites," followers of Elder John "Jack" Vickers, viciously attacked Two-seedism and fatalism at every opportunity. While not a large group, the Jackites survived into the next century. Finally, yet another schismatic faction appeared in 1872 in the Ochlocknee Association behind the preaching of Elder J. R. Battle in Georgia and Florida. The "Battleites" permitted acceptance of missionary Baptists without rebaptism, implying the acceptance of missionary doctrines. In the twentieth century, "come-outerism" continued with the Towaliga (Georgia) Association, that had long prided itself in being "everywhere spoken against," exhibiting openness to musical instruments, membership in lodges, and making footwashing (the sacred rite of Primitive Baptists) optional. In the last several decades, the Wiregrass Baptists have declined in most categories, in some instances dramatically. They now number about one thousand members in several small associations.[9]

The Impact of C. H. Spurgeon

If schism was inherent in certain regions of Baptist life in the United States, the larger tendency toward come-outerism was given much impetus and credibility by the ministry of the British Prince of Preachers, Charles Haddon Spurgeon. There are elements in Spurgeon's background to suggest why he behaved the way he did at the peak of his career. Raised only in part in his natural family, he had a checkered religious heritage: his father was a part-time Independent pastor, his grandfather was an Old Dissenter with strong Puritan leanings, Charles was converted in a Primitive Methodist Chapel where he dropped by on a snowy day.[10] Experiencing a call to ministry, Spurgeon desired to attend the Baptist College at Stepney (later Regent's Park College), but was denied admission because of a missed interview with the principal, Joseph Angus.[11] Self-taught, he assumed the pastorate of the Baptist Church at Carter Lane, London, that later moved to New Park Street. His effectiveness as a preacher was soon recognized and he rose to meteoric heights in Victorian London. He preached to throngs in the Crystal Palace and his congregation erected a massive edifice, the Metropolitan Tabernacle, at Elephant and Castle to accommodate the increased attendance at his weekly services. Throughout his ministry, Spurgeon watched cautiously the rapprochement of the Particular and General Baptists and he gradually came to see their union as wholly unsatisfactory to evangelical religion as he understood it.

How Spurgeon moved toward schism is worthy of attention. As early as 1856–59 London's great Protestant orator became the principal antagonist to the publication of a collection of hymns that Thomas Toke Lynch compiled, entitled *The Rivulet*. Spurgeon and other evangelicals found the hymns devoid of the essentials of vital

Christianity with no recognition of the divinity of Christ. Spurgeon openly denounced the collection and urged, "The time is come for sterner men than the willows of the stream can afford; we shall soon have to handle truth, not with kid gloves, but with gauntlets – the gauntlets of holy courage and integrity. Go on, ye warriors of the cross, for the King is at the head of you."[12]

Attempts have been made to cast the Down Grade Controversy as a personal battle for supremacy between Spurgeon and John Clifford, the prominent English General Baptist. Spurgeon denied this, as did Clifford, and it appears the entire saga was a negative reaction of Spurgeon to modern trends in social and intellectual thinking. According to the most plausible accounts, Spurgeon was gravely troubled at the perceived departure from traditional Calvinism that he noticed among his preacher colleagues in the Baptist Union of Great Britain. In particular, he saw an unwarranted reinterpretation of the doctrine of eternal punishment and the substitutionary atonement; as well, many teachers were rethinking the inspiration of Scripture. Spurgeon urged conformity to a doctrinal standard such as that of the Evangelical Alliance as an antidote. In 1887, two articles appeared in his monthly magazine the *Sword and Trowel* under the title "The Down Grade" that suggested apostasy from truth. Although the articles were written by Robert Schindler at Addlestone, they carried Spurgeon's approval as a not-so-covert attack upon General Baptists. Spurgeon later joined the editorial barrage directly and questioned the benefits of being aligned with a "confederacy of evil" as he characterized the Union. He called for the expulsion of prominent pastors in the Union or he would withdraw. When this did not occur, Spurgeon withdrew the Tabernacle from fellowship in the Union, and after repeated attempts at conciliation, his decision remained final. He advised other congregations to "let the hampering ropes be cut clean away, and no more lines be thrown out until we know that we are alongside a friend who sails under the same glorious flag."[13] Like many who would come after him, Spurgeon remained outside the mainstream of British Baptists, sad and isolated, according to one historian.[14]

Spurgeon was of course well known by the 1890s in both the United States and Canada. One of his earliest publications, *Lectures to My Students*, was produced in the United States as early as 1875. Abridged editions of his sermons appeared beginning in 1887 and in 1891 a small booklet, "The Greatest Fight in the World," reached North America. His magazine, the *Sword and Trowel*, had numerous subscribers in North America, as well as being available in libraries and reading rooms. Volumes of his sermons were available through US publishers as well as British editions in Canada. In 1898 the American Baptist Publication Society published an octavo edition of Spurgeon's autobiography that included his interpretation of the Down Grade Controversy. Philadelphia Baptist Temple pastor, Russell H. Conwell, for whom Spurgeon was a role model, had published a biography of the British preacher in 1892 that was widely circulated in the American evangelical community. At least one relative of the great preacher, Muriel Spurgeon Carder, showed up in Canada and drew attention to her connection with Spurgeon as she became the first ordained woman among Baptists in Canada. There can be little doubt that the early Baptist fundamentalists were aware of the positions that C. H. Spurgeon had taken, creating for him heroic status in international evangelical circles.

Spurgeon's influence among evangelical and fundamentalist Baptists continued to be evident into the twentieth century. First, the Metropolitan Tabernacle under Spurgeon's successors continued to carry many of Spurgeon's concerns and stood outside the Union. Second, in the mid-1920s president of the Union, T. R. Glover, drafted a study pamphlet with the title "The Fundamentals" in which he appeared to question the substitutionary theory of the atonement. The controversy that erupted in the pages of the *Baptist Times* and the *Sword and Trowel* was known internationally as a second Down Grade. It was recognized that many of Spurgeon's contemporaries were still living and the wounds of the 1880s survived. This led to similar controversies in the US and Canadian Baptist communities. Among the leadership of the General Association of Regular Baptist Churches (GARBC) in the 1930s, for instance, David Otis Fuller, editor of the *Baptist Bulletin,* reminded his readers of the stand for truth against apostasy that Spurgeon had taken decades before. Quoting Spurgeon he said, "I can be ridiculed; I can be abused; but I cannot be false to my Lord." Like Spurgeon, Fuller saw the situation facing Regular Baptists as either denying Christ or separating from apostasy.[15] A generous gift from a college donor enabled William Jewell College in Missouri to purchase Spurgeon's library in 1905 for display in a permanent exhibit, further boosting his reputation to a new generation of Reformed Baptists.

The twentieth century turned out to give even greater license to Baptists to "come out." Given the sweeping cultural changes occurring in the urbanization of life in North America, coupled with the intellectual currents that entailed new ideas like socialism, an enlarged role for government, the rise of the social sciences, professional specialization, and an overall optimistic view of humanity, the natural role for religion became for many one of conservation. Baptists, whose epistemology rested on Scripture and the primitive church, naturally gravitated to a protectionistic mode, and many pastors and lay persons were unwilling to adopt new ideas or accept challenges to traditional religious values.

As the main streams of Baptists experimented with a new language for the faith, and joined other Protestants in their quest for a relevant and contemporary understanding of Christianity, clusters and groups of Baptists opted for their own organizations that vouchsafed their principles. C. H. Spurgeon's principles reached far and wide indeed.

McMaster University and the Storm in Canada

Among the earliest manifestations of come-outerism that had roots in the Down Grade was the attack upon McMaster University in Ontario, Canada. From its beginnings in Montreal as a British-founded theological college in Canada, McMaster emerged as the principal university-level institution among Baptists in Canada. It had all the prestige of Toronto as a location and the investment of Senator William McMaster who bequeathed to the institution the largest sum of money given to a denominational school in Canadian history to that date. Its prestige was further enhanced by connections with the University of Toronto, the center of education in central Canada.

McMaster entered the twentieth century as a multiple-purpose institution, equally serving its denominational pastoral and missionary needs as well as providing a strong arts program. By 1912 the arts course had outdistanced the theological degree enrollments and the institution under Howard P. Whidden sought to realize its potential in the humanities and sciences. Two appointments in particular, in 1901 of George Cross in Church History and later in 1904 of Isaac G. Matthews as professor of Old Testament, raised serious questions about the spirituality of the university as a Baptist school. The leader of the antagonistic forces was Elmore Harris, pastor at Toronto's Walmer Road Baptist Church who was joined by Thomas Todhunter Shields, pastor of Jarvis Street Baptist Church in Toronto. In 1909 Harris brought charges to the University Senate against Matthews that he consistently made disparaging remarks about the early chapters of Genesis as well as other contradictions in the Old Testament. Matthews was vindicated in both the Senate and in the following year at the Baptist Convention Assembly. The Rev. Harris, who had been appointed to the editorial committee in the United States to produce the series of doctrinal tracts called *The Fundamentals* (see chapter 5), was not amused to see the Senate report state that Professor Matthews was sound in the "fundamentals."

Elmore Harris died in 1912 while on a mission trip to Burma. The battle for McMaster had been given over to T. T. Shields. For the next decade he relentlessly pursued McMaster for its supposed lack of orthodoxy. Although Prof. Matthews resigned in 1919 to move to New Haven, Connecticut and eventually to Crozer Seminary near Philadelphia, Shields continued to hone his skills as a warrior for orthodoxy. He cherished the thought of becoming a successor to C. H. Spurgeon as pastor of the Metropolitan Tabernacle in London when the pulpit came open in 1919. Admirably gifted and self-taught like the Prince of Preachers, Shields was naturally combative and an opponent of liberalism wherever it raised its head. He was exceedingly disappointed when he did not receive the call to the Tabernacle. McMaster historian Charles Johnston believes Shields redoubled his attacks upon McMaster in light of losing the Spurgeonic opportunity. The pastor of Jarvis Street had plenty of reason to be enraged when McMaster in 1923 granted an honorary degree to Brown University president William H. P. Faunce, an internationally known advocate of religious liberalism and the target of fundamentalist investigators in the Northern Baptist Convention. Shields took this move as an affront to conservative evangelicals in the Ontario and Quebec Convention, and it became the first issue of his new campaign to take control of McMaster. A second major eruption occurred in 1925 over yet another faculty appointment to McMaster, that of L. H. Marshall to the chair in pastoral theology. Although Dean Jones Farmer defended Marshall as an exponent of cherished Baptist principles, Shields presented evidence against him from English sources that he was guilty of modernistic teaching. Again the Senate gave Marshall a clean bill of health and the subsequent session of the Baptist Convention of Ontario and Quebec (BCOQ) likewise turned down a potential investigation of Marshall's theology, producing a sharp slap in the face for the overzealous Shields. Shields was ready for the outcome and had amassed a following that we shall see below produced a new come-outer brand of Baptists in Canada.

Rift in the Northern Baptist Convention

Fundamentalism gave birth to four new Baptist groups, two born in the Northern Baptist Convention, one in the Southern Baptist Convention, and one in the Canadian Baptist context. From the Northern Baptists came the General Association of Regular Baptists and the later Conservative Baptist Association. From the Southern Baptists the World

Baptist, the Baptist Bible Fellowship, and the Southwide Baptist Fellowship made new roads in Baptist identity.

The General Association of Regular Baptist Churches, formed in 1932, was the direct heir to the fundamentalist movement of Northern Baptists in the 1920s. As discussed in chapter 5, the militant fundamentalists in the NBC coalesced into the Baptist Bible Union (BBU) in 1923. This provided a forum for about five years, but then lost its effectiveness due to lack of success in pressing their agenda in the NBC annual meetings, embarrassment over the collapse of Des Moines University, and the personal failures of J. Frank Norris. Most problematic was the organizational nature of the BBU, comprised of individuals rather than congregations. T. T. Shields in Canada, William Bell Riley, J. Frank Norris, and Robert Ketcham were all in search of a more effective means to carry forth the objectives of Baptist fundamentalism. The last meeting of the BBU was held in 1930, though after a lackluster annual meeting in Buffalo the previous year, the Union was practically finished.

In his paper, *The Gospel Witness*, T. T. Shields issued a call to the "Regular Baptist Brotherhood" in April 1932 to meet in Chicago to set forth a more adequate organization. At the Belden Avenue Baptist Church in Chicago a new body was born, the General Association of Regular Baptist Churches. As far as records go, Shields first used the terminology "Regular Baptists" in an editorial to characterize those Baptists who held the high spiritual principles for which Baptists have stood from apostolic days down to the present, principally the inspiration, inerrancy, infallibility, and authority of the Bible.[16] Following terminology in the time-honored Edward T. Hiscox's *Standard Manual for Baptist Churches* (1890), Robert Ketcham stressed the nature of the Association as a voluntary society that is entirely of human creation for mutual support and outreach. Of course it was a general association to cover all regions and local associations and to avoid the frequent use of the term "national" amongst Northern Baptists. One analysis has stressed that the strongest sentiment among those organizing the GARBC was the separationist stance against the perceived apostasy of the Northern Baptist Convention.[17] The first years would witness a continual struggle to find a positive direction out of what seemed to be an overly negative raison d'être.

As the Association took shape it was sharply defined theologically: revelation over rationalism, creationism over evolutionism, trinitarianism over unitarianism, and regeneration over reformation. Three doctrinal confessions were at first accepted: the London, Philadelphia, and the

New Hampshire Confessions of Faith. Practically, churches related to the GARBC were to be independent of the Northern Convention and dedicated to the spread of the gospel in all the world. Unlike its predecessor, the Association purposed to assist churches to secure safe, sound, and satisfactory pastors and needy churches. Following the lead of the New Hampshire Confession, the Association was local-church in orientation and strongly premillennial.

Personalities played a large role in the first decades of the GARBC. The principal leader was Robert Ketcham, pastor of Central Baptist Church, Gary, Indiana. Ketcham (1889–1978) was among the most forceful proponents of militant fundamentalism in the BBU of the later 1920s. Joining him were Harry Hamilton of First Baptist, Buffalo, New York; Earl Griffith of Toledo, Ohio; and David Otis Fuller, the first editor of the *Baptist Bulletin*. Ketcham was the president and guiding light of the Association in its early history, criticized by many as a "one-man outfit." In 1938, largely at the behest of Ketcham, then in his fourth term, the annual meeting delegates created a Council of Fourteen to make policy and supervise the GARBC. Ketcham continued on the Council and as editor of the paper, ultimately overshadowing titanic personalities like William Bell Riley, J. Frank Norris, and T. T. Shields, who made attempts to secure the Association's influence in the northern states for themselves. Norris was especially threatening to the survival of the Association and to President Ketcham, whom he referred to as a "smart alec . . . with a large waistband."[18] Ketcham responded by demonstrating to the Association Credentials Committee that Norris's application for membership in the Association was bogus, and the application was denied.

Having resolved its theological identity, the Council of Fourteen (later Eighteen) turned to matters of ministerial training and missions. Dismissive of universities and theological schools as promotive of theological liberalism, the GARBC adopted the Bible college pattern for its leadership training. Beginning in 1932 as the Association itself was taking shape, the Baptist Bible Seminary was founded in Johnson City, New York. In 1968 the school moved to Clark's Summit, Pennsylvania, and became Baptist Bible College, inclusive of a graduate school in theology, added in 1972. Its faculty has been much influenced by Dallas Theological Seminary and an early dean and fundamentalist Baptist theologian, Emery Bancroft. A second school, founded in 1927 and recognized by the GARBC, was Los Angeles Baptist Theological Seminary; after some realignments in the 1940s it moved to Tacoma, Washington, as the Northwest Bible Seminary. In 1941 the Baptist Bible Institute of Grand Rapids opened with approval from GARBC, later to evolve as a Bible college and seminary. In Ohio, the Baptist Bible Institute of Cleveland began in 1942, later to become Cedarville College, the first accredited liberal arts school of Regular Baptists. In the southwest, where a number of Regular Baptists had retired, the Phoenix Bible Institute was established in 1935, later relocating to Oakland, California, and still later to Salem, Oregon. Lastly, the Omaha Bible Institute affiliated with the GARBC in 1956 and was renamed Faith Baptist Bible College in Ankeny, Iowa. For much of the twentieth century, the ideal of education in GARBC schools was Bible instruction from a conservative evangelical, premillennial perspective, essentially to train evangelistic Christian workers, missionaries, and church planters.

As the missionary enterprise had been basic in the critique of Northern Baptists, Regular Baptists were careful to scrutinize their engagement with theologically sound organizations. At the outset, the Association did not seek to create a new missions society, in large part because financial resources were lacking and also because two organizations had come into being that met the expectations of fundamentalist Baptists, Baptist Mid-Missions (1920) and the Association of Baptists for World Evangelism (1927). Instead, the GARBC created an ongoing accrediting process whereby each year mission organizations are assessed and if possible GARBC representatives have served on the respective boards. The first approved was the General Council of Cooperating Baptist Mid Missions, the second was the Association of Baptists for Evangelism in the Orient. Later, the Evangelical Baptist Mission (1938), the Hiawatha Baptist Mission (founded 1921), and the Fellowship of Baptists for Home Missions (founded 1941) were added to the list of approved organizations. To administer its work, at first the Association worked from the location of its presidents, typically in churches. The Association built its headquarters at Schaumburg, Illinois, in 1977. The International Resource Center includes Regular Baptist Press and executive offices for program divisions. The geographical spread of the Association has been essentially in Pennsylvania, New York, the Great Lakes, and California.

As the General Association of Regular Baptists wrestled with its future in the 1930s and 1940s, another progeny of Northern Baptist fundamentalism came forth. Those fundamentalists who had followed William Bell Riley in his long pursuit to claim a position in the NBC for fundamentalists, plus the more moderate wing of the movement, wearied after repeated attempts to change the course of liberal trends. The Conservative Baptist movement was a long-term reaction of more moderate fundamentalists to policies of the Northern Baptist Convention. Early on, it amounted to a reaction against the so-called inclusive policy of foreign mission appointments in the American Baptist Foreign Mission Society. That dimension is discussed at length in chapter 9 below.

What began as the Fundamentalist Fellowship, whose leaders included prominent pastors and the leading Baptist editor of the northern states, was planned as a recognized cooperating agency within the NBC. This proved to be unacceptable as a potentially competitive and divisive force in an already galvanized denominational family. Stage Two saw the Fellowship become the Conservative Baptist Foreign Mission Society, and Stage Three came naturally as numbers of congregations withdrew their support from NBC programs. Among the burning issues were the 1944 purchase by the convention-related American Baptist Publication and Education Society of Lawsonia, an estate in Wisconsin that became the American Baptist Assembly and national retreat center. Many felt the purchase was fiscally unwise in a time of war and criticized Luther Wesley Smith, head of the Publication Society and recently merged Board of Education. Another divisive issue was the redoubled membership of the Northern Baptist Convention in the Federal Council of Churches and international ecumenical organizations like the Faith and Order and Life and Work movements. In 1946 the Fellowship officially became a new Baptist subdenomination, the Conservative Baptist Fellowship. Myron Cedarholm, an early executive of the Conservative movement, characterized this new coalition as "a confessional body, and a fellowship of independent churches with no organic relations to the organizations its churches support."[19] A strong-willed fundamentalist, Chester E. Tulga, became research director and chief apologist for the group, writing a series of booklets critical of rising ecumenism in the NBC.

In the 1950s, the Conservative Baptist Fellowship continued to strengthen its identity. The Conservative Baptist Home Mission Society was formed in 1948 and began work in Alaska, and among Indian tribes. Next came educational initiatives, the first being the establishment in 1950 of the Conservative Baptist Seminary in Denver, Colorado by Vernon Grounds. John Marvin Dean, associated with Northern Baptist Seminary in Chicago, had founded Western (Conservative) Baptist Seminary in 1927 in Portland, Oregon, that joined forces with the Conservative Baptist movement in 1951. The umbrella national organization came to be the Conservative Baptist Association of America (CBA) and, through its visionary executive leadership, it resolved the perpetual problem of independent congregations and central organizations.

The CBA was destined to suffer one additional defining schism that pertained to theological confessionalism, interaction with liberal organizations, and separationist missions, the latter discussed in chapter 9 below. Younger, leading pastors opposed the executive directions of the CBA, in particular calling for a premillennial doctrinal stance, less openness to scholarship, social activism, and the neo-evangelical movement rising around theologians like Bernard Ramm and Carl F. H. Henry. This new "militant minority" was headed up by Richard Clearwaters, Monroe Parker, and G. Archer Weniger. Clearwaters, from his Minnesota pastoral base, criticized Billy Graham and the National Association of Evangelicals as he pushed toward a new organization, the New Testament Association of Independent Baptist Churches, founded in 1964. He also spearheaded a new seminary of his own style, Central Baptist Seminary in Minneapolis.

History Repeats Itself Among Southern Baptists

Among Baptists in the South, the come-outer potential had equally disintegrative effects similar to those among the northern Baptist churches. A precursor movement could be seen in the Landmarkist coalitions around the turn of the century. Benjamin Marquis Bogard was the leading agitator of the renewed Landmarkists. Bogard (1868–1951), was a feisty local church protectionist from Kentucky, and came to take offense at several aspects of what he called "conventionism."[20] Often compared to Abraham Lincoln in his humble upbringing, he was poorly educated. The great Landmarkist, J. R. Graves, whom Bogard thought to be the most influential thinker among Baptists in America, convinced him to give up the convention system; during his early pastoral ministry, Bogard had observed the ever-present tendency among Baptists in his region to lapse back into conventionism. He learned more as an editor of the *Arkansas Baptist*. In 1904 he became its sole editor. From the pages of his paper and other publications like *Pillars of Orthodoxy or Defenders of the Faith* (1900) and *The Baptist Way-Book* (1908) he made a case for Bible Christianity, a regenerate church membership, absolutely independent, democratic congregations with equality in membership and in the ministry.[21] Following closely the tradition of J. R. Graves and Amos Dayton, Bogard wrote, "The church is never larger than a local congregation that can meet in one place. The local individual church is the only kind of church God has on this earth today. There are thousands of churches of God on earth. Each individual Baptist church is a church of God. NO OTHERS ARE."[22] In over two hundred public debates he railed against the overly authoritarian tendencies of the Southern Baptist Convention and defended Baptist principles as he held them against Campbellism (see below), Whitsettism (see chapter 4), and conventionism. He founded a publishing company, a national association of Landmark Baptists in 1905, a Sunday School Concern, and aided two Baptist colleges and a new Landmarkist seminary. In the latter years of his ministry he advocated prohibition and was vehemently antievolution.

Bogard's contribution to the come-outer tradition of Baptists had been set in the context of the contemporary history of the Southern Baptist Convention. From the mid-1890s he had served southern Baptist-related congregations in Missouri and Arkansas. The Arkansas State Convention became the immediate context in which his antagonisms surfaced. In 1901 he strenuously opposed the creation of a secretary for home mission work and identified strong currents of voting manipulation and "wire-pulling" that he labeled ecclesiastical politics and "conventionism." It seemed to Bogard and other Landmarkists that the Convention was seeking to establish an authority over the local churches. He and a group of younger pastors organized a new body in 1902, the General Association of Arkansas Baptist Churches, realizing there was no hope of working with the convention because of the principles involved. The historian of Baptist life in Arkansas noted that this separation from the mainstream state convention was a turning point: as churches and associations split, the institutional cohesion of Baptists in the state was destroyed, and a formal organization of Landmarkists was born.[23] Over a hundred and fifty congregations, many of whom called themselves "missionary Baptists," joined the breakaway body. For a time a "Peace Plan" seemed possible, but ultimately, the feelings of enmity were too great and the General Association refused to disband, a key demand of the Convention. Bogard himself began to create a publishing empire as editor of the *Arkansas Baptist* and producer of Sunday school literature. He visited the Southern Baptist annual meeting in Nashville in 1904 and concluded that the SBC was drifting toward episcopacy. His next move was to call for a national organization of Landmarkists. The initial meeting of the Baptist General Association of the United States met at Texarkana and elected Bogard as clerk. When the SBC rejected the demands that Bogard presented to them in 1905, the breach that then involved one hundred congregations and 12 states was permanent. Over the next two decades, Bogard sought to bring the other major Landmarkist organization, the Baptist Missionary Association in Texas, into the national body. He enunciated "Baptist principles" like regenerate membership, the independent democratic nature of local churches, and the equality of membership and ministry in his maturing thought.[24] Apparently Bogard was too energetic in his design to unite all Landmark Baptists, because he became embroiled in 1915–16 in a bitter debate with S. H. Slaughter in Texas and offended the Baptist Missionary Association. Moreover in 1918, Bogard himself was accused of being publicly drunk in Princeton, Arkansas, an offense to the teetotalism of most Baptists in the South. Other leaders, less sullied with controversy, with Bogard's support, created a unification movement in 1920 that bore fruit in 1924 with the coalition of Landmark Baptists from Kentucky and Tennessee, the General Association based in Arkansas, and the BMA in Texas, as the American Baptist Association (ABA). The ABA was doctrinally fundamentalist in every point, plus in its own unique Landmarkist positions that the Great Commission was given to the churches only, and that all cooperative bodies should be servants of the churches. Bogard assisted the Association in establishing the Missionary Baptist Seminary in 1924 and the related Missionary Baptist Printery. The American Baptist Association has continued through the turn of the next century to safeguard Landmarkist theology and a regional form of Baptist witness confined largely to the Southwest. Bogard himself demonstrated that the rising Southern Baptist Convention was not immune to schism and he provided an important model for the come-outers.

Yet another schism developed among Landmark Baptists in the 1950s. Never entirely satisfied with the Texas/Arkansas amalgamation that led to the formation of the ABA, a group of dissident Texas pastors met at Little Rock in 1950 and formed the North American Baptist Association. Describing itself as evangelical, missionary, fundamental, and premillennial, it had all the marks of blending historic Landmark tenets with recent fundamentalism. Historian Leon McBeth has also pointed out that a succession of churches since Christ became a doctrinal tenet with this group. In the 1950s and 1960s, slowly the process of institutionalization took place with the creation of women's and men's auxiliaries, publishing, colleges, camps, and a seminary at Jacksonville, Texas. Eschewing the term "north" because of its connection with ecumenism, modernism, and kindred evils, in 1969 the Association took the new name, Baptist Missionary Association of America (BMAA). Though in recent decades the BMAA has spread into 29 states, its strength is still in Texas and Arkansas.

Contemporary with Bogard and the Landmarkists, J. Frank Norris provided the next example of Baptist come-outerism among Southern Baptists. Emerging from the fundamentalist crusades of the 1920s,

Norris of Fort Worth conducted a bitter and often personal crusade against the leadership of the Southern Baptist Convention. As a student at Baylor University, Norris had locked horns with J. B. Gambrell, and the bitterness continued over time and distance as Gambrell became the leader of the Baptist General Convention of Texas and Norris became pastor at First Baptist, Fort Worth. Norris had further joined forces with northern and Canadian fundamentalists in the World's Christian Fundamentals Association (1919) and later within the fundamentalist Baptist fold, the Baptist Bible Union (1923). Under the latter umbrella, he spearheaded a project to assume control of Des Moines (Iowa) University to make it a center of American fundamentalism. In his rise to leadership of dissident factions, Norris was ousted from the Southern Baptist Pastor's Conference in 1914, from the Tarrant County Baptist Association in 1922, and from the Baptist General Convention of Texas in 1924. A born leader and motivator, Norris formed his own movement, the Premillennial Fundamental Missionary Fellowship, in 1931. This later became the World Fundamental Baptist Missionary Fellowship, and still later the Bible Baptist Fellowship, inclusive of a "seminary" and a mission-sending program. From 1935 to 1951, Norris served concurrently First Baptist, Fort Worth, and Temple Baptist Church in Detroit, Michigan, as well as broadcasting regularly on the radio.

Norris's brand of Baptist fundamentalism was a combination of unflinching biblical literalism and antimodern social and political positions. He was a staunch defender of the verbal plenary inspiration of the Scriptures, a position that Prof. Louis Gaussen of Geneva and others espoused in the nineteenth century in the face of biblical criticism. Norris wrote, "the big issue is the verbal inspiration of Scriptures and if there is no verbal inspiration we have no inspiration."[25] Norris defended a premillennialist interpretation of the return of Christ, built upon a strong doctrine of inspiration, that was a powerful, threatening tool of evangelism. The premillennialist view is the only missionary motive . . . ," he wrote, "not to clean out the stables, but to redeem the individual men and women."[26] This led Norris to accept a Zionist perspective on the future of Israel, which often turned into anti-Semitic rhetoric. Characteristic of his southwestern Southern Baptist context, Norris was vehemently "local church" in his ecclesiology. He rejected denominationalism in any form except that which he controlled. As he observed the movement toward ecumenical cooperation and even the formation of a Baptist world alliance, he denounced "unionizing tendencies" and referred to the BWA as "the biggest cuckoo framework ever known among Baptists."[27] His social objective was simply to restore the nineteenth century as a time of homogeneous values within an evangelical orthodoxy. Like other firebrands of fundamentalism, he railed against evolution, alcohol consumption, the New Deal, foreign alliances, German militarism (which he equated with German scholarship), communism, and higher education. Ever the flamboyant promoter of his causes, Norris staged a public funeral for "John Barleycorn" upon passage of the Eighteenth Amendment (Prohibition), and a baptism in the Detroit River which 40 thousand people attended. In his original Southern context, J. Frank Norris conducted a battle royal against the forces of modernism that threatened his culture and he became the most belligerent fundamentalist in the land, according to *The Christian Century*.[28] He had, most observers would agree, shifted the thrust and force of Baptist fundamentalism from the North to the South.

A major rift in Norris's movement occurred in 1949–50 when his song-leader and copastor, G. Beauchamp Vick, broke away and led in the formation of the Baptist Bible Fellowship (BBF). The disagreement was bitter and Norris vilified Vick in cartoons and editorials. With the breach of 1950, a new generation of fundamentalists thus grew from the Norris taproot. In 1952 Norris turned the control of his pastorates and the administration of Bible Baptist Seminary and the Arlington Baptist Schools in Fort Worth over to Louis Entzminger, his Sunday school superintendent in Fort Worth. The Norris movement itself withered and became a relatively minor player in the religious politics of southern fundamentalism. On the other hand, Beauchamp Vick was able to unite anti-Norris churches across the Midwest and South in the new Fellowship. He began a school in Springfield, Missouri, the Baptist Bible College, that became the leading institution of its type among Baptists.[29] The BBF was as militantly fundamentalist as Norris had been, but also highly successful in planting new megacongregations in strategic cities. Graduates of the Baptist Bible College became known for "soul-winning evangelism" and extraordinary means like school bus ministries to build up large Sunday schools. Model congregations sprang up in the 1960s in Connersville and Anderson, Indiana; Riverdale, Maryland; Decatur, Georgia; and Lynchburg, Virginia, the latter of which Jerry Falwell began in 1956. While continuing to relate to the Baptist Bible Fellowship, Falwell in turn created his own movement, the Liberty Baptist Fellowship, in 1977, to enlarge the outreach of his church,Thomas Road Baptist, and his own sociopolitical agenda.[30] The main thrust of the Liberty Baptist Fellowship is a pastors' conference and support of Liberty University, over which Falwell has served as chancellor. In the late 1990s, Falwell began to identify himself with the reorganized Southern Baptist Convention and has for several years been on the speaking circuit among prominent SBC churches and institutions. Thus from J. Frank Norris, three major Baptist subgroups are derived: the World Baptist Fellowship, the Baptist Bible Fellowship, and the Liberty Baptist Fellowship.

Another come-outer group from Southern Baptist ranks was the Southwide Baptist Fellowship (SBF). The SBF was born in the disaffection of Lee Roberson, pastor for over five decades of the Highland Baptist Church in Chattanooga, Tennessee, with the Southern Baptist Convention. Roberson, once the confidant of Southern Baptist luminaries Robert G. Lee and W. A. Criswell, came under the influence of Bob Jones University in Greenville, South Carolina and John R. Rice, a militant fundamentalist editor of the *Sword of the Lord* newspaper. Roberson started the Tennessee Temple Schools, inclusive of a high school, a college, and a seminary, to train independent-minded Baptist preachers and workers, and he used his pulpit to attack evidences of liberalism and ecumenism in the SBC. Roberson soon became a pariah in SBC circles and was eventually voted out of the local Baptist association. His response was to create in 1956 the Southwide Baptist Fellowship, at first a voluntary fellowship of 147 independent Baptist churches, many of which had also been ejected from SBC associations. By 2000, the SBF encompassed local churches in the Southeast and Deep South, numbering about one thousand churches; it focuses its energies on inspirational rallies, Bible conferences, and great preaching. For many years Roberson was the leading figure in the Fellowship, especially targeting neo-evangelicals whom he thought had infiltrated, for the worse, the ranks of the mainstream conventions. In 2003, after Roberson's death, discussions between the SBF, the Baptist Bible Fellowship, and the World Baptist Fellowship, generated interest in greater cooperation among Baptist fundamentalists in the South. This led to the creation in September 2004 of the International Baptist Network, composed of the three groups. An immediate negative reaction occurred to the Network among those loyal to the *Sword of the Lord* and Bob Jones University. The latter faction opposed cooperation with Southern Baptist Convention leaders and churches and maintains a strict separationist stance with respect to cooperation with any other groups.

Spillover Back to Canada

Similar to the context of emerging fundamentalism in the United States, Baptists in central and western Canada identified with and joined the efforts of the Baptist Bible Union and other manifestations of the militant form of the movement. The leader of this trend, T. T. Shields, had led the attack upon McMaster University and the Convention through his paper, the *Gospel Witness*, and his new theological school, Toronto Baptist Seminary. Shields so deeply antagonized the leadership of the Baptist Convention of Ontario and Quebec, that by 1926 the BCOQ approved a resolution to censure him if he refused to apologize for his virulent attacks on the Convention. The BCOQ then applied to the provincial legislature to change its charter to allow for disciplinary action upon unruly congregations. With this new authority, plans were laid to expel up to 11 congregations. Shields met the inevitable by calling a meeting of those interested in forming a "missionary convention" early in 1927. With the support of some prominent Toronto Baptist citizens, Shields organized the Regular Baptist Missionary and Educational Society of Canada, clearly a come-outer effort. The choice of the terminology "Regular Baptists" was intended to cast aspersion upon the Convention Baptists who, Shields held, had taken on a liberal character and become "irregular" in their practice of Baptist principles. "Regular" became synonymous with "evangelical." The new organization sought alternative directions in home and foreign missions, and in 1927 Toronto Baptist Seminary opened as an evangelical alternative to McMaster University.

Fundamentalist Baptists also began to emerge in the life of the Baptist Union of Western Canada in the early 1920s. Again, the charges of liberal teaching in a Baptist school were leveled against Brandon College in Manitoba in 1920–21, where Professor Harris MacNeill was accused of undermining historic Christianity. MacNeill was exonerated but the evangelical coalition led by Andrew Grieve hardened its stance and would not allow the issues to die. In 1925, the evangelicals formed the British Columbia Missionary Council to work within the Convention, much as moderate fundamentalists had done in the United States. The Council began publication of its own magazine, *The British Columbia Baptist*, and began to accept affiliating congregations that numbered 16 within a year. Soon notices appeared of an executive committee, a missionary budget, young peoples' and women's organizations. At the 1926 British Columbia Baptist Convention, the evangelical attempt to assert a doctrinal statement was defeated and the separation took definite shape. The following year, the BC Missionary Council members withdrew from the Convention to constitute the Convention of Regular Baptist Churches of British Columbia. The historic meeting to organize western fundamentalist Baptists was held at Mount Pleasant Baptist Church in Vancouver on Dominion Day, July 1, a memorable occasion for Canadians. As historian Leslie Tarr reported, 1,600 members, or about one third of the membership of the British Columbia Baptist Convention, joined the new movement.[31]

By the end of 1927 important steps had been taken to create a Trans-Canada fellowship of fundamentalist Baptists. Soon after the creation of the Regular Baptist Missionary and Educational Society, it evolved into a chartered body, the Union of Regular Baptist Churches of Ontario and Quebec, virtually imitating the BCOQ. Shields was elected president of the Union for much of its history until 1949. He controlled the *Gospel Witness* from Jarvis Street Church and the Toronto Baptist Seminary was based at the church. Even so, the Union claimed 10,000 members in 89 congregations by 1930. Domestic missionary work moved ahead with focus upon French Canada and southwestern Ontario. Likewise, foreign efforts included Liberia and Europe. But Shields's authoritarian leadership in the Union began to create rifts that threatened its vitality. In 1931 nine ministers left the Union. In 1948 Shields dismissed the dean of the Seminary, W. Gordon Brown, who promptly started a new school, Central Baptist Seminary, also in Toronto. Support for Shields's leadership declined and the epicenter moved away from Jarvis Street Church in 1950. The Union office was shifted to Montreal, a new paper, the *Union Baptist Witness,* came into publication, and Jarvis Street Church left the Union to become independent. Shields had run a similar course to that of his old fundamentalist friend, J. Frank Norris toward the conclusion of his career.

A second major come-outer group emerged from the rift in the BCOQ and the Union: the Independent Baptist Fellowship. Commencing in 1931 three hundred Baptists from 23 churches gathered at a rally in Brantford, Ontario to form a Baptist Fellowship among some of the churches that had withdrawn from Shields's Union. In September 1933 they constituted themselves the Fellowship of Independent Baptist Churches of Canada at a meeting at Eglinton Baptist Church in Toronto. This group adopted a fundamentalist doctrinal statement that was also premillennial, much like the GARBC in the US. The Fellowship planted congregations across the country, was open to cooperation with the Union, and the churches of the Baptist General Conference in Canada. A paper, the *Fellowship Baptist,* maintained communications among the churches, a pastor's pension fund was started, and many of the pastors were educated at Central Baptist Seminary. One of the assets of the Fellowship was the Muskoka Baptist Conference retreat center, purchased in 1931. An energetic effort was made to plant churches in francophone Quebec and this outdistanced the efforts of Convention Baptists that were older and broader.

The Union of Regular Baptist Churches of Ontario and Quebec, freed from Shields's control, recognized its theological and practical affinities with the Fellowship of Independent Baptist Churches and by 1950 the two fundamentalist organizations of churches began to discuss closer relationships. Several joint meetings of pastors and rallies of youth led to discussion of a merger of "Bible-believing Baptists into a solid-front Evangelical Baptist testimony in Canada."[32] This was effected on June 18, 1953 and the first joint meeting of the Fellowship of Evangelical Baptist Churches of Canada with 200 congregations and 15,000 members was held in Cooke's Presbyterian Church in Toronto. Their stated objective was to plant a Baptist church in every community in Canada. Since 1953 the Fellowship has progressed to include the Regular Baptist Missionary Fellowship in the West (1963) and the Convention of Regular Baptist Churches of British Columbia (1965). The Fellowship has spawned educational institutions, the Western Baptist Bible College in Alberta, and the London Baptist Bible College in southwestern Ontario. Later, in 1993 the London school and Central Baptist Seminary would merge into the Heritage Baptist College and Seminary in Cambridge, Ontario. The Fellowship's institutional manifestation also includes a central headquarters site that has remained in Toronto at "Fellowship House," and later in enlarged facilities that were built in honor of the national centennial in 1967. As the official historian observed in 1968, "The expanding Fellowship operation required more adequate facilities,"[33] thus marking its maturing status as a major subgroup of Baptists in Canada.

Individual Come-outers

Not all Baptist examples of come-outers remained within a Baptist frame of reference. Some notable personalities, in their efforts to modify Baptist principles to their liking, bolted from the Baptist fold altogether. Generally speaking, most held onto certain Baptist traces, notably biblical authority, congregational independence, and vivid religious experience.

One of the most far-reaching examples of Baptist come-outerism occurred in the pilgrimage of Thomas and Alexander Campbell. Thomas, a pastor in Ireland of a Seceder Presbyterian Church, emigrated in 1807 to western Pennsylvania for reasons of health. He settled among Scotch-Irish Seceders in Washington County but fell into disagreement with them over doctrinal issues. He formed a new body called the Christian Association of Washington, dedicated to church cooperation, the use of the Bible over creeds, and voluntary support for Christian endeavors. His son, Alexander Campbell, fresh from study at Glasgow University and work under the Haldane Brothers in Edinburgh, lent support to his father's cause. Unsuccessful in linking up with local Presbyterians, the Campbells faced the question of baptism and were immersed, along with several members of their congregation, at Brush Run. Essentially a Baptist church at that point, the congregation applied for membership in the Redstone Baptist Association and was accepted in 1813.

During the next decade and a half of the Campbell's sojourn among Baptists, sharp differences emerged. The Campbells did not like doctrinal examinations prior to baptism and practiced the Lord's Supper every week, as was the custom in the New Testament. Alexander Campbell did not recognize the validity of the Old Testament Law, but chose to live under the covenant of grace, and he denied that regeneration occurred prior to faith. More seriously for mainstream Baptists, he began in the 1820s to advocate baptismal regeneration. In a famous debate with a Presbyterian minister of Kentucky, Campbell asserted, "The water of baptism, then, formally washes away our sins. The blood of Christ really washes away our sins . . . Paul's sins were really pardoned when he believed. Yet he had no solemn pledge of the fact, no formal acquittal, no formal purgation of his sins until he washed them away in the water of baptism."[34] In an era of rapid development of schools and missionary societies, Campbell referred to clergy as "hireling priests," theological schools as "priest factories," and associations as "tyrannous." His chief forums were public debates and his newspaper, the *Christian Baptist.*

Between 1825 and 1830, the Campbellite movement was a serious deterrent to missionary work because Alexander had opposed societies external to the local church. A significant number of Baptist congregations came out of their associations to join Campbell. Gradually, Baptist associations took action against Campbellism and in 1830 Campbell himself reorganized his followers as "Disciples of Christ." The greatest impact of Campbellism came in western Pennsylvania, Ohio, Kentucky, Indiana, and Illinois in the United States, as well as in Upper Canada. For the most part, Baptists declared Campbell's teachings heretical, as they did the similar movement of Barton Stone called the "Christians."

Sidney Rigdon exemplifies how far-ranging a Baptistic orientation can extend. In 1817 Rigdon joined a Regular Baptist church in Ohio and for two years lived with Adamson Bentley, a Baptist minister at Warren, Ohio. Bentley mentored Rigdon and the latter was ordained there in 1821. That same year Rigdon was called to be the pastor at

First Baptist, Pittsburgh, Pennsylvania, where he served for three years. Within a short time he developed an interest in the primitive New Testament churches and began to influence the congregation to move to a simpler order of worship. The church did not accept Rigdon's ideas on the ancient order and he resigned in 1824 to follow closely the teachings of Alexander Campbell, whom he had come to know in the region. He returned to Ohio and served Campbellite churches at Mantua and Mentor before breaking with Campbell. Rigdon by then had developed his own ecclesiology that entailed a communal society and a belief in a literal reign of Christ on earth, neither one of which was compatible with Campbell's beliefs. In 1826 he accepted the call of an independent church at Kirtland, Ohio, and there he met Joseph Smith of the newly organized Church of Jesus Christ of the Latter Day Saints. Rigdon supported Smith's interpretations and affirmed the supernatural origins of the Book of Mormon. He invited Smith to move to Ohio where the two became leaders in the evolution of the Latter Day Saints. As far as Rigdon's Baptist background is concerned, he is mentioned only tangentially in Pittsburgh Baptist history.

Baptists had long had an interest in eschatological matters and this has come to a peak at several points in their history: during the Cromwell Protectorate in England 1648–60, at the turn of the nineteenth century in writings of pastors like Isaac Backus, and in the mid-nineteenth century. The primary advocate of renewed interest in this doctrine in the US was William Miller, a lay pastor in the Baptist church at Low Hampton, New York. Raised a Calvinistic Baptist, licensed to preach at Low Hampton (on the state border with Vermont), and in constant correspondence with a New York Baptist pastor, Truman Hendryx, and Elders Smith and Fuller in Vermont, Miller was described as a conservative student of the Bible, always tending toward the literal interpretation, and aided only by his concordance. Miller's 1822 interpretation, that "I believe the second coming of Jesus Christ is near, even at the door, even within twenty one years, or on or before 1843,"[35] conflicted with common Baptist postmillennialism, the belief that after the churches evangelized the world, Christ would return to establish his kingdom. Miller actually calculated that the Return of the Lord would take place on March 21, 1843, a date he later modified to October 22, 1844. He lectured widely 1834–44 and drew vast crowds to his gatherings. Often, it was better-educated Baptist clergy who became his worst critics, and this reinforced Miller's anticlerical bias from his early career as a lay preacher. Oddly, Miller is not to be classed with other Baptist revivalists or ultraists in the New York State of his era, whom he referred to as "fire-skulled, visionary, fanatical, treasonable, suicidal, demoralizing, hot-headed" abolitionist types that he deemed were descended from the Antimasons. Such reckless enthusiasts repulsed him.[36] Many Baptists also joined the Millerites, including Elon Galusha, a leader among New York State Missionary Baptists. Though the disappointment that ensued was great when Miller's date(s) did not materialize, many congregations continued their interest in the question and were bolstered by Plymouth Brethren teachings later in the century. Although it was possible to remain within the Baptist fold and hold premillennial views,[37] some congregations in the Northeast came out of their denominational relationship and became independent or Brethren in orientation. Millerism made such an impact upon New Jersey Baptists that the Central Association in 1843 was compelled to warn its churches not to be deceived by "men who have spread the report that Jesus would return in 1843." The Circular Letter refrained from any dogmatic interpretation of the Millennium, except to assert that it would be a state of great happiness and glory to Christians and Jews, perhaps brought to reality by the Bible and Mission Societies that are the forerunners of the "happy, bright and glorious day."[38] As to Miller's later pilgrimage, he had no organizational plans beyond 1844 and returned to Low Hampton to write his story. In 1845 his cohorts held a conference of "Adventists" to consider next steps.

In the twentieth century a well known come-outer from the Baptists was James Robison. Robison began his career as a Southern Baptist pastor and evangelist who held revival meetings in smaller cities in the Southwest in the 1960s and 1970s. Dubbed "God's Angry Man" because of his vituperations against liberalism, higher education, and many in the Southern Baptist Convention, Robison displayed a personal anger that spoke of his troubled upbringing. With the support of Texas Baptists and Billy Graham, Robison founded his own evangelistic association and took to television quite successfully. In 1982 he began to interact with Pentecostals and Charismatics and restyled his work as a "Day of Restoration" by which he hoped to unite fundamentalists and Pentecostals. His public rhetoric softened and he apologized to many whom he had earlier targeted. He appeared with prominent Pentecostals like John Wimber and Jamie Buckingham and, in so doing, he turned away many of his Baptist supporters. In yet another switch of emphases in the 1990s, he and his wife Betty organized Life Reach International, a Christian nondenominational outreach that responds to crises like famine and civil strife, as well as advocating a healthy lifestyle by dietary control and the use of nutritional supplements. His pilgrimage has thus led to a "coming out" of traditional Baptist relationships, while maintaining a militantly biblicist foundation.

Legacy: Biblical Literalism and Baptist Identity

The establishment of the Baptist Bible Union carried forth in denominational terms what had been codified earlier in 1917 by the World's Christian Fundamentals Association, namely an understanding of Scripture as an icon in itself: "The inspiration [of the Bible] includes not only all the books of the Bible in general but in detail, the form as well as the substance, the word as well as the thought."[39] A vocabulary of inerrancy, infallibility, and literalism emerged in the statements of all the fundamentalist groups and each of the mainstream Baptist bodies reflected at length on their understanding of the Bible in defining the faith. What became the standard for conservative evangelicals was an uncompromising view of the Bible as a supernatural book. It is supernatural in its origin (inspired by God which for the common understanding really means a kind of dictation process based upon an interpretation of II Peter 1: 21). It is supernatural in the revelation of its meaning, and it may produce supernatural effects upon its readers. Finally, Baptists believe the Bible is to be revered as a holy, sacred book in itself as articulated in the Pledge of Allegiance to the Bible, said by thousands of Bible school children every summer: "I believe in the Bible as God's Holy Word, a lamp unto my feet and a light unto my path, that I might not sin against God."

Baptist evangelicals came quickly to conclude that missionary endeavor, preaching, philanthropic work, and denominational programs must be based solidly on an authoritative Word of God. At times this was mediated through the language of an anti-Catholic bias such as referring to the Roman papacy as "church tyrants for which the Dark Ages were distinguished," as contrasted with universal education and an "intelligent Christianity."[40] Consequently, when the Northern Baptist Convention refused such doctrinal statements, its educational institutions, missionary societies, and denominational relationships were called into question. The successors in the "come-outer" Baptist groups were transparent in their application of an authoritative word of God to every aspect of Christian endeavor.

On the other hand, a permanent "loyal opposition" of progressive to liberal Baptists finally came into the light of day. Beginning in the scholarship of eighteenth-century Baptist pastor-theologians like Elhanan Winchester, Jonathan Maxcy, and Asa Messer, a less dogmatic approach to Scripture was noticeable among Baptist congregations in the East coast cities. By the 1830s younger Baptist theological teachers like Barnas Sears at Madison University were able to visit Europe and imbibe higher critical understandings of the Bible. This led to a more evolutionary process for how the ancient texts were prepared, edited, and compiled across many centuries. In the seminaries of the nineteenth century, Baptists began to hear about the documentary hypothesis of the origins of the Pentateuch, the multiple authorship of Isaiah, source theories of the Gospels, metaphorical interpretations of the books of Daniel and Revelation, and naturalistic interpretations of Old Testament stories like the parting of the Red Sea and Jonah's "whale." Most startling, perhaps, was the questioning of the miracles of Christ and his Virgin Birth. The Chicago School blatantly asserted the evolutionary nature of all religions and William Newton Clarke, son of a Baptist parsonage, jettisoned his father's proof-text faith for an improved meaning of doctrine mediated through religious experience. Southern Baptist theologian E. Y. Mullins, the most reticent of the turn-of-the-century Baptist theological educators, carefully concurred.

Notes

1 John Smyth, *The Differences of the Churches of the Seperation: Containing A Description of the Leitourgiue and Ministerie of the Visible Church in The Works of John Smyth, Fellow of Christ's College, 1594–8,* ed. W. T. Whitley (Amsterdam: 1608; repr. Cambridge, UK: Cambridge University Press, 1915), I: 271.

2 John Smyth, *Principles and Inferences Concerning the Visible Church* (Amsterdam: 1607; repr. Cambridge, UK: Cambridge University Press, 1915), I: 263.

3 Thomas Helwys to the Singelkirk Mennonite Congregation, 1609 (Correspondence files, City Archives, Amsterdam).

4 Howard Dorgan, *The Old Regular Baptists of Central Appalachia: Brothers and Sisters in Hope* (Knoxville, TN: The University of Tennessee Press, 1988), 152–3.

5 Ibid., 214–15, 223–6.

6 "Wiregrass" refers to the tough grasses that naturally abounded along the low coastal regions.

7 "Minutes of the Richland Creek Church" (1835), quoted in John G. Crowley, *Primitive Baptists of the Wiregrass South: 1815 to the Present* (Gainesville, FL: University Press of Florida, 1998), 71. The term "hetridose" is a colloquialism for "heterodox."

8 For an assessment of these several groups, see John G. Crowley, *Primitive Baptists of the Wiregrass South: 1815 to the Present* (Gainesville, FL: University Press of Florida, 1998), 112–33.

9 Ibid., 164.

10 C. H. Spurgeon: *The Early Years 1834–1859: A Revised Edition of His Autobiography, Compiled by His Wife and Private Secretary* (London: Banner of Truth Trust, 1962), 2, 46, 78.

11 Spurgeon was in one room, the principal in another for up to two hours. Spurgeon at first blamed it on an incompetent maid, but later credited the providence of God. See *C. H. Spurgeon: The Early Years*, 209.

12 Ibid., 480–1.

13 Quoted in Ernest A. Payne, *The Baptist Union: A Short History* (London: The Carey Kingsgate Press, 1959), 142.

14 Ibid.

15 Curtis Wayne Whiteman, "The General Association of Regular Baptist Churches 1932–1970" (PhD dissertation, St. Louis University, 1982), 175.

16 *Gospel Witness* 11 (May 5, 1932), 12.

17 Whiteman, "The General Association of Regular Baptist Churches," 163–4.

18 Quoted in J. Murray Murdoch, *Portrait of Obedience* (Schaumberg, IL: Regular Baptist Press, 1979), 177–8.

19 Bruce L. Shelley, *History of the Conservative Baptists* (Denver, CO: Conservative Baptist Theological Seminary, 1960), 68.

20 A useful biography of Bogard is by Jonathan K. Pratt, "A Landmark Baptist Ecclesiology: Ben M. Bogard and Local Church Protectionism" (PhD dissertation, Baylor University, 2005).

21 Earlier titles reveal his tendencies: *Four Reasons Why I Am A Baptist* (1892) and *Christian Union, or The Problem Solved* (1894).

22 *Orthodox Baptist Searchlight* (August 25, 1939), cited in Pratt, "A Landmark Baptist Ecclesiology," 3.

23 E. Glenn Hinson, *A History of Baptists in Arkansas 1818–1978* (Little Rock, AR: Arkansas Baptist State Convention, 1979), 244. For the Convention Baptists, BMA was a term of derision.

24 *Baptist Commoner*, August 20, 1914, quoted in Pratt, "A Landmark Baptist Ecclesiology," 31.

25 Quoted in C. Allyn Russell, *Voices of Fundamentalism: Seven Biographical Studies* (Philadelphia, PA: Westminster Press, 1976), 26.

26 Ibid., 27.

27 Ibid., 38.

28 See Barry Hankins, *God's Rascal: J. Frank Norris and the Beginnings of Southern Fundamentalism* (Lexington, KY: The University Press of Kentucky, 1996), 28ff.

29 Later institutions include a Baptist Bible College in the Northeast and the Baptist University of America in Doraville, Georgia.

30 Falwell also started the Moral Majority, an evangelical group of activist Christians dedicated to changing public policy toward a strict interpretation of the constitution and the advocacy of conservative moral values.

31 Leslie J. Tarr, *This Dominion, His Dominion: The Story of Evangelical Baptist Endeavour in Canada* (Willowdale, ON: Fellowship of Evangelical Baptist Churches, 1968), 92.

32 Ibid., 130.

33 Ibid., 146.

34 Quoted in Robert G. Torbet, *History of the Baptists* (Valley Forge, PA: Judson Press, 1963), 272.

35 Quoted in Francis D. Nichol, *The Midnight Cry: A Defense of the Character and Conduct of William Miller and the Millerites, Who Mistakenly Believed that the Second Coming of Christ Would Take Place in the Year 1844* (Takoma Park, DC: Review and Herald Publishing Association, 1944), 37.

36 Ibid., 54.

37 Premillennialism experienced a resurgence under the influence of A. J. Gordon, pastor of Clarendon Street Baptist Church in Boston, 1869–95.

38 Norman H. Maring, *Baptists in New Jersey: A Study in Transition* (Valley Forge, PA: Judson Press, 1964), 152–3.

39 James M. Gray, "The Inspiration of the Bible – Definition, Extent and Proof." In *The Fundamentals*, vol. II (Los Angeles, CA: Bible Institute of Los Angeles, 1917), 15.

40 John Mockett Cramp quoted in George Rawlyk (ed.), *The Canadian Protestant Experience 1760–1990* (Burlington, ON: G.R. Welch Co., 1990), 83. Cramp was a long-term Canadian Baptist who had emigrated from England.

Chapter 8
The Uniqueness of African American Baptists

Comprising four major and several minor groups, African American Baptists presently total over 15.7 million members or 46 percent of all Baptists in North America. Of all the Baptist groups, black Baptists are perhaps the most baptistic of all, blending freedom and religious experience. As we have seen, some of their origins lie in congregations gathered in the eighteenth-century slave communities. As they developed an associational life, in a unique consciousness they exhibited both classic Baptist traits and a character directly attributable to their culture. There is a long and substantive debate among historians as to where the black Baptist movement actually commenced. Did it emerge from informal religious gatherings on the plantations, or in the black subcongregations that were included in the white churches, north and south, or in the fully constituted churches that existed with white sanctions at the end of the eighteenth century? The very character of the black experience in North America is at stake in the identification of the proper origins of black Baptist life: black Baptists presently represent 44 percent of the total population of African Americans in the United States.

Initial Coalitions of Black Baptists

As noted earlier, the Separate Baptist experience formed the crucible for the emergence of black Baptists. As important assessments have demonstrated, by emphasizing an inward conversion experience, the Awakening de-emphasized the outward character of individuals in matters of social standing, economic rank, gender, and color. Preaching for an emotive experience was to present a universalistic dimension for the gospel.[1] A scant record exists of white preaching, doubtless Separates, among the slaves in South Carolina as early as 1742. Some time in the 1750s Phillip Mulkey and William Murphy, two Separate Baptist evangelists working in south central Virginia, gathered what is likely the oldest known black slave congregation in the Colonies. It was located on the plantation of William Byrd III on the Bluestone River at Mecklenburg, Virginia. While little is known of that moment, a church was in fact constituted there in 1772 and it has been connected with the Petersburg, Virginia, Church of the 1820s. One of the problems raised in the definition of the Byrd Plantation "church" is that there is a distinct difference between preaching New Light experiences and gathering a congregation under the discipline of a covenant or confession. Historian Albert Raboteau has argued that in the case of slaves, both the experiential and the noetic were complementary for a sustained Christian life.[2] Records suggest that slave attendance was sporadic and that continuity of any kind of church experience such as that of the Caucasian community in the colonies was dubious at best. Preaching to the slaves was, as one contemporary account characterized it, more like filling the heads of slaves "with a parcel of Cant-Phrases, Trances, Dreams, Visions and Revelations."[3]

The next major identifying development occurred in 1773 with the conversion of George Leile, a slave born in Virginia but relocated with his master, Henry Sharpe, to Burke County, Georgia. Sharpe's pastor at Buckhead Creek Baptist Church, Matthew Moore, was the catalyst in Leile's conversion during a sermon he preached in Georgia that much resembled the metaphors in Jonathan Edwards' famous sermon, "Sinners in the Hands of an Angry God." Leile traveled in the Savannah River region, establishing regular preaching points at places like Tybee Island, Yamacraw, and on several plantations. During the Revolution, Leile was freed by virtue of the death of his master and British friends advised him to leave Georgia for the West Indies. Eventually he settled at Kingston, Jamaica, where he pioneered the black Baptist movement there.

In the early 1770s the first congregations of African American Baptists formally emerged in the larger culture. Many argue that the earliest was the congregation which was planted at Silver Bluff, South Carolina. It became the first type of black Baptist congregation in which black preachers led the congregations. Silver Bluff was a trading station near Aiken, about 12 miles from Augusta, Georgia. Among those involved in trade with the backcountry and Indian tribes was George Galphin. Slaves were active in the community tending the extensive warehouse of Galphin. One of the slaves who actually hailed from tidewater Virginia was David George. A conscientious man, he was also a religious seeker. He responded warmly to various preachers who visited the Silver Bluff community and held services there. Both George Leile and Wait Palmer, a Separate Baptist from Connecticut, visited on several occasions. In his journal David George told of his religious conversion under Palmer's preaching and how, when Palmer constituted an African congregation somewhere between 1773 and 1775, David George was part of it. This congregation is rightly credited with being one of the oldest African American Baptist churches in North America, solely under the aegis of black Baptists. In 1775, David George was persuaded to become the first pastor of this historic Silver Bluff Church. A prominent historian of the last century also heralded the compassion and generosity of George Galphin who freed Leile and allowed the meetings on his property.[4]

Another congregation that lays claim to being the first black Baptist church in North America was in the vicinity of Savannah, Georgia. In 1783 en route to Jamaica, the famed black preacher George Leile stopped at Tybee Island in the Savannah River and there preached to slaves, baptizing among others, Andrew Bryan and his family. Bryan and his brother, Sampson, preached and baptized new converts in swamp meetings and on plantations when allowed to do so. The brothers frequently suffered beatings and incarcerations. In 1788 Abraham Marshall of Kiokee, a noted black preacher, visited the region and organized them into a church, recognizing Andrew Bryan as pastor. From 1790–94 the congregation met on the Bryan Plantation, at Brampton, and later within the city suburbs. Eventually the Georgia Baptist Association, organized in 1784, officially recognized the church as the First Colored (later First Bryan) Baptist Church. Marshall became pastor in 1815 and under his ministry the number of the congregation swelled to over three thousand. The construction of a substantial wooden meetinghouse building in 1794 was to become a symbol of the architectural simplicity of early black Baptist churches:

> The building was very plain, without any attempt at architectural beauty: almost square and box-like, high pitched roof, with small windows; one wide door in the West center of the building, and two smaller doors near each end on the south side, leading into the open space of the lot between the praise-house, as the smaller building was then called, and the pulpit in the East center, built very plain, shaped like an acorn, with a raise from the floor of about three feet, plain board front, a neat cushioned pad for the Bible, and board seat which would accommodate three. No part of the building inside was ceiled, rafters and studs in their rough state, straight-back pews without doors; and the only pretension

to neatness was in the smoothing of the backs and seats and rounding and beading the edges and tops. No part of the building was painted or whitewashed, but plain and pure as from the carpenter's hands.[5]

In Augusta, Georgia, the Springfield Baptist Church also lays claim to being the "oldest independent African American church in the nation." An historical marker at the present site indicates that it was organized in 1787 by Jesse Peters (also called Jesse Peters Galphin) as an outgrowth of the Silver Bluff church.[6] Rather than following George Leile to Jamaica, Jesse Peters returned to slave status after the British evacuation, and served as an ordained person at Silver Bluff. He remained at Silver Bluff until about 1791 when the congregation vanished and he moved 12 miles away to Augusta, Georgia. There he apparently continued as the pastor of a black congregation that he thought of as a successor to Silver Bluff. The Springfield church thereafter has a continuous history as the mother congregation of the Augusta black community. In 1867 Morehouse College was founded as Augusta Institute in the basement of Springfield Church.

One instance of a black Baptist congregation that has missed the attention of many surveys is the slave congregation in Welsh Neck Church in South Carolina. For historians, it constitutes a second type of congregation, characterized by white Baptist pastors in charge of the congregation. During 1779 the newly installed pastor, Elhanan Winchester, had a "summer of great success" in which a revival occurred that produced 240 new members for the church. According to Winchester, his antislavery views were an inducement to local plantation slaves in the Pee Dee River region:

About this time I began to find uncommon desires for the conversion and salvation of the poor Negroes, who were very numerous in that part of the country; but whom none of my predecessors, that I could learn, had ever taken pains to instruct in the principles of Christianity; neither had any single slave, either man or woman been baptized . . . One evening seeing a number of them at the door of the house where I was preaching, I found myself constrained as it were, to go to the door, and tell them that Jesus Christ loved them, and died for them, as well as for white people, and that they might come and believe in him . . . There were about thirty from one plantation in the neighborhood present (besides others); these returned home, and did not even give sleep to their eyes . . . until they had settled every quarrel among themselves, and according to their form of marriage, had married every man to the woman with whom he lived; had restored whatever one had unjustly taken from another . . . I continued to instruct them, and within three months from the first of June, I baptized more than thirty blacks belonging to that plantation, besides many others, as in the whole made up one hundred, of which sixty three were men, thirty seven were women, all of which were born in Africa, or immediately descended from such as were natives of that unhappy country.[7]

Having baptized the slaves (whom he called "servants"), Winchester assisted them in forming a separate congregation in 1779. He preached to them each week, likely on Sunday afternoons. Unfortunately, the pastor who followed Winchester, Edmund Botsford, claimed that many of those whom Winchester had baptized were "ignorant of true religion" and he subsequently excommunicated many of them in 1782.[8] The remainder of the black members were examined by a committee of the Welsh Neck congregation and admitted to that body. In the period 1780 to 1810, the slave congregation-white pastor type would become the dominant model in Virginia and Georgia. According to historian David Benedict, by 1846 blacks outnumbered whites in the Welsh Neck Association in Georgia by two to one.[9]

David George's history as a pioneering black Baptist continued in British North America. Introduced earlier in the context of separatist Baptist preaching, George sided with the British in the evacuation of Charleston in 1780. He and his family and several other former slaves accepted the offer of the British to relocate to Nova Scotia in what came to be the Maritime Provinces. By 1782, he became the catalyst for a black Baptist congregation at Birchtown, near Shelburne on the South Shore. In Nova Scotia they were greeted by inhospitable whites who at one point burned a structure in the black community. This congregation survived the harsh elements and racial prejudice for a little less than a decade when David George led a company of blacks to resettle in Sierra Leone, West Africa.

Coming of Age Under Challenging Circumstances

The first half of the nineteenth century was determinative for black Baptist identity. One denominational historian has called it "the Heroic Age."[10] Through 1845 32 black congregations were established in the South and about 30 were created in the northern and midwestern states. In the next two decades through the end of the Civil War, an additional 38 were established in the North and 68 in the southern states.[11] The congregations in the North were mostly composed of families that had successfully fled the Fugitive Slave laws, and the churches in the South were the products of both white evangelism and separation of blacks from white congregations.

In this period, the evolution of the first African Baptist Church in Richmond, Virginia, is another important milestone in the emergence of black Baptist identity. Here may be seen a third type of black Baptist congregation: the racially mixed congregation that grew substantially in numbers of black worshipers. As early as the 1780s slaves were permitted to worship at First Baptist. Lott Carey emerged from this congregation in 1815 and the church was instrumental in founding the Richmond African Missionary Society. During the ministry of Jeremiah Jeter, the number of slaves increased dramatically so that the building could not accommodate the worshipers. A decision was made, in view of the predominantly African population of the congregation, to separate the two races by deeding the building of First Baptist to the slaves while the white congregation erected a new church in 1838–41. Under Virginia law, the white leadership determined that it was permissible to have a black church if it was served by a white minister. Consequently, Robert Ryland, president of Richmond College, served the First African Baptist Church from 1841 until 1866 when he was succeeded by the first black pastor. Under Ryland's ministry the church increased from a few hundred members to over three thousand.

Significant development of congregational life in northern cities occurred in the first decades of the nineteenth century. In Boston, Samuel Stillman was baptizing and admitting black ministers as early as 1772. Thomas Paul, a free black who was born and educated in New Hampshire, moved to Boston and was ordained by Stillman at First Baptist Church. In 1805 when "people of colour in west Boston" desired to be set apart as a church, First Baptist Church offered support and helped to raise a subscription of $1,500 for a meetinghouse. In an act of reverse discrimination, Stillman, who had baptized numerous blacks during a recent revival, attempted to dissuade the black leaders from admitting white members, lest their quality of being an "African" church be sacrificed. Thus the First African Baptist Church of Boston was born, later to become under Thomas Paul, the Joy Street Baptist Church.[12] Two years later in Burlington, Ohio the Macedonia Baptist Church was formed from slaves that had escaped from Kentucky across the Ohio River. It was the first African American congregation west of Pennsylvania. In 1808 First Baptist Church in New York City requested Thomas Paul of Boston to form a black congregation of 16 honorably dismissed members of First Church. This congregation became Abyssinian Baptist Church. Likewise First African Baptist Church in Philadelphia was organized in 1809.

Beyond the local congregations, associations of churches also sprang forth. Reflecting the pattern of support and cooperation that prevailed among other Baptists, the outgrowth congregations of the Bryan Church at Newington, Ogeechee, Black Creek, Lot's Creek, and Second, Savannah in 1802 organized the Savannah River Association. The membership in these congregations ranged from 75 to almost five hundred, even though served officially by white pastors. The historians of these early congregations were quick to point out their orthodoxy: closed communion, the use of Watts's and Rippon's hymns, sermons sound in doctrine, congregations evangelical in faith and missionary spirit, baptism by immersion, and proof of Christian marriage.[13] But there was a side to the associations that historians of slavery have not missed, namely the capability of white churches and pastors to control black slave congregations. This was ironic, because from the earliest development of Baptist associations on either side of the Atlantic, the associations had no superior authority over local congregations. Fear of insurrection, the prospects of racial parity, and social anxiety in general caused southern white Baptists to monitor congregations and general meetings carefully. For some individuals this meant a kind of dismissive presence at worship and business meetings, for others it created regular accountability through supervised congregational and associational meetings, and in some instances racial demarcation meant ownership of land and identification of pastors. The association thus became a disciplinary body necessary to the very survival of black congregations.

Key to congregations and associations were the black Baptist preachers. Many of the preachers, for reasons of social control, were never ordained. Yet they created an institution that defined their medium. Lay preaching or "exhorting" was common, especially after the Nat Turner Rebellion in 1822. Typically not allowed in the pulpits, blacks preached in the white churches in the afternoons after white services, or in graveyard "brush arbors." Some were called "chairbackers" because they used chairs as props, or "floor preachers" because they spoke from the floor of the congregations as opposed to the raised pulpits. Surviving examples of antebellum black Baptist preaching are rich in the use of metaphors and emotional devices, much more so than even white revivalistic preachers.

As seen from this survey, the origins of the black Baptist movement were varied and complex. What is clear by 1840 is that there were over 50 black congregations identified from New England to the Deep South and west to the Mississippi.[14] A definite form of church life or polity was evident by the mid-nineteenth century among black Baptist churches,

slave and free. Several commentators have written on the response of
the black community to Baptist principles and this needs to be underscored again. Both the structure and style of Baptist life were amenable
to the black circumstance. As noted earlier, Baptist worship favored
experience over knowledge and this boded well for a preliterate community. Further, black preachers were more characterized by gifts and
style than training, of which there was little to none available. Finally,
constituting a black congregation or association was relatively simple.
Rules of order were minimal and the stress was again on preaching. No
bishops, or elaborate confessions of faith, or published minutes were
required for the sustenance of affairs. Charles Lyell, a visiting geologist
from Scotland, provided one of the best windows on the vitality of
black congregations at Savannah, Georgia, in January 1846. The only
white person present, he observed a congregation consisting of about
six hundred persons:

> As soon as I entered I was shown to a seat reserved for strangers, near
> the preacher. First the congregation all joined, both men and women,
> very harmoniously in a hymn, most of them having evidently good ears
> for music, and good voices. The singing was followed by prayers, not
> read, but delivered without notes by a negro of pure African blood, a
> gray-headed, venerable-looking man, with a fine sonorous voice, named
> Marshall. He, as I learnt afterwards, had the reputation of being one of
> their best preachers, and he concluded by addressing to them a sermon,
> also without notes, in good style, and for the most part in good English;
> so much so, as to make me doubt whether a few ungrammatical phrases
> in the negro idiom might not have been purposely introduced for the
> sake of bringing the subject home to their family thoughts ... He also
> inculcated some good practical maxims of morality, and told them they
> were to look to a future state of rewards and punishments in which God
> would deal impartially with "the poor and the rich, the black man and
> the white."[15]

Emergence of a Black Denomination for Black People

Black Baptists were the immediate beneficiaries of the abolitionist crusade, the Civil War itself, and Reconstruction. Organizational life among
black Baptists had originated in segregated associations in the South. In
1833 the Ohio Baptist Convention appointed Robert Townshend of
Meigs County to work among freed slaves, and he helped form the
Providence Antislavery Missionary Baptist Association in 1834, oldest

among the northern states. It was clearly related to the existing white Tees Valley Association. Two years later the Union Baptist Antislavery Association in the Cincinnati area was formed, comprising 22 congregations and spreading its influence throughout the state. The Union Association was careful to maintain a strong relationship with white antislavery churches in Ohio. A third, the Wood River Association of southwestern Illinois, was formed in 1839 from the labors of a free black preacher, John Livingston, and with the blessing of a white missionary of repute, James Lemen. Lemen was a founder of the Illinois Friends of Humanity and moderator of the Illinois Union Baptist Association. Churches were added to this association as far distant as Racine, Wisconsin, and Leavenworth, Kansas.[16] Additionally, just across the river from Detroit in Upper Canada in 1841 the Amherstburg Association catered to churches safely across the Canadian border. It came to include churches in Michigan and Canada. Finally, one historian includes the association of churches in Louisiana that an ex-slave, Father Willis, formed in 1837. This body was racially mixed and was dominated by the white membership.[17]

The Amherstburg Association deserves special attention in African American Baptist history. The historian of the AfriCanadian movement reflected upon the plight of those who went to Canada:

> Poverty-stricken, they had to compete with those who had always known the blessings of a home and reaped the fruits of labour; black of skin and recent slaves, they were forced to live alongside whites who had always been free; illiterate, they were thrust into a society which had a long tradition of education. In their attempts to adapt themselves to the new environment, they encountered a rising tide of colour prejudice which could not be overcome by the change in their legal status.[18]

Comprised mostly of former slaves who made it to freedom in Upper Canada via the Underground Railroad, the Association was originally made up of only 47 members and shared work with black churches in Michigan. Although free politically, black Baptists were still to face huge prejudices from the white community at the crossing village of Amherstburg and in the region at large. The clerk of the new association summed it up: "we cannot enjoy the privileges we wish with the white churches in Canada . . . we invite all the Christian churches of the same faith and order to unite with us in the great Celestial cause. . . ."[19]

The Association grew to a membership of over 1,000 in 14 congregations by 1861. Through much of its early history it was unsuccessful in uniting efforts with any white association in Canada, though during the 1850s it affiliated with the American Baptist Free Mission Society that gave it new credibility and international recognition. Amherstburg also suffered schism, when the Canadian Antislavery Association was formed; in 1857 the two groups reunited under an antislavery banner. Significant numbers of members in the association returned to the US during the Civil War to aid in the cause of freedom, while also depleting the churches in Canada. After the War, the Association grew to include churches in Hamilton and Toronto and in 1876 it voted to join the Baptist Convention of Canada West where it became a fully integrated association with the predominantly white associations west of the Ottawa River. Over the years of its existence ministers were drawn heavily from the southern Michigan region and educated at black institutions.

Another significant beginning in the antebellum years was at important urban congregations like Abyssinian Baptist Church in New York, where the American Baptist Missionary Convention (ABMC) was formed in 1840. The ABMC actually had its origins in a disagreement over the degree of antislavery fervor and missions to Africa among those in the Baptist antislavery community. When formed, it included the Abyssinian and Zion Baptist churches in New York City plus Union Church in Philadelphia. Two outstanding black leaders emerged in the Convention: Sampson White, pastor of Abyssinian, and John Berry Meachum, pastor of First African Baptist Church in St Louis. Individual members, churches, associations, and missionary societies could join this convention for nominal contributions that, as James Washington showed, could be sent via the mails, thus allowing blacks in the slave states to join.[20] Strong statements came from the annual meetings, like the resolution in 1853 that put forth a united effort for the abolition of slavery, the annihilation of the Colonization Society, and the removal of all forms of intemperance. Some leaders in the ABMC also urged missionary work in Africa in order to create a black Christian civilization that would prepare for the overthrow of the abominable slave trade there. In 1863 President Abraham Lincoln authorized appointees of this group to go behind enemy lines and minister to the black community.

A similar body of antislavery Baptists in Boston formed the American Baptist Free Mission Society (ABFrMS) in 1843 to support black congregations and missionary work. Tremont Temple Baptist Church in Boston was the initial meeting place and an important support congregation for the Society. This organization was essentially a white dominant group of abolitionists who included Cyrus P. Grosvenor of First Baptist, Hartford, Connecticut, Albert Post, John Duer, and William H. Brisbane, a prominent former slaveholder from South Carolina. The

Free Mission Society sent black ministers to preach shortly after the fall of Fort Sumter. Deep in South Carolina, congregations were gathered and ties were made with northern churches for support.

The third major convention body formed before Emancipation was the Western Colored Baptist Convention, created in 1853. This body was called forth from among the Wood River Association in Illinois to include congregations north of slave states and west of St Louis. It met each year from 1853 to 1859 and suspended meetings during the early years of the war. Delegates from 26 congregations in eight states convened anew in 1864 to build a strategy for what had become an "open South." They renamed the Western Colored Baptist Convention the "Northwestern and Southern Baptist Convention." Prominent among their leaders were William Newman (formerly a pastor in Cincinnati), Richard deBaptiste, pastor of Olivet Baptist in Chicago, and William Troy from Canada West. Among the concerns of the new Convention were the training of ministers and the distribution of confiscated church properties in southern states. As a relatively impoverished body of former slaves and lacking political clout, it would be outdistanced in these areas by the northern Baptist societies.

Along with the American Baptist Free Mission Society, the American Baptist Home Mission Society (ABHMS) laid plans for extensive work among the southern black population during and immediately following military hostilities. Missionaries were appointed during the war to work among immediately freed slaves. Joanna Patterson Moore, appointed by the Society to Island No. 10 near Helena, Arkansas, gained much notoriety among the local white community for teaching slaves to read. Still others participated in the Port Royal Experiment in South Carolina. In 1864 the Society announced plans to initiate a network of educational institutions in each southern state to enable the training and empowerment of the emancipated slaves. Of the over two dozen schools, five centers emerged as important leading black institutions of the New South: Richmond Theological Seminary (which became Virginia Union University), Shaw University in Raleigh, North Carolina, Morehouse College in Atlanta, Simmons University in Kentucky, and Bishop College in Texas. In this mission the Freewill Baptists also had a share, starting one of the earliest schools, Storer College at Harper's Ferry, West Virginia.

During the era of Reconstruction, state communities of black Baptists became important organizational foci for the freedman community. Kentucky was the first to organize a black convention in 1865, followed by North Carolina, Virginia and Arkansas, Alabama, Mississippi, Georgia, Tennessee and Louisiana, Texas, and, finally among the

southern Reconstruction districts, South Carolina in 1876. The importance of the black state conventions lay in their identification with laws
and programs of support and improvement for freedmen, plus the
court system to protect their rights. Reorganization of state governments under Radical Republican rule seemed to go hand in hand with
black Baptist conventions. A generation of leadership giants emerged
from these state Baptist families. Typical of the regions were Kentucky
and Arkansas. William J. Simmons (1849–90) was an exemplar of the
high caliber of black leaders. He was educated at Madison University
and Howard University and later served pastorates in Washington, DC
and Kentucky. As president of State University (later Simmons University) in Kentucky, he did much to encourage black Baptist identity and
organizational independence. When the impetus for a national organization of black Baptists came to a head in 1895 and the Consolidated
American Baptist Missionary Convention merged with the American
National Baptist Convention to form the National Baptist Convention
in the United States of America (NBCUSA), Simmons was elected first
president of the Convention.

Arkansas likewise became the permanent home for a reported 122,169
black Americans by 1870. One of the outstanding leaders of the
Arkansas Black Baptist community was E. C. Morris (1855–1922).
Morris moved to Helena on the Mississippi River in 1877 and became
pastor of Centennial Baptist Church there. A person of great oratorical
and organizational gifts, Morris soon became active in the local black
Baptist organization: the Phillips, Lee, and Monroe County Association. He quickly became a leader among the congregations, particularly
in the stewardship of financial resources toward home and foreign
missionary work. A staunch Republican with a southern pedigree, he
steered between the fractious competition that James White, a northern
black and George Robinson, a southerner, had created in the early
development of a state black Baptist community in Arkansas.[21] In 1880
Morris was chosen secretary of the Baptist State Convention of Arkansas, formed in 1867. He took pride in the rise of black Baptists in the
state from 30,000 in 1882 to 70,000 in 1900. He understood their
needs and set about accomplishing a comprehensive plan. Morris was
the chief catalyst in starting five high schools, the Arkansas Baptist
College at Little Rock, a publishing business for Sunday Schools, and a
weekly paper, the *Baptist Vanguard,* all of which radiated from Little
Rock, the capital of the state. But there was also a cautionary trend
among Arkansas black Baptists, as witnessed in the case of Wilson
Brown in Little Rock who opposed black involvement in political matters, lest they draw the wrath of the white community.

Ultimately it was Morris and the progressive faction that took the lead among Arkansas black Baptists. Thus began the rise of the most populous organization of black Baptists in the United States. Morris would observe:

> We decided that instead of begging the means from the good white people of the North, who had given so much for like causes, we would endeavor to buy and build from the means given by our own people, thereby giving ourselves a practical knowledge of such a work, and that would be an inspiration to those who are to follow.[22]

In the 1890s black Baptists across the United States would turn to the Rev. E. C. Morris to give shape to a national organization, based upon the heritage in Arkansas.

The Grand Accomplishment: 1895

The roots of a national Baptist organization among black Baptists are manifold. Less direct but nevertheless significant were the associations and state conventions of churches across the South and in the North and Midwest. A succession of 10 conventions and scores of associations across the South, Midwest, and Northeast provided both organizational paradigms and leaders. Second, certainly, was the effort of the ABHMS, that desired a viable black church community to assume support, if not control, of its nascent institutions in the southern states. Third were the fragile attempts at a national organization from 1840, like the Consolidated American Baptist Missionary Convention and the Northwestern and Southern Baptist Convention, formed in 1853. Finally, new leaders of stature such as William J. Simmons, missionary, educator, promoter, and master ecclesiastical politician and E. C. Morris of equal attainment held out the vision of a united black Christian family in the Baptist tradition.

Of direct relation to the national project, there were five organizations that preceded the grand gathering of 1895. Historians of the black Baptist tradition refer to this as the "convention era." The Consolidated American Baptist Missionary Convention (formed 1867, defunct in 1879) was the vision of William P. Newman (1815–67), a former slave from Virginia who served a congregation in Cincinnati, and thereafter lived in Canada in the Amherstburg community. Newman eventually became a missionary in Haiti, from which he returned in 1864 to become president of the Northwestern and Southern Baptist

Convention, a black Baptist body. His dream of a united black organization was realized by Nelson G. Merry of Nashville, Richard deBaptiste of Chicago, and William Troy of Amherstburg, Canada. The desire of this group was to become a national, truly integrated denominational body from Maine to the Gulf of Mexico, integrally related to the three great white missionary bodies, the ABHMS, American Baptist Publication Society, and the American Baptist Free Mission Society. In its two decades of work the Consolidated Convention demonstrated the governance and financial problems as well as the leadership styles that plagued black Baptists in the 1870s and 1880s.

Two additional black Baptist national organizations belong to the decade of the 1880s. The first was the Baptist Foreign Mission Convention of the United States, formed at Montgomery Alabama, in 1880; the second was the American National Baptist Convention, established in St Louis in 1886. The creation of a national umbrella for those interested in furthering the cause of black evangelization of Africa was admittedly a secondary interest of the black Baptist community, but it did further the awareness of black unity and black Baptist unity. It was overshadowed by the rise of the American National Baptist Convention that was carried out by heavyweight pastors and educators like William J. Simmons, Richard DeBaptiste, and Elias Camp Morris. DeBaptiste joined the effort as a statistician and collected valuable data about the rise of the African Baptist community. Simmons was the widely recognized educator from Louisville who linked positively with the Home Mission and Publication societies, and of course Morris carried an impeccable reputation as a promoter and organizer at the state level. From its beginning, the American National Convention focused its efforts at unification and took a giant step in this direction in 1888 with a fraternal "joint meeting." Representatives to the Nashville gathering included most of the stakeholders in a possible national union: the Baptist Foreign Mission Convention, the American National Baptist Convention, the American Baptist Home Mission Society, and the American Baptist Missionary Union. The next year much the same delegation met at Indianapolis with the American Baptist Publication Society also represented.

Haltingly, against a backdrop of negotiations between the northern Baptist societies and the Southern Baptist Convention that would lead to a comity agreement and the withdrawal of the ABHMS from its southern strategy, nationalists continued unabated in their pursuit of unity. Unhappily, it became obvious in the early 1890s that the American National Baptist Convention, in itself, lacked the credibility to be the drawing force. Signaling a new direction, a national periodical, the

National Baptist Magazine, was launched in Washington DC in 1894. In its pages, a general invitation went forth to all black churches and leaders to meet the following year to work towards a better organization. As associations met, representatives were chosen, as well as organizations and congregations and delegates from every state. They traveled to Atlanta to attend the historic organizing convention. Under the wise and prophetic leadership of Elias C. Morris, the National Baptist Convention in the USA was launched.

It has been estimated that in 1890 there were approximately 1.4 million black Baptists in the US, as compared with about 800,000 black Methodists of several kinds. Other Christian denominations had appreciably fewer black adherents: Roman Catholics, 100,000; Christian Churches, 25,000; Episcopalians, 20,000; and Presbyterians, 20,000. Baptists owned and operated over 50 schools and colleges. Even with their numerical superiority, however, black Baptists faced formidable challenges. James Washington in his masterful study chose the term "frustrated fellowship" to describe the history of black Baptists in a quest for social power. By this, he meant to point out that there have long been serious divisions among black Baptists over personality and property and internal and external political issues. This would play itself out vividly in the first century of black Baptist development.

The Dividing Lines Within a Tradition

As seen in the preceding narrative, before the last shots were fired in the Civil War, it was evident there would be a variety of organizations of black Baptists in the South. It was naïve to think that one comprehensive body could reflect all of the differing perspectives and dreams of the aspiring leaders. The new National Baptist Convention USA was not alone for long. The American Baptist Home Mission Society claimed the missionary responsibility for the black population, and from this position developed a generous but paternalistic attitude toward what the Society did accomplish. It provided funds for training leaders that it hoped would be loyal to the Society, plus capital grants to construct buildings for the black colleges. "Cooperationists" openly courted ABHMS support and accepted its sometimes harshly paternalistic policies. The ABHMS remained a key player in the development of the black Baptist community well into the twentieth century. Other organizations, like the Consolidated American Baptist Missionary Convention, the Baptist Foreign Mission Convention (BFMC), and the American National Baptist Convention, had wanted to be independent of white control. In 1886 the BFMC turned aside an offer of support from the Baptists of the North, holding "that to continue our work as an organization will develop qualities and powers in us as a people that will not be developed if we go into another organization."[23] This attitude of separationism was reflected in the character of the National Baptist Convention from its inception. The Southern Baptists constituted a third interested group, hoping to forestall a coalition of blacks in the South with the northern Baptist societies or the emergence of any organizations antagonistic to white Baptists. Southern Baptists looked for opportunities to support missionaries among the black congregations and to link up with the general organization. To no one's surprise, most black leaders following the Civil War concluded that the best future for black Baptists was also the best opportunity for black people. E. C. Morris argued that a black Baptist organization with a publishing house, and so forth, was important for employment and scholarship, as an outlet for the development of the race, as a bequest to posterity, and to demonstrate the business acumen of blacks.[24]

The National Baptist Convention USA grew dramatically during the first decades of the new century. When organized, the membership was about one million; within 15 years it exceeded three million. While there were black Baptist associations in 15 states, the greatest numbers of black Baptists in 1900 were located in Virginia (230,000), with Georgia (221,000) and Mississippi (200,000), close behind.[25] Organizational growth followed membership growth. In 1899 a Young People's Union became a permanent constituent board. It spawned a Baptist Training Union for persons of all ages in the churches. Similarly, the Baptist Women's Missionary League started and a year later it joined the Convention as the Women's Auxiliary. In 1903 a Home Mission Board was organized to extend credit to needy churches or those near bankruptcy. A related project dear to the NBCUSA was the establishment, with support from the Southern Baptist Convention, of the American Baptist Theological Seminary in Nashville. This school sought to focus on various theological degrees that supplemented the education in the historically black colleges. Much of the success of the NBCUSA in its first two decades was due to the excellent leadership of E. C. Morris, Lewis G. Jordan, and Richard H. Boyd.

The National Baptist Convention proved to be a fragile enterprise. State conventions often competed with the national organization for loyalty and stewardship of the churches. A second major stream of black Baptist life came to be associated with Richard H. Boyd and the National Baptist Convention of America. Boyd, a gifted preacher and administrator from Texas, felt that black churches needed a distinct literature from either the Southern Baptist Sunday School Board or the American Baptist Publication Society. In 1897, under the auspices of the NBCUSA, he began the National Baptist Publishing Board in Nashville and was instantly successful in business terms. Gradually he came to lead the National Baptist Home Mission Board and several other enterprises, including furniture manufacturing and creation of black dolls. In 1915 the leadership of the National Baptist Convention became concerned about his various ministries and his own career aspirations, and they demanded financial accountability. Boyd refused and a major legal action ensued that ran on for years. Boyd retained personal control of his enterprises, and started a new national body, the National Baptist Convention of America (NBCA). The NBCUSA incorporated itself to cover all of its auxiliary enterprises and Boyd continued to operate under the corporate status of his National Baptist Publishing Board, with the NBCA unincorporated.

Following the embarrassing schism of 1915, National Baptists exhibited many of the same institutional tendencies of other parts of the Baptist denominational family, centralizing their denominational boards and agencies in Nashville. Arthur M. Townsend, a distinguished medical doctor and president of Roger Williams University, became head of the newly organized National Baptist Publishing Board and turned it into a major denominational press within a decade. He secured a prominent plot of land within view of the Tennessee State Capitol, and using a distinguished African American architectural firm, designed and built the Morris Memorial Building, in memory of the first National Baptist president, E. C. Morris. The building was, at $700,000, a major project for the denomination, housing a bookstore, cafeteria, staff offices, and printing plant. It was said to be the most magnificent structure owned by black people in the United States, and became the virtual center of National Baptist life for decades. Among the most prized accomplishments of the publishing house were the *Standard Baptist Hymnal*, that contained scores of spirituals, and the *Baptist Voice*, a national newspaper for black Baptists.

L. K. Williams led the NBCUSA through turbulent times in the 1930s and 1940s. Not only were there severe racial troubles across the South that called for leadership and diplomacy skills from the largest group of black Christians, but also funds were mostly in deficit. Williams forged creative relations with the Home Mission Board of the Southern Baptist Convention, resulting in joint projects such as church extension and the establishment of the American Baptist Theological Seminary in Nashville. Throughout his presidency, he built strong ties of cooperation with the northern Baptist societies. D. V. Jemison followed in

Williams's footsteps as president of the Convention, until poor health forced his resignation in 1953. Jemison is remembered for his forth-right stance against segregation: "Our Lord and Master is not inter-ested in any particular race, except the human race," he wrote. "The Negro is human, and deserves the treatment of human being just as any other race or nation."[26] Jemison also placed a high value on the history of black Baptists, supporting the preparation of several schol-arly accounts of black Baptist development. Still, however, frustration remained high within the Convention because the aspirations of black Baptists in this era remained largely unfulfilled on the social and polit-ical fronts. George W. Lucas, a pastor from Bethel Church in Dayton, Ohio, observed at the end of this decade, "American Baptists and Negro Baptists would have agreed that Southern Baptists were highly bigoted; Negro and Southern Baptists labeled American Baptists as spiritually barren; and American and Southern Baptists would have agreed that Negro Baptists were sadly belated."[27]

Similarly, the National Baptist Convention of America (NBCA) made advances in the next phase of its development. Throughout the 1920s, 1930s, and 1940s, the chief energies of the Convention were seen in the Publishing Board. In the 1950s, under successive generations of Boyd family executives (earning it the sobriquet the "Boyd Baptist Convention"), the Board produced a major amount of Sunday school materials and held Sunday School and Training Union congresses with attendance sometimes in excess of 20,000 delegates. The Boyd execut-ives were primary leaders in the life of the Convention as well. The NBCA took a sympathetic view of the civil rights crusades at the end of the 1950s and embraced the work of Martin Luther King, Jr. and supported Jesse Jackson for president in 1984. Eventually the national headquarters of the NBCA was established at Shreveport, Louisiana, where ministries include missionary, benevolent, stewardship, and pub-lishing concerns. The Convention actively supports religious liberty, doctrinal authenticity (essentially the New Hampshire Confession of Faith), social justice, and economic development. The most visible expressions of the NBCA are found in the annual conventions and national study sessions.

Beginning in 1987, leadership quarrels beset the NBCA and led to another major schism among black Baptists. The Convention presi-dent, E. Edward Jones, proposed sweeping changes in the objectives and structure of the Convention, and attempted to bring the National Baptist Publishing Board under its auspices. The Boyd family rallied its support, mounting an all-out campaign against centralization, and pointed to the successes of the Sunday School Congresses. In 1988 the

Boyd supporters convened a "Restoration Meeting" in Dallas, Texas, to organize a new national body, the National Missionary Baptist Convention of America. The elected president, S. M. Lockridge, declared his support for an independent National Baptist Publishing Board and the Board shifted its alignment from the National Baptist Convention of America (NBCA) to the National Missionary Baptist Convention of America (NMBCA). The new organization claimed the full heritage of the National Baptist movement back to 1895.[28] Headquartered in Los Angeles, California, the geographic strengths of the NMBCA lie in Texas and California. Yet a further leadership split occurred in 1998, when a Texas faction led by H. J. Johnson of Dallas withdrew and formed the International Missionary Baptist Convention of America.

In 1953 Joseph Harrison Jackson became president of the National Baptist Convention USA; this signaled an active era of mainstream African American Baptist advancement. Jackson was a graduate of Jackson College, Colgate Rochester Divinity School, and Creighton University. He served pastorates in Mississippi and Pennsylvania before assuming leadership at Chicago's historic Olivet Baptist Church in 1941. Jackson led his denomination in relief projects, became a confidant of American presidents, and represented NBCUSA at major ecumenical events of the Baptist World Alliance and the World Council of Churches. Jackson was a gradualist or "accommodationist" in the civil rights movement of the 1960s and he opposed the nonviolent resistance of Martin Luther King and Ralph Abernathy. While he later reminded his detractors that the Convention had lent its support to the Montgomery Improvement Association in 1956, he much favored working through political channels. In 1957 Jackson organized a Convention-wide drive to support the civil rights legislation of President Dwight Eisenhower called the "Urge Congress Movement." Simultaneously he sponsored a self-help and training project, Freedom Farm, in Somerville, Tennessee. To the existing nine committees of the Convention, President Jackson added a bewildering array of 13 new departments, many of which overlapped responsibilities. Collectively, these cost him support as Convention president, and in 1960 there was an abortive attempt to unseat him led by Gardner Taylor of Brooklyn and Marshal Shepard of Philadelphia. Jackson triumphed, but the dissidents left the National Baptist family and formed a new coalition, the Progressive National Baptist Convention (PNBC). Jackson continued as president until 1982, when he retired, and was succeeded by T. J. Jemison, son of his predecessor. Henry J. Lyons, Jemison's successor in 1994, was convicted of using the Convention's funds for personal purposes and served a prison term. William J. Shaw of Philadelphia succeeded to the presidency in 1999, and has rebuilt the denomination of 30,000 congregations and eight million members around objectives of vision, integrity, structure, and accountability. One of the enduring legacies of the Jackson era was the creation in 1973 of the Joseph H. Jackson Library for the historical study of African American Baptists, a national center adjacent to Olivet Church in Chicago.

The Progressive Convention came into being with high-powered leadership. In 1960 Martin Luther King, Sr. had listed five serious concerns in his critique of the Jackson era in the NBCUSA: restoration of denominational harmony, unification of the parent body and the auxiliaries, commitment to civil rights, information on financial matters regularly reported to pastors, and re-establishment of tenure as a principle for leadership. In many ways this became a charter for the new organization. Lavaughn Venchael Booth of Zion Baptist, Cincinnati, was the leading political figure, and Gardner Taylor of Brooklyn, New York, was clearly the great orator and idealist of the new movement, being dubbed one of America's most outstanding preachers. Essential to the Progressive identity was an ecumenical stance that was realized in the joint affiliation of many of its congregations with the American Baptist Churches in the USA. At the first meeting of the Convention, the delegates adopted the motto, "Unity, Service, Fellowship, and Peace." It would quickly move its focus to "the least, the lost, and the left out."[29] Many black leaders also welcomed the energetic support the Progressive Convention gave to Dr King and the Southern Christian Leadership Conference in advancing civil rights. Within a decade, the Progressive National Baptist Convention included about 1,000 churches, and at the end of the century, just under 2,000, most of which are dually aligned. Under President Thomas Kilgore, the ending of segregation became a major platform of the PNBC. Four decades into its history, Gardner Taylor and Bennett Smith have called the PNBC the last and best hope for black Baptists in the US and Baptists in general because of its correction of many of the aberrations perceived in the earlier history of black Baptists.[30]

Organizationally, the modern black Baptist spectrum in the United States includes both theologically conservative and ecumenical bodies. Most of the organizational history turns on personal leadership differentiation, and now allows for cooperation and dual alignments that may encompass other black Baptist as well as historically Caucasian Baptist groups. In Canada there have been different nuances to black Baptist identity in the past quarter century. The first reality is a declining membership in black Baptist congregations. Second, the two centers in Ontario and Nova Scotia are isolated from each other. Third, there is a small but identifiable influx from the Caribbean islands, and another directly from Africa, that have different heritages from the original British Loyalists and Underground Railroad congregations. Fourth, the training of ministers is mostly in Bible colleges in the United States, and part-time. This last factor has limited a Canadian consciousness and inhibited congregational growth. There are two associations of black Baptists in Canada: the Amherstburg in southwestern Ontario and Toronto, and the association centered in Dartmouth, Nova Scotia. Together they comprise about 3,500 members in 20 congregations. Both clusters of "AfriCanadians" have joined the mainstream Caucasian conventions and are loosely involved in that work.

A moment of high significance to all black Baptists was achieved on January 27, 2005 when over 10,000 African American Baptist leaders met in a single convention gathering. Plans for the meeting had been laid for over a year among the executives of the four major groups: NBCUSA, NBCA, PNBC, and NMBCA. This occurred in Nashville, Tennessee across four historic days. Among the leading speakers were Gardner Taylor, Jesse Jackson, and William J. Shaw. The show of unity expressed the hopes of 13 million black Baptists, the largest ever assemblage of African Americans. While no firm details about a possible merger were forthcoming, this meeting bodes well for a more united future than in the previous 90 years with its three major schisms.

Legacy: The Wedding of Freedom, Religious Experience, and Social Justice

In the North American context, achieving religious freedom has been a major theme of Baptists. No other part of the Baptist tradition more vividly evinces the struggle for freedom than the black Baptist communities. At the profoundest level, their struggle for freedom involved a human right – freedom from bondage to other humans. For some, like the former slave, Israel Campbell, who became a pastor and leader of black Baptists in Texas, that right came from escape or removal to the territories of freedom; for most, it came in the abolition of slavery in British dominions in 1833 and the US Emancipation Proclamation in 1864. Freedom thus being achieved, blacks next faced serious obstacles to their expression of religious values. They were discouraged from worshiping as a community. Later acts of discrimination came against organizations and schools. Even in the northern Baptist community where freed blacks were welcomed by whites, they were fed at separate tables and expected to sleep on the floor. No one better illustrates this part of the struggle than Andrew Bryan of the famous congregation at Savannah, Georgia who with his brother, Sampson, and 50 others in 1782 were brought before city magistrates on charges of illicit worship. They were imprisoned and beaten so severely, it is said, that Andrew bled abundantly. Like Obadiah Holmes in a previous century, Bryan told his persecutors that he would gladly suffer death for the cause of Jesus Christ.

No observer can be oblivious to the proclivity of black Baptists toward ecstatic religious experience. For some it is rooted in the pre-American African cultures; for others it is a part of the Separate evangelical preaching that brought the first converts to the Baptist movement in the eighteenth-century Awakening. Both factors influence the worship, and it still forms the core of black Baptist worship and spirituality. While social advancement and mainstream Protestantism have quieted the meetinghouses of other Baptists, black Baptists still sing boisterously, shout, respond to exhortation, and prophesy.

Finally, a permanent feature of black Baptist witness is social justice. Hardly a theological proposition or a denominational program, social justice (or the lack thereof) is *felt* among black Baptists. Being deprived of freedom and basic needs, living in a color-bound society, and being the targets of laws that codified segregation and discrimination, black Baptists have cried out from their pulpits with words of Scripture to identify God's role among the oppressed. They have marched on institutions and sat in jail cells on behalf of justice. Furthermore, black Baptists have organized permanent voluntary associations to continue to address the concerns of an unjust society, like the Southern Christian Leadership Conference and Jesse Jackson's Rainbow/PUSH Coalition. In the struggle for social justice, some like Martin Luther King, Jr., have paid the ultimate price as martyrs for the practical pursuit of these ideals.

Notes

1   Albert J. Raboteau, *Slave Religion: The "Invisible Institution" in the Antebellum South*, updated edn (New York: Oxford University Press, 2004), 148.
2   Ibid., 150.
3   Mechal Sobel, *Trabelin' On: The Slave Journey to an Afro-Baptist Faith* (Princeton, NJ: Princeton University Press, 1979), 102.
4   Walter H. Brooks, "The Priority of the Silver Bluff Church and its Promoters," *Journal of Negro History* 7/2 (April 1922): 181.

5   Rev. James M. Simms, *The First Colored Baptist Church in North America* (New York: Negro Universities Press, 1969), 34.

6   I am grateful to Mr Philip Calderwood of Augusta, Georgia, for securing this information.

7   Edwin Martin Stone, *Biography of Rev. Elhanan Winchester* (Boston, MA: H. R. Brewster, 1836), 35–6.

8   Edmund Botsford, the pastor, attached this inadequacy to Winchester's movement away from election to universalism. On the Welsh Neck church, see Joe M. King, *A History of South Carolina Baptists* (Columbia, SC: R. L. Bryan, 1964), 44, and "Minutes of the Welsh Neck Baptist Church", 1777–82 (original in Special Collections, Furman University Library, Greenville, SC).

9   David Benedict, *A General History of the Baptist Denomination in America and Other Parts of the World* (New York: Lewis Colby, 1848), 710.

10 Owen D. Pelt and Ralph Lee Smith, *The Story of the National Baptists* (New York: Vantage Press, 1960), 34.

11 Estimates found in Sobel, *Trabelin' On*, 182, 187.

12 Nathan E. Wood, *The History of the First Baptist Church of Boston (1665–1899)* (Philadelphia, PA: American Baptist Publication Society, 1899), 297.

13 James Simms, *The First Colored Baptist Church in North America, Constituted at Savannah, Georgia January 20, 1788* (New York: Negro Universities Press, 1969), 42–4.

14 Here one is indebted to the recent thorough work of Henry Mitchell, *Black Church Beginnings: The Long Hidden Realities of the First Years* (Grand Rapids, MI: Eerdmans, 2004), 182–92.

15 Sir Charles Lyell, *A Second Visit to the United States of North America*, 2 vols (London: John Murray, 1850), II: 14.

16 Mitchell, *Black Church Beginnings*, 115–16.

17 Ibid., 118.

18 Dorothy Shadd Shreve, *The AfriCanadian Church: A Stabilizer* (Jordan Station, ON: Paideia Press, 1983), 26.

19 "Minutes of the Amherstburg Baptist Association," 1841, quoted in Shreve, *The AfriCanadian Church*, 47.

20 James Melvin Washington, *Frustrated Fellowship: The Black Baptist Quest for Social Power* (Macon, GA: Mercer University Press, 1986), 40.

21 Ibid., 113–14.

22 E. C. Morris, *Sermons, Addresses, and Reminiscences and Important Correspondence* (Nashville, TN: National Baptist Publishing Board, 1901; repr. New York: Arno Press, 1980), 177.

23 Quoted in Washington, *Frustrated Fellowship*, 138.

24 "The Demand for a Negro Baptist Publishing House" in Morris, *Sermons, Addresses, and Reminiscences*, 56–61.

25 *American Baptist Yearbook 1900*, ed. J. G. Walker (Philadelphia, PA: American Baptist Publication Society, 1900), statistical tables, 57–101.

Alabama, North Carolina, South Carolina, and Texas had conglomerate church memberships in excess of 100,000 each.

26   Joseph H. Jackson, *A Story of Christian Activism: The History of the National Baptist Convention, USA* (Nashville, TN: Townsend Press, 1980), 186.

27   George W. Lucas, "Negro Baptists Sail a Stormy Sea," *Foundations* 4/3 (July, 1961): 214.

28   Its story is told in Bobby L. Lovett, *A Black Man's Dream: The First One Hundred Years – Richard Henry Boyd and the National Baptist Publishing Board* (Nashville, TN: Mega Corporation, 1993).

29   Albert A. Avant Jr., *The Social Teachings of the Progressive National Baptist Convention, Inc., Since 1961* (New York: Routledge, 2004), 4, 5.

30   Ibid., 8.

Chapter 9
Baptists and the Missionary Impulse

Following the lead of their English and Scottish forebears, Baptists in North America have been aggressive in their pursuit of Jesus's Great Commission. Among all the dissenters of the seventeenth century, Baptists took Matthew 28: 19–20 to themselves as a special challenge: "Go therefore and make disciples of all nations, baptizing them in the name of the Father, and of the Son, and of the Holy Spirit, and teaching them to observe everything that I have commanded you. And remember, I am with you always, to the end of the age" (NRSV). The connection of teaching all nations and trinitarian baptism was not lost on any but the small groups of hyper-Calvinistic Baptists described above, who thought evangelism was God's work alone. Sociopolitically and organizationally, the missionary endeavors of Baptists in the United States and Canada reflect an aggressive extension of North American religious values.

Mission history is a dominant motif in Baptist historiography. To tell the story organizationally is to draw the map of the extension of Baptist financial commitment and influence from North American bases to virtually every corner of the globe. Most Baptist mission history, however, is recounted as biography. In country by country, mission historians follow the dramatic steps of pioneering men and women far removed from native cultures who labor for decades in various sorts of evangelical work. More important than confessional statements is the experience of missionaries who often died on the fields. Mission history is exceptionally important for women in Baptist history, because it was one of the first open doors to service and leadership that women enjoyed from the mid-nineteenth century.

The first efforts of American Baptists in evangelism and missions occurred at the congregational level. Baptist ministers frequently engaged in preaching to potential converts. They recognized no parish boundaries or pre-existing church relationships. The much-repeated story of Obadiah Holmes and John Clarke in 1651 (see chapter 1 above) illustrates how Baptists often took risks to conduct evangelism. With Toleration, Baptists actively traveled from one colony to another, as with the Philadelphia Baptist Association in 1755, when its representatives commissioned two full-time seasonal evangelists to visit the southern colonies. Later, in 1771, Morgan Edwards was appointed evangelist-at-large, and others followed him in church planting work in the Carolinas and Virginia. On the moving frontier as families penetrated the Ohio Valley, the Old Northwest, and the Mississippi Valley, church planting required preaching for conversion. Baptists joined Methodists and Presbyterians in particular, in reaching the distant homesteads and isolated "heathen."

Baptists were clear about their organizational commitments to missions. While the associations were often useful in assisting mission work within their bounds and in special circumstances, new organizations cropped up to meet the challenge of consistent support for missions. Local mission societies based upon models in British Baptist and American Congregationalist efforts, sprang forth in New York, Boston, and Philadelphia. In upstate New York, a strong missionary effort was launched among three overlapping societies. The first fields were on the frontiers of American settlements in New York, New England, Appalachia, and the South, as well as a concern for local problems in northeastern cities. When one field seemed to close, another opened, and the missionary societies redeployed their resources. No other body better illustrates this than the Massachusetts Baptist Missionary Society, founded in 1802. It combined available pastors who could afford six weeks away from home pulpits per year, and available unassigned preachers on an approved list, with resources garnered from individual supporters, church contributions, and sporadic local gifts from the field. The Massachusetts Society developed methods and strategies that later national boards would emulate (see chapter 3 above).

The Expansion to Overseas Mission

Baptists were not pioneers in the "foreign" missionary enterprise. Preceding them were Roman Catholic orders, the Church of England, Pietists, and Congregationalists. In terms of Baptist engagement from North America, two influences were direct and pronounced: the Baptist Missionary Society and the Congregationalists. The Baptist Missionary

Society, formed in 1792, was the genius of the English Baptist mission-ary William Carey and English friends like Andrew Fuller at Kettering and John Sutcliff of Olney. Following an early lead of John Thomas, Carey convinced enough supporters (actually a fabled 13 original par-ticipants) to form a voluntary society and raise the funds to pay for his travel and initial upkeep in India. His tract, *A Solemn Enquiry* (1792), clearly indicated his appreciation for earlier efforts among the Danish and the evangelical Anglicans. By 1793 the exploits of Carey, and later Joshua Marshman and William Ward, were well-circulated in North America among the Baptist community and beyond. Among those who read of Carey were Adoniram Judson, Luther Rice, and others in the formative period of the American Board of Commissioners for Foreign Missions. Essentially a Congregationalist Reformed mission-sending group, this Board would play a major role in the development of Baptist overseas missions.

Carey's exploits were reported in the United States and Canada through copies of the *Periodical Accounts* that were widely circulated among the American Evangelical community. These annual papers drew from Carey's own reports and letters from other sources. They created an image of the overseas missionary as a sacrificial person who placed the gospel ahead of all else, including family. Sacrificial service de-served sacrificial giving and much prayer, since it was ultimately God's work. Local pastors used the *Accounts* to illustrate their sermons, and laypersons began in the 1790s to create voluntary associations in sup-port of Carey's mission at Serampore in West Bengal. Carey himself corresponded with Baptist leaders in the United States and was helpful in organizing the interest in mission work overseas. All of the first generation of American Baptist missionaries knew of William Carey and esteemed him highly.

As we have seen in the early history of the General Missionary Convention, there was no clear delineation in domestic and foreign missions among the first generation of organizers. It was only the limited financial resources that forced a priority and later a distinction between the needs in North America and those beyond. Theologically to missionary Baptists, the world was filled with the heathen, some closer to home than others. The strategy of American Baptists overseas was much the same on every continent. Derived largely from experi-ence with observation of other denominations and the English Baptists, American Baptist missionaries first worked for religious toleration to secure their permanent opportunities. Next, following Carey's and Judson's example, translation projects consumed their efforts, in part to teach missionaries the languages involved and, in part, to leave a lasting cultural heritage. Along the way, most missionaries engaged in church planting, though these efforts were limited in results. More impressive were the printing establishments, schools, dispensaries, and universities that were established and largely staffed by American resources and missionary faculty until well into the twentieth century. A final stage has turned out to be the clustering of churches into associations or conventions that can amass resources and make most decisions for themselves. From time to time, assessments were made of the overseas work and these were published for mission education and to cultivate interest in Baptist work overseas. Among the most erudite of these was Howard Malcolm's *Travels in Southeastern Asia* (1839) and A. H. Strong's *A Tour of the Missions* (1918).

The fields of American Baptist missions opened up in a kind of logical order. First came Burma, then Thailand, the Chinese in Thailand, and later China itself, India, Africa, Europe, and Latin America. These footholds constituted the first generation of missionary outreach from Baptists in North America. A second generation commenced with subgroups of Baptists embarking upon missions in Africa, China, India, and Latin America. Finally, Baptist missions from the North American sending agencies proliferated greatly in the mid-twentieth century as conservative and fundamentalist boards commissioned missionaries to virtually every country on the map open to westerners as well as a few clandestine places.

While it is not the intent of this survey of Baptists to record an exhaustive history of Baptist missions, mention of some major contributions sheds light upon the evolving nature of Baptists in the United States and Canada. Among the characteristics of the denomination that surfaced in relation to missions were: organized benevolence to a central, national program; gender and racial/ethnic diversity in appointments both to service and support; theological and social relevance for Baptist values; and national political and social integration with missiological objectives. The very first Baptist missionaries reflect many of these enduring characteristics.

Adoniram and Ann Judson, it will be recalled, energized Baptists on the home front in 1814 with the announcement of their conversion to Baptist principles. What they (and the second and third wives of Adoniram) accomplished in Burma clearly articulated Baptist ideals in American context. From the outset of his mission to Ava and later Tavoy, Adoniram had skills and opportunities to bridge cultures. His translation work on the Bible, completed in 1840, and accompanying linguistic tools, made him unique in the Burman Empire. He was called upon to be a translator, a diplomatic courier, and a reluctant negotiator of the peace between the Burmans and the British. With his second wife, Sarah Boardman, Judson continued to introduce western ideas to tribes in remote areas of the country. In his life devoted to missions, Judson defined the missionary vocation as well as anyone in any denomination. His New England education provided a foundation in language training and cultural understanding that the Baptist Board of Missions virtually adopted as policy, and that influenced the American Board of Commissioners for Foreign Missions as well. The sacrificial work of his wives, retold by Emily, his third wife, set a pattern for women missionaries not only as spouses but as gifted translators and scholars themselves. Finally, Adoniram Judson's advocacy of religious toleration, that reflected the democratic forces in Jacksonian America, generated an international appreciation for both Baptists and the United States.

Judson helped to orient and train a score of pioneer Baptist missionaries in his pattern, including George Dana Boardman, Cephas Bennett, Eugenio Kincaid, and Jonathan Wade. Boardman opened up the field with the Karen tribes and was succeeded by Francis Mason and Jonathan Wade. C. H. Carpenter began work in 1868 with the isolated hill Karens at Bassein. The Carpenters established schools that were quite effective in the evangelization process, and in 1876 could report the establishment of a Karen Baptist Home Mission Society that gradually assumed leadership for the work. This had been Carpenter's great dream. Between India and Burma, Baptists moved into the province of Assam. Nathan Brown, a linguistic genius the equal of William Carey, targeted the Shan peoples and then turned to Assamese. Later Josiah Cushing and his wife, Ellen, took up the translation challenge among the Shans. Likewise, Ola Hanson worked among the Kachin people. Later, American Freewill Baptists also worked in Bengal, Orissa, and Bihar, complementing the Regular Baptists from the US. The Nagaland Mission was so successful that at the end of the twentieth century a substantial portion of the Naga people was Christian and Baptist. While the actual conversions seem small – fewer than 4,000 in Burma by 1914 – the impact of the American Baptist presence in Burma was broad and long term in light of educational institutions and linguistic achievements.

Related to American Baptist work in Burma and Assam was the opening of their stations in India proper. It was among the Telugu tribes that American Baptists made a major impact in India. First a Freewill Baptist mission started by Amos Sutton, it turned to an effort by a Canadian, Samuel Stearns Day, and E. L. Abbott, an American. Nellore and Madras were chosen as the stations. Great enthusiasm was to accompany what became known as the "Lone Star Mission," from a poem by Samuel F. Smith, the author of "America!" In its first three quarters of a century, over 40,000 converts were baptized, making it one of the best efforts of American Baptists. Later in the century, at Ongole in 1866, John E. Clough, who was influenced by the work of Walter Rauschenbusch, took charge of a section of the Buckingham Canal construction project and so astutely supervised the work that he countered a starvation epidemic and reoriented the social and economic patterns of the local population. In one day at Ongole, July 3, 1878, 2,222 converts were baptized, with a continuing significant number through the remainder of the year. In 1925, the membership of the Ongole congregation was in excess of 10,000 persons. With the encouragement of American Baptists, a Telugu Baptist Home Mission Society assumed the leadership of the work of church planting after 1919. The Baptist witness in Madras and Nellore has evolved in an ecumenical pattern, with Baptists fully cooperating in educational and health care institutions.

Next to Adoniram Judson and the south Asian fields must come Johann Gerhard Oncken (1800–84). German born but raised in England and Scotland, Oncken nevertheless reflected American Baptist ideals about culture and missions. He served as a Bible colporteur for the British Continental Society and the Edinburgh Bible Society during the 1820s and came into contact with Barnas Sears, a theological professor from Hamilton, New York, who was on sabbatical in Europe in 1834. Sears interviewed Oncken and, satisfied with his basic convictions and baptistic orientations, baptized him in the River Elbe. Sears foresaw the potential impact of Oncken and immediately recruited him for an American relationship and service. Oncken became a long-term appointee of the American Baptist Foreign Mission Society and was a frequent contributor to the *American Baptist Magazine* for almost half a century.

Oncken was an evangelist and church planter. He established a base at Hamburg and that congregation became the center of wide travels and church development. Oncken administered the connection from Hamburg, where he established a press and newspaper. He itinerated among preaching stations in the German states, into Poland and Russia, and south to the Balkan states, Hungary, and Romania. He is seen as the pioneer Baptist in virtually every region of central and northern Europe along with his colleagues, Julius Köbner and Gustave Lehmann. Together they were called the "Kleeblatt" or "cloverleaf." Oncken and Köbner in particular studied American democratic ideals and focused upon the principle of separation of church and state, widely advocating these positions during the revolutionary era in Europe. Oncken wrote that the highest achievements in statehood had been reached both in Britain and the United States, especially the latter, where religious liberty prevailed. In 1848, just months after Karl Marx published his "Communist Manifesto," Köbner produced a "Manifesto of Free Primitive Christianity for the German People." The authorities were so antagonized by the document that they sought to destroy all extant copies and thwart the movement toward disestablishment. Oncken and Köbner were persistent, often suffering much harassment from local authorities, and more than once being imprisoned in Germany. More than any other single person, Oncken is credited with being a catalyst for religious toleration and, ultimately, freedom of religion in the principal German states. At one point, a story circulated that when asked to distinguish between the number of Baptist adherents and those who were formally missionaries, Oncken replied to a magistrate, "every Baptist is a missionary!" These words have become a part of the Baptist psyche over the years, creating a strong missionary impulse among Baptist believers worldwide and making Oncken a virtual hero among Baptists in the United States.

In the wake of Oncken's own far-reaching travels, American Baptists pursued a fairly aggressive policy in Europe. Often, there were crosscurrents with immigrant communities in the US. In Scandinavia, for instance Gustaf Shroeder, a Swedish sailor, established a Mariner's Mission in New York in 1844 that reached back to Sweden as well as to Illinois. F. O. Nilson, another Swede, had connections in Sweden and Minnesota, as did Anders Wiberg. Bethel Seminary became a center of Swedish-American Baptist missions, fostering a similar institution in Sweden. A Baptist congregation was started in Norway in 1860 by F. K. Rymker, who had been baptized in the United States. Denmark was largely the field of Julius Köbner. Baptists from the United States were minor players in Russia and the Baltic States, though strong efforts were made among those immigrant communities in the United States and Canada. The Mission Board of Ontario and Quebec fostered Russian churches in Ontario and Saskatchewan. In southeastern Europe, American Baptists were active at several points in Greece from 1836–86, and various regions of the Austro-Hungarian Empire among Romanians, Yugoslavs, Bulgarians, and Hungarians.

The American Baptist mission presence in the Far East was to assume a major role in the outreach of the Baptist community in North America. Beginning with a base in Southeast Asia, the Chinese community was targeted as an important priority in the 1830s and the Baptist Board for Foreign Missions appointed John Taylor Jones to Bangkok in 1832; two years later William Dean arrived to continue the mission. When treaties opened the Port of Hong Kong to foreign trading, J. Lewis Shuck began efforts there, followed by William Dean. Dean focused his time on Bible translation and a pastoral ministry among the Tie Chiu in Hong Kong. Eventually, he built upon the strong linguistic foundation he received at Madison University to launch a long-term Bible translation project that was uniquely Baptist in its nuances about believer's baptism. Dean was sensitive to Confucian thought and he pursued a careful literalism in translation. Those who followed in his train included William Ashmore in Swatow, South China, who assisted in the establishment of the first western university in China. Other missionaries in China sent out by the American Baptist Missionary Union (ABMU, formerly the General Missionary Convention and its Baptist Board of Foreign Missions) were Josiah Goddard in East China at Ningpo, William Upcraft and George Warner in West China, and Joseph Adams in central China. In 1914, American Baptists were supporting 72 missionaries in 21 stations across China.[1] Related to the work in China was the work that opened up in Japan as a result of Commodore Mathew Perry's voyages, allowing Jonathan Goble, and later Nathan Brown and C. H. Carpenter, both of whom had moved from earlier fields in the region, to commence evangelism and church planting. One of the most colorful Baptist efforts was that of Captain Luke Bickel, a merchant marine captain who commanded a "gospel ship" in the outer islands of Japan from 1899 to 1914. Illustrative of the "two-way principle" of missions, the work in China was the base from which Baptists began work among Chinese immigrants in California and Oregon at mid-century. The First Chinese Baptist Church in San Francisco was founded as the result of a furlough of American Baptist missionaries from China.

American Baptists were active in pursuit of missions in Africa from 1817, when the General Missionary Convention appointed the former slave Lott Carey to Liberia. Carey's work was well-received, but owing to the interplay of politics in the coastal regions, Carey lost his life in a military attack and American Baptists continued a sustained effort through the American Colonization Society for a few years. They returned to the central part of Africa when English Baptists found themselves unable to carry on their work. In 1878 the Livingstone Inland Mission was offered to Northern Baptists in the US and with the urging of Boston's Clarendon Street pastor, A. J. Gordon, the ABMU took over the field. Outstanding results in evangelization were soon forthcoming as illustrated by Catherine L. Mabie's heroic itinerant medical mission with almost no up-to-date medical supplies, and the

"Pentecost on the Congo" during which missionary Henry Richard baptized 11,000 converts from 1921 to 1924. American Baptists decided for much of the twentieth century to concentrate their efforts in the Congo, through good times and revolutions.

Southern Baptists were the second Baptist group in North America to pursue overseas missions work energetically. Historians of SBC life point to the high priority Southern Baptists have always given to evangelism and missions. This has led to an unfortunate isolation from cooperation with other Baptists, but at the same time countless achievements that are uniquely Southern Baptist. From the Convention's beginnings in 1845, a Foreign and a Domestic Mission Board were launched. The first field was China where J. Lewis Shuck was already established. Next came Nigeria where in 1854 the board made several appointments who could not withstand the tropical environment. Under extremely difficult health circumstances, W. J. David and William Colley in 1874 re-established a permanent mission at Lagos in conjunction with the Colored Baptist Convention of Virginia. Southern Baptists staked out their southern European claim with the appointment in 1871 of a medical doctor, W. M. Cote, in Rome. Cote hoped to build upon Italian political unification and extend a more liberal religious policy in the government of King Victor Emmanuel. Even more energizing to the Southern Baptists of the Southwest was the decision of the Foreign Mission Board in 1876 to enter Mexico; tragedy struck however when John Westrup was killed, and the plan to enter Mexico was slowed until 1880. Further Southern Baptist overseas growth occurred in 1871 with the first Baptist church constituted in Brazil under the guidance of Z. C. and Anne Taylor and W. B. and Kate Bagby. Cuba became an interesting challenge to the Southern Board as the American Baptist Home Mission Society laid plans for Baptist missions in that island. Eventually a comity agreement in 1898 held that the American Baptist Home Mission Society (ABHMS) would work in eastern Cuba while Southern Baptists continued in the western reaches of the island.

A third major Baptist missionary effort from North America has been associated with black Baptist development. As noted in chapter 3 above, Lott Carey and Colin Teague were appointed to Africa in 1819 jointly by the American Colonization Society and the General Missionary Convention. They established a beachhead for Baptist missions in Africa. Assuming the African mission from northern Baptists, in 1846 the Southern Baptist Board appointed two black Baptists, A. L. Jones and John Day, to West Africa. By mid-century, this led to a Southern Baptist mission force of 13 missionaries, seven ministers, and six teachers. Liberia was the first station, followed by Nigeria in the 1850s. The

Southern Baptist mission was built of blacks, because "They would be more acceptable to their own race; they would be more likely to live in Africa, and could be more cheaply sustained."[2] After the Civil War, Northern Baptists renewed their interest in Liberia and sustained 14 preachers and teachers in West Africa.

Because of its obvious connection with the origins of black Americans, Africa was the primary objective of black Baptist overseas missions from North America. Among black Baptists, there were four foci to the outreach: personal evangelism, personal piety, colonization, and establishing a Christian civilization in Africa. Between 1880 and 1883 part of the program of "uplifting the African race" involved missions to Africa. This gave rise to the Baptist Foreign Mission Convention (BFMC) in 1880 in Montgomery, Alabama. An outgrowth of black Baptist support, especially from Virginia, South Carolina, and North Carolina, the Convention was urged into reality by W. W. Colley who had served under the SBC in Africa and returned home to travel extensively among the black churches. The BFMC was cooperative with the American Baptist Missionary Union, the primary sending agency of the northern Baptist churches. It commissioned a number of black missionaries to Africa in the 1880s, a source of great pride to the black Baptist community.[3] Although the BFMC made attempts to become a national organization, receipts were insufficient for the program and the work in Africa suffered into the 1890s as a result.

As we have seen previously, the need for a national, comprehensive black Baptist organization was critical; the National Baptist Convention in the United States of America (NBCUSA) became a reality in 1895. Virginia black Baptists soon had cause to be concerned, however, because the location of the headquarters of the Foreign Mission Board was moved from Richmond to Louisville, Kentucky, and the NBCUSA decided to publish its own literature rather than use the material provided by the American Baptist Publication Society. Virginia was the locus of most support funding for foreign missions and the Virginia black Baptist community was upset with these changes. Consequently, those churches and pastors, primarily in Virginia and North Carolina, who wanted to cooperate with white Baptists, and who were disgruntled over the relocation of the Foreign Mission Board, met with others from the Middle Atlantic States at Shiloh Baptist Church in Washington, DC, in December 1897 to organize what became the Lott Carey Baptist Foreign Mission Convention (LCC). For the next decade, the Lott Carey personalities debated with the National Baptist Convention over cooperation in foreign missions, as well as waging sharp disagreements among many of the black Baptist state conventions, notably Virginia. Some semblance of reunion of the opposing parties was achieved in an agreement between the NBCUSA and the LCC in 1905, but this was short-lived. The two main supporters of black Baptist missions to Africa would inevitably follow separate courses. This proved to be a benefit to African missions, as historian Sandy D. Martin has shown. The Lott Carey contingent directed their support to Liberia and West Africa, while the National Baptist Convention focused upon southern Africa.[4] In the twentieth century, the LCC would work closely with the American Baptist Convention, while the National Baptists of both conventions (incorporated and unincorporated) would pursue separate mission strategies. The NBCUSA would in fact commence missions in other black areas like Haiti, the Bahamas, and Jamaica.

Demonstrative of the diversity among Baptists in North America with respect to overseas missions is the involvement of Seventh Day Baptists in missionary activity. Growing out of any early nineteenth-century interest in domestic missions, in 1824 a Seventh Day Baptist Board of Missions was formed. Four years later the independent American Seventh Day Baptist Missionary Society was chartered. Gradually, Seventh Day Baptists looked to conducting missions among other Christians and Sabbath-keeping Jews. From this secondary interest grew a mission to Palestine that operated until 1859. China was chosen as a major thrust of Sabbath-keeping work and this carried on from 1846 when Solomon and Lucy Carpenter sailed for China. The Seventh Day Baptist movement in China grew at a faster pace than in the United States, with its center in Shanghai where the largest sabbatarian congregation in the world (670 members) was located before the Communist takeover in 1949.[5] Other fields of Seventh Day Baptists were opened in Guyana, the Netherlands, Germany, Australia, Brazil, Jamaica, Malawi, India, and Mexico. The chief benefit from all of the mission effort of these Sabbath-keeping Americans overseas was the formation in 1964 of the Seventh Day Baptist World Federation, an interconnecting family that was ahead of other Baptists in building cooperative international relations.

In the overseas mission context, Baptists from the United States learned at length to interact with other kinds of Christians, in some instances with very positive results. There was a definite sense of democratic imperialism and colonialism that prevailed at first. This was gradually superseded by a cooperative partnership in the Northern Baptist context, while Southern Baptists retained tighter control over their missionary work, preferring to support a hierarchical leadership from the base in Richmond, Virginia, that was under full-time appointment of the Board. The continuing appointive power structure was to have ramifications, especially as observed by T. P. Crawford and others.

Missions Reflect Tensions Within the Baptist Family

Almost immediately upon the organization of the Southern Baptist Convention in 1845, the Baptist program in missions reflected political and organizational strife. In the South, there were those who favored a replication of the mission work of the General Missionary Convention, so aggressive steps were taken to recruit certain missionaries from the American Baptist Foreign Mission Society to the new Foreign Mission Board. There was a second group in the new convention that desired an entirely new scheme of missionary organization that was practically centralized and Southern Baptist in ethos. They looked to developing new fields and a new generation of personnel. In the North, as already noted, the General Missionary Convention was reorganized in 1846 as the American Baptist Missionary Union and it implemented the long-standing program of stations in Europe, Burma, China, and for a time among Indian tribes in the western United States. As historian Robert Torbet suggested 50 years ago, the Society before 1845, and the American Baptist Missionary Union thereafter, seemed to be perpetually in debt, with more funds committed than in hand, and this apparently had a salubrious effect upon the stewardship demands of the churches. Churches, Torbet maintained, responded more generously to a board in need than to clever administrations that kept balanced books.[6]

Among Baptists in the North, the slavery issue again had its impact. A movement to lodge missionary endeavor as one of the great moral issues confronting American society had its origins in the social reform movements of New England, western New York, and the Old Northwest. Baptists had responded enthusiastically to antimasonry, temperance, and peace in the 1830s and were organized around local coalitions opposed to slavery. The burgeoning antislavery movement was led by a number of Baptists or former Baptists, notably William Lloyd Garrison. Many in the more committed congregations believed action had to be taken and in 1843 they formed the American and Foreign Missionary Society. Outspoken reformers like William H. Brisbane and Albert Post had pressed their case against slavery to both the home and foreign mission societies, but to little avail. Some missionaries in the Burma field were of similar sentiments and also disagreed with the educational policies of the Society; they withdrew from the American Baptist Foreign Mission Society and joined cause with the new antislavery body called the American Baptist Free Mission Society in 1848. Not only did the Free Mission Society make its case against allowing a connection between slaveholding and missions through its publications and annual meetings, but it also raised a considerable amount of financial support in both Canada and the United States for overseas personnel in Burma, Japan, and Haiti. The well-known missionary to Japan, Nathan Brown, became the corresponding secretary for the Society through its years of service. In 1872, in recognition that the old issues had passed into history, the American Baptist Free Mission Society merged its programs and personnel with the American Baptist Missionary Union and the Consolidated American Baptist Missionary Convention (African American), thus bringing unity once again to the mission effort of Baptists in the northern states.

A serious threat to the unity of Southern Baptist missions erupted in 1877. Called the "Gospel Mission" movement, it originated in the Landmarkist tradition among Southern Baptists. Tarlton P. Crawford and his wife, Martha Foster Crawford, Southern Baptist missionaries appointed in 1851 to China encountered difficulties with J. B. Hartwell and Henry A. Tupper at the Foreign Mission Board. Further, the Crawfords noted large problems among Chinese mission workers involved in money-laundering and Bible distribution. Crawford also objected to the use of educational and humanitarian institutions to conduct evangelism and he came to prefer direct personal evangelism. Having invested heavily in real estate ventures, the Crawfords became independently wealthy and concluded that missionaries should be self-supporting. Crawford boldly opposed "subsidy" expenditures, claiming "the subsidy load is made up of costly chapels, costly schools of various kinds, native preachers, colporters [sic], Bible women, dispensaries, hospitals, patients and other hangers-on to mission funds generally." Instead, he argued that "the work of foreign missions should not embrace all sorts of good things, as the public has been led to believe; but, it should be confined to preaching the gospel to every creature, etc., according to the command of Christ."[7] Their views were presented in scholarly papers at a council in China of Protestant missionaries in 1877 and were generally well received. This followed their Landmarkist theological leanings and the Crawfords initiated a self-supporting plan for missions that made great inroads among Southern Baptist churches as they itinerated while on furlough in 1878–79. By the mid-1890s T. P. Crawford had become such a problem for the board that his resignation was sought and he stepped down from his appointment to the North China field in 1889. In his resignation, he clearly asserted Landmarkist ecclesiology:

> Having long ago taken the New Testament as the standard of my Christian faith and as the guide-book of my religious life, I cannot acknowledge the right of any Central Board or general committee of individuals to take official control over any part of its ministry and gospel work. In my candid judgment there is no provision in its pages, expressed or implied, for such a body.[8]

Mrs Crawford continued to serve the Board for mission support and set a precedent that would influence later independent missionary work.

The fundamentalist controversy of the 1920s had a serious impact upon Baptist missions in the oldest sending organization. The American Baptist Foreign Mission Society gave the impression during and after World War I that it was primarily oriented toward education and humanitarian work in schools and hospitals with a lessening interest in evangelism. Fundamentalists were quick to find quotations from field personnel that appeared to deny key doctrines of the faith like the deity of Christ or the final authority of the Scriptures. It seemed as if the Society was sending out both orthodox and unorthodox missionaries indiscriminately with a greater emphasis upon educational qualifications than spirituality. To fend off the critics, the chairman of the Society's Board of Managers, Frederick L. Anderson, announced what later became an appointment policy for the ABFMS:

> Guided by the facts that Baptists have always been known as evangelicals, and that the gospel is the most important message of the Scriptures, we have demanded that all our officers and missionaries be loyal to the gospel. We will appoint only suitable evangelical men and women; we will appoint evangelicals, and we will not appoint nonevangelicals. And by the gospel we mean the good news of the free forgiveness of sin and eternal life . . . This salvation is graciously offered on the sole condition of repentance and faith in Christ and has in it the divine power of regeneration and sanctification through the Spirit. The only reason we have for accepting this gospel is our belief in the deity of Christ . . . a faith founded on the trustworthiness of the Scriptures, and the fact that we have experienced this salvation in our own hearts.[9]

In general, moderate fundamentalists accepted the definition for the time being. The more staunchly committed fundamentalists labeled the Anderson Plan the "Inclusivist Policy," left the Convention, and looked for other avenues to fulfill their missionary imperative.

The leading Baptist mission thrusts that reflected radical fundamentalist theology were Baptist Mid-Missions (BMM), the Association of Baptists for World Evangelism (ABWE), and the Conservative Baptist Foreign Mission Society (CBFMS). ABWE represented a moderate form of fundamentalism, BMM a more strident critique of mainstream Baptist missions, and CBFMS a later mainstream evangelical response. These organizations became major players in the development of Baptist overseas missionary work in the twentieth century.

Baptist Mid-Missions was born in the Northern Baptist tradition. The lead role was played by William Haas (1873–1924), a high-school-educated Baptist minister and evangelist from Michigan. Haas was pastor of Union City Baptist Church in Michigan, and then Manchester Baptist Church in Caldwell, Ohio. In a third pastorate in Columbus, Ohio, Haas felt a call to full-time mission work in Africa and sought appointment from the American Baptist Foreign Mission Society in 1908. He had serious reservations about the Northern Baptist Convention (probably over educational requirements) and they expressed no interest in starting a new field in Africa. Haas turned to the independent Africa Inland Mission and there found support for his appointment to French Africa where he could establish Baptist churches. Haas arrived in mid-Africa in 1912, eventually reaching French Equatorial Africa where he and his wife traveled widely and distributed Bibles while they preached. They returned to the United States in 1916 and 1920 to raise additional support for their proposed work.[10]

Haas observed what he believed were unbiblical tendencies in the Northern Baptist community and he gravitated toward the fundamentalist faction led by William Bell Riley and others. He visited Riley's Northwestern Schools and Moody Bible Institute where he found support for his call to Africa. In Cleveland, Ohio, he met Edwin S. Carman, a wealthy businessman and Baptist layman who was taken with Haas's proposals. In September 1920, amid the fundamentalist storm in the Northern Baptist Convention, Haas, Carman, and 10 others formed the General Council of Cooperating Baptist Missions of North America upon strictly evangelical principles. The field name of the organization became "Mid-Africa Mission," and eventually by the 1930s, Baptist Mid-Missions.

Slowly during the Great Depression the work of Baptist Mid-Missions grew to include several stations in Africa and then Latin America. Given the number of congregations in the United States and Canada that had withdrawn from the Northern Baptist Convention and the Baptist Convention of Ontario and Quebec, scores of independent fundamentalist Baptist churches moved to identify Mid-Africa

Missions as their foreign missionary sending agency. In 1931 the board of the mission affirmed an independent Baptist stance, committed to local church autonomy and biblical separationism. Haas had always maintained that the council was advisory only and that policy making was reserved to the supporting churches. A momentous step was taken in 1932 when the General Association of Regular Baptist Churches was formed and immediate approval was given to Mid-Africa Missions as an approved orthodox mission. The partnership resulted in greater attention to the administrative details of Baptist Mid-Missions, providing for field representatives to raise funds, public financial reports, scrutiny of personnel health records, and designated funds for administration in the home office.[11]

The Association of Baptists for World Evangelism (ABWE) was a moderate fundamentalist response to the Northern Baptist inclusive policy and interdenominational cooperation in missions. In 1926 when Dr Raphael C. Thomas, a medical missionary of the American Baptist Foreign Mission Society since 1904, was reprimanded for open advocacy of evangelism over social service, he resigned from the ABFMS and returned to the US to raise support from friends. Lucy W. Peabody, who was Thomas's mother-in-law, and Marguerite Treat Doane, daughter of the hymnist William Howard Doane, joined Thomas's support and gave birth to ABWE in 1927–28. The new scheme, called Association of Baptists for Evangelism in the Orient, was a voluntary association of confessional supporters rather than a denominational board. It was identified with Curtis Laws, Frank Goodchild, J. C. Massee, and others who had founded Eastern Baptist Theological Seminary only two years before. The first field of ABWE was the Philippines, where Thomas's work continued at Iloilo on Panay Island. Latin American appointments followed as a major field in due course, and as a result, the name was changed in 1939 to Association of Baptists for World Evangelism (ABWE). ABWE stations were also established by the 1960s in Hong Kong, Chile, Japan, and Pakistan. Headquartered in Harrisburg, Pennsylvania, ABWE employs around 1,100 workers in 75 countries and adheres to a theologically evangelical confession of faith. It is the largest of the fundamentalist Baptist sending organizations.

A third major theologically driven agency that emerged from the Northern Baptist Convention was the Conservative Baptist Foreign Mission Society. When the American Baptist Foreign Mission Society held its course under existing appointment policies in the late 1930s and early 1940s, stalwart Northern Baptist evangelicals wondered if they could in good conscience remain within convention structures. In response to a call to all "conservatives" from Earl Pierce and John W.

Bradbury, the Fundamental Baptist Fellowship was formed in 1943 and included a substantial number of NBC churches. At first an attempt was made to become a recognized agency of the Northern Baptist Convention but this was rejected by the NBC leadership who observed that due process of recognition had not been followed. In late 1943 the Fellowship became the Conservative Baptist Foreign Mission Society. One historian calculated that in its first five years, the CBFMS sent over one hundred missionaries to 30 stations in India, China, Japan, the Philippines, Latin America, central Africa, and Europe.[12] Theological strife continued as the Conservative Baptist movement found its way and a further split occurred in 1961 whereby a radical conservative branch left the CBF and followed pastors like Richard Clearwaters of Minnesota. Ultimately, Clearwaters assumed an independent missions stance and many of the affiliated congregations came to support the missionary work of Baptist Mid-Missions.

New Paradigms of Mission for Baptists

The American Baptist missionary effort sought an intentional ecumenical posture early in the twentieth century. Following the lead of the newly organized Northern Baptist Convention, that became a charter member of the Federal Council of Churches of Christ, the ABFMS cooperated with other evangelical agencies as long as compromise of principles was not at stake. This cooperation included joint personnel appointments on the fields like in China and India, membership in the Foreign Missions Conference, the Missionary Education Movement, the Laymen's Missionary Movement, the International Missionary Council, the Student Christian Movement, and the Student Volunteer Movement. Administratively, American Baptists participated in cooperative medical assessments of overseas personnel, transportation arrangements, and various conferences to share information and strategies. Ultimately, major ecumenical cooperation occurred in Europe through various councils of churches, in India where American Baptists cooperated with the Church of North India, and, later in the century, in the People's Republic of China with the Amity Foundation and The China Christian Council.

Southern Baptists rejected cooperation on the foreign fields. In 1914, as the Foreign Mission Board elected new leadership under executive secretary J. F. Love, important decisions were made that would affect Southern Baptist missions for generations to come. The church union movement that included both ecumenical organizations and increased cooperation on the mission fields troubled many Southern Baptists, particularly those with a bent toward Landmarkism. In 1916, after a two-year study of the matter, the Southern Baptist Foreign Mission Board recommended to the Convention that the denomination remain true to New Testament principles and preserve the unity of the denomination by enlisting its own forces for the holy cause of missions. What this meant was that Southern Baptists declined participation in missionary endeavor with other Christian bodies as well as other Baptists. Although they had been singularly successful in comity agreements at the turn of the century, the new policy ruled out future boundary disputes in missions by essentially claiming all fields open to Southern Baptist witness. As Secretary Love stated, "Baptists can render the greatest help to those who carry missionary burdens by faithfully carrying their own."[13]

Southern Baptists expanded their roster of commissioned missionaries in the twentieth century, concentrating first on fields in China, Nigeria, and Latin American nations. The Board's efforts picked up momentum after World War II, under the leadership of M. Theron Rankin and Baker James Cauthen, both former missionaries to China. Expansion became the watchword, with efforts being made in over one hundred new countries on every continent from 1948 through 1990. Rankin stressed indigenous work wherever possible, religious liberty in countries where it was essentially denied, and an overall advance in the number of missionaries under appointment. At the conclusion of Rankin's secretariat, the Board had appointed over 650 missionaries and there were over 900 in active service. Cauthen worked hard at missionary education on the home front, promoting the Baptist Jubilee Advance and Bold Mission Thrust among Baptists in North America and reorganizing the entire administrative staff to allow for international area secretaries. Cauthen also fostered a program of missionary associates and Missionary Journeymen who, as volunteers, complemented the appointed missionaries. While Southern Baptists coordinated massive relief efforts with governments, the long-standing policy against cooperation with other Christian bodies remained largely intact: when the Foreign Missions Conference of North America in 1943 joined the National Council of Churches, the SBC withdrew its support; an invitation to participate in the Church of Christ in Japan in 1940–43 was refused, and overtures to join the uniting churches of India in the 1950s and 1960s were rejected. Symbolic of the emerging prestige of the Foreign Mission Board was the erection in 1957 of a new world headquarters building in Richmond, Virginia, that has in recent years been substantially enlarged.

The Ebb and Flow of Missions

For American Baptists, the period between 1980 and 2000 was a time of sharp retrenchment and new understandings of how to do missions. A combination of factors led to these changes, including a downturn in funding for missions due to reduced money available to the national boards, competition between American Baptist educational ministries and home missions, changing geo-political circumstances, and a disastrous downturn in the invested income of the Society. The overall overseas missionary force was reduced from about 200 in 1980 to about 120 after 2000.

Recognizing that the most expensive way to conduct missions overseas was to appoint career missionaries, in the 1980s the American Baptist Board of International Ministries (BIM) began to redefine its work. While still maintaining full-time mission personnel in strategic areas and historic American Baptist fields like Zaire, Thailand, Hong Kong, Japan, and Haiti, they made grants of support to other fields and Baptist unions to "indigenize" the work. The Baptist Council on World Mission was created in 1968 among American Baptist partners, and relations through the Baptist World Alliance were strengthened to communicate and coadminister programs with mission partners. An important form of American Baptist support went to institutions like colleges and seminaries overseas. Unstable political activities in Africa and Asia led to reduction of staff, while the downfall of the Soviet Union opened unprecedented opportunities in the new republics of central Asia. The interaction of new ideas of cooperation with diminished investment and contribution funding led to numerous cooperative ventures with European Baptists, Cooperative Baptists, and Canadian Baptists, to mention a few. Under John A. Sundquist, a former executive minister in Ohio, BIM redefined itself and celebrated several milestones in its long history. Overall, however, the number of traditional missionaries was dramatically reduced. American Baptist statistical reports for this period routinely included figures for a combined membership "of one denomination." In fact there were as many Baptists claiming to be related to the ABC overseas as in the homeland in 1980. Further, American Baptists counted overseas associational organizations as part of their denominational structures. Currently, American Baptists have missions in 29 countries with 169 mission partnerships.

Much American Baptist attention was given to matters of social justice in mission and overseas relationships. The continuing apartheid situation in South Africa is a prime example. Here the work of the Rev. Leon Sullivan, pastor of Philadelphia's Zion Baptist Church, became definitive. As a means of placing economic pressure on the South African government to end segregation, Sullivan proposed six principles, among which were: fair employment, pay equity, appointment of black managers in industries, and job training programs that would guide the future of South Africa. He further urged the American Baptist General Board to desist from investing in any South African corporation until apartheid ended. In the end, when the South African government was changed, the Sullivan Principles were a triumph for social justice in missions.

Major changes in Southern Baptist outlook toward missions occurred, beginning in 1980, when R. Keith Parks took over as executive director. Parks was a career missionary and was familiar with the existing paradigms. When Parks succeeded Baker J. Cauthen, he set about reorienting Southern Baptists from a denominational strategy to a Global Evangelization strategy. This meant that the new objectives of the Foreign Board (after 1997, the International Mission Board) were evangelism and church planting, particularly in areas not reached by the gospel. This required specialization at the center, and so Parks convened regular consultations in the Richmond offices with world missions specialists referred to as "Great Commission" sending agencies; he also secured the services of David Barrett, a prominent Church of England mission statistician, to keep pace with world needs. One noticeable change under Parks was the adoption of a corporate model where a series of vice presidents took responsibility for the work divisions and Parks himself became president of the Board.

Although highly qualified for his role and energetic in his pursuit of objectives, Parks presided over the demise of the Southern Baptist foreign mission enterprise as it had been shaped over the previous half century. His initiatives included: an office of intercessory prayer; Bold Mission Thrust as a comprehensive mission strategy; "Seven Controlling Principles" that entailed a primary objective of evangelism, emphasis upon career missionaries, an indigenous principle of church and leadership development, and strong communications with the SBC constituency; a missionary learning center; and a redoubled recruitment of volunteers. With a relentless postmillennial fervor, Parks and Southern Baptists held to the objective of preaching the gospel to the entire world by 2000, in fulfillment of Matthew 24: 14. But Parks had to contend with an increasingly conservative Board of Trustees who began to manage the work of missions itself. Perhaps the most troubling issue was centered on the Southern Baptist seminary located in

Rüschlikon, Switzerland. Founded in 1949 to train leaders for postwar Europe, its faculty was an amalgam of European scholars and Southern Baptist missionaries. It developed a reputation for European-style theology that offended increasing numbers of conservatives at home. In 1991, an investigation of the program at Rüschlikon was undertaken and funds were withheld, crippling the school's program. Tensions mounted between the Board and Parks, who supported the seminary, and between Southern Baptists and European Baptists. A deep rift opened between Southern Baptists and all of their European partners when support for the seminary was withdrawn completely and Parks himself, along with two prominent vice presidents, left the Board's service in 1992. Suspicion of the trustworthiness of commitments by the International Mission Board swept through the Baptist world in the 1990s, as the fundamentalist takeover at home continued unabated. As of 2005, the International Mission Board employs 5,220 career missionaries plus 30,000 volunteers in an overseas church membership of over seven million, a considerable outreach of American Christian culture.

Historians of Canadian Baptist missions note substantial changes in their outreach during this same era.[14] For much of the twentieth century, Canadian overseas missions had been concentrated in a limited number of fields: Bolivia, India, and Africa. As Bolivia and India matured in organizational terms, Canadian Baptists, according to a plan first developed by Orville Daniel, planned to pull back support gradually in these areas and develop new fields in cooperation with other boards. The major efforts were made in Brazil, Eastern Europe, Indonesia, and Asia. A funding crisis in the 1990s resulted in the amalgamation of the Canadian Baptist International Ministries organization with the Canadian Baptist Federation, leading to a comprehensive redistribution of denominational effort. The new leadership of the overseas mission, Canadian Baptist Ministries, came to include prominent Canadian Baptist pastors along with career missionaries.

In recounting the advance of North American missions in the last half of the twentieth century, one is tempted to limit the discussion to mainstream boards. Doing so misses the important growth of theologically defined missionary work that outdistanced the work of older agencies and parts of the denomination. ABWE, for instance, became the largest Baptist sending agency in North America. Primarily involved in evangelism and church planting, it has remained a confessional pan-Baptist organization, Second to ABWE is Baptist Mid-Missions, that represents the fundamentalist churches of the GARBC and the Fellowship of Evangelical Baptists in Canada. With headquarters in Cleveland,

Ohio, and Moncton, New Brunswick, BMM employs over a thousand workers in 50 countries. Again with emphasis upon evangelism, BMM also works in aviation, radio, publications, translation, and camping ministries. Third, CB International, the modernized form of Canadian Baptist Foreign Missions, has stations in 60 countries and employs five hundred missionaries, more than double that of the ABFMS from which it originated in 1944.

Legacy: Whose Interpretation of the Gospel Prevails?

In being faithful to the Great Commission, Baptists in North America have seen themselves as uniquely qualified and enabled to evangelize the rest of the world. The "qualification" stems from their fidelity to scriptural Christianity, and they are "enabled" by virtue of their growth and financial resources that far outdistance other Protestant groups. Part of the reality of mission in the twentieth century, however, is that Baptists do not agree on the interpretation of the gospel that best advances their group interests and identity.

At the root of the interpretation of the gospel lies the thorny issue of how one understands the authority of Scripture. Since the 1920s in the Northern/American Baptist denomination, there has been disagreement over whether missionaries who accept a higher critical view of Scripture were trustworthy exponents of the gospel. Not accepting an infallible Bible limits their ability to communicate an authoritative evangelical message, it has been argued. For this reason, conservative evangelicals, and later fundamentalists, would not support most missionary candidates from schools like Colgate, Rochester, Crozer, or the University of Chicago, where more progressive views of the Bible were taught. Instead, they preferred to support candidates who had completed a Bible course at Gordon Missionary Training School, Moody Bible Institute, or the Bible Institute of Los Angeles. Here an educational differentiation subtly emerged, namely the American Baptist Foreign Mission Society basically preferred a bachelor's degree plus seminary for full-time appointment, while fundamentalists approved candidates with unaccredited Bible college degrees or less.

Embedded within the Southern Baptist disinclination to cooperate with other mainstream Baptists on the mission fields was the authority of Scripture issue. Since the turn of the last century, Southern Baptists have defended their denominationally exclusive stance on the basis of their strict advocacy of New Testament Christianity, as they understand New Testament principles. Even more, SBC policy statements have delineated sharp lines between SBC understandings of the gospel and those of other religious groups, presumably the Northern/American Baptist Convention. A 1914 Southern Baptist report read in part, "We believe that the highest efficiency of the Southern Baptist Convention in the propagation of the Gospel can be attained . . . by preserving a complete autonomy at home and abroad, unembarrassed by entangling alliances with other bodies holding to different standards of doctrine and different views of church life and order."[15] This was due in large part to the participation of Northern Baptists in ecumenical discussions as well as wholesale adoption of higher criticism and the principles of the social gospel and religious pluralism.

Another differentiating factor was the debate over the objective of missionary work. From the adoption of the Judsons as the first American Baptist missionaries, the primary work of the missionary was preaching the gospel, starting new churches, and translating the Bible. Judson's inability to win many converts in his first few years, which mirrored the experience of William Carey from England, was rationalized by pointing out the great contribution he made in Scripture translation. As time went on, and more missionaries went overseas, a virtual Baptist foreign service emerged. This required field administrators and area supervisors at home in New York, Richmond, or Toronto. More importantly, the objectives of missionary work expanded to embrace education, both undergraduate and theological schools; Christian associations and organizations; medical work; and even clerical and support personnel. T. P. Crawford was among the first to question the purpose of sending missionaries overseas to perform tasks that were better accomplished by indigenous persons. Increasingly after the turn of the twentieth century, American Baptist missionary heroes came to include those who engaged in major educational missions, like William Ashmore in China, or humanitarian projects, like John E. Clough in India. Clough was praised as an extension of his wife's brother, Walter Rauschenbusch. Similarly, among Canadian Baptists, Archibald Reekie and a train of missionaries educated at McMaster University dominated Canadian Baptist missions in Bolivia. In contrast, however, Northern Baptist missionaries like Rafael Thomas objected to this social gospel trend or engagement in political activities and pressed the ABFMS Board to appoint him to a strictly evangelical assignment.

A survey of the work of fundamentalist Baptist missions outside of North America demonstrates that the fundamentalist sending agencies that served groups like the GARBC, Conservative Baptist Missions, the World Baptist Fellowship and the Fellowship of Evangelical Baptists in

Canada, have concentrated on "evangelical" missions, that is, preaching and planting churches. Where they have ventured beyond those basic activities, it has been in support of a seminary or Bible college to train indigenous pastors and workers, such as in Africa or the Philippines.

The legacy of the North American Baptist missionary outreach also portrays cultural factors. For instance, Northern/American Baptists began to make appointments of single women in the late nineteenth century through their Woman's American Baptist Foreign Mission Societies. By the 1980s, women held appointments in almost all phases of American Baptist work. Southern Baptists, on the other hand, appointed women to nonpastoral roles and continue to refuse women as candidates for ordained ministries. Fundamentalist Baptists uniformly oppose appointing women to ordained or pastoral responsibilities and make this a mark of their mission work. In addition to the claimed lack of scriptural evidence in support of women in ministry, those opposed to the practice argue that appointing women in positions of spiritual leadership overseas would offend the receiving countries, many of whom would be Hindu, Muslim, or Buddhist. Women may be appointed to teach women in overseas schools, to serve as nurses, and to translate the Scriptures among these groups. Likewise, Baptist missions from North America have exhibited a distinct racial exclusivity. There are few non-Caucasians in the overseas staffs of any major or minor Baptist overseas sending agency, nor are there any nonblack appointees from a black Baptist organization.

An intriguing symbolic feature of Baptist presence overseas lies in the development and construction of mission institutions. Not only did North American mission agencies transplant their associational networks to the fields, but also the terminology of organizations reflected the Baptist vocabulary. English language terms like "association," "union," and "alliance" were transliterated into a variety of languages, not to speak of the insistence upon the Baptist language of immersion for "baptism." Perhaps most vivid in this respect were the physical structures North American Baptists built overseas: the Reekie Memorial Church in Oruro, Bolivia, strongly resembled that of First Baptist, Halifax, Nova Scotia; the Shanghai and Tengchow Baptist churches in China imitated Southern Baptist church buildings in Kentucky and Virginia, respectively; and the New England Baptist chapel that A. J. Gordon sent in sections ready to be assembled to Banza Manteke in 1886, required African Christians to carry 700 loads 60 miles up the Congo River, sometimes making as many as five arduous trips per carrier.

Finally, the issue of control reflects a not-so-subtle attitude of North American cultural superiority among many Baptist-sending agencies. One of the reasons why administrative functions were handled largely in North America for so long was the matter of money. Baptists at home were slow to trust overseas administrators in spending money, so the decisions as to how the funds were to be allocated were made "at home" upon recommendations of field personnel. Other administrative practices in the selection of local officers of the missions, program emphases, and the public image of overseas mission endeavor continue to emphasize North American priorities. This has been somewhat mollified in light of consultations like the Lausanne Congress on World Evangelization, and other meetings that have stressed the need to co-operate and "partner" with churches on a global basis. Also the rise of larger and more extensive evangelical mission efforts has forced the older Baptist sending organizations to modify their programs.

Notes

1   Robert G. Torbet, *Venture of Faith: The Story of the American Baptist Foreign Mission Society and the Woman's American Baptist Foreign Mission Society 1814–1954* (Philadelphia, PA: Judson Press, 1955), 294.
2   *Annual and Proceedings, The Southern Baptist Convention*, 1869, 36.
3   Sandy D. Martin, *Black Baptists and African Missions: The Origins of a Movement 1880–1915* (Macon, GA: Mercer University Press, 1989), 77.
4   Ibid., 184.
5   Don A. Sanford, *A Choosing People: The History of Seventh Day Baptists* (Nashville, TN: Broadman Press, 1992), 184, 287.
6   Torbet, *Venture of Faith*, 152, 176.
7   T. P. Crawford, *Evolution in My Mission Views, or Growth of Gospel Mission Principles in My Own Mind* (Fulton, KY: J. A. Scarboro, 1903), 52, 81.
8   Ibid., 159.
9   Quoted in Robert G. Torbet, *History of the Baptists* (Valley Forge, PA: Judson Press, 1963), 399–400.
10 The history of the mission is told in Polly Strong, *Burning Wicks: The Story of Baptist Mid-Missions* (Cleveland, OH: Baptist Mid-Missions, 1984).
11 Strong, *Burning Wicks*, 149–50.
12 Torbet, *History of the Baptists*, 401.
13 Quoted in William R. Estep, *Whole Gospel, Whole World: The Foreign Mission Board of the Southern Baptist Convention 1845–1995* (Nashville, TN: Broadman Press, 1994), 194.

14 Harry A Renfree, *Heritage and Horizon: The Baptist Story in Canada* (Mississauga, ON: Canadian Baptist Federation, 1988), 303–15; Donald H. Fraser, "An Evolving Partnership: Canadian Baptist Missions in Bolivia" in William H. Brackney (ed.), *Bridging Cultures and Hemispheres: The Legacy of Archibald Reekie and Canadian Baptists in Bolivia* (Macon, GA: Smyth and Helwys Publishers, 1997), 40–7.
15 "Report on Denominational Efficiency," *Annual of the Southern Baptist Convention 1914*, 77.

Chapter 10
Social Concerns and Mores: The Legacy of an Evangelical Tradition

As the organizational maturation of Baptists in North America transpired, churches, associations, and individuals exhibited a profile of social concerns. More than a simple profession of doctrinal standards, these concerns placed Baptists often at the head of applied Christianity in North America. Not all Baptists at all times held to the characteristics discussed below; in fact some Baptists oppose the major tenets of mainstream churches and leaders. It is by looking across time and comparing the Baptist experience to others in the American and Canadian Protestant mainstreams, that a balanced profile of the greater portion of Baptists in North America emerges.

Cultural Issues That Defined Baptists

Religious liberty

As far as Baptists are concerned, religious liberty is the foundational human right. From their beginnings, Baptists have been leaders in the struggle to achieve religious freedom for all peoples, regardless of race, creed, social status, or gender. Baptists in North America inherited this libertarian bent from their English forebears, notably the General Baptists. It was Thomas Helwys who first asserted "Let them be heretics, Turks, Jews, or whatsoever, it appertains not to the early power to punish them in the least measure."[1] Likewise, Roger Williams, who bridged the Old Country and the New World, wrote in his classic *Bloudy Tenent of Persecution for Cause of Conscience* (1644), "God requires not a uniformity of religion to be enacted and enforced in any civil state . . . toleration of [erroneous persons] ought to continue till doomsday . . . persecution for cause of conscience, is most evidently and lamentably contrary to the doctrine of Jesus Christ, the Prince of Peace. . . ."[2] In their discourse about the subject, Baptists have used the terms "religious toleration," "religious freedom," and "religious liberty," as well as "soul freedom" and "soul liberty," sometimes interchangeably. Basically, toleration was a key term in the seventeenth century for Baptists as they more or less accepted the reality of a religious establishment. Toleration was also sought in the missionary context in Asia and Latin America where existing governments had failed to recognize the human rights of minorities. "Soul freedom" and "soul liberty" have been connected especially with Roger Williams and his spiritual descendants. Beginning in the eighteenth century, Baptists came to be more vocal about their right to religious liberty and sought through various means to achieve religious freedom. Conceptually the phrase "religious liberty" is an all-encompassing term.

In the narrative above, we have seen how Baptists stood against colonial ecclesiastical harassment over the baptism of children, enforced registration of religious groups, and taxation for support of state churches in Massachusetts, Connecticut, and in the South, Virginia, Carolina, and Georgia. At first this was focused upon specific and usually local instances as in Bristol, Massachusetts in 1729 when 30 persons, Baptists, Churchmen, and Quakers, were committed to the Bristol Jail, "by reason of their refusing to pay ye minister's rate."[3] But, by the mid-eighteenth century, in situations like the Ashfield, Massachusetts, case in 1769–71 when Baptists were denied tax exemption certificates for their status as dissenters, local grievances became general concerns and a full-blown case for religious freedom was made. By the 1770s in the work of Isaac Backus and John Leland, the larger issue of religious freedom became highly focused as a campaign to ensure the separation of church and state. For Baptists there would be two major achievements from the eighteenth century effort: the ratification of the First Amendment to the US Constitution that provided for "no law respecting an establishment of religion, or prohibiting the free exercise thereof," and the gradual abolition of state-supported churches in Massachusetts, Connecticut, New Hampshire, and Vermont.

Among all US denominations of Christians, Baptists have continued to be vigilant in pursuit of religious liberty and separation of church and state. This happened in the nineteenth century through the missionary outreach of the Baptist communities, mostly the American Baptist Missionary Union. Major accomplishments were noted in Burma, India, Latin America, Europe, and China for a time.

In the twentieth century, religious liberty concerns were once again focused in the decade after World War I as new governments settled in central and eastern Europe and totalitarian regimes emerged in Italy, Germany, and Japan. However, Baptists were equally concerned about the tendency of the Roosevelt presidency officially to recognize the Vatican as a political state. This overall anxiety produced in 1939 the "American Baptist Bill of Rights," a powerful, united statement affirming religious liberty. The statement, ratified by the Northern Baptist Convention, the Southern Baptist Convention, and the National Baptist Convention, USA, in part read:

> No issue in modern life is more urgent or more complicated than the relation of organized religion to organized society. The sudden rise of the European dictators to power has changed fundamentally the organic law of the governments through which they exercise sovereignty, and as a result, the institutions of religion are either suppressed or made subservient to the ambitious national programs of these new totalitarian states . . . Standing as we do for the principle of voluntariness in religion, grounded upon the competency of the human soul, Baptists are essentially antagonistic to every form of religious coercion or persecution . . . Believing religious liberty to be not only an inalienable human right, but indispensible to human welfare, a Baptist must exercise himself to the utmost in the maintenance of absolute religious liberty for his Jewish neighbor, his Protestant neighbor, and for everybody else. Profoundly convinced that any deprivation of this right is a wrong to be challenged, Baptists condemn every form of compulsion in religion or restraint of the free consideration of the claims of religion. We stand for a civil state, "with full liberty in religious concernments."[4]

The long-term outcome of this unusual cooperation among the three major Baptist groups was later to become the Baptist Joint Committee on Public Affairs (BJC). As much as any other factor, the joint effort was catalyzed by a desire to have an impact upon current government policies, while not allowing the reverse to take place. The constitution, adopted in 1946, was the work of its founder, Joseph M. Dawson, who saw its purpose as:

> to act in the field of public affairs whenever the interests or rights of the cooperating conventions which constitute the Committee call for conference or negotiation with the government of the United States or with any other Governments, or whenever Baptist principles are involved in, or jeopardized through, governmental action. . . .[5]

BJC leaders evolved from part-time advocacy in Rufus Weaver and W. W. Everett in the 1940s to a full-time professional staff: Joseph M. Dawson, C. Emmanuel Carlson, James E. Wood, Jr., James Dunn, and Brent Walker.[6] Located in the shadow of the US capitol, over seven decades the BJC has studied legislation for possible infringements of religious liberty, offered *amicus curiae* briefs on Supreme Court and other cases, and provided public education on matters of religious liberty and the separation of church and state. Its work has been described as research, education, and "watchdog." Nine groups participated in the Baptist Joint Committee from its establishment in 1939 to 1991,[7] when the SBC withdrew and some former Southern Baptists rejoined through two new national organizations (Alliance of Baptists and Cooperative Baptist Fellowship) and three Southern Baptist-related state organizations (Texas, Virginia, and North Carolina). The Religious Liberty Council is also now a member. Among the solid accomplishments of the BJC are: advocacy of separation of church and state in the appointment of a US ambassador to the Vatican, public school religious exercises, aid to parochial schools, undergirding of US foreign policy with human rights, and support for the Helsinki Final Accord; position papers on the meaning of religious liberty, tax exemption for churches, scholarly conferences on public funding for religious institutions, right to privacy, religious discrimination in employment, civil religion and nationalism, and human rights. To its credit on the issue of religious liberty, the Baptist Joint Committee for a decade in the 1950s also included a representative from the Canadian Baptist Federation. In 2005 the organization changed its name to the Baptist Joint Committee for Religious Liberty, sharpening its focus on first amendment constitutional concerns.[8]

In Canadian history, Baptists were also leaders in the struggle for religious freedom. In the Maritime Provinces it was manifested in the discrimination that dissenters in the first three decades of the nineteenth century faced in launching their own chartered educational institution. Presbyterians did not follow their announced plan to allow Baptists a faculty position in Dalhousie University in Halifax and when Baptists again tried to create their own school in the Annapolis Valley, both Presbyterians and Anglicans fought it. At length, the charter of Acadia College in 1838 was a victory in achieving religious freedom in a context dominated by the religious establishment. Similarly, until well into the twentieth century, Quebec was entirely resistant to Protestants, or "evangelicals" as they were called. Not only was it difficult to evangelize in the Roman Catholic communities, but outright persecution against fledgling institutions, such as the destructive fire at Grande

Ligne in 1837, were signs of local opposition to Baptists. In central Canada during the 1840s, Baptists joined Methodists and other dissenters in opposing the distribution of the Clergy Reserves lands only among the established churches. After a prolonged legislative debate in which Baptists like Robert A Fyfe figured significantly, a "voluntary" plan was adopted whereby a recognized number of institutions from the major Christian denominations of the province were to receive funds toward the support of degree candidates. Many Baptists felt that no funds should be allocated to denominational schools under a "separationist" plan similar to that in the United States, but ultimately Baptists accepted their share of the provincial distributions.

Human rights

Baptists have been activists for human rights in a broader sense. This has taken shape in the North American context and beyond in missionary endeavor. The crusade against slavery is perhaps the most evident example of the denomination's struggle to achieve human rights. Next in priority would be the efforts of domestic missionaries like Isaac McCoy and Isabel Crawford on behalf of Native Americans, and Silas Rand among the Micmacs in Canada. As we have already noted, there were impressive efforts in the overseas mission context of Baptist advocacy of human rights.

Baptists, like other Protestant communities, spread across the South well before the Revolution. This placed them squarely among the planter classes that owned slaves in Virginia, the Carolinas, and Georgia. Major congregations in the southern cities, notably First Baptist, Charleston, included significant numbers of members who were slaveholders. The venerable Richard Furman was raised on a plantation and became a slaveholder in his own right. His social peers at High Hills of the Santee and Charleston included many of the planter/slaveholding class. Little wonder, then, in 1822 in the wake of the Denmark Vesey Rebellion in Charleston, that Furman, as president of the South Carolina Baptist Convention, upheld the legitimacy of slaveholding:

> On the lawfulness of holding slaves, considering it in a moral and religious view ... the right of holding slaves is clearly established in the Holy Scriptures, both by precept and example ... the Divine Law never sanctions immoral actions ... Cruelty is, certainly, inadmissible; but servitude may be consistent with such degrees of happiness as men usually attain in this imperfect state of things ... Slavery, when tempered with

humanity and justice, is a state of tolerable happiness; equal, if not superior, to that which many poor enjoy in countries reputed free.[9]

Another leading Baptist of antebellum Alabama, Basil Manly, Sr., in a sermon on "patriarchal government" to his parishioners, affirmed the master/slave relationship as biblically mandated: "God has made you their masters – placed them under your protection, made you their guardians, the conservators of their lives and happiness."[10]

As early as the 1780s Baptist voices against slavery were heard. John Leland, the Connecticut itinerant to Virginia, was among its most vocal critics. In the Strawberry Association in 1789 Leland crafted a resolution that targeted both slaveholders and the state legislature:

> Resolved that slavery is a violent deprivation of the rights of nature, and inconsistent with republican government, we therefore recommend it to our brethren, to make use of every legal measure to extirpate this horrid evil from the land; and pray Almighty God that our honorable legislature may have it in their power to proclaim the great Jubilee, consistent with the principles of good policy.[11]

Even more vehement was the sentiment among many northern churches and spokespeople. Ebenezer Smith, the pastor of the Baptist church at Ashfield, Massachusetts in 1773 wrote to his friend Isaac Backus, "We complain of Bondage [to the established authorities], and shall we at the same time keep our fellow men in bondage?" In 1794 the members of the Clifton Park, New York congregation exhibited a prophetic clarity about the peculiar institution: "We believe that all mankind are born Equally free and that none has the right to Enslave or hold them in Bondage, let their Colour be what it may and we have no fellowship with such unfruteful works of Darkness."[12]

One of the strongest voices in support of emancipation was Morgan John Rhees, the Welsh immigrant who toured the United States in 1794–95. Rhees found it difficult to reconcile American commitments to liberty while slaveholding persisted. In Virginia he urged Baptists to free their slaves and in Georgetown, South Carolina, he addressed the House of Representatives on slavery, fraternity, and the signs of the times. Rhees developed a fairly sophisticated argument that connected human capacity with emancipation and he worked at practical solutions. For instance in 1795 when he encountered Andrew Bryan and his persecuted African congregation at Savannah, Rhees assisted in preparing a petition to allow the blacks to worship God in freedom. He wrote of the free gift of God (civil rights) to every rational creature and when the congregation erected their meetinghouse, Rhees contributed the name, "Beth-Shallom."[13] In addition he urged the support of the Philadelphia Association for the cost of the building and wrote to John Rippon in England and created his own published account of the Savannah church for Welsh readers. From Charleston and Savannah he wrote his *Letters on Liberty and Slavery* (1797) in which he advocated immediate emancipation as a corollary to repentance and warned that while he was afraid of a slave insurrection as much as any person, he was more afraid of God's judgment: "a dreadful revolution must soon take place, unless the slaves are instructed and gradually emancipated."[14] In fact, Morgan John Rhees stands out among most abolitionists as he was among the first to recognize the challenges of freed blacks meeting the burdens of freedom.

In the Jeffersonian era the institution of slavery became firmly imbedded in the Southern economy and many Baptists, like other southern Christians, tried to separate what to them seemed a political issue from the spiritual realm of the churches. For instance, after Leland left Virginia in 1791 the tide turned against antislavery and the Virginia Baptist Association rescinded an earlier position and supported placing the question in the context of the legislature. In Charleston, South Carolina, the Association voted not to encourage marriage among blacks because in their mind slaves were not entitled to the privileges of freemen. Some Baptists in this period explored the option of joining the Colonization Movement, but this proved to be of little interest.

Baptist antislavery sentiments developed on the western frontier as well. Within the Elkhorn Association in Kentucky, several congregations were not pleased with the noncommittal position of the Association and agitation began in earnest in 1805. Two years later, a forthright emancipation movement began, known as the Friends of Humanity Association. Its influence spread to Illinois and Indiana as well. The prime mover in the frontier Baptist communities was Elder Carter Tarrant, pastor of the New Hope, Kentucky, church. "Tarrant's Rules," that governed the movement, precluded slaveholders from joining the Friends except in the cases of widows, debilitated persons, and women married to slaveholders; the purchase of slaves was also forbidden. To meet the objection that the Friends of Humanity mingled politics with religion, Tarrant also asserted that there was no alteration in their understanding of the gospel. In addition to taking a stance in favor of emancipation in the border states, the Friends offered practical training and moral instruction to free blacks and mulattos and addressed injustices against those still captive to slavery. David Barrow, a member of the North District Association in Kentucky, in 1816 published a paper,

The Abolition Intelligencer, among an estimated 12 congregations and three hundred members of the Friends in Kentucky. His tract, *Involuntary, Absolute, Hereditary Slavery Examined on the Principles of Nature, Reason, Justice, and Scripture* (1808) became a key handbook of the Friends of Humanity.

While the Friends of Humanity movement languished in Kentucky by 1816, in Illinois it prospered. In that state, James Lemen, a long-time friend of Thomas Jefferson from their common Virginia past, took up the cause to create a constitution for the new state of Illinois that prohibited slavery. Lemen canvassed and circularized the pioneer Baptist congregations and, starting in 1820, formed associations of churches bearing the name "Friends to Humanity." At the high point of Friends' influence, the historian David Benedict recorded 39 churches and in excess of 13 hundred members in the Illinois Friends. The propaganda campaign they launched, that drew upon Baptist leaders like John Mason Peck, halted the attempts of proslavery advocates to control the new state constitution and exerted a powerful influence in Missouri as well. As the critical nature of antislavery shifted toward the colonization movement and the constitutional debates ended, the Friends shifted their emphases to fighting other forms of infidelity such as deism, atheism, Campbellism, Mormonism, Parkerism (see chapter 3), and drunkenness, through camp meeting revival experiences. Their millennial sense continued to drive their ultraism: "It is more than probable that the present age in which it is our lot to be placed will exhibit the most stupendous, momentous, and interesting displays of Divine Providence that ever will transpire, till the second coming of the Judge of the Quick and the Dead."[15] While relatively short-lived and limited in scope essentially to an upper South public, the Friends of Humanity movement was a unique Baptist chapter in the moral crusade against slavery.

Given the inherent tendency among Baptists in the United States to link freedom with antislavery, support for the human rights of slaves needed only a catalyst to launch into a national phenomenon. That catalyst was the urgency presented from the English Baptist community, both Particular and General Baptists. William Knibb, the famous English Baptist missionary, along with widespread support from Baptists like Joseph Ivimey and John Howard Hinton, and the Parliamentary Reformers, became the champion of abolishing slavery in the British Empire by 1833. Almost immediately the English Baptist community began correspondence with their American counterparts, first with the Board of the General Missionary Convention, then with prominent individuals, to bring about a concerted stance against slavery. The initial response of the American Board was to assert the limitations of its authority as a national voluntary association that then enjoyed a "pleasing degree of union" among its churches.[16]

Undaunted and aware of growing support for the antislavery position, English Baptists kept up the correspondence in 1834–35. A high watermark of English influence upon American Baptists was reached in 1835 when Francis Cox and James Hoby visited the Baptist communities in North America on behalf of the Baptist Union largely to advocate the "sacred cause of Negro emancipation."[17] Upon their return to England and the publication of their journals in book form, English Baptist associations passed resolutions and sent letters to various parts of the Baptist constituency in the United States. By 1836 American Baptists understood that English Baptists wanted no union with those who approved slavery. Baron Stow, a prominent Boston Baptist pastor who was active in the General Missionary Convention, urged patience but believed God was on the side of abolitionists and the cause would prevail. In 1840 a group of American Baptist pastors reciprocated the Cox and Hoby visit in attending the World Antislavery Convention in London and speaking in area churches. Historian Robert Baker observed that they "imbibed the spirit of English immediatism."[18]

During the 1840s Baptist antislavery in the North evolved into abolitionist urgency. Most of the black Baptists in the North were generally from the lower class of exslaves. Pastors readily joined the crusade and committed themselves and their congregations to the cause. As early as 1834 the African Baptist Church in Albany, New York was involved in regular prayer meetings for their "Southern brethren." Certain Baptist newspapers were known to support abolition in their editorials. Some states were stronger than others in their sentiments. Maine, for instance, in 1833 formed an antislavery society in which Baptists were prominent members. Numerous meetings were held in Baptist churches across the state. Southern Baptist historian Robert Baker estimated that 180 of the over two hundred Maine Baptist ministers were abolitionists by 1840.[19] Likewise New Hampshire Baptists, who formed a denominational antislavery society in 1838, almost unanimously supported the cause, and Vermont Baptists produced Alvin Sabin of Georgia, Vermont, a leader in the Shaftsbury Baptist Association, a long-time member of the state legislature, and a national voice for antislavery. From Massachusetts to New Jersey, Baptist engagement in antislavery was strong and sustained, with Pennsylvania being the most tepid community of Baptists on the issue.

Antislavery sentiments could also be found among Baptists in the southern states. William H. Brisbane, a physician and plantation owner in South Carolina, read Francis Wayland's book, *Elements of Moral Science* (1835), and concluded that Christians could not morally be slaveholders. Local opposition to his views was so severe that Brisbane moved to Ohio and later Wisconsin, where he continued to speak and write on abolition. During the Civil War, he returned to South Carolina first to help organize the Port Royal Experiment, and also as a later chaplain in the Wisconsin Cavalry stationed in that state. During Reconstruction, Brisbane served as a tax commissioner and helped to ameliorate the conditions of freedmen. His 1847 book, *Slaveholding Examined in Light of the Holy Bible*, was intended for the South but received much attention in the northern evangelical community.

The most intense phase of the Baptist drive for human rights in antebellum America was during the creation of a national Baptist anti-slavery society. In 1839 editorial agitation toward concerted action appeared in various denominational newspapers. At the annual meeting that year of the American Antislavery Society in which several Baptists played a prominent role, the Baptist delegates met to plan strategies. A call was issued to Baptists north and south to meet at McDougal Street Baptist Church in New York, April 28–30, 1840 to form their own antislavery body. Responding to the names of Cyrus P. Grosvenor, Elon Galusha, Nathaniel Colver, and Robert Turnbull, seven hundred Baptists from 13 states threw in with the cause. The American and Foreign Missionary Society, later the American Baptist Free Mission Society, was thus formed and its members set about attempting to influence Baptists in the South to give up slavery and Baptists in the North to unite in the General Missionary Convention and national societies to cease cooperation with slaveholders. Southern Baptists were instructed to confess the sin of slavery and work to change the legal basis of the system. If they failed, they were encouraged to move to Free State territory in the North. "Ultraism," as the new extreme demands were labeled, caused Baptist churches, associations, and editors in the South to resolve to protect their social institutions and constitutional rights in the Baptist organizations in the next four years. The antislave/abolitionist sentiments were intense at the Baltimore national triennial meeting in 1841 and a temporary compromise was reached. In the next four years the relentless moral pursuit of slavery by the Free Mission Society and others doubtless produced the high anxiety that led to the severance of southern Baptist churches from the national societies in 1845 described in chapter 3 above.

Historians agree that the high watermark of Baptist defense of human rights in the slavery controversy occurred in 1844–45 with the publication of editorial debates between Richard Fuller and Francis

Wayland. Fuller, a Harvard-trained pastor at Beaufort, South Carolina, began the exchange with a letter to the *Christian Reflector* in which he held that the "anathemas and excommunications against every Christian at the South" were ill-directed fulminations of "monomaniacs."[20] Fuller defended slavery as a biblically recognized institution and argued further that the Bible made no assertion of the sinfulness of slavery. His essay was in part directed to the case made by Francis Wayland in his book, *Elements of Moral Science,* and Wayland was quick to respond in a series of published essays on the points that Fuller made. Essentially, Wayland retorted that slavery was wrong because "it conflicted with the relations designed at first by God between man and man." Further, Wayland concluded that slavery is by the word of God forbidden and that the word of God intended to remove it by applying the principles of the gospel to human consciences and, thus, by changing the sentiments of society, it would gradually and kindly be exterminated.[21] The two authors revised their respective contributions and published the entire exchange in an 1845 book produced by the leading religious publisher in New York, Lewis Colby, and a similar house in Boston: Gould, Kendall, and Lincoln. The collection became a handbook on the differences of opinion between the sections of Baptists, north and south, and was referred to often in local debates and editorials. Wayland continued to serve Brown University and Fuller moved to the city of Baltimore where, after the Civil War, he advocated reconciliation between the two great families of Baptists.

Baptists continued to be advocates of human rights in the area of racial equality long after emancipation of slaves in the United States. For instance, the effort of the American Baptist Home Mission Society in providing financial assistance, leadership development, and institutions of higher education during the Reconstruction era was an act of affirming human and civil rights. The work of Walter Rauschenbusch and George Cross at Rochester Seminary and Sankey L. Blanton and George W. Davis at Crozer Seminary was a key factor in the formation of human rights thinking and praxis in leaders like Mordecai Johnson, M. L. King, and Howard Thurman. During the civil rights crusades of the 1950s and 1960s, American Baptists like M. Forrest Ashbrook, Harvey Cox, Dean Wright, and Howard Rees displayed courage and consistency in support of Martin Luther King, Jr., Ralph Abernathy, and later Adam Clayton Powell, Jr. by publicly joining marches in Selma and Montgomery, Alabama, and providing grants to civil rights causes from the Ministers and Missionaries Benefit Board. Because of this stance, a significant number of black Baptist congregations dually affiliated themselves with the National Baptist Convention, USA or the

Progressive National Baptist Convention, as well as with the American Baptist Convention in the 1960s and 1970s. Black Baptists, often using different strategies, lent support for the same causes. Joseph H. Jackson, president of the National Baptist Convention, USA, a gradualist, used his position among politicians like Lyndon Johnson and Hubert Humphrey to effect improved conditions for black Americans, while Martin Luther King and Gardner C. Taylor preferred a more aggressive type of assertion of rights and social improvements. Socially concerned Southern Baptists must not be excluded from the twentieth-century Baptist witness for human rights, notably Henlee Barnette at Southern Seminary and Carlyle Marney, a pastor in North Carolina who identified with civil rights issues in the South.

Opportunities and vocation for women

Women have been active leaders in Baptist congregations virtually from the beginnings of the tradition. In the General Baptist congregations there are records of "she-preachers" and at Broadmead Church, Bristol, the redoubtable Dorothy Hazzard served as leader during a critical period in the congregation's history. Opportunities for women in leadership were sharply curtailed, however, in the 1640s. At that time some women, such as Margaret Fell, became Quakers. In the colonial American scene, women played important roles in evangelism, church planting, and organization of mission work, notably Martha Stearns Marshall and Rachel Scammon, mentioned above (chapters 2 and 1, respectively).

Mary Webb exemplifies the accomplishment of early Baptist women in mission. She was a faithful member of Second Baptist, Boston, where her pastor, Thomas Baldwin, stressed the importance of missions. Confined to a wheelchair all of her life, she rose above her limitations to organize Boston women in the Boston Female Society for Missionary Purposes in 1800. At first it planned work among Native Americans, then considered support for William Carey's mission in India. Later in 1815 Miss Webb formed two other efforts, the Female Mite Society, and the Boston Baptist Female Education Society, both of which focused upon the needs of women in the New England region. Mary Webb was also a promoter of a women's concert of prayer for missions.

Another almost forgotten woman leader in the early nineteenth century was Charlotte H. White. Mrs White was a widow from Pennsylvania who applied to go to Burma and assist the Baptist mission printer, George H. Hough. She offered to donate her property to the Baptist Board of Foreign Missions; that amounted to about 15 hundred dollars. Her request caused much debate and soul-searching in the Board because they had no intention of appointing single female missionaries, and some even resigned over the matter. Eventually she accompanied the Houghs to Burma as part of his appointment, but at the same time making history for the emerging role of women among Baptists. The Board was spared a prolonged discussion of the matter of women in leadership when Mrs White married an English Baptist missionary, Joshua Rowe, in India.

The mission context provided an impetus for women to become involved not only in Christian endeavor but also in the social network. The women missionaries themselves were among the first of their gender to assume roles of leadership. Adoniram Judson's first wife Ann took over the mission during her husband's incarceration in Burma; his second wife, Sarah Boardman, traveled extensively in the back country after the death of her first husband, superintended schools, organized Bible classes and prayer meetings, and then translated a good deal of material into Burmese, Talain, and Peguan. The third Mrs Judson, Emily Chubbock, braved the Burmese frontier, assisted with the Ann Judson biography, and raised more children for Adoniram, as well as overseeing his memoirs after his death. Their lives of sacrifice, extolled in such hagiographic accounts as Daniel Eddy's *The Three Mrs. Judsons, and Other Daughters of the Cross* (1859) became suggestive of the opportunities that waited young Baptist women in mission. One historian has called this the "Apostolate of Women" because of the impact it had on redefining the role and perception of women in Christian work.[22]

By later in the century, due in part to the reluctance of the American Baptist Missionary Union and the American Baptist Home Mission Society to appoint single women missionaries, and yet the declared need for teachers, Bible readers, nurses, and workers, women's organizations grew up. The first was an interdenominational group in which Baptists participated, the Woman's Union Missionary Society of America for Heathen Lands, founded in 1861. Joining the chorus of Presbyterians, Congregationalists, and Methodists who formed boards in the later 1860s, Baptists moved in that direction as well. Hannah Maria Norris, a Canadian Baptist woman, was among the first to organize local societies in support of women missionaries. In a remarkable effort in 1870 she actually formed 32 societies across the Maritime Provinces in three months. Two years later at the urging of Mrs. C. H. Carpenter, the Woman's Baptist Foreign Mission Society of the East was formed at Clarendon Street Church in Boston. In response to this move, women in the West formed the Woman's Baptist Missionary Society of the West at First Baptist Church of Chicago. Other regional societies were formed in California, Washington, DC, and Oregon. Each took responsibility for a different location overseas to avoid duplication. From 1903 to 1913 several combinations of regional women's organizations occurred among northern Baptists, spurred on in part by the coalition of the Northern Baptist Convention itself. In 1914, the two great women's societies, East and West, held their final separate meetings and the Woman's American Baptist Foreign Mission Society, related to the Northern Baptist Convention, became a reality. A leading voice in this development was Helen Barrett Montgomery, who served as the organization's first president, and later as the first woman president of an American religious denomination, the Northern Baptist Convention. One of Mrs Montgomery's great achievements in the field of missions was her advocacy of the World Day of Prayer in 1913, which she helped to institute after a round the world visit.

Likewise in the South, women had organized around missions as early as 1812 in South Carolina, and in Richmond a Female Missionary Society began in 1813. Organizations of women grew up in most states, beginning in Georgia in 1817, through to Texas by 1832. A major national meeting was held in 1868 under the call of Ann Baker Graves, mother of a Southern Baptist missionary in China. In the next decade, Southern Baptist women were moved by the example of women in the North, meeting as early as 1883 in support of the financially burdened mission boards. In 1888 the Women's Missionary Union (WMU), a permanent auxiliary to the Southern Baptist Convention, was officially organized with its home in Baltimore. Turned aside as messengers to the annual SBC meetings, women were doubtless anxious for action. The new organization defined its role sharply, declining to appoint its own missionaries and desirous of raising support for existing missions. The outstanding leaders for two generations of the WMU included Annie Armstrong and Kathryn Mallory. Charlotte "Lottie" Moon, the much-celebrated Southern Baptist missionary in China, became the leading inspiration for the new organization and in 1918 the annual offering for missions was named in her honor, as was a parallel offering for home missions named for Annie Armstrong. Like their northern Baptist counterparts, Baptist women in the South found many leadership opportunities in the WMU system, both as volunteers and administrative staff.

The real focus, of course, for many Baptist women in North America, came to be upon the ordained ministry. Here, the record is scant until later in the twentieth century. Among the Freewill Baptists, Ruby Bixby in Iowa was licensed in 1846, A. Gerry was ordained by a Freewill local church process in 1869, and the Seventh Day Baptists ordained

Experience Randolph in the 1880s in New York State. The first denominationally recognized ordination of a woman occurred in 1893 when Elmira Heights (NY) Baptist Church ordained Libby C. Griffin and her husband to the ministry. Griffin had been a Freewill missionary to India. American Baptists, following trends in North American Protestantism in general, systematically supported women in ministry, beginning in the 1960s. Colgate Rochester and Andover Newton accepted female candidates for the ministry degrees in the 1960s and those graduates began to appear in pastoral and denominational roles in the 1970s.

One of the initial places where women (many of whom were ordained) reached leading roles in American Baptist life was in higher education: Blanche Parks served as dean and instructor at Berkeley Baptist Divinity School in the 1920s; Catherine Thompson at Eastern Baptist Seminary and Ruthella Rodeaver at Northern Baptist Seminary both taught religious education in the 1930s, followed by Martha Leypoldt at Eastern, Phyllis Trible at Andover Newton, and Beverly Gaventa at Colgate Rochester in the 1960s and 1970s. Women assumed executive responsibilities in national program boards and institutions in the 1980s with Shirley Jones in Educational Ministries, Cheryl Wade in the Ministers and Missionaries Benefit Board, Martha Barr in the Office of General Secretary, Doris Anne Younger at American Baptist Women, and Roberta Hestenes as president of Eastern College. In 1984 the National Commission on the Ministry initiated a Task Force to ascertain the progress of women in American Baptist ministry. Called the Study of Women in Ministry (SWIM), it determined that about a third of American Baptist seminary students were women, 16 percent of churches were served by women, about half of the Christian educators in the churches were women, over five hundred women were included in the national personnel database, and that generally male pastors were becoming more sympathetic to women in ministry. Soon after the Report, the Rev. Linda Spoolstra was named executive of the national American Baptist Commission on the Ministry, and Kathryn Baker was named executive minister of the Niagara Region in 1985, the first women executive at the regional level.

The Southern Baptist story of women in ministry has absorbed more opposition and yet has had impressive results. It is noteworthy that one of the first women to engage in ministry in North America did so in the South, Martha Stearns Marshall among the Separates. The hiatus was long between Mrs Marshall in the eighteenth century and Addie Davis who was ordained at Watts Street Baptist Church in Durham, North Carolina, in 1964. The next decade brought another short-lived candidate, Shirley Carter of Kathwood Church, Columbia, South Carolina; she was ordained in 1971, only to have the action rescinded by the church the following year. As more seminary candidates entered Southern Baptist schools, the issue would not go away. Among Southern Baptist congregations in Virginia, New York, Texas, and Tennessee, women were ordained in the next two decades. A celebrated instance was Nancy Sehested who was elected pastor of the Prescott Memorial Baptist Church in Memphis, Tennessee, in 1987, only to have the Shelby Baptist Association disfellowship the congregation. Accompanying the ordination of women to pastoral ministry came more ordination of women deacons; the first congregation known to have done so was First Baptist, Waco, Texas.

Southern Baptist Convention opposition to women in ministry built to a fever pitch in the 1970s and 1980s and became a major divisive debate. In 1972 Oklahoma Baptists declared their opposition to ordaining women as ministers or deacons, and in 1977 official opposition was expressed in Arkansas. As the SBC moved to become more accepting of minorities, their breadth was tested by the acceptance of Druecillar Fordham, a black Baptist pastor in Harlem whose congregation was admitted in 1972 to the local Southern Baptist-related association. Beginning in 1983, the growing number of Southern Baptist women in ministry or seeking ministry began to organize in Louisville, Kentucky where they formed Southern Baptist Women in Ministry to encourage women, provide a support system, and explore new models of ministry for Southern Baptists. Louisville became the location of a Center of Women in Ministry, housed at Crescent Hill Baptist Church. Unfortunately, more opposition appeared; Carl F. H. Henry, exercising his floor rights as a messenger to the 1984 Convention, moved a resolution that excluded women from pastoral ministry on the basis of an interpretation of the first chapters of Genesis and passages from the pastoral epistles.

One of the principal reasons for the great divide among Southern Baptists in the 1990s was the issue of women in ministry. As resurgent confessionalists took over the management of both the Convention agencies, many of the colleges and all of the seminaries, the exclusion of women from pastoral ministry and from the diaconate seemed inevitable. To no one's surprise in 2000 when the "Baptist Faith and Message" was revised and reissued, it read, "While both men and women are gifted for service in the church, the office of pastor is limited to men as qualified by Scripture."[23] This became a ground rule for institutions, SBC agencies, staff, and missionaries to affirm without reservation.

In response to this position of the SBC, the new organizations of southern Baptists like the Alliance of Baptists and the Cooperative Baptist Fellowship came out strongly in favor of women in ministry. In the new schools like Baptist Theological Seminary at Richmond, McAfee School of Theology, and George W. Truett Theological Seminary, women were recruited both as students and to fill faculty positions. Recently, a woman president, Molly Marshall Green, has been appointed at Central Baptist Theological Seminary in Kansas, jointly related to the American Baptist Churches and the Cooperative Baptist Fellowship.

Although barred from the ordained ministry for much of their early history, black Baptist women have made historic strides toward full recognition as well. Jennie Johnson, a Canadian Free Baptist, was ordained in Michigan in 1909. Rosetta O'Neal was ordained to serve a congregation in Windsor, Ontario in 1975 and later was elected president of the Baptist Convention of Ontario and Quebec in 1998. Among American Baptists, Ella Mitchell was ordained in California in 1978 after many years of ministry, and Suzanne Johnson was ordained in 1982 at Mariners Temple Church in New York, a congregation dually aligned with National Baptists.

Baptist women in Canada have made progress in becoming recognized in ministry. Muriel Spurgeon Carder, a McMaster University graduate, in 1948 was the first Baptist woman to be ordained in central Canada, followed by Mae Benedict Field in the West in 1959. Urged along by McMaster professor of ministry, Lois Tupper, the first full-time female faculty member of a theological school in Canada, McMaster Divinity College recruited a number of women in the period 1975 to 1990, most of whom were ordained and served churches in the Baptist Convention. Similar progress was made in the Maritimes in the 1990s and in the West during the same period. A report on the plight of Baptist women among the Baptist Convention of Ontario and Quebec that was issued in the 1990s was still sharply critical of attitudes and practices among the churches with respect to women in leadership.

It must be noted that even the sporadic success of the recognition of women among American and Southern Baptists cannot offset what is a difficulty for Baptist women elsewhere. Among the black Baptist traditions and the fundamentalist groups, women are either not encouraged to seek licensing or ordination or it is forbidden. Leadership is male-exclusive, except for limited missionary work where males still dominate females in the administrative process. There is a clear division among Baptists in Canada between the "convention" Baptists who universally support and recognize women in ministry, and those in the

Fellowship of Evangelical Baptist Churches who regard it as a biblically unsound practice. The mission field remains a challenge for North American Baptist women who face opposition from the indigenous cultures with respect to female leadership.

Baptists Define Issues of Relevance to the Culture

Beginning with the first decades of the nineteenth century, several social concerns emerged in American and Canadian life and society that defined a number of cultural patterns. Religious groups were often the purveyors of these values and, conversely, the values helped to define religious groups. Baptists were no exception as they faced the concerns of temperance, secret societies, and peacemaking. How they defined their posture in this context helped to create mores for an emerging tradition.

Temperance

For the most part, Baptists have reflected cultural patterns commensurate with their social status. No other issue reflects this better than temperance. It is evident from a reading of early Baptist records in England and the American colonies, that Baptists drank wine and it was used at the celebration of the Lord's Supper. Some prominent Baptists were involved in the industrial production of beer, notably the Englishman William Kiffin in the seventeenth century and Matthew Vassar and John J. Jones in the nineteenth century. It is unlikely that Baptists were major consumers of spirituous liquors during the colonial period because of the exorbitant prices and taxation. Baptist ministers did imbibe liquor at special occasions, including ordination ceremonies. There is no eighteenth-century literature inveighing against Baptist use of liquor.

As American society became more aware of the effects of drunkenness on family life in the lower socioeconomic groups in the 1820s, editorials encouraging restraint and temperance appeared in religious literature, including those of the Baptist community. Typically, evangelical churches joined the temperance chorus, led by Congregationalists and Methodists. Lyman Beecher at Yale College was a leading exponent in the formation of local temperance societies that included a modest number of Baptists. A new phase of the temperance movement emerged in the 1840s as the Washingtonian Societies, and among the most ardent leaders were Baptists Jacob Knapp of New York and William F. Broaddus of Virginia. Some associations even went so far as to require abstinence tests for fellowship. In the Northeast, temperance became a part of what social reformers called "ultraism."

In the 1880s the temperance cause became more easily acceptable in religious circles with the development of grape juice. A debate among northern Baptists ensued over whether Scripture mandated wine or some form of it as a "fruit of the vine." Generally, Baptists, with other evangelicals, followed a nonalcoholic understanding officially. By the American Prohibition campaign after 1910, Baptists, especially fundamentalists, were wholly devoted to the practice of abstinence. George B. Cutten, president of Colgate University, and Harry Emerson Fosdick, were among those advocating temperance in the Northern Baptist family. One of the most effective devices in establishing a widespread abstinence position among Baptists was the oft-quoted covenant phrase that the American Baptist Publication Society distributed, beginning in 1836: "We will abstain from the use of intoxicating beverages." It continues to be included in many Baptist hymnals for congregation recitation.

Secret societies

Membership in secret societies and associations after the Revolution was an important part of socialization in the new nation. Former military officers were part of the Society of the Cincinnati and many women joined the Daughters of the American Revolution. Ever popular across the United States was the Freemasonic fraternity. Baptist joined local lodges in New England and across New York in the first decades of the nineteenth century, mostly as a socializing vehicle in village-sized communities. Baptists were also known to be prominent members of city lodges in Boston, New York, and Philadelphia.

Scandal erupted among the Masons in western New York in 1826. William Morgan, a stonemason from the village of Canandaigua, New York was denied membership in a local lodge and he retaliated by writing an exposé of Freemasonry. Morgan was apprehended by local Masons, put through a mock trial, and then harried off to Fort Niagara where he was never seen again, and was presumed dead. An investigation was held and rumors of a major political conspiracy ran across the Northeast. The evangelical community picked up the issue and took a fairly uniform stance against membership in secret societies. Baptists in New York divided sharply, as among the Chautauqua Association that split over whether to disfellowship churches where members continued their lodge relationships. Baptists supported statewide conventions in New York, Vermont, Massachusetts, and Pennsylvania, calling upon Masons to renounce their fraternal ties, much like revivalists called upon their hearers to renounce their evil ways.

Those Baptists who joined in the antimasonic crusade did so largely because they were social and religious egalitarians. The extreme form of the movement was only modestly successful among Baptists. Associations as widely dispersed as Shaftsbury in Vermont and Sandy Creek in North Carolina took strongly worded stances against lodge membership. However, Christian members valued the socialization the lodges provided and studies have shown that in the larger towns of the northeast, Baptist lodge membership continued. Likewise in the South, significant numbers of Baptist pastors joined the fraternity, along with prominent laymen. The greatest impact of the crusade to prevent the spread of Freemasonry occurred in rural churches in New York, Michigan, and Ohio. Those congregations identified with the Second Awakening and/or New Measures campaigned in support of antimasonic candidates for local, state, and national offices through the end of the history of the Antimasonic Party (1835). Many of them then joined the evangelical trend against secret societies that characterized such associations as counterfeit Christianity and unfavorable competition with the values and objectives of gospel churches. Historian Robert Torbet thought that the antimasonic crusade of the 1830s was a major factor in the social division of the Baptist movement.[24]

Peacemaking

An important category of social concern from the early nineteenth century in the United States was peace. Advocates of nonviolence and peace have always been present in the Baptist community, but not predominant. Baptists, unlike their historical cousins the Society of Friends and the Brethren, are not one of the historic peace churches. Yet a strong witness shows up in each generation. Early American Baptists like Henry Holcombe, Francis Wayland, Howard Malcolm, and George Dana Boardman, Jr. held positions articulating peace concerns: Holcombe was a member of the African Baptist Peace Society in Philadelphia following the War of 1812, and Wayland was president of the American Peace Society at the outbreak of the Civil War. In contrast, of course, there were numerous Baptist voices in support of the war with Mexico in the 1840s and widespread Baptist engagement in the Civil War. Among Baptists in general, there has not been any type of cogent biblical hermeneutic or theological case for peacemaking that has carried a significant following in a very diverse tradition.

For the most part, peace concerns emerged among North American Baptists during World War II. Support for conscientious objectors was demonstrated among Baptist families, notably the Northern Baptists, National Baptists, and less so among Southern Baptists. Edwin M. Poteat among Southern Baptists, and Harry Emerson Fosdick and Edwin Dahlberg among Northern Baptists, helped to form the Baptist Pacifist Fellowship in 1939. In 1984 the Baptist Peace Fellowship of North America was formed, initially reflecting both theologically liberal and conservative Baptists from Canada and the United States. In recent years, however, the BPFNA has come to be associated with socially liberal Baptist congregations and is an effective minority movement among the several conventions of Baptists. It holds annual conferences and publishes a newsletter, the *Baptist Peacemaker*. During the United States military intervention in Afghanistan and the subsequent war with Iraq, when the expectation was high that greater numbers of Baptists would identify with BPFNA, a significant number of congregations and the Southern Baptist Convention have preferred the terminology, "peacekeeping," that signals an openness to pre-emptive military action.

Perhaps the largest contributions to peacemaking among Baptists have been made by Harry E. Fosdick and Martin Luther King, Jr. Fosdick had served with the American Expeditionary Force in France during World War I. The carnage he witnessed in France forever changed his mind about war:

> I renounce war. I renounce war because of what it does to our men. . . . I renounce war because of what it compels us to do to our enemies . . . I renounce war for its consequences, for the lies it lives on and propagates, for the underlying hatreds it arouses . . . I renounce war and never again, directly or indirectly, will I sanction or support another![25]

In a different vein, King cast the issue of peace in a beloved community that he saw threatened by the Vietnam War. "Peace," he wrote, "is not merely the absence of some negative force – war, tension, confusion, but it is the presence of some positive force – justice, goodwill, the power of the kingdom of God."[26]

Thomas Kilgore, president of the Progressive National Baptist Convention in the late 1970s, articulated a vision for peace that contained implications for "virile, positive, and creative force." He conceived of peace within the framework of an organization to pertain to democratic process, such as tenure in office, avoiding dictatorial leadership, and promoting free and open debate. Kilgore eschewed "bitterness," hostility, and antagonism as contrary to "a reverence for law, order, and decency, honor and justice."[27]

Toward Defining Baptists in North America

Two major, but subtle characteristics were powerfully definitive from the later nineteenth century and forward, in understanding who Baptists have come to be. One pertains to a sociotheological set of factors – cultural assimilation – while the other is an ecclesial matter: ecumenism.

Cultural assimilation

In the last decades of the nineteenth century the American Baptist Home Mission Society (ABHMS) placed a new emphasis upon reaching immigrants to the United States. What emerged from this effort was a broadened perspective on Baptist attitudes of race/ethnicity. For many Baptists, Christianity became synonymous with American democratic ideals. Baptists widely adopted the notion that North America was a continent blessed of God essentially for English-speaking Caucasians. Henry Vedder, a Baptist historian at the turn of the twentieth century, summarized the goals of this "Americanization" ideal:

> 1. Freedom under law, not lawless freedom; 2. High standard of social morality, no double standard in sex or business; 3. Good social habits – no spitting on sidewalks, no scattering of rubbish, no reckless driving of cars; consideration always to be given the other man; 4. Genuine loyalty to American institutions; 5. Freedom of speech, combined with responsibility for all utterances.[28]

Among the first of the new groups to be evangelized east of the Mississippi in 1887 were the Czechs or Bohemians who settled in the East coast cities and around the Great Lakes. Mission efforts among the Portuguese commenced in 1888 in California and Massachusetts; by 1920, the mission totaled over five hundred members. A Polish work was started the same year in Detroit, Michigan, that spread through most of the northeast and produced a strong union of churches by 1930. In 1891, the ABHMS commissioned a missionary among the

Finns in Massachusetts. Within a decade, this resulted in a Finnish Baptist Union of over one hundred members. In 1894 a mission to Italians began in Buffalo, New York. This spread to New York City and smaller urban areas in New England and New Jersey. The success of efforts among Italians led Colgate University to begin in 1907 a theological studies program that became its Italian Department in Brooklyn, New York. By 1920 with indigenous American leadership, the Italian Association claimed over three thousand members and a flourishing newspaper, *L'Aurora*. Other efforts were made by the Society in 1901 among the Russians in North Dakota, and later in Pennsylvania, Connecticut, and Manitoba. The same year in Cleveland, Ohio, a Hungarian mission started. A decade later Romanian missions were started in Pennsylvania.

The Society was also active in the West. During the 1880s and 1890s thousands of Japanese and Chinese settled in fishing villages and cities on the Northwest coast. From the 1840s Baptists had supported a Chinese ministry in San Francisco, but the increased demand for labor on the railroads and in cottage industries led to redoubled efforts in the 1880s. Joint efforts between the state conventions and the ABHMS resulted in special efforts among the warring gangs of Chinese, and the creation of inner-city and children's centers. Chinese laborers were heavily employed in the construction of the Northern Pacific Railway. Baptist missionary work began among the Japanese in 1905 in Seattle and later extended to California.

The evolution of opium gangs within Chinese neighborhoods became especially acute. The Chinese situation prompted a special concern over the nature of witness among new Americans. In the 1880s widespread opposition toward Asian peoples on the West Coast broke out in a number of violent incidents. Scores of Chinese were massacred, property was destroyed, and Chinese families were scattered. The ABHMS and Southern Baptist Home Mission Board stepped up their mission among the Chinese. Support for protective legislation was given, buildings for Chinese communities were constructed and safe houses for women were designated. In Berkeley, California, the Chung Mei Home for Chinese Boys received national attention. The strength of the Baptist effort was evident in the cross-involvement of former missionaries to China, like C. R. Shepherd, who returned to the US in 1919 to direct the work of Northern Baptists among Chinese across the nation.

The result of this flurry of missionary work among ethnically diverse peoples was the establishment of new foreign language associations: French-Speaking Baptist Conference (1894), Italian Baptist Convention (1898), Hungarian Baptist Union (1908), Czechoslovak Baptist

Convention (1912), Polish Baptist Conference (1912), Romanian Baptist Association (1913), Russian and Ukrainian Baptist Union (1919). Howard B. Grose, a leading Baptist home mission specialist in the early twentieth century, put the task plainly:

> Let us seek to make the foreigners Christian, give them the Bible, and set them an example of the brotherhood of believers. Then the immigrants will become believers and join the brotherhood . . . God has set for American Christianity the gigantic task of the ages . . . nothing less than the assimilation of all these foreign peoples who find a home on this continent into a common Americanism so that they shall form a composite American nation – Christian, united, free, and great.[29]

Ecumenism

The view of Baptist origins that one maintains often creates a perspective on Baptist relationships with other Baptists and other Christians. For instance, maintaining a successionist understanding of Baptist origins leads to an exclusivist position that can create the impression that Baptists are the only true Christians. Holding to an Anabaptist kinship theory, as W. R. Estep has shown,[30] will foster a love for religious liberty, individual freedom, congregational independence, and a strong sectarianism. This has been witnessed in the Southern Baptist family in particular in the twentieth century. If one adopts the so-called Puritan Separatist hypothesis, one is inclined to recognize the multiplicity of Baptist origins in the greater English Reformation, thus creating an openness to relationships with Anglicans, Presbyterians, and Congregationalists in particular and other Free Church Protestants in general. It is noteworthy that in the much-quoted Second London Confession of Faith, republished as the Philadelphia Confession of Faith (1677, 1742), the signatories observed: "although we do differ from our brethren who are Paedobaptists . . . yet we would not be from hence misconstrued, as if the discharge of our own consciences herein, did any ways disoblige or alienate our affections, or conversations from any others that fear the Lord."[31]

Baptists in North America inherited this irenic tendency from their British forbears and this has manifested itself in some significant ways. In the colonial period, Baptists in New England and the Middle Colonies often shared common cause with Quakers in the face of religious persecution. During the eighteenth century, New Light Baptists (prorevival) and Old Regular Baptists demonstrated that they could lay aside their differences for addressing matters of common grievance with the colonial and revolutionary governments. The "merger" of Separates and Regulars in Virginia and through the Appalachian frontier in 1800 showed a capacity for real union in the face of historic differences. In British North America, the blending of American, English, Scottish, and Scotch Baptists in the central provinces, [32] though often painfully marred by disputes over closed communion, demonstrated that unity was highly desirable in the face of so great a territory for mission.

Of all the Baptists in North America, Northern/American Baptists have led in relating to other Christian groups. For many, a cherished dream after the War Between the States, was a reunion of the two great separated parts of the Baptist family. Other possibilities developed as mission organizations often paralleled each other in domestic work. In scholarly discussions like the Baptist Congress, regular space was devoted to church union discussions. As we have seen, just three years after the formation of a national convention, the NBC voted to join the Federal Council of Churches. In 1911 Northern Baptists merged with the Free Baptist General Conference. For several decades, fundamentalist battles within the NBC kept any discussion of merger at bay, until after World War II. At that point, in the midst of the formation of the World Council of Churches, union possibilities again rose to prominence, notably with the Disciples of Christ. American Baptists have also exchanged fraternal delegates with the Church of the Brethren and of late are engaged in informal discussions toward greater cooperation. As the Southern Baptist family has become dysfunctional, greater cooperation with the Alliance of Baptists, the Cooperative Baptist Fellowship, and Mainstream Baptists has been seen in theological education at Central Baptist Seminary and as limited numbers of Southern Baptist students have done work at Andover Newton and Harvard Divinity School. However, on the negative side, under mounting pressure from the opponents of the World Council of Churches, a growing number of American Baptists have declined to support their denominations' commitment to membership in the National Council and World Council. This has produced an annual listing of congregations whose financial support is not to go toward either organization. During the 1980s an alternative strategy was investigated, namely that the American Baptist Churches would also seek to relate to the National Association of Evangelicals, but this proved fruitless because membership in the NAE was granted to individuals, not denominations, and because NAE members frowned upon holding memberships in other theologically definitive organizations like the ecumenical movement.

The most serious possibility of union among major Baptist groups has involved a long-term conversation between Northern/American Baptists and the Disciples of Christ. Historians of the denominations point out that as early as 1841 there were overtures of cooperation between the two groups, particularly in the arena of Bible publication. In 1866 and again in 1871 Disciples entertained discussions with both Regular Baptists and Free(will) Baptists. A widely reported set of discussions occurred in the 1890s and in 1904 as the Free(will) Baptists, Northern Baptists, and Disciples all considered joint action for the new century. As noted in chapter 5 above, the merger of the two Baptist groups was consummated, but the talks with Disciples languished. After World War I, again the national offices of both denominations set about joint discussions, in 1941 using the terminology "cooperation" rather than merger. This produced a joint magazine, devotional guide, and hymnal. Progress being the order of the day, an official Joint Commission on Baptist and Disciples Relations was authorized in 1947 as the Northern Baptists numbered 6,300 congregations with in excess of 1.5 million members in 36 states and the Disciples about 8,000 congregations with 1.8 million members in 41 states. Both had a benevolence budget of approximately $80,000 annually. Between 1949 and 1952 concrete steps were taken toward actual union: joint ministerial conferences in 1950, up to two hundred pulpit exchanges per year in 1948–50, simultaneous national convention meetings in 1952, the presentation of a "Plan of Union" in 1954, and the plan for a formal vote scheduled for 1955.

An observer to the process maintained that it was the Baptists who gradually withdrew support from the discussions. Powerful individual voices, particularly in the Midwest, came out in opposition to merger. One minister conducted a personal survey and published the results. Significant numbers of churches in Kansas and southern California indicated that they would withdraw from the NBC if the merger talks proceeded. Opposition crystallized around four concerns: Baptists wanted to remain Baptists, more division in the Northern Convention after the Conservative Baptist schism was not healthy, many churches in the southern states would join the Southern Convention, and all hope of reunion between Northern and Southern Baptists would be lost. At the base of the distress was a continuing opposition to the Disciples' understanding of baptismal regeneration and their weekly observance of the Lord's Supper, neither of which Baptists could easily accept. Wisely, the Joint Commission itself voted to drop the timetable and by 1952 it was discharged short of any further recommendations.[33] While no later move toward merger was taken up, Disciples and

American Baptists maintained friendly relations through various channels including the National Council of Churches and a study group sponsored by the Pew Foundation in the 1980s. Baptists were wise not to have voted officially against merger, and this opened the possibility of local and regional cooperation.

Next to the American Baptist Churches, USA, the National Baptist Convention, USA, has a long record of support for ecumenical engagement. We have noted the close cooperation that existed in the formative years of black Baptist national development between the northern Baptists and various black conventions, state and national. To a lesser degree, National Baptists worked jointly with Southern Baptists in the South. In 1924 a project reflecting what historian Joseph Jackson called the "highest peak" of cooperation with Southern Baptists occurred in the establishment of the American Baptist Theological Seminary in Nashville, Tennessee, to train black Baptist leaders.[34] Also noteworthy under the auspices of NBCUSA President L. K. Williams, who carefully fostered intradenominational relationships, was the joint declaration on religious liberty in 1939.

On every platform of the Baptist World Congresses since 1905 have been speakers representative of the National Baptist Convention: in 1960–65 President Jackson served as a vice president of the Alliance. Jackson, a thoroughgoing ecumenist, was a member of the Central Committee of the World Council of Churches, a denominational member of the National Council of Churches, and many regional ecumenical organizations in the Midwest. He led National Baptists in a personal visit to Rome in 1961 with Pope John XXIII to discuss world peace and the upcoming Vatican Council, and to Washington with both Republican and Democratic presidents to interact and advise on the concerns of the black community. Jackson was deeply supportive of the National Association for the Advancement of Colored People (NAACP), and reminded his critics that, although he was reluctant to join forces with the Southern Christian Leadership Conference (SCLC), many National Baptists leaders had been involved.[35]

In the mainstream Canadian Baptist family during the twentieth century, there was a consistent pattern of close cooperation among Protestants that reached a peak in the 1960s. Baptists in the Ontario and Quebec Convention cooperated fully in the establishment of the Toronto School of Theology in 1970 and their theological school, McMaster Divinity College, was thoroughly ecumenical in student body and faculty makeup by the 1990s. An increasing number of congregations in the Baptist Convention of Ontario and Quebec (BCOQ) expressed their sense of Christian unity by training pastors in the pan-denominational Ontario Theological Seminary in Toronto or in similar schools in the upper US, notably Trinity Evangelical Divinity School. Unfortunately, the surge of evangelicalism experienced across Canada in the 1980s and 1990s came against the social positions of the United Church of Canada and the presence of the Baptists in the Canadian Council of Churches was called into question, with only the BCOQ ultimately remaining in the Council. Joint Church School literature publishing with the United Church was dropped (as was a later publishing venture with American Baptists); membership in the Evangelical Fellowship of Canada took precedence over the Council of Churches; and contributions to ecumenical organizations slipped sharply. One writer credits this "personality problem" to the influx of Southern Baptists into Canada,[36] while in the Maritimes and the Western Union the evidences of fundamentalism were a major contributing factor.

An irenic spirit has not been limited to the progressive or liberal wings of the Baptist movements. Among strict separationist Baptists, the General Association of Regular Baptist Churches (GARBC) has made several overtures to like-minded Christians. In 1941 militant Presbyterian and founder of the Bible Presbyterian movement, Carl MacIntire, formed the American Council of Christian Churches to speak on behalf of Bible-believing Christians against the apostasy of the Federal Council of Churches in the US. Later, in 1948 in response to the founding of the World Council of Churches, he formed the International Council of Christian Churches. Leaders like Paul Jackson in the GARBC encouraged membership in the American and International Councils, as long as it did not infringe upon the rights of local churches or compete with the programs of the Association. Denunciation of apostasy and political activism were mutually beneficial: fundamentalist preachers had easy access to free radio time, and fundamentalist chaplains were recognized in the armed forces in World War II. Eventually, the uncompromising dictatorial style of MacIntire brought an end to the GARBC cooperation. The GARBC also considered cooperation with the National Association of Evangelicals (NAE), founded in 1940 by Stephen Paine and Harold J. Ockenga to affirm the truths of supernatural Christianity across denominational lines. Because the NAE did not openly oppose the Federal Council of Churches and denounce apostasy, the leadership of the GARBC did not lend support to its churches to participate in the NAE.

When the Conservative Baptist Fellowship coalesced in 1943, many thought it was an excellent opportunity to unite the fundamentalist voices formerly among the Northern Baptist family. Robert Ketcham, president of the GARBC, proposed to the Conservative Baptist leadership that the two groups affiliate. This was followed by an invitation from the GARBC Council of Fourteen that suggested a possible union date of 1950. The Council of Fifteen from the Conservative Baptist Fellowship did meet with the Council of Fourteen from the GARBC in 1948, and a statement on organic separation from apostasy was adopted and union looked possible. However, the statement presented to the CBA churches in its first national meeting was toned down to allow for those churches that continued to hold membership in the NBC to do so. Further, the CBA encouraged membership in the less militant National Association of Evangelicals. By the early 1950s dialogue between the Conservative Baptists and Regular Baptists ceased and each was left to follow its own independent organizational course.[37]

Progressive National Baptists perhaps reflect the most extensive ecumenical commitment among Baptist national organizations. In the formation of the PNBC in 1961, its leaders had been clear about their relationship to other Christians, "acknowledging a mutual desire to be in close Christian fellowship and to witness together and cooperate in mission together wherever feasible."[38] As a result, a large percentage of congregations identified with the PNBC are dually affiliated, mostly with the American Baptist Churches, USA. Direct links with other bodies have been achieved, notably the Baptist World Alliance, National Council of Churches, and the World Council of Churches. The Convention is a constituent member of the Congress of National Black Churches that enables investment, credit, and communications in the black communities toward infrastructure development and family revitalization. Other important cooperative endeavors that enjoy PNBC support are Revelation Corporation of America, a group devoted to black home ownership, and comprising over 43,000 churches and 20 million members, and the Interdenominational Theological Center in Atlanta, Georgia, that equips ministers for black churches. In 1996 the PNBC joined American and Southern Baptist representatives in a conference to combat the sin of racism, that produced fraternal presidential visits to denominational meetings and a litany of reconciliation that could be used in church worship: "We commit ourselves as blood bought Christians who are Baptist by choice to do justice, love mercy, and walk humbly before our God. We commit ourselves to reject Racism as a principle and actively attack it as a practice whenever and wherever we encounter it."[39]

Finally, Canadian Baptist involvement in interchurch relations is an important illustration of Baptist ecumenism in North America. In the early years of Maritime Baptist development, Baptists worked with Presbyterians and Anglicans to forge an educational plan for the

region. Similarly, we have seen where Baptists in central Canada cooperated in a scheme to build a support base for church-related colleges.
This in turn led to cooperative theological education in the twentieth
century that has fostered trust and strong relationships among Baptists,
other Protestants, and Catholics. In 1944, when the Canadian Council
of Churches was founded, Convention Baptists were a constituent
member and the inaugural service was held at Toronto's Yorkminster
Park Baptist Church. Convention Baptists across Canada have all joined
the multidenominational Evangelical Fellowship of Canada, and Convention Baptists enthusiastically endorse the Canadian Bible Society.
The collectivist ethos of Canadian culture tends toward greater natural
cooperation than is the case for many Baptists in the United States.

In the last analysis, Baptists historically have had much to contribute
to the larger Christian family, including faithfulness to the authority of
Scripture, insisting upon liberty, possessing no binding creeds or liturgies,
and understanding ministry as properly belonging to the entire church.[40]

Notes

1   Thomas Helwys, *A Solemn Declaration of the Mistery of Iniquity*, edited
    by Thomas Groves (Macon, GA: Mercer University Press, 1998), 53.
2   Roger Williams, *The Bloudy Tenent of Persecution for Cause of Con-
    science* (London: 1644; repr. Macon, GA: Mercer University Press, 2001),
    3, 57, 180, 263.
3   *The Diary of John Comer*, ed. C. Edwin Barrows (Providence, RI: Rhode
    Island Historical Society, 1893), 62.
4   Quoted in William H. Brackney (ed.), *Baptist Life and Thought: A
    Sourcebook* (Valley Forge, PA: Judson Press, 1999), 423–7.
5   "Constitution of the Baptist Joint Committee on Public Affairs," in
    Annual, Southern Baptist Convention, 1961, 68.
6   All the executives but Carlson were Southern Baptist; he came from the
    Baptist General Conference. The staffs also included American Baptists
    and National Baptists.
7   Southern Baptist Convention, American Baptist Churches, National Bap-
    tist Convention, USA, National Baptist Convention of America, Progres-
    sive National Baptist Convention, National Missionary Baptist Convention,
    North American Baptist Conference, Baptist General Conference, Seventh
    Day Baptist Conference
8   Southern Baptists formed their own agency, the Ethics and Religious
    Liberty Commission, in 1988 from the former Christian Life Commission.
9   Richard Furman, "Exposition of the Views of the Baptists Relative To
    The Coloured Population of the United States in a Communication to the
    Governor of South Carolina," quoted in James A. Rogers, *Richard Furman:*

Life and Legacy (Macon, GA: Mercer University Press, 2001), 277, 279, 285.

10 Basil Manly, "Duties of Masters and Servants," in *Sermons on Duty* (Basil Manly Sermons and Notes, Boyce Library, Southern Baptist Theological Seminary).

11 Quoted in Brackney, *Baptist Life and Thought*, 143.

12 Ibid., 144.

13 The best account of Rhees's antislavery is in Hywel Davies, *Transatlantic Brethren: Rev. Samuel Jones (1735–1814) and His Friends: Baptists in Wales, Pennsylvania and Beyond. Bethlehem* (PA: Lehigh University Press, 1995), 217–21.

14 Ibid., 222.

15 Quoted in William W. Sweet, *Religion on the American Frontier: The Baptists* (New York: Henry Holt), 1931, 100.

16 Quoted in Robert Andrew Baker, Relations Between Northern and Southern Baptists (Ft.Worth, TX: Seminary Press, 1954), 41.

17 Quoted in Baker, *Relations Between Northern and Southern Baptists*, 42.

18 Baker, *Relations Between Northern and Southern Baptists*, 43.

19 Ibid., 44.

20 *Domestic Slavery Considered as a Scriptural Institution: in a Correspondence Between the Rev. Richard Fuller of Beaufort, S.C. and the Rev. Francis Wayland of Providence R.I.* (New York: Lewis Colby, 1845), 12.

21 Ibid., 245, 248–9.

22 Joan Jacobs Brumberg, *Mission for Life: The Dramatic Story of the Family of Adoniram Judson* (New York: The Free Press, 1980), 79–106.

23 *The Baptist Faith and Message: A Statement Adopted by the Southern Baptist Convention June 14, 2000* (Nashville, TN: Lifeway Church Resources, 2000), 13.

24 Robert G. Torbet, *History of the Baptists* (Valley Forge, PA: Judson Press, 1963), 276–8.

25 Harry Emerson Fosdick, "The Unknown Soldier," quoted in Brackney, *Baptist Life and Thought*, 376.

26 Martin Luther King, Jr., "When Peace Becomes Obnoxious," quoted in Paul R. Dekar, *Baptist Peacemakers* (Macon, GA: Smyth and Helwys Publishers, 1993), 235.

27 Albert A. Avant, Jnr., *The Social Teachings of the Progressive National Baptist Convention, Inc., Since 1961: A Critical Analysis of the Least, the Lost, and the Left-out* (New York: Routledge, 2004), 102, 103.

28 Henry C. Vedder, *A Short History of Baptist Missions* (Philadelphia, PA: Judson Press, 1927), 489–90.

29 Howard B. Grose, *Aliens or Americans?* (New York: American Baptist Home Mission Society, 1906), 288–9, 298–9.

30 William R. Estep, *The Anabaptist Story* (Nashville, TN: Broadman Press, 1963), 209.

31 Quoted in W. J. McGlothlin, *Baptist Confessions of Faith* (Philadelphia, PA: American Baptist Publication Society, 1911), 275.

32 The term "Scotch" was applied to McLeanite Baptists in Scotland to distinguish them from mainstream Scottish Baptists. Many Scotch Baptists evolved in Canada to became Disciples of Christ congregations.

33 See Franklin E. Rector, "Behind the Breakdown of Baptist-Disciple Conversations on Unity," *Foundations* 4/2 (April, 1961): 120–37.

34 J. H. Jackson, *A Story of Christian Activism: The History of the National Baptist Convention, USA, Inc.* (Nashville, TN: Townshend Press, 1980), 172.

35 Ibid., 276–86.

36 G. Gerald Harrop, "Canadian Baptists in Their North American Context," *Foundations* 4/3 (July, 1961): 223.

37 Much of this discussion is derived from Curtis Whiteman's "The General Association of Regular Baptist Churches 1932–1970." Ph.D. dissertation, St. Louis University, 1982, 309–18.

38 "Progressive National Baptist Convention and American Baptist Convention in Associated Relationship," quoted in Brackney, *Baptist Life and Thought*, 430.

39 Quoted in Avant, *The Social Teachings of the Progressive National Baptist Convention, Inc*, 131.

40 So stated distinguished professor John E. Skoglund in "American Baptists and the Ecumenical Movement After Fifty Years," *Foundations* 4/2 (April 1961): 118.

Chapter 11
Baptists Face Modernity

This survey and analysis began with the identity questions, "What are the Baptists? or Who are the Baptists?" We have seen through almost four centuries how Baptists in North America have evolved from "hole-in-the-wall" dissenters to a major denomination of Christians in the United States and Canada. Their identity, as a diverse collection of over 110,000 churches in excess of 34 million members (2004)[1] that yearn for religious freedom, eschew authority beyond the bounds of their congregations, who can be militantly evangelistic and who demonstrate a high level of personal stewardship, is informed at every point in their character by the Bible. That was important in the first two centuries of Baptist development, but it became problematic in the last two centuries as a battle over the interpretation of the Bible emerged among Baptists. Fundamentalism, we have seen, was exceedingly damaging to mainstream Baptists, yet productive of whole new Baptist fellowships at the same time. Some Baptists, as a result, came to look like mainline Protestants in Canada and the United States, while others rejected all forms of denominationalism. How well have Baptists survived the era of "antidenominationalism" and "postdenominationalism"? The early years of the fifth century of Baptist development have been characterized by disintegration and regrouping. How does one understand this?

As a tradition, Baptists in North America at present are in a state of disarray. Their historic emphases have been taken up by many other Christian groups in North America: for instance, believers' baptism by immersion is practiced by many evangelical groups; congregational governance is observed by most Protestants and even the Catholic episcopacy in North America; and virtually all Christian groups hearken back to the authority of Scripture as the foundation of their faith and practice. Therefore, one is forced to ask the question, "What is unique among Baptists: their theological perspective? . . . their organizational patterns? . . . their socioeconomic identity?"

With the passing of commonly held confessions of faith in the eighteenth century, Baptists lost their overall theological consensus. Their divisions into Regular, Freewill, Separates, and Old Schoolers signaled a permanent set of Baptist denominations, as different as Baptists are from Methodists, Presbyterians, and Lutherans. The resurgence of confessionalism among Baptists in the twentieth century has not reunified the tradition, but hardened the lines of demarcation around the Baptist denominations. It has taken harsh disciplinary methods to maintain many of these "sub" denominations, as well as a constant critique of alternatives. Most Baptists in the United States and Canada would like to think of themselves as "evangelical," meaning that the gospel of Jesus Christ is central to their identity as Christians. Within the evangelical category, there are fundamentalist Baptists and liberal evangelical Baptists. There are also many Baptists in both countries for whom the term "evangelical" is problematic. This is either because it stands at counterpoint with the historic definition of being Baptist or because evangelicals from numerous denominational traditions have organized their work in competition or contradistinction to any existing denomination. Moderate Baptists in the American South, and many Convention Baptists in central Canada, would not use "evangelical" terminology to describe their theological identity.

Baptist organizational identity, called "polity," used to be part of their genius. It was characterized by a maximum of freedom and a minimal bureaucracy. Baptist associations in North America performed an admirable set of tasks in a rapidly developing frontier context. State conventions and national societies secured the resources to extend Baptist horizons virtually around the world. In all of the expansion of polity, Baptists have always reminded themselves that the local congregation is the heart of their organization. The other side of the voluntary style of organization, however, is that it lacks authority and accountability and it can lead to obscurantism. Many Baptists yearn for the equivalent of a bishop, and some have even empowered their regional ministers and executives with episcopal authority. More than once, a deep chasm of misunderstanding has opened between Baptist congregations and extraparish organizations that seem to rely upon endowments and financial investments more than local church stewardship. This has been the basis of antimissionism, anticonventionism, and much of fundamentalist reaction to mainstream Baptist agencies and institutions. The placement of scriptural authority in the context of a voluntary association of enthusiastic or controlling leaders can be a recipe for dysfunctional isolationism. The most effective Baptist denominations, notably the Freewill Baptists and Seventh Day Baptists in the United States, have found ways to imitate more connectional polities, while still affirming principles of freedom and flexibility. The local church protectionism that characterizes Baptist polity and practice seems to guarantee that resolution of controversies will be difficult, if not impossible.

When one observes the socioeconomic make-up of Baptists, some commonalities across the family of denominations begin to emerge. One study of early English and North American Baptists demonstrates that the vast majority of Baptists were drawn from the lower levels of English-speaking society. This was augmented in the black Baptist experience and new immigrants to the United States and Canada in the nineteenth century. To be sure, Baptists have not attracted the numbers of converts that other Protestants and Catholics have from the immigration pools, but their growth among new Americans and new Canadians has been significant in Baptist demography. In the twentieth century, Baptist growth among Asian peoples and Hispanics from several locations has been the most pronounced statistical increase. One is much persuaded, therefore, to accept the hypothesis of Kenneth Scott Latourette, a Baptist historian and missiologist, who four decades ago asserted, "Baptists have come chiefly from lower educational and economic levels of older American stock. That is a cause not for shame or apology but for humble gratitude."[2] The Baptist communities in both the United States and Canada have apparently been fitting nurseries for individuals who prize freedom, an essentially Protestant/Free Church religious perspective, and socialization among persons who value education and vocational advancement. Baptists appear to be a "value-added" sort of denominational choice rather than a permanent spiritual home for the desperately poor and socially outcast. There has been no noticeable major attempt in any Baptist denomination in Canada or the United States to pursue the permanent enlistment of those who are desperate and oppressed, only stories of heroic individuals whose witness has been spent in such circumstances.

What is left for the Baptist tradition in North America as a mild-to-aggressive conversionist form of Christianity at the beginning of a new millennium? Doubtless, the continuing forms of traditional biblical interpretation will be subjected to cultural critique. Consequently, Baptist apologetics that stress the authority of Scripture need to be continually qualified. In many ways, mainstream Baptists are no longer distinct from other nondescript varieties of middle-class Protestantism.

Baptists look and behave like Congregationalists, Methodists, the United Church of Canada, and Presbyterians in many ways. Another problem for Baptists is their seeming close proximity to national ideals; this is particularly a problem for Baptists in the United States who in large numbers support the platforms of one political party over another. The decline of membership and loss of stewardship support for Baptist denominational programs and collective outreach is a serious problem for the overly optimistic corporate dreams of a half-century ago. No Baptist denomination better illustrates this than American Baptists and Canadian Convention Baptists. Future Baptists will have to rely upon the resources primarily of the faith communities in local churches, something Baptists should understand from their beginnings. Perhaps the most negative challenge Baptists in North America face is their reputation for extreme theological and ethical positions coupled with disruptive and schismatic tendencies. In the past two decades, Southern Baptists have taken a lead in this regard.

On the positive side, Baptists have historically exercised exemplary forms of dissent. They have carried a torch for the value of individuals, religious freedom as a human right, and toleration of other religious beliefs. Baptists understand the importance of voluntary associations and local religious communities. Like most dissenters, they practice a variety of religious experience and recognize the relevance of symbols over superstition. They make constant reference to the Bible. Like most Christian "true believers," Baptists draw inspiration from a personal God in Jesus Christ who is specially incarnated in communities that began in ancient Israel and continue in believers' churches across North America and beyond.

Notes

1 As of 2005, in Canada there are 235,000 members in 2,028 Baptist congregations, including Convention Baptists, Fellowship Baptists, and smaller groups like Freewill, Southern, and ethnic conferences. In the United States, Baptists represent 1 percent of the population; in Canada, 0.007 percent of the population.

2 Kenneth Scott Latourette, "Epilogue," in *Baptist Advance: The Achievements of the Baptists of North America for a Century and a Half* (Nashville, TN: Broadman Press, 1964), 489.

Bibliography

Reference Works

Brackney, William H. *Historical Dictionary of the Baptists*. Lanham, MD: Scarecrow Press, 1999.

Burgess, G. A. and Ward, J. T. *Free Baptist Cyclopedia: Historical and Biographical*. Chicago, IL: Free Baptist Cyclopedia Company, 1889.

Cathcart, William. *The Baptist Encyclopedia*. Philadelphia, PA: Everts, 1887.

Cox, Norman Wade (ed.), *Encyclopedia of Southern Baptists*, vols. 1 and 2. Nashville, TN: Broadman Press, 1958.

Leonard, Bill J. (ed.), *Dictionary of Baptists in America*. Downer's Grove, IL: Intervarsity Press, 1994.

May, Lynn E., Jr., and Woolley, Davis C. (eds), *Encyclopedia of Southern Baptists*, vols. 3 and 4. Nashville, TN: Broadman Press, 1971, 1982.

Starr, Edward C. *A Baptist Bibliography*, 25 vols. Rochester, NY: American Baptist Historical Society, 1976.

General Surveys of Baptist History in the United States

Barnes, William Wright. *The Southern Baptist Convention, 1945–1953*. Nashville, TN: Broadman Press, 1954.

Benedict, David. *A General History of the Baptist Denomination in America and Other Parts of the World*. New York: Lewis Colby, 1848.

Brackney, William H. *The Baptists*. Westport, CT: Greenwood Press, 1988.

Brackney, William H. (ed.), *Baptist Life and Thought: A Sourcebook*. Valley Forge, PA: Judson Press, 1999.

Fletcher, Jesse. *The Southern Baptist Convention: A Sesquicentennial History*. Nashville, TN: Broadman Press, 1994.

Leonard, Bill J. *Baptist Ways: A History*. Valley Forge, PA: Judson Press, 2003.

McBeth, H. Leon. *The Baptist Heritage: Four Centuries of Baptist Witness*. Nashville, TN: Broadman Press, 1988.

Newman, Albert H. *History of the Baptists in the United States*. Philadelphia, PA: American Baptist Publication Society, 1898.

Torbet, Robert G. *History of the Baptists*. Valley Forge, PA: Judson Press, 1963.

Vedder, Henry C. *A Short History of the Baptists*. Philadelphia, PA: American Baptist Publication Society, 1907.

Smaller Baptist Groups

Baxter, Norman A. *History of the Freewill Baptists: A Study in New England Separatism*. Rochester, NY: American Baptist Historical Society, 1957.

Hassell, Cushing Biggs. *History of the Church of God, From the Creation to A.D. 1885, Including Especially the History of the Kehukee Primitive Baptist Association*. Middletown, NY: Gilbert Beebe's Sons, 1886.

Latch, Ollie. *History of the General Baptists*. Poplar Bluff, MO: The General Baptist Press, 1972.

Olson, Adolf. *A Centenary History, As Related to the Baptist General Conference of America*. Chicago, IL: Baptist Conference Press, 1952.

Rogers, Albert N. *Seventh Day Baptists in Europe and America*, 3 vols. Plainfield, NJ: Seventh Day Baptist Publishing House, 1972.

Sanford, Don A. *A Choosing People: The History of Seventh Day Baptists*. Nashville, TN: Broadman Press, 1992.

Stiansen, Peder. *History of the Norwegian Baptists in America*. Philadelphia, PA: American Baptist Publication Society, 1939.

Woyke, Frank H. *Heritage and Ministry of the North American Baptist Conference*. Oakbrook Terrace, IL: North American Baptist Conference, 1979.

English Backgrounds to Baptists in North America

Briggs, John. *The English Baptists in the Nineteenth Century*. Didcot, UK: Baptist Historical Society, 1994.

Brown, Raymond. *The English Baptists of the Eighteenth Century*. London: The Baptist Historical Society, 1986.

Burrage, Champlin. *The Early English Dissenters in Light of Recent Research*, 2 vols. Cambridge, UK: Cambridge University Press, 1912.

Crosby, Thomas. *The History of the English Baptists, From the Reformation to the Beginning of the Reign of King George I*, 2 vols. London: Crosby, 1738–40.

Thomas, Joshua. *A History of the Baptist Association in Wales, from the Year 1650 to the Year 1790*. London: Dilly, Button, & Thomas, 1795.

Underwood, A. C. *History of the English Baptists*. London: Carey Kingsgate, 1947.

White, B. R. *The English Separatist Tradition*. Oxford: Clarendon Press, 1971.

White, B. R. *English Baptists in the Seventeenth Century*. Didcot, UK: Baptist Historical Society, 1983.

The Colonial Era

Backus, Isaac. *A History of New England with Particular Reference to the Denomination of Christians Called Baptists*, 2 vols. Newton, MA: Backus Historical Society, 1871.

Barrows, C. Edwin (ed.), *Diary of John Comer*. Providence, RI: Rhode Island Historical Society, 1893.

Davies, Hywel. *Transatlantic Brethren: Rev. Samuel Jones (1735–1814) and His Friends: Baptists in Wales, Pennsylvania and Beyond*. Bethlehem, PA: Lehigh University Press, 1995.

Edwards, Morgan. *Materials Towards a History of the American Baptists*, 2 vols. Philadelphia, PA: 1770, 1792.

Hudson, Winthrop S. "Documents on the Association of Churches," *Foundations* 4/4 (October 1961): 332–9.

Keen, William W. *The Bicentennial of the Founding of the First Baptist Church, Philadelphia*. Philadelphia, PA: American Baptist Publication Society, 1899.

Maring, Norman H. *Baptists in New Jersey: A Study in Transition*. Valley Forge, PA: Judson Press, 1964.

McLoughlin, William G. *New England Dissent, 1630–1833: Baptists and the Separation of Church and State*, 2 vols. Cambridge, MA: Harvard University Press, 1971.

Ryland, Garnett. *The Baptists of Virginia, 1699–1926*. Richmond, VA: The Baptist Board of Missions and Education, 1955.

Semple, Robert B. *History of the Rise and Progress of Baptists in Virginia*. Richmond. VA: Pitt and Dickinson, 1894.

Spencer, David. *Early Baptists of Philadelphia*. Philadelphia, PA: William Syckelmoore, 1877.

Torbet, Robert G. *A Social History of the Philadelphia Baptist Association*. Philadelphia, PA: Westbrook Publishing Co., 1945.

Wood, Nathan E. *The History of the First Baptist Church of Boston (1665–1899)*. Philadelphia, PA: American Baptist Publication Society, 1899.

Nineteenth Century

Babcock, Rufus (ed.), *Memoir of John Mason Peck D.D.* Carbondale, IL: Southern Illinois University, 1965.

Baker, Robert A. *Relations Between Northern and Southern Baptists*. Fort Worth, TX: Seminary Press, 1948.

Benedict, David. *A General History of the Baptist Denomination in America and Other Parts of the World*, 2 vols. Boston, MA: Manning and Loring, 1811.

Benedict, David. *Fifty Years a Baptist*. Glen Rose, TX: Newman and Collings, 1913.

Brackney, William H. (ed.), *Dispensations of Providence: The Journal and Selected Letters of Luther Rice*. Rochester, NY: American Baptist Historical Society, 1984.

Cady, John F. *The Origin and Development of the Missionary Baptist Church in Indiana*. Franklin, IN: Franklin College, 1942.

Cox, Francis A. and Hoby, James. *The Baptists in America*. New York: Leavitt, Lord, 1836.

Flynt, Wayne. *Alabama Baptists: Southern Baptists in the Heart of Dixie*. Tuscaloosa, AL: University of Alabama Press, 1998.

Gardner, Robert G. *A Decade of Debate and Division: Georgia Baptists and the Formation of the Southern Baptist Convention*. Macon, GA: Mercer University Press, 1995.

Mills, Randy. *Christ Tasted Death for Every Man: The Story of America's Frontier General Baptists*. Poplar Bluff, MO: Stinson Press, 2000.

Payne, Ernest A. *The Baptist Union: A Short History*. London: Carey Kingsgate Press, 1959.

Posey, Walter B. *The Baptist Church in the Lower Mississippi Valley, 1776–1845*. Lexington, KY: University Press of Kentucky, 1957.

Putnam, Mary B. *The Baptists and Slavery: 1840–1845*. Ann Arbor, MI: George Wahr, 1913.

Smith, Justin A. *A History of Baptists in the Western States East of the Mississippi*. Philadelphia, PA: American Baptist Publication Society, 1896.

Sweet, William W. *Religion on the American Frontier: The Baptists*. New York: Henry Holt, 1931.

Taylor, John. *A History of Ten Churches*. Frankfort, KY: J. H. Holeman, 1823.

Vedder, Henry C. *A History of the Baptists in the Middle States*. Philadelphia, PA: American Baptist Publication Society, 1898.

Williams, Michael E., Sr. *Isaac Taylor Tichenor: The Creation of the Baptist New South*. Tuscaloosa, AL: University of Alabama Press, 2005.

Twentieth Century

Duncan, Leland, and Runyan, Edwin. *The Journey with General Baptists*. Poplar Bluff, MO: Stinson Press, 2005.

Hankins, Barry G. *J. Frank Norris and the Beginnings of Southern Fundamentalism*. Lexington, KY: The University Press of Kentucky, 1996.

Maring, Norman. *American Baptists: Whence and Whither?* Valley Forge, PA: Judson Press, 1968.

Padelford, Frank W. *The Kingdom in the States: A Study of the Missionary Work of State Conventions.* Philadelphia, PA: Judson Press, 1928.

Shurden, Walter B. *Baptist Identity: Four Fragile Freedoms.* Macon, GA: Smyth and Helwys, 1993.

Stackhouse, Perry J. *Chicago and the Baptists.* Chicago, IL: University of Chicago Press, 1933.

Torbet, Robert G. and Hill, Samuel S. *Baptists North and South: What Keeps Baptists Apart?* Valley Forge, PA: Judson Press, 1964.

Whiteman, Curtis W. "The General Association of Regular Baptist Churches 1932–1970," Ph.D. dissertation, St. Louis University, 1982.

Woolley, Davis Collier (ed.), *Baptist Advance: The Achievements of the Baptists of North America for a Century and a Half.* Nashville, TN: Broadman Press, 1964.

Baptist Theology

Brackney, William H. *A Genetic History of Baptist Thought, with Particular Reference to Britain and North America.* Macon, GA: Mercer University Press, 2004.

Freeman, Curtis W., McClendon, James William, Velloso da Silva, C. Rosalee (eds), *Baptist Roots: A Reader in the Theology of a Christian People.* Valley Forge, PA: Judson Press, 1999.

Garrett, James Leo, Jr. *Systematic Theology: Biblical, Historical, and Evangelical,* 2 vols. Grand Rapids, MI: Eerdmans, 1990, 1995.

George, Timothy and Dockery, David S. (eds), *Baptist Theologians.* Nashville, TN: Broadman Press, 1990.

Mullins, Edgar Y. *The Christian Religion in its Doctrinal Expression.* Philadelphia, PA: Judson Press, 1917.

Newman, Albert H. "Recent Changes in the Theology of Baptists," *American Journal of Theology* VI/3 (October 1906): 587–609.

Patterson, W. Morgan. *Baptist Successionism: A Critical View.* Valley Gorge, PA: Judson Press, 1969.

Strong, Augustus H. *Systematic Theology.* New York: A. C. Armstrong, 1886; reissued Philadelphia, PA: Judson Press, 1915.

Wood, Nathan E. "Movements of Baptist Theological Thought During the Nineteenth Century." In A. H. Newman (ed.), *A Century of Baptist Achievement.* Philadelphia, PA: American Baptist Publication Society, 1901, pp. 428–38.

Religious Liberty, Social and Ethical Issues

Bancroft, George. *History of the United States,* 2 vols. New York: D. Appleton Co., 1902.

Batten, Samuel Zane. *The New World Order*. Philadelphia: American Baptist Publication Society, 1919.

Cobb, Sanford H. *The Rise of Religious Liberty in America*. New York: The Macmillan Co., 1920.

Dawson, Joseph M. *A Thousand Months to Remember*. Waco, TX: Baylor University Press, 1964.

Dekar, Paul R. *For the Healing of the Nations: Baptist Peacemakers*. Macon, GA: Smyth and Helwys Publishers, 1993.

Falwell, Jerry. *Listen, America!* Garden City, NY: Doubleday, 1980.

Gaustad, Edwin S. *Proclaim Liberty Throughout All the Land: A History of Church and State in America*. New York: Oxford University Press, 2003.

Goen, C. C. "Baptists and Church-State Issues in the Twentieth Century," *American Baptist Quarterly* 6/4 (December 1987): 226–53.

Handy, Robert T. "The Principle of Religious Freedom and the Dynamics of Baptist History," *Perspectives in Religious Studies* 13/4 (1986): 23–4.

Hinson, E. Glenn. *Religious Liberty: The Christian Roots of Our Fundamental Freedoms*. Louisville, KY: Glad River Publications, 1991.

King, Martin Luther, Jr. *Strength to Love*. Philadelphia, PA: Fortress Press, 1963.

Mecklin, John M. *The Story of American Dissent*. New York: Harcourt, Brace, and Co., 1934.

Northcott, Cecil. *Religious Liberty*. New York: The Macmillan Co., 1949.

Pfeffer, Leo. *Church, State, and Freedom*. Boston, MA: Beacon Press, 1953.

Smith, Elwyn A. *Religious Liberty in the United States: The Development of Church-State Thought Since the Revolutionary Era*. Philadelphia, PA: Fortress Press, 1972.

Stokes, Anson P. *Church and State in the United States*, 3 vols. New York: Harper Brothers, 1953.

Sullivan, Leon H. *Moving Mountains: The Principles and Purposes of Leon Sullivan*. Valley Forge, PA: Judson Press, 1998.

Truett, George. *God's Call to America*. New York: George Doran, 1923.

Weaver, Rufus. *The Road to Freedom*. Washington, DC: Joint Committee on Public Relations, 1944.

African American Baptists

Avant, Albert A. *The Social Teachings of the Progressive National Baptist Convention, Inc., Since 1961: A Critical Analysis of the Least, the Lost, and the Left-out*. New York: Routledge, 2004.

Booth, William D. *The Progressive Story: New Baptist Roots*. St Paul, MN: Braun Press, 1981.

Fisher, Miles Mark. *A Short History of the Baptist Denomination*. Nashville, TN: Sunday School Board, 1933.

Jackson, J. H. *A Story of Christian Activism: The History of the National Baptist Convention, USA, Inc*. Nashville, TN: Townshend Press, 1980.

Jordan, Lewis G. *Negro Baptist History, USA*. Nashville, TN: Sunday School Board of the National Baptist Convention, 1930.

Lovett, Bobby L. *A Black Man's Dream: The First 100 Years: Richard Henry Boyd and the National Baptist Publishing Board*. Nashville, TN: Mega Corporation, 1993.

Martin, Sandy D. *Black Baptists and African Missions: The Origins of a Movement, 1880–1915*. Macon, GA: Mercer University Press, 1989.

Mitchell, Henry M. *Black Church Beginnings: The Long-Hidden Realities of the First Years*. Grand Rapids, MI: Eerdmans, 2004.

Pelt, Owen D. and Smith, Ralph L. *The Story of the National Baptists*. New York: Vantage Books, 1960.

Raboteau, Albert J. *Slave Religion: The 'Invisible Institution' in the Antebellum South*. New York: Oxford University Press, 2004.

Scherer, Lester B. *Afro-American Baptists: A Guide to Materials in the American Baptist Historical Society*. Rochester, NY: American Baptist Historical Society, 1985.

Simms, James M. *The First Colored Baptist Church in North America, Constituted at Savannah, Georgia January 20, 1788*. New York: Negro Universities Press, 1969.

Washington, James Melvin. *Frustrated Fellowship: The Black Baptist Quest for Social Power*. Macon, GA: Mercer University Press, 1986.

Baptists in Canada

Bentall, Shirley. *From Sea to Sea: The Canadian Baptist Federation 1944–1994*. Mississauga, ON: Canadian Baptist Federation, 1994.

Bill, Ingraham E. *Fifty Years with the Baptist Ministers and Churches of the Maritime Provinces of Canada*. St John, NB: Barnes and Co., 1880.

Brackney, William H. "The Planter Motif among Baptists from New England to Nova Scotia, 1760–1850." In William H. Brackney and Paul S. Fiddes (eds), *Pilgrim Pathways: Essays in Baptist History in Honour of B. R. White*. Macon, GA: Mercer University Press, 1999, pp. 283–302.

Clark, S. D. *Church and Sect in Canada*. Toronto, ON: University of Toronto Press, 1948.

Gibson, Theo T. *Robert A. Fyfe: His Contemporaries and His Influence*. Burlington, ON: G. R. Welch, 1988.

Harrop, G. Gerald. "Canadian Baptists in Their North American Context," *Foundations* 4/3 (July 1961): 216–24.

Ivison, Stuart and Rosser, Fred. *The Baptists in Upper and Lower Canada Before 1820*. Toronto, ON: University of Toronto Press, 1956.

McLaurin, C. C. *Pioneering in Western Canada: A Story of the Baptists*. Calgary, AB: The Author, 1939.

Rawlyk, George (ed.), *The Canadian Protestant Experience 1760–1990*. Burlington, ON: G. R. Welch Co., 1990.

Renfree, Harry A. *Heritage and Horizon: The Baptist Story in Canada.* Mississauga, ON: Canadian Baptist Federation, 1988.

Tarr, L. K. *This Dominion, His Dominion: The Story of Evangelical Baptist Endeavour in Canada.* Willowdale, ON: Fellowship of Evangelical Baptist Churches, 1968.

Walker, James W. St. G. *The Black Loyalists: The Search for a Promised Land in Nova Scotia and Sierra Leone, 1783–1870.* New York: Africana Press, 1976.

Congregational Life

May, Lynn E. *The First Baptist Church of Nashville, Tennessee, 1820–1970.* Nashville, TN: First Baptist Church, 1970.

McBeth, Leon. *The First Baptist Church of Dallas: Centennial History (1868–1968).* Grand Rapids, MI: Zondervan Publishing House, 1968.

Paris, Peter J. *The History of the Riverside Church in New York City.* New York: New York University Press, 2004.

Tupper, Henry A. (ed.), *The First Century of the First Baptist Church of Richmond, Virginia 1780–1880.* Richmond: Carlton McCarthy, 1880.

Tupper, Henry A. *Two Centuries of the First Baptist Church of South Carolina 1683–1883, with Supplement.* Baltimore, MD: R. H. Woodward and Co., 1889.

Wood, Nathan A. *History of the First Baptist Church of Boston.* Philadelphia, PA: American Baptist Publication Society, 1899.

Select Baptist Educational Institutions

Alley, Reuben E. *History of the University of Richmond 1830–1971.* Charlottesville, VA: University Press of Virginia, 1977.

Cady, John F. *The Centennial History of Franklin College.* Franklin, IN: The College, 1934.

Chessman, G. Wallace. *Denison: The Story of an Ohio College.* Granville, OH: Denison University, 1957.

Daniel, Robert Norman. *Furman University: A History.* Greenville, SC: Furman University, 1951.

Dowell, Spright. *A History of Mercer University 1833–1953.* Macon, GA: Mercer University Press, 1958.

Guffin, Gilbert E. (ed.), *What God Hath Wrought: Eastern's First Thirty-Five Years.* Philadelphia, PA: Judson Press, 1960.

Guild, Reuben Aldridge. *Early History of Brown University, Including the Life, Times, and Correspondence of President Manning 1756–1791.* Providence, RI: Brown University, 1897.

Kayser, Elmer Louis. *Bricks Without Straw: The Evolution of George Washington University.* New York: Appleton-Century-Crofts, 1970.

Lycan, Gilbert. *Stetson University: The First 100 Years.* Deland, FL: Stetson University Press, 1983.

Marriner, Ernst C. *The History of Colby College.* Waterville, ME: Colby College, 1963.

Mueller, William A. *A History of the Southern Baptist Theological Seminary.* Nashville, TN: Broadman Press, 1959.

Murray, Lois Smith. *Baylor at Independence.* Waco, TX: Baylor University Press, 1962.

Starr, Edward C. "William Staughton: Baptist Educator," *The Chronicle* 12/3 (October 1949): 166–77.

Storr, Richard J. *Harper's University: The Beginnings.* Chicago, IL: University of Chicago Press, 1966.

Williams, Howard. *A History of Colgate University.* New York: Van Nostrand, 1969.

Young, Warren C. *Command What You Have Heard: A History of Northern Baptist Theological Seminary 1913–1988.* Wheaton, IL: Harold Shaw Publishers, 1988.

Baptist Missions

Beers, G. Pitt. *Ministry to Turbulent America: A History of the American Baptist Home Mission Society Covering its Fifth Quarter Century, 1932–1957.* Philadelphia, PA: Judson Press, 1957.

Burton, Joe W. *Epochs of Home Missions.* Atlanta, GA: Southern Baptist Home Mission Board, 1945.

Estep, William R. *Whole Gospel, Whole World: The Foreign Mission Board of the Southern Baptist Convention 1845–1995.* Nashville, TN: Broadman and Holman Publishers, 1994.

Freeman, Edward A. *The Epoch of Negro Baptists and the Foreign Mission Board.* Kansas City, KS: Central Baptist Seminary, 1953.

Jordan, L. G. *Up the Ladder in Foreign Missions.* Nashville, TN: National Baptist Publishing Board, 1901.

Merriam, Edmund F. *A History of American Baptist Missions.* Philadelphia, PA: Judson Press, 1913.

Torbet, Robert G. *Venture in Faith: The Story of the American Baptist Foreign Mission Society and the Woman's American Baptist Foreign Mission Society 1814–1954.* Philadelphia, PA: Judson Press, 1955.

Vedder, Henry C. *A Short History of Baptist Missions.* Philadelphia, PA: Judson Press, 1927.

White, Charles L. *A Century of Achievement.* Philadelphia, PA: Judson Press, 1932.

Appendix: List of Baptist Groups in the United States and Canada

United States

Alliance of Baptists (1987)

American Baptist Association (1924)

American Baptist Churches in the USA (1972; formerly American Baptist Convention)

American Baptist Convention (1950; formerly Northern Baptist Convention)

American Baptist Evangelicals (1992)

Antimissionary Baptists (1817; also called Hardshell or Primitive Baptists)

Baptist Bible Fellowship (1950)

Baptist Bible Union (1923)

Baptist Church of Christ (1825; also called Duck River and Kindred Baptists)

Baptist General Conference (1856; also known as Swedish Baptists)

Baptist Missionary Association of America (1969)

Bible Baptists (1944)

Caucus Nacional Bautista Hispano (1970)

Conservative Baptist Association (1947)

Conservative Baptist Fellowship (1965)

Cooperative Baptist Fellowship (1991)

Czechoslovak Baptist Convention (1909)

Danish Baptist General Conference (1910)

Finnish Baptist Union (1901)

Free Communion Baptists (1840)

Freewill Baptists (1781; later known as Free Baptists)

French-Speaking Baptist Conference of New England (1895)

Fundamental Baptist Fellowship (1974)

Fundamental Baptist Missionary Fellowship (1939)

General Association of General Baptists (1870)

General Association of Regular Baptist Churches (1932)

General Six Principle Baptists (1670)
Great Commission Baptists (2005)
Hampton [University] Ministers Conference (1914)
Hardshell Baptists (1820; also known as Primitive Baptists)
Hungarian Baptist Union (1908)
Independent Baptist Fellowship International (1984)
Independent Baptists (1756)
Italian Baptist Association of America (1898)
King James Only Baptists (1950)
Liberty Baptist Fellowship (1977)
Lott Carey Baptist Foreign Mission Convention (1897)
Mainstream Baptists (2001)
Mexican Baptist Convention of Northern North America (1910)
Missionary Baptists (1901)
Moderate Baptists (2000)
National Association of Freewill Baptists (1935)
National Baptist Convention of America (1915)
National Baptist Convention USA, Inc. (1895)
National Baptist Missionary Convention (1988)
New Testament Association of Independent Baptist Churches (1974)
Norwegian Baptist Conference of America (1864)
North American Baptist Association (1950)
North American Baptist Conference (1851; also known as German Baptists)
Northern Baptist Convention (1907; later American Baptist Convention (1950)
    and still later
American Baptist Churches, USA (1972)
Old Regular Baptists (1892)
Old School Baptists (1832)
Pentecostal Freewill Baptist Church (1959)
Polish Baptist Conference (1912)
Portuguese Baptist Conference (1919)
Premillennial Baptist Missionary Fellowship (1933)
Primitive Baptists (South: 1827; North: 1832)
Progressive National Baptist Convention (1961)
Regular Baptists (1707)
Rogerenes (1674)
Romanian Baptist Association of America (1913)
Russian and Ukrainian Evangelical Baptist Union (1919)
Separate Baptists (1754)
Seventh Day Baptists (1653)
Southern Baptist Convention (1845)
Southwide Baptist Fellowship (1956)
Two Seed in the Spirit Double Predestinarian Baptists (1817)
Welcoming and Affirming Baptists (1993)
World Baptist Fellowship (1950; formerly the Premillennial Baptist Missionary
    Fellowship)

Canada

AfriCanadian Baptists (1782)
Amherstburg Association (1841)
Association of Regular Baptist Churches (1957)
Atlantic Baptist Fellowship (1970)
Baptist Convention of Ontario and Quebec (1888)
Baptist Federation of Canada (1944; later called Canadian Baptist Ministries)
Baptist General Conference of Canada (1906; originally Swedish Baptists)
Baptist Union of Western Canada (1905)
Canadian Convention of Southern Baptists (1985)
Convention of Baptists in Atlantic Canada (1846)
Fellowship of Evangelical Baptist Churches (1953)
Free Baptists (1832; also known as Freewill Baptists)
Gathering of Baptists (1994)
North American Conference Baptists (1902; originally German Baptists)
Primitive Baptists (1875)
Reformed Baptists (1886; later joined the Wesleyan Church)
Regular Baptists (1925)
Scotch Baptists (1816)
Seventh Day Baptists (1978)
L'Union d'Eglises Baptistes Françaises au Canada (1966)

Glossary of Terms in Baptist Usage

Antipaedobaptist. Literally, one who is opposed to the baptism of infants and children. In the seventeenth century there were those who stood against the sacrament of baptism but had not yet adopted Baptist principles. For others, antipaedobaptism was a stage in the development of full baptistic identity.

Association. The basic pattern of Baptist regional organization of congregations. Usually composed of five or six churches and effective in relationships when not more than 25–30 miles in radius. The purpose of associations is mutual support, fellowship, and recognition of clergy. Associations may be called upon to offer advice to congregations. Associations have no power over local congregations.

Baptism. The denominating article of Baptists as a Christian group. A religious rite for believers administered upon profession of faith in Christ. Since the 1640s it has been immersion in water to signify obedience to Christ's command (Matthew 28: 19) and as a depiction of the gospel (Romans 6: 3–4). Baptisms may take place in creeks, rivers, ponds, or lakes, or in indoor baptisteries. Baptism is typically according to a Trinitarian formula and sometimes by triune immersion.

Church. The local congregation, composed of baptized believers, has all the authority and gifts from Jesus Christ to be the fullness of the church (*ecclesia*) as in the New Testament. A church may be as small as two or three gathered in Christ's name or several thousand members. Churches are said to be independent or autonomous, yet also interdependent. Baptists do not refer to associations or conventions as the "church."

Confession of Faith. From their earliest history Baptists have produced confessions of faith as individuals, congregations, or groups like associations. Confessions of faith are summaries of doctrinal beliefs, usually with accompanying

Scripture texts. The confessions are used to guide the groups who produce them in study, nurture, and correction. Sometimes some Baptist groups have used confessions to discipline or exclude members or congregations from fellowship.

Convention. The larger organizational entity of Baptists in a state, province, or region. The first in the US was in South Carolina and in Canada in Nova Scotia and New Brunswick. It includes associations, churches, and benevolent organizations in its scope.

Council. An advisory body called within the congregation or association to offer counsel or ratification of a decision by a congregation or association. In several Baptist groups, a council administers denominational policy for the member congregations. A council is restricted to the body that authorizes it.

Covenant. The agreement that members of a Baptist congregation have among themselves to be faithful to the gospel. Covenants generally articulate the bases of belief, doctrine of the church, ethical and moral expectations, and membership requirements. Covenants may be revised from time to time and used to reaffirm the congregational commitment at services of baptism or celebration.

Deacon. The lay office in a congregation that oversees the care of the congregation and advises the pastor on spiritual matters. In larger congregations, deacons may constitute a board or diaconate. In some Baptist groups, deacons are limited to men only, while in others, men and women serve in the capacity.

Elder. Term denoting the leader of a congregation from the eighteenth through the nineteenth centuries, the equivalent of the title "reverend" in other denominations. Since the twentieth century, a multiplicity of eldership leads some congregations, while in others the elders are spiritual laypersons who rank above deacons and below pastors.

General Baptist. Those Baptists who hold to a position that Christ died for the salvation of all humankind. Their view of the atonement of Christ is general, meaning inclusive. In the early development of Baptists, this term applied formally to groups in England and the US.

Member. The role that baptized believers have in the life of a congregation. One becomes a member by believer's baptism and election by the congregation, by transfer of a letter of membership from another congregation, or by statement of Christian faith and vote by the congregation. In many congregations, members take vows to support the church by their prayers, service, and financial support. As the decision makers of the congregation, members constitute the body politic of the church

Ordinances. Describes those rites taught by Christ to be observed in the churches, mainly baptism and the Lord's Supper. Some Baptists recognize footwashing and the laying on of hands at ordination and following baptism as ordinances. Early Baptists used the term synonymously with sacraments.

Ordination. The formal recognition of a person for ministry in the local congregation. Candidates for ordination present their gifts and experience to a congregation for ratification, and a formal ceremony of the laying on of hands in a public service completes the rite of ordination. Some Baptists ordain deacons as well as pastors.

Pastor. The spiritual leader of a congregation. May be paid or volunteer. Pastors reside in parsonages, if owned by the congregation. In some Baptist groups, the pastoral ministry is limited to men, while in others, both men and women may serve as pastors.

Regular Baptist. In the eighteenth century, Regular Baptists were mainstream, Calvinistic Baptists who accepted the Second London or Philadelphia confessions of faith. In the early nineteenth century, Regular Baptists contrasted with Separate Baptists in their adherence to confessions over religious experience. Later, in the fundamentalist groups, Regular Baptists were those who maintained historic Baptist principles in light of the perceived apostasy of other Baptist groups.

Separationism. The ethical position assumed particularly by Primitive (Old School) and fundamentalist Baptists, that biblical injunctions forbid relationships with liberal or apostate groups of Christians or other Baptists.

Index